CFSA
Certified Financial Services Auditor®

Examination Study Guide
Volume 1
(Two-volume Set)

Authors:
Albert J. Marcella Jr., Ph.D., CFSA, CISA
William J. Sampias, CISA, CFSA
James K. Kincaid, CIA, CGAP, CFSA

Contributing Authors:
Don Caniglia, CISA, CISM
Frank O'Brien, CIA, CPA

30 YEARS 1976–2006
IIA RESEARCH FOUNDATION

Disclosure

The IIA publishes this document for informational and educational purposes. This document is intended to provide information, but is not a substitute for legal or accounting advice. The IIA does not provide such advice and makes no warranty as to any legal or accounting results through its publication of this document. When legal or accounting issues arise, professional assistance should be sought and retained.

The Professional Practices Framework for Internal Auditing (PPF) was designed by The IIA Board of Directors' Guidance Task Force to appropriately organize the full range of existing and developing practice guidance for the profession. Based on the definition of internal auditing, the PPF comprises Ethics and Standards, Practice Advisories, and Development and Practice Aids, and paves the way to world-class internal auditing.

This guidance fits into the Framework under the heading Development and Practice Aids.

The mission of The IIA Research Foundation (IIARF) is to be the global leader in sponsoring, disseminating, and promoting research and knowledge resources to enhance the development and effectiveness of the internal auditing profession.

ISBN 0-89413-529-9
06261 04/06
(Two-volume Set)
First Printing

Table of Contents

Volume 1 of 2

Volume 2 of 2

Appendices

Reviewers and Contributors

The authors wish to acknowledge The Institute of Internal Auditors (IIA) for permission to use various IIA publications. The willingness of this professional body to permit use of these materials contributed greatly to the development of this study guide. In addition, we wish to thank *Bonnie Ulmer* of The IIA for her support throughout the project.

The authors also wish to specifically acknowledge *Don Caniglia*, Senior Associate at Campbell and Associates, for his work in developing materials in the Banking Discipline section, and *Frank O'Brien*, Director of Financial and Operational Audits for the Olin Corporation, for his role in developing materials for the Securities Discipline section of this guide. Their efforts were instrumental to the successful completion of the project.

The authors wish to extend a special acknowledgment to thank the Securities Industry Association, the Internal Auditor's Division (SIA/IAD), for their support of our research and their generous consent and permission to reprint significant portions of the Association's Internal Audit Guidelines. The authors hope that the addition of these guidelines in this study guide will better assist the candidate in preparing for the CFSA examination. Further information about the Securities Industry Association can be found online at www.siaiad.com, by writing the Association at 120 Broadway, New York, NY 10271-0080, or by calling +1-212-618-0534.

Dedication

Special thanks go to our families, spouses, parents, and children, whose continuing support, love, and patience have been a source of strength and motivation.

With heartfelt thanks,

AJM
WJS
JKK

About the Authors

Albert J. Marcella, Jr., Ph.D., CFSA, CISA, COAP, CQA, CSP, CDP, president of Business Automation Consultants, LLC, (www.businessautomationconsultants.com) is an internationally recognized public speaker, researcher, and seminar leader with over 25 years of experience in IT audit, security and assessing internal controls. He has contributed numerous articles to audit-related publications and has written over 27 books on critical and timely IT audit and IT audit-related subjects.

A recipient of the 2000 Leon R. Radde Educator of the Year award, conferred by The Institute of Internal Auditors and recognizing contributions to the advancement of internal auditing and education in colleges and universities, Dr. Marcella provides information technology (IT) management consulting and IT audit and security reviews and training for an international clientele. He has taught IT audit seminar courses for The Institute of Internal Auditors, and teaches for the Information Systems Audit and Control Association.

Dr. Marcella's additional professional experiences include IT auditing responsibilities for Dun & Bradstreet, providing internal systems consulting services to the Hartford Insurance Group, and the design and execution of operational, financial, and information technology audits for the Uniroyal Corporation, both in the United States and abroad.

William J. Sampias, CISA, CFSA, has been involved in the auditing profession for the past 20 years with a primary emphasis on audits of information systems. He is the co-author of the *Certified Government Auditing Professional® (CGAP) Examination Study Guide* and the *Certification in Control Self-Assessment® (CCSA®) Examination Study Guide,* as well as many other IIA publications on topics such as effective written communications, ethics, disaster contingency planning, end-user computing, and fraud. He is currently director of an Information Systems Audit group for a governmental audit agency. He holds an MBA from the University of Illinois at Springfield.

James K. Kincaid, CIA, CGAP, CFSA, is manager of the Public Services Division of the Illinois Office of Internal Audit. He has over 20 years of auditing experience and has written numerous audit-related publications. He is the co-author of the *CGAP* and *CCSA Examination Study Guides,* a writing manual for auditors, and several other instructional materials on topics such as fraud, business ethics, and information technology. He has also written articles published in *Internal Auditor* and other periodicals. He has taught writing at the university level and spoken at several audit conferences. His educational background includes a BA in Economics and Business Administration from Illinois College, an MA in English from the University of Illinois at Springfield, and an MBA from the University of Illinois at Springfield.

Preface

The purpose of this study guide is to help you prepare to pass the Certified Financial Services Auditor® (CFSA) Examination. The guide provides a general overview of the topics that will be covered in the exam. However, it is critical that you perform additional study in areas where your experience or background dictates the need for additional review. A list of reference materials is included to provide additional resources to supplement your study.

This study guide refers to U.S.-specific laws and organizations, unless otherwise specified.

The guide was created using an outline developed and published by The Institute of Internal Auditors (IIA) Web site on September 29, 2005. The outline is included in the section in the guide titled "Domains for the CFSA Examination."

Please forward suggestions, corrections, and comments concerning typographical errors, etc., to The Institute of Internal Auditors. Appendix A of the Guide can be used to note corrections and comments. We appreciate any feedback, as it will help us improve future editions of the guide.

Good luck on the CFSA exam.

Information on The Institute of Internal Auditors[1]

About The Institute

Established in 1941, The Institute of Internal Auditors (IIA) serves over 115,000 members in internal auditing, governance and internal control, IT audit, education, and security from more than 165 countries. The world's leader in certification, education, research, and technological guidance for the profession, The IIA serves as the profession's watchdog and resource on significant auditing issues around the globe.

Presenting important conferences and seminars for professional development, producing leading-edge educational products, certifying qualified auditing professionals, providing quality assurance reviews and benchmarking, and conducting valuable research projects through The IIA Research Foundation are just a few of The IIA's many activities.

The IIA also provides internal auditing practitioners, executive management, boards of directors, and audit committees with standards, guidance, and information on internal auditing best practices.

The IIA is a dynamic international organization that meets the needs of a worldwide body of internal auditors. The history of internal auditing has been synonymous with that of The IIA and its motto, "Progress Through Sharing."

Mission Statement

The IIA's mission is to be the primary international professional association, organized on a worldwide basis, dedicated to the promotion and development of the practice of internal auditing.

The IIA is committed to:

- Providing, on an international scale, comprehensive professional development activities, standards for the practice of internal auditing, and certification.

- Researching, disseminating, and promoting to its members and to the public throughout the world, knowledge and information concerning internal auditing, including internal control and related subjects.

[1]Information taken from The Institute of Internal Auditors (IIA) Web site http://www.theiia.org/.

- Establishing meetings worldwide in order to educate members and others as to the practice of internal auditing as it exists in various countries throughout the world.

- Bringing together internal auditors from all countries to share information and experiences in internal auditing and promoting education in the field of internal auditing.

About the Profession

Internal auditing is an independent, objective assurance and consulting activity designed to add value and improve an organization's operations. It helps an organization accomplish its objectives by bringing a systematic, disciplined approach to evaluate and improve the effectiveness of risk management, control, and governance processes.

Internal auditing reviews the reliability and integrity of information, compliance with policies and regulations, the safeguarding of assets, the economical and efficient use of resources, and established operational goals and objectives. Internal audits encompass financial activities and operations, including systems, production, engineering, marketing, and human resources.

The IIA believes that an organization is best served by a fully resourced and professionally competent internal auditing staff that provides value-added services that are critical to the efficient and effective management of an organization.

According to the National Commission on Fraudulent Financial Reporting (Treadway Commission), every public corporation should have an internal audit function. The New York Stock Exchange also requires an internal audit function for companies traded on their exchange.

IIA Certifications

Certified Internal Auditor® (CIA®)
For more than 30 years, The IIA's premier certification, the Certified Internal Auditor (CIA) designation, has reflected competence in the principles and practices of internal auditing and has served as the only internationally accepted designation for internal auditors. Over 45,000 internal auditors hold the CIA designation the world over.

Certification in Control Self-Assessment® (CCSA®)
The Certification in Control Self-Assessment is the specialty certification for practitioners of control self-assessment (CSA) — the first specialty certification to be offered by The IIA. The CCSA certification program identifies the skill sets needed by successful practitioners of CSA, measures understanding of CSA, and provides guidance for CSA initiatives.

Certified Government Auditing Professional® (CGAP®)
The IIA recognizes the important contributions of government auditors and has developed a certification program that distinguishes leaders in public sector auditing — the Certified Government Auditing Professional (CGAP). Auditors from various levels of government who recognize that auditing in the public sector has unique challenges developed the program.

Certified Financial Services Auditor® (CFSA)
The Certified Financial Services Auditor (CFSA) exam tests a candidate's knowledge of current auditing practices and understanding of internal audit issues, risks, and remedies in the financial services industry. The revised format allows candidates a choice of emphasis in one of three financial services disciplines: Banking, Insurance, and Securities.

Information on the CFSA Examination

CFSA Exam Information

The Institute of Internal Auditors (IIA) has developed a CFSA page on its Web site (www.theiia.org) to provide detailed and updated information on the CFSA exam. We advise you to check this site for the most up-to-date information on the CFSA program. You can also contact The IIA's Customer Service Center (custserv@theiia.org) or Certification Department (certification@theiia.org) for answers to your questions.

- The Certified Financial Services Auditor® (CFSA) is one of The IIA's specialty certifications that measures an individual's knowledge of, and proficiency in, audit principles and practices within the banking, insurance, and securities financial services industries. The exam format offers candidates a choice of three financial services disciplines — banking, insurance, and securities.

CFSA Eligibility Requirements

By applying to become a CFSA candidate, an individual agrees to accept all conditions of the program, including eligibility, exam confidentiality, ethics, and continuing professional education requirements, along with other conditions enacted by The IIA's Board of Regents or Certification Department.

Eligibility Requirements: A CFSA candidate must meet the following eligibility requirements:

- Education: A CFSA candidate must have a bachelor's (four-year) degree or educational equivalent. Two years of post-secondary schooling with an accredited organization plus three years of financial services experience may be substituted for a bachelor's degree. A copy of the degree or transcripts must accompany the application.
- Character Reference: A CFSA candidate must exhibit high moral and professional character and must submit a character reference form signed by a CFSA, a Certified Internal Auditor (CIA), a CCSA (Certification in Control Self-Assessment), a CGAP (Certified Government Auditing Professional), or the candidate's supervisor. The completed character reference form must accompany the application.

- Work Experience: A CFSA candidate must obtain two years of auditing experience in a financial services environment. Work experience must be verified by a CFSA, a CIA, a CCSA, a CGAP, or the candidate's supervisor. The experience verification form may accompany the application or be submitted before or after taking the exam. However, the form must be completed and received by The IIA before a candidate can become certified and use the CFSA designation.

Special Consideration for CIAs, CCSAs, and CGAPs Who Wish to Take the CFSA Exam: *Based on previously met requirements, individuals who hold the CIA, CCSA, or CGAP designations are assumed to have met the education and character requirements of the CFSA program. These individuals will only be required to submit proof of auditing experience in a financial services environment in order to meet the eligibility requirements to sit for the CFSA exam and earn the CFSA designation.*

Eligibility Period: The IIA's approval of a candidate's CFSA application and eligibility allows the candidate to participate in the CFSA program for two years from the date that the application is approved. In addition, each time a candidate sits for the exam, the candidate's eligibility period is extended two years from the date of the last exam taken. A candidate's eligibility expires only if the candidate does not take a single exam within any two-year period.

Exam Non-disclosure and Confidentiality: The CFSA exam is a non-disclosed exam, which means that current exam questions and answers are not published or divulged. Candidates in the CFSA program agree to keep the contents of the exam confidential and therefore may not discuss the specific exam content with anyone except The IIA's Certification Department. Unauthorized disclosure of exam material will be considered a breach of The IIA's Code of Ethics and may result in disqualification of the candidate or other appropriate censure.

Code of Ethics: CFSA candidates agree to abide by the Code of Ethics established by The IIA.

IIA Membership: In most cases, a candidate does not have to be an IIA member to take the exam or receive the CFSA designation. (Requirements may vary in certain countries where the exam is administered under the direction of an IIA affiliate. Please refer to the list of countries with special registration instructions in the "CFSA Registration" section on the following page.) However, there are immediate and long-term member benefits and special offers that a nonmember CFSA candidate may wish to consider, such as:

- Discounts on The IIA's CFSA review materials.
- No charge for Continuing Professional Education (CPE) reporting.
- Access to The IIA's online auditing standards, ethics, and guidance information.
- Access to local IIA affiliates for professional development opportunities.

IIA membership provides access to exclusive member resources and up-to-date information on current issues, a network of more than 120,000 members in hundreds of affiliates and institutes worldwide, professional standards, certification, research, and education. In order to provide an additional forum for financial services auditors, The IIA also offers membership in the Financial Services Auditor (FSA) Group, which serves as a network and communication clearinghouse for FSA guidance and training opportunities.

CFSA Registration

Individuals seeking to take the CFSA exam in Australia, Austria, Belgium, Brazil, China, Czech Republic, France, Germany, Greece, Indonesia, Israel, Italy, Japan, Korea, Malaysia, Morocco, The Netherlands, New Zealand, Norway, Philippines, Singapore, South Africa, Spain, Sweden, Switzerland, Taiwan, Thailand, or Turkey should refer to the special registration instructions on The IIA's Web site (www.theiia.org).

All other CFSA candidates must complete and submit the CFSA application form to The IIA by e-mail, fax, or mail, along with the appropriate fees and other required documentation.

The IIA cannot guarantee a candidate's right to sit for the examination if the required procedures are not followed. The exam fee will be refunded to candidates who are denied entrance into the program.

Exam Testing Sites: Candidates should choose the most convenient location from the exam site list and enter the appropriate site number on the application. The IIA makes every attempt to accommodate site requests. In the event that the requested site is not available, The IIA will assign candidates to the nearest available site. If the assigned site is not acceptable and the candidate chooses not to sit for the exam, the exam fee will be refunded. The exam site in any city changes from one exam cycle to another based upon the group size. Therefore, it is not possible for The IIA to provide candidates with the exact exam site until all applications have been processed and the exam site is selected and secured, which is typically three weeks prior to the exam.

Authorization Letter: Approximately three weeks before the exam date, candidates will receive an authorization letter with a candidate identification number, the exam site number and address, the date and time to report to the site, and the time that the exam will begin and end. This letter is needed for admission to the exam site. Candidates should review the letter for accuracy and report any errors or questions to The IIA's Certification Department at +1-407-937-1323 or e-mail certification@theiia.org. When contacting The IIA, please refer to the candidate identification number. Any candidate who has not received an authorization letter two weeks before the examination date should contact The IIA immediately.

Materials Allowed at the Exam Site: To be admitted to the exam site, a candidate must have the authorization letter and a valid photo identification. Candidates should bring their own pencils and erasers (recommend 2 or 3) to the exam. Pens may not be used.

Candidates also may bring the following items to the exam site:

- A nonprogrammable six-function calculator with only addition, subtraction, multiplication, division, square root, and percentage functions can be used during the examination. Calculators with additional functions (other than numerical memory) will not be allowed.
- A translation dictionary is allowed if the exam is not in the candidate's native language. However, only non-electronic translation dictionaries may be used. Regular (single-language) dictionaries may not be used.
- A drink with lid.

No other items (papers, electronic devices, food, etc.) are allowed at the exam site.

Exam Misconduct: The IIA and its Board of Regents consider candidate misconduct related to the certification process to be a serious offense. If the exam site chairpersons, exam proctors, or IIA Certification Department staff determine that misconduct has occurred, the Board of Regents will immediately refer the case to the International Ethics Committee for action. Reportable offenses include, but are not limited to:

- Copying another candidate's answers during the exam.
- Assisting another candidate during the exam.
- Using unauthorized material during the exam.
- Removing exam booklets, in whole or part, from the exam site.
- Discussing exam questions with anyone other than The IIA Certification Department staff.
- Submitting false credentials.

Actions by the International Ethics Committee may include: invalidation of exam results, disqualification from participation in all IIA certification programs, and publication of the results of their due process in an IIA publication. If evidence of misconduct is discovered after a candidate has been awarded an IIA certification, it may be revoked.

CFSA Exam Schedule and Fees

The CFSA exam is a prepaid event. All fees are due at the time of registration.

CFSA Exam Schedule

The CFSA exam is offered in May and November, with other special offerings at various times during the year in conjunction with certain events, such as IIA conferences. The registration deadline for the May exams is March 31, and the registration deadline for the November exams is September 30. Please refer to The IIA's Web site (www.theiia.org under Certification/CFSA) for more information on exam schedules and registration deadlines.

CFSA Exam Fees*

Regular Exam Fee — *includes $50 non-refundable application fee and $175 test fee.*	US $225
Retest Exam Fee — *includes $175 test fee only.*	US $175
Canadian Exam Site Tax (percent of total fees paid)	GST - 7%; HST - 15%
*Prices are subject to change.	

1. Exam dates and fees are subject to change.
2. All fees must be prepaid.
3. Fees may vary in certain countries where the exam is administered under the direction of an IIA affiliate. Please refer to the list of countries with special registration instructions in the "CFSA Registration" section on page 7.
4. Candidates who are paying with a wire transfer, direct deposit, or separate company check must include a copy of the transaction form with their application.
5. Requests for a receipt for reimbursement purposes should be sent to The IIA's Customer Service Center at custserv@theiia.org.
6. Exam results will be withheld pending payment of any outstanding fees.

CFSA Application Fee Waiver: If a candidate is a member of The IIA, has attended The IIA's Financial Services Conference, and is planning to take the CFSA exam for the first time, The IIA will waive the $50 non-refundable application fee. To take advantage of this special offer, the candidate should include the Continuing Professional Education (CPE) letter from the conference with the CFSA application and ask for the waiver. This offer is not retroactive. The $50 application fee waiver can only be used if the candidate attended the course within one year prior to sitting for the exam.

Refunds: Test fees are refundable with a written request by the application deadline. A US $25 processing fee will be charged.

Deferrals, Changes, Cancellations, or No-shows: Candidates must notify The IIA in writing (via mail, fax, or e-mail) to make changes to their registration, such as changing examination sites, deferring to sit at a later examination, or canceling the registration. Payment of any required fees is due at the time the change is made.

Deferrals, changes, or cancellations may be made at no cost if written notice is received by the application deadline. However, a US $25 fee will be charged for any exam fee refund requests. A US $35 fee will be charged for deferrals, changes, or cancellations received after the deadline. This fee increases to US $100 beginning on the Wednesday of the week before the exam date. Please note that The IIA will not accept or process any exam site change requests beginning on the Wednesday of the week prior to the exam date. Deferrals, changes, or cancellations will not be accepted without receipt of the appropriate payment, and requests may not be submitted separately from payments. Any remaining monies will be held in the candidate's account pending further instructions. Monies left in the account after a candidate's eligibility period expires are subject to forfeiture.

Professional Recognition Credit for Part IV of the Certified Internal Auditor® (CIA®) Exam

The IIA's Board of Regents has approved the CFSA designation for Professional Recognition Credit for Part IV (PRC-IV) of the CIA exam.

CIA candidates who have successfully completed the CFSA examination are eligible to receive credit for Part IV of the CIA exam. CIA candidates who attain PRC-IV and pass Parts I, II, and III will have satisfied the examination requirement for the CIA designation.

To apply for PRC-IV, CIA candidates who have passed the CFSA exam should check the PRC-IV box on the CIA application/registration form or request PRC-IV through The IIA's Customer Service Center (custserv@theiia.org) and should indicate that they have passed the CFSA exam. The PRC-IV administrative fee is waived for CIA candidates who request PRC-IV based on the CFSA exam.

CFSA Exam Grading and Results

Concerns Regarding Exam Questions: Candidates who have concerns regarding exam questions or the testing experience should submit their comments by fax (+1-407-937-1313) or by e-mail to certification@theiia.org. These comments must be received within 96 hours of completion of the exam so that they will be available to the Board of Regents for review before grading begins. Comments on exam questions must identify the general content of the question and briefly outline any perceived flaw. Candidate input is gratefully acknowledged and considered in the evaluation of the exam and the testing program.

Exam Grading Process: The Board of Regents and the Certification Department staff strive to maintain fairness and consistency in grading the CFSA exam. Exam questions are graded with an optical scanner, and any irregularities are thoroughly researched. The grading process includes both a pre-exam review of the suggested responses and a post-exam review of the statistical performance of exam questions. Based on this review, appropriate scoring modifications and adjustments to the grading scale may be made.

Passing Score: Statistical information from pre-tested questions is used to maintain comparable difficulty from one CFSA exam to the next. Because the exact number of questions required to pass the exam may adjust slightly from one exam to the next, all raw scores are converted to a reporting scale of 250 to 750 points in order to ensure a common standard. A scaled score of 600 points or higher is required to pass the CFSA exam. (A scaled score of 600 would be the equivalent of achieving 75 percent correct on an exam of appropriate difficulty.)

Exam Results: Exam results are mailed by July 15 for May exams and by January 15 for November exams. Specific passing scores are not reported. Requests for copies of grade letters will not be accepted until two weeks after these dates. Access to grade information is limited to The IIA's Certification Department, and grades cannot be released by telephone or posted on The IIA's Web site. Due to the extensive exam review process outlined above, changes to candidates' scores are not possible after grades are released. Re-grades are not available.

Reapplication: In order to retake the CFSA exam, candidates must reapply by completing the reapplication registration form that accompanies the grade letter or by contacting The IIA's Customer Service Center: e-mail: custserv@theiia.org, fax: +1-407-937-1101, tel: +1-407-937-1111. The candidate must also pay the appropriate exam fee.

Certificates: Once a candidate has successfully completed the CFSA exam and met all program requirements, The IIA mails the CFSA certificate to the local IIA affiliate for presentation to the successful candidate. A listing of IIA affiliates may be found by visiting "The IIA" at www.theiia.org.

Exam Performance Awards: Awards are conferred annually to candidates who achieve outstanding exam performance.

Continuing Professional Education

Upon certification, CFSAs are required to maintain their knowledge and skills and stay abreast of improvements and current developments in the financial services auditing environment through Continuing Professional Education (CPE). CFSAs must acquire 40 hours of CPE every two years and report these hours in compliance with CPE reporting requirements. In acknowledgment of the study time required to successfully complete the CFSA exam, the CPE requirement is waived for the year the exam is passed and for the subsequent year.

If a CFSA is also a CIA, the CPE reporting that the CFSA completes for the CIA program satisfies the CPE reporting requirement for the CFSA certification. IIA members can report their CPE hours at no cost. Nonmembers incur a US $50 fee for CPE reporting. Further information on the CPE requirements is available on The IIA's Web site (www.theiia.org).

Financial Services Auditor Group

A Special Membership Section Exclusively for Financial Services Audit Professionals

The Financial Services Auditor (FSA) Group is a special subsection of The IIA membership, providing auditors in banking, brokerage, and insurance with specific guidance and hands-on assistance to help them navigate through the sea of regulations and requirements. The following mission statement has been developed for the Financial Services Auditor Group and the *FSA Times* newsletter.

Financial Services Auditor Group Mission Statement

The mission of The Institute of Internal Auditors' Financial Services Auditor Group is to enhance, promote, and represent the internal audit professional in the financial services industry. Through its partnership with The IIA, the Financial Services Auditor Group will offer the following high-quality services to accomplish its mission:

- Sponsor a comprehensive certification program.
- Provide effective, cost-beneficial training.
- Develop quality internal audit educational products and research.
- Communicate and share best practices with members through a quarterly newsletter.
- Provide networking opportunities for its members, including an annual directory.

FSA Times Mission Statement

The *FSA Times* quarterly newsletter helps keep members of the Financial Services Auditor Group current on emerging issues within the financial services industry and profession, and provides news, instructional articles, and links to Web resources about auditing financial services.

A Financial Services Advisory Board has been established to oversee the FSA Group. The chairman of the Advisory Board is Thomas J. Beirne, CFSA, Protiviti Inc.

Members are:

Mark E. Arning, New York Life Insurance Company
Jennifer F. Burke, Crowe Chizek and Company LLC
Steven E. Jameson, CIA, CFSA, Community Trust Bank
Frederick Purser, Friedman Billings Ramesy Group Inc.
Leo M. Stenson, CIA, Bryn Mawr Trust Company
Michael V. Trieste, CFSA, HSH Nordbank
Edward C. Weiss, CFSA, Protiviti Inc.
Scott D. White, CIA, CFSA, John Hancock Financial Services

Please contact the members of the advisory board if you have ideas or suggestions for improving the benefits or services of the FSA Group.

Section Membership

The Financial Services Auditor Group is open to members of The IIA and is only US $40 per year in addition to IIA membership dues. If you have further questions, please e-mail karen.ryland@theiia.org.

Some program services will be provided via e-mail to ensure that you receive the information you need in a timely manner.

CFSA Exam Content and Format

The CFSA exam tests a candidate's knowledge of current auditing practices and understanding of internal audit issues, risks, and remedies in the financial services industry.

- The exam consists of 125 multiple-choice questions.
- The testing period is three hours and thirty minutes.
- Exam questions are all multiple-choice (objective) with four-answer choices.
- The first 100 questions cover general financial services auditing activities and topics in all three financial services disciplines at the awareness level.
- The remaining 25 questions specifically address the candidate's chosen discipline — banking, insurance, and securities — at the proficiency level.
- CFSA candidates may choose any one of the three disciplines as part of their CFSA exam.
- Candidates may not choose to be tested on more than one discipline.
- The CFSA designation does not distinguish one chosen discipline from another.

The CFSA exam core content covers four domains:

Domain I – Financial Services Auditing *(25-35 percent)*
Domain II – Auditing Financial Services Products *(25-35 percent)*
Domain III – Auditing Financial Services Processes *(25-35 percent)*
Domain IV – The Regulatory Environment *(10-20 percent)*

Individual Financial Services Discipline Sections *(25 Questions - Proficiency Level)*

- Banking: Products, Processes, and The Regulatory Environment
- Insurance: Products, Processes, and The Regulatory Environment
- Securities: Products, Processes, and The Regulatory Environment

Domains for the CFSA Examination

Domain I — Financial Services Auditing (25-35% Proficiency Level)

A. IIA Professional Practices Framework
B. Internal Control/Risk Management/Governance
   1. Internal Control Frameworks
   2. Risk Management Frameworks
   3. Governance Models
C. Audit Process
   1. Audit Planning
   2. Audit Fieldwork
      a. Risk Assessment
      b. Analytical Review
      c. Data Gathering and Evaluation
      d. Testing
      e. Tools and Techniques (e.g., CAAT)
   3. Audit Communications
   4. Monitoring Outcomes
D. Implications of Information Technology
E. Auditing Financial Statement Elements
   1. Balance Sheet
   2. Statement of Cash Flows
   3. Income/Expense Statements
   4. Off-balance-sheet Items

Domain II — Auditing Financial Services Products (25-35% Awareness Level)

A. Lending/Loans
B. Deposits
C. Trusts
D. Annuities
E. Derivatives
F. Electronic Services
G. Cash Management Services
H. Stocks
I. Bonds
J. Commodities
K. Mutual Funds
L. Employee Benefits

M. Capital Market Products
N. Securities Lending
O. Insurance Policies
P. Insurance Products
Q. Foreign Exchange
R. Asset Management (e.g., supervision of fund managers' portfolios and valuations)
S. Money Market Products

Domain III — Auditing Financial Service Processes (25-35% Awareness Level)

A. Risk Management
   1. Asset/Liability Management
   2. Trading Market Risk
   3. Credit, Liquidity, Operational Risk
   4. Allowance for Loan and Lease Losses
   5. Reserves
B. Underwriting
   1. Loans
   2. Securities
   3. Insurance
   4. Private Placement
   5. Initial Public Offerings
C. Securitizations
D. Treasury Operations (e.g., Cash Management)
E. Back-office Operations
F. Marketing Sales and Distribution (e.g., Insurance Agencies, Bank Branches, Brokers)
G. Claims
H. Investments
I. Broker-dealer Activities
J. Rating Advisory Service
K. Mergers and Acquisitions
L. Loan Operations (e.g., Collateral Issues, Perfecting Liens)

Domain IV — The Regulatory Environment (10-20% Awareness Level)

A. Overview of the Regulatory Environment
   1. Function of Central Bank
   2. Function of Insurance Regulators
   3. Function of Securities Regulators
B. Laws and Regulations
   1. Equal Credit Opportunity/Antidiscrimination
   2. Home Mortgage Disclosure

3. Reserve Requirements
4. Insider Transactions
5. Lending Disclosure
6. Deposits Disclosure
7. Real Estate Sales Disclosure
8. Self-assessment of Internal Controls/Risk Management
9. Investor/Depositor Protection
10. Financial and Personal Information Privacy
11. Anti-money Laundering

C. Stock Exchanges and Other Markets
D. Money and Banking
   1. Role of Money and Banking
   2. Bond and Stock Markets
   3. Effect of Interest Rate Movements
   4. Monetary Management Theories

Individual Financial Services Discipline Sections (25 Questions - Proficiency Level)

Banking (25 questions at the proficiency level)

A. Financial Statement Application
   1. Assets
      a. Cash and Due from Banks
      b. Federal Funds Sold and Securities Purchased under Resale Agreements
      c. Interest-bearing Accounts
      d. Trading Securities
      e. Securities Available for Sale
      f. Loans
         i. Commercial
         ii. Residential
         iii. Consumer
         iv. Leases
         v. Credit Card
         vi. International
      g. Allowance for Loan Losses
      h. Premises and Equipment
      i. Customer Acceptances (Letters of Credit)
      j. Intangible Assets
      k. Other Assets

2. Liabilities and Shareholders Equity
   a. Deposits
      i. Non-interest Bearing
      ii. Interest Bearing
      iii. Savings
      iv. Time
   b. Securities Sold under Repurchase Agreements
   c. Other Borrowed Funds
   d. Long-term Debt
   e. Preferred/Common Stock
   f. Retained Earnings
   g. Treasury Stock
3. Other Services/Operations
   a. Payroll/Employee Benefits
   b. Automated Clearing House Wire Transfer
   c. Branch Operations
   d. Trust
      i. Personal
      ii. Corporate
      iii. Employee Benefit
      iv. Transfer/Registrar
   e. Investment Products
   f. Asset/Liability Management
   g. Use of Derivatives
   h. Statement of Cash Flows
4. Money and Banking
   a. Role of Money and Banking
   b. Bond and Stock Markets
   c. Effect of Interest Rate Movements
   d. Monetary Management Theories

B. Laws/Regulations and Regulatory Environment
1. Overview of the Regulatory Environment
   a. Federal Reserve System
   b. Office of the Comptroller of the Currency
   c. FDIC
   d. State Regulatory Systems
   e. National Credit Union Administration (NUCA)
2. Laws and Regulations
   Regulation A - Borrowing by Depository Institutions
   Regulation B - Equal Credit Opportunity Act
   Regulation C - Home Mortgage Disclosure Act

Regulation D - Reserve Requirements
Regulation E - Electronic Funds Transfer Act
Regulation F - Limitations on Interbank Liabilities
Regulation G - Disclosure and Reporting of CRA-related Agreements
Regulation H - Membership of State Banking Institutions in the Federal Reserve System
Regulation I - Issue and Cancellation of Capital Stock of Federal Reserve Banks
Regulation J - Collection of Checks and Other Items
Regulation K - Edge Act
Regulation L - Interlocks Act
Regulation M - Consumer Leasing
Regulation N - Relationships with Foreign Banks and Bankers
Regulation O - Loans to Executive Officers
Regulation P - Bank Protection Act
Regulation Q - Interest on Deposits
Regulation S - Reimbursement for Providing Financial Records
Regulation T - Credit by Brokers and Dealers
Regulation U - Credit by Banks for Purchase of Margin Stocks
Regulation V - Fair Credit Reporting
Regulation W - Transactions Between Member Banks and Their Affiliates
Regulation Y - Bank Holding Company Act
Regulation Z - Truth in Lending
Regulation AA
Regulation BB - Community Reinvestment Act
Regulation CC - Availability of Funds and Collection of Checks
Regulation DD - Truth in Savings
Regulation EE - Netting Eligibility for Financial Institution
Regulation FF - Obtaining and Using Medical Information in Connection with Credit

Insurance (25 questions at the proficiency level)

A. Products
  1. Individual/Group
     a. Whole Life
     b. Term Life
     c. Universal Life
     d. Endowments
     e. Property and Casualty
     f. Health
     g. Managed Care
     h. Disability
     i. Flood Insurance

j. Dental
k. Utilization Management
l. Long-term Care
m. Other
2. Pensions
a. Qualified Plans
b. Individual Retirement Plans
c. Savings Plans
d. Vesting
e. Fiduciaries
f. Annuities
3. Reinsurance

B. Processes
1. Risk Management
a. Reinsurance
b. Reserves
c. Asset/Liability Management
d. Investments
e. Actuarial
2. Underwriting
3. Treasury Operations (e.g., Cash Management)
4. Back-office Operations
5. Proof/Items Processing and Settlement
6. Claims
7. Policy Loans
8. Marketing Sales and Distribution (e.g., Insurance Agencies)
9. Mergers and Acquisitions

C. The Regulatory Environment
1. Overview (e.g., Function of Insurance Regulators)
2. Laws and Regulations
a. Reserve Requirements
b. Financial and Personal Information Privacy
c. Self-assessment of Internal Controls/Risk Management
d. Securities and Exchange Commission

Securities (25 questions at the proficiency level)

A. Products
   1. Trusts
      a. Personal
      b. Corporate
      c. Employee Benefits
      d. Transfer/Registrar
   2. Annuities
      a. Fixed
      b. Variable
      c. Real Estate
   3. Derivatives
      a. Swaps
      b. Options
      c. Other Components (e.g., Structured, Credit, Interest, Futures, Forwards)
   4. Stocks
      a. Common
      b. Preferred
      c. Warrants
      d. Debt Securities
      e. Options
   5. Bonds
      a. Convertible
      b. Straight
   6. Commodities
   7. Mutual Funds
      a. Income
      b. Stock
      c. Growth
      d. Balanced Funds
      e. Specialized Funds
   8. Capital Market Products
      a. Real Estate Investment Trust
      b. Repurchase Agreements
   9. Securities Lending
   10. Asset Management (e.g., supervision of fund managers' portfolios and valuations)
   11. Money Market Products

B. Processes
   1. Risk Management
      a. Trading Market Risk
      b. Asset/Liability Management
      c. Reserves
   2. Underwriting
      a. Securities
      b. Initial Public Offerings
   3. Securitizations
   4. Treasury Operations
   5. Back-office Operations
   6. Marketing Sales and Distribution (e.g., Brokers)
   7. Investments
   8. Broker/Dealer Activities
   9. Mergers and Acquisitions

C. The Regulatory Environment
   1. Overview (e.g., Function of Securities Regulators)
   2. Laws and Regulations
      a. Reserve Requirements
      b. Insider Transactions
      c. Self-assessment of Internal Controls/Risk Management
      d. Investor Protection
      e. Financial and Personal Information Privacy
      f. Anti-money Laundering
   3. Financial Markets
      a. Overview
         1) Brokers and Dealers
         2) Types of orders
         3) New issues
         4) Clearing and settlement process
      b. Stock Exchanges
      c. Over-the-Counter (OTC) Market
      d. Future and Options Markets
   4. Money and Banking
      a. Theories on the Effect of Interest Rate Movements
      b. Monetary Management Theories

Note: *Exam topics and/or format are subject to change as approved by the Board of Regents.*

Proficiency Level — Candidates must exhibit proficiency (thorough understanding; ability to apply concepts) in these topic areas.

Awareness Level — Candidates must exhibit awareness (knowledge of terminology and fundamentals) in these topic areas.

Domains and Disciplines Matrix

The following matrix identifies topics that are addressed in a domain (I, II, III, IV) and also addressed in more detail in the Banking, Insurance, and/or Securities Discipline sections.

The large column on the left mirrors the outline of each of the individual domains. If material is covered in the domain is also covered in a discipline section, a reference to the appropriate outline is included.

		DISCIPLINES		
	Domain I – Financial Services Auditing	**Banking**	**Insurance**	**Securities**
D	**A** IIA Professional Practices Framework			
O	**B** Internal Control/Risk Management/Governance			
M	**B.1** Internal Control Frameworks			
A	**B.2** Risk Management Frameworks			
I	**B.3** Governance Models			
N	**C** Audit Process			
S	**C.1** Audit Planning			
	C.2 Audit Fieldwork			
	C.2 a Risk Assessment			
	C.2 b Analytical Review			
	C.2 c Data Gathering and Evaluation			
	C.2 d Testing			
	C.2 e Tools and Techniques (e.g., CAAT)			
	C.3 Audit Communications			
	C.4 Monitoring Outcomes			
	D Implications of Information Technology			
	E Auditing Financial Elements			
	E.1 Balance Sheet			
	E.2 Statement of Cash Flows			
	E.3 Income/Expense Statement			
	E.4 Off-balance-sheet Items			

		DISCIPLINES		
	Domain II – Auditing Financial Services Products	**Banking**	**Insurance**	**Securities**
D	**A** Lending/Loans	A.1		
O	**B** Deposits	A.2		
M	**C** Trusts			A.1
A	**D** Annuities			A.2
I	**E** Derivatives			A.3
N	**F** Electronic Services	A.3, B.5.d		
S	**G** Cash Management Services			
	H Stocks			A.4
	I Bonds			A.5
	J Commodities			A.6
	K Mutual Funds			A.7
	L Employee Benefits	B.5.a		
	M Capital Market Products			A.8
	N Securities Lending			A.9
	O Insurance Policies			
	P Insurance Products		A.	
	Q Foreign Exchange	A.4		
	R Asset Management (e.g., supervision of fund manager's portfolio and valuations)	A.5		A.10
	S Money Market Products			A.11

		DISCIPLINES		
	Domain III – Auditing Financial Services Processes	**Banking**	**Insurance**	**Securities**
D	**A.** Risk Management	B.1	B.1	B.1
O	**A.1** Asset/Liability Management	B.1.c	B.1.c	B.1.b
M	**A.2** Trading Market Risk	B.1.e		B.1.a
A	**A.3** Credit, Liquidity, Operational Risk	B.1.a		
I	**A.4** Allowance for Loan and Lease Losses	B.1.b		
N	**A.5** Reserves	B.1.b	B.1.d	B.1.c
S	**B** Underwriting	B.2	B.2	B.2
	B.1 Loans	B.2.a		
	B.2 Securities			B.2.a
	B.3 Insurance		B.2	
	B.4 Private Placement	B.2.b		
	B.5 Initial Public Offerings			B.2.b
	C Securitizations			B.3
	D Treasury Operation (e.g., Cash Management)	B.4	B.3	B.4
	E Back-office Operations	B.5	B.4	B.5
	F Marketing Sales and Distribution (e.g., Insurance Agencies, Bank Branches, Brokers)	B.6	B.8	B.6
	G Claims		B.6	
	H Investments		B.1.d	B.7
	I Broker-dealer Activities	B.10		B.8
	J Rating Advisory Service	B.7		
	K Mergers and Acquisitions	B.8	B.9	B.9
	L Loan Operations (e.g., Collateral Issues, Perfecting Liens)	B.9		

		DISCIPLINES		
	Domain IV – The Regulatory Environment	**Banking**	**Insurance**	**Securities**
D	**A**. Overview of Regulatory Environment	C.	C.	C.
O	**A.1** Function of Central Bank	C.1		
M	**A.2** Function of Insurance Regulators		C.1	
A	**A.3** Functions of Securities Regulators			C.1
I	**A.5** Reserves	B.1.b	B.1.d	B.1.c
N	**B** Laws and Regulations	C.2	C.2	C.2
S	**B.1** Equal Credit Opportunity/Antidiscrimination	C.2.a		
	B.2 Home Mortgage Disclosure	C.2.b		
	B.3 Reserve Requirements	C.2.c	C.2.a	C.2.a
	B.4 Insider Transactions			C.2.b
	B.5 Lending Disclosure	C.2.d		
	B.6 Deposits Disclosure	C.2.e		
	B.7 Real Estate Sales Disclosure	C.2.f		
	B.8 Self-assessment of Internal Controls/ Risk Management	C.2.g	C.2.c	C.2.c
	B.9 Investor/Depositor Protection	C.2.e		C.2.d
	B.10 Financial and Personal Information Privacy	C.2.h	C.2.b	C.2.e
	B.11 Anti-money Laundering	C.2.i		C.2.f
	C Stock Exchanges and Other Markets			C.3.b,c,d
	D Money and Banking	C.3		C.4
	D.1 Role of Money and Banking	C.3.a		
	D.2 Bond and Stock Markets			A.4, A.5
	D.3 Effect of Interest Rate Movements	C.3.b		C.4.a
	D.4 Monetary Management Theories	C.3.c		C.4.b

Additional Review Materials to Supplement This Guide

Additional Potential References for CFSA Exam from The IIA's Web Site
(Refer to The IIA's Web site for the most current list)

The CFSA exam is a self-study exam and does not require a prescribed curriculum. Candidates may choose their own method of preparing for the exam.

Sample Questions: The IIA provides a limited number of sample questions on its Web site at Certification/CFSA to give candidates an understanding of the types of questions that typically appear on the CFSA exam.

Other Books: The IIARF bookstore offers several books on general financial services auditing. While these books are not written as CFSA exam study guides, they may assist candidates in preparing for the CFSA exam.

- *Auditing Derivative Strategies*, Davison, Barbara (The Institute of Internal Auditors, 2000)
- *Auditing Investments*, Davison, Barbara (The Institute of Internal Auditors, 1999)
- *The Broker-Dealer Audit Guide*, Ross, Richard (The Institute of Internal Auditors, 2001)
- *Economic Value Management – Applications and Techniques*, Bloxham, Eleanor (John Willey & Sons, 2003)
- *Financial Shenanigans: How to Detect Accounting Gimmicks and Fraud in Financial Reports*, Schilit, Howard (McGraw Hill, 2002)
- *Mergers, Acquisitions, and Divestitures: Control and Audit Best Practices*, Selim, Georges, Sudarsanam, Sudi, and Lavine, Michael (The Institute of Internal Auditors Research Foundation, 2002)
- *Understanding the Mergers and Acquisition Process*, Davison, Barbara (The Institute of Internal Auditors, 2001)

IIA Seminars: The IIA offers the following seminars on financial services auditing practices and principles. While these are not exam review courses, they may be helpful to candidates in preparing for the CFSA exam:

- Auditing Investment Activities
- Fighting Fraudulent Financial Reporting

Additional Suggested References for CFSA Exam Recommended by the Authors of This Guide

Audit and General Resources

Sawyer's Internal Auditing, 5th Edition,
Lawrence B. Sawyer, JD, CIA, PA, Mortimer A. Dittenhofer, Ph.D., CIA, James H. Scheiner, Ph.D., with contributions from Anne Graham, Ph.D., and Paul Makosz
Altamonte Springs, FL: The Institute of Internal Auditors, 2003
(Book included for coverage of general audit process, fraud, statistical sampling, etc.)

Business Risk Assessment
McNamee, David
Altamonte Springs, FL: The Institute of Internal Auditors, 1998

IS Audit

Control Objectives for Information and Related Technology (Cobit 4.0)
Information Systems Audit and Control Association and Foundation, 2005

Systems Auditability and Control
Altamonte Springs, FL: The Institute of Internal Auditors

Banking

Cannon Financial Institute, Inc.,
Internal Audit II
University of North Carolina-Charlotte, 1999

Internet Resources

The Institute of Internal Auditors (IIA)
http://www.theiia.org/

Information Systems Audit and Control Association (ISACA)
http://www.isaca.org/

American Institute of Certified Public Accountants (AICPA)
http://www.aicpa.org/index.htm

Association of Certified Fraud Examiners
http://www.cfenet.com

Auditnet
http://www.auditnet.org

Code of Federal Regulations
http://www.gpoaccess.gov/

U.S. Securities and Exchange Commission
http://www.sec.gov

The Financial Markets Association
http://www.aciforex.com

Financial Accounting Standards Board
http://www.fasb.org

Federal Reserve Bank of New York
http://www.ny.frb.org

Comptroller of the Currency, Administrator of National Banks
http://www.occ.treas.gov

International Securities Lending Association
http://www.isla.co.uk

Preparing to Pass the CFSA Examination

1. Begin preparing well in advance of the test date.
2. Secure the proper study materials. A list of supplemental books and materials is provided in this study guide.
3. Find a suitable place to study.
4. Familiarize yourself with the exam site and surrounding facilities.
5. Relax and get plenty of sleep the night before the test.
6. Arrive at the exam site in plenty of time before the test begins.
7. Dress comfortably.

Test-taking Tips

1. Read the entire question slowly and carefully before attempting to answer it.
2. Answer the questions in which you are certain of the answer first, then go back and spend the remainder of the available time working on the other questions.
3. Budget your time.
4. Read answer choices carefully.
5. Answer all questions. The number of correct answers determines your final score on the CFSA examination. Therefore, there is no penalty for providing a wrong answer. Guessing is better than not answering a question at all.

Sample CFSA Questions

The 14 sample questions below are provided to give candidates a preview of the format and content of the CFSA exam questions. These questions may not have been pre-tested and may therefore vary in difficulty from the pre-tested questions used on the CFSA exam. While these sample questions are intended to be generally representative of those on the CFSA exam, a candidate's results on this small group of questions should not be taken as a guarantee of performance on the CFSA exam.

The solution for each question is included in the following section of the guide.

1. Which of the following situations would **not** impair audit objectivity?

   A. An auditor is assigned to audit a business function that the auditor was responsible for nine months ago.
   B. An individual temporarily assigned to the internal audit activity because of the individual's expert knowledge in a particular business function is assigned to audit an activity that the individual was responsible for just prior to transferring to the internal audit activity.
   C. An auditor is assigned to perform a post-implementation review on a system for which the auditor participated in the design of controls during the system's design process.
   D. An auditor is assigned to perform a post-implementation review on a system for which the auditor performed a procedure review and made control recommendations prior to the system's implementation.

2. Compliance testing is designed primarily to:

   A. Hold detection risk to an acceptable level.
   B. Determine whether policies and procedures have been followed.
   C. Determine that account balances exist, are accurate, and are properly classified.
   D. Provide evidence about monetary misstatements.

3. Which of the following are typical information systems controls that are used to ensure properly authorized transactions?

   I. Online validation routines that check dollar authority limits.
   II. Online user access controls.
   III. Automated balancing and reconciliation routines.
   IV. Edits that validate full completion of data input fields.

   A. I and II only.
   B. II and III only.
   C. III and IV only.
   D. I, II, and IV only.

4. Commercial banks create money by:

   A. Making loans.
   B. Selling government bonds to the public.
   C. Placing reserves at the Federal Reserve Bank.
   D. Repurchasing their stock on the open market.

5. Which of the following are generally considered to be characteristics of savings deposits?

   I. Interest bearing.
   II. No stated maturity.
   III. Penalty for withdrawal.

   A. I and II only.
   B. I and III only.
   C. II and III only.
   D. I, II, and III.

6. The time that a new group member must wait before becoming eligible to enroll in a group insurance plan is known as the:

   A. Actively-at-work provision.
   B. Probationary period.
   C. Eligibility period.
   D. Enrollment period.

7. An entity that purchases and sells securities on its own behalf is acting as:

   A. A broker.
   B. A dealer.
   C. An agent.
   D. A principal.

8. Which of the following statements about the over-the-counter market is **false**?

   A. Mutual funds and other new issues are initially issued over the counter.
   B. Security prices are determined through auction bidding.
   C. Broker dealers must be registered.
   D. Securities are traded at many locations throughout the country.

9. Which statement is correct concerning commercial letters of credit?

   A. A letter of credit is not a negotiable instrument, and the contract of sale between the buyer and seller is independent of the letter of credit.
   B. A letter of credit is not a negotiable instrument, and the contract of sale between the buyer and seller is dependent on the letter of credit.
   C. A letter of credit is a negotiable instrument, and the contract of sale between the buyer and seller is independent of the letter of credit.
   D. A letter of credit is a negotiable instrument, and the contract of sale between the buyer and seller is dependent on the letter of credit.

10. If a corporation has an asset sensitive gap in a rising interest rate environment, which of the following would be considered an appropriate hedging strategy to prevent a decrease in net interest income?

A. Take no action.
B. Purchase an interest rate floor.
C. Enter into an interest rate swap to receive fixed and pay floating rate payments.
D. Enter into an interest rate swap to receive floating and pay fixed rate payments.

11. Which of the following statements about endowments is correct?

A. Endowment insurance pays a benefit amount only if the insured dies during the specified term of coverage.
B. Premiums vary throughout the term of an endowment policy.
C. An endowment can be purchased with a single premium or with a series of premiums over a limited period of time.
D. Unlike permanent life insurance policies, endowment policies do not steadily build cash values.

12. Which of the following would **not** generally be a responsibility of an underwriting department?

A. Helping policy owners with requests for information, interpreting policy language, answering questions regarding policy coverage.
B. Verifying that the mortality/morbidity rates of the company's insureds do not exceed the rates assumed when the premiums were calculated.
C. Considering the applicant's age, weight, physical condition, personal/family history, and other factors to determine the degree of risk.
D. Negotiating and managing reinsurance agreements.

13. In which of the following ways are call and put options used by the options investor in purchase and sales transactions?

I. A long call allows the investor to purchase the underlying security at the specified strike price after the option expiration date.
II. A long put allows the investor to sell the underlying security at the specified strike price until the option expiration date.
III. An investor who is short a call is obligated to sell the underlying security at the specified strike price if a call option is exercised after the option expiration date.
IV. An investor who is short a put is obligated to buy the underlying security at the specified strike price if a put option is exercised by the option expiration date.

A. I and II only.
B. I and III only.
C. II and III only.
D. II and IV only.

14. In which of the following ways would the writer of an uncovered call usually make a profit?

    I. The call expires.
    II. The underlying stock splits.
    III. The underlying stock goes up in price.
    IV. The underlying stock goes down in price.

    A. III only.
    B. I and IV only.
    C. II and IV only.
    D. I, II, and III only.

Suggested Solutions to Sample CFSA Questions

Question 1
Solution: D

A. Incorrect. Practice Advisory 1130.A1-1 states that "objectivity is presumed to be impaired when internal auditors perform an assurance review of any activity for which they had authority or responsibility within the past year." "Persons transferred to or temporarily engaged by the internal audit activity should not be assigned to audit those activities they previously performed until a reasonable period of time (at least one year) has elapsed."
B. Incorrect. Practice Advisory 1130.A1-1 states that "persons transferred to or temporarily engaged by the internal audit activity should not be assigned to audit those activities they previously performed until a reasonable period of time (at least one year) has elapsed."
C. Incorrect. Practice Advisory 1130.A1-1 states that "the auditor's objectivity is considered to be impaired if the auditor designs, installs, drafts procedures for, or operates ...systems."
D. **Correct.** Practice Advisory 1130.A1-1 states that "the internal auditor's objectivity is not adversely affected when the auditor recommends standards of control for systems or reviews procedures before they are implemented."

Question 2
Solution: B

A. Incorrect. Ensuring that risk is at an acceptable level is a characteristic of substantive testing.
B. **Correct.** Compliance testing is designed primarily to determine whether policies and procedures have been followed.
C. Incorrect. Reviewing account balances for existence, accuracy, and correct classification are components of substantive testing.
D. Incorrect. Providing evidence related to monetary misstatements is a component of substantive testing.

Question 3
Solution: A

A. **Correct.** Online validation routines that check dollar authority limits is a control that ensures that individuals do not input amounts exceeding a predefined limit, and is therefore a control to ensure that only authorized transactions occur. Online user access controls are controls to ensure only authorized users will be granted access.
B. Incorrect. Online user access controls are controls to ensure only authorized users will be granted access. However, automated balancing and reconciliation routines are controls which ensure that transactions are complete and accurate.

C. Incorrect. Automated balancing and reconciliation routines are controls which ensure that transactions are complete and accurate. Edits which validate full completion of data input fields is control to ensure the completeness of processing.
D. Incorrect. Online validation routines that check dollar authority limits is a control that ensures that individuals do not input amounts exceeding a predefined limit, and is therefore a control to ensure that only authorized transactions occur. Online user access controls are controls to ensure only authorized users will be granted access. However, edits which validate full completion of data input fields is control to ensure the completeness of processing.

Question 4
Solution: A

A. **Correct.** Commercial banks create money through loans.
B. Incorrect. Money decreases as banks sell government bonds to the public. Instead, money is created when banks buy government bonds from the public.
C. Incorrect. Placing reserves at the Federal Reserve Bank only transfers money from one account to another account on the bank's balance sheet. Money is not created.
D. Incorrect. Repurchasing their stock on the open market only moves money from the bank to the seller. No money is created.

Question 5
Solution: A

A. **Correct.** Savings accounts are interest bearing and do not have a stated date of maturity. Dates of maturity refer to dates on which debts must be repaid.
B. Incorrect. Savings accounts are interest bearing. However, penalties for withdrawal are not associated with savings accounts. They are associated with time deposit accounts.
C. Incorrect. II is correct because savings accounts do not have dates of maturity. Dates of maturity are associated with repayments for debts. However, III is not correct in that penalties or withdrawal are not associated with savings accounts. They are associated with time deposit accounts.
D. Incorrect. Savings accounts are interest bearing and do not have a stated date of maturity. Dates of maturity refer to dates on which debts must be repaid. However, penalties or withdrawal are not associated with savings accounts. They are associated with time deposit accounts.

Question 6
Solution: B

A. Incorrect. The actively-at-work provision requires that the employee is only eligible for coverage if the employee is actively at work.
B. **Correct.** The probationary period is the time that a new group member must wait before becoming eligible to enroll in a group insurance plan.
C. Incorrect. Eligibility period, also known as the enrollment period, is the time during which a new group member may first enroll for coverage.

D. Incorrect. The enrollment period, also known as the eligibility period, is the time during which a new group member may first enroll for coverage.

Question 7
Solution: B

A. Incorrect. A broker would buy and sell securities of others.
B. **Correct.** A dealer purchases and sells securities on its own behalf.
C. Incorrect. An agent acts on behalf of a principal but has no role in the buying and selling of securities.
D. Incorrect. A principal would be the party on whose behalf the agent is acting. This does not apply to the purchase and sale of securities.

Question 8
Solution: B

A. Incorrect. This statement is true.
B. **Correct.** This statement is false. Knowledge in the over-the-counter market security prices is determined through negotiation; not auction bidding.
C. Incorrect. This statement is true.
D. Incorrect. This statement is true.

Question 9
Solution: A

A. **Correct.** A letter of credit is not a negotiable instrument and the contract of sale between the buyer and seller is independent of the letter of credit.
B. Incorrect. Although a letter of credit is not a negotiable instrument, the contract of sale between the buyer and seller is independent of the letter of credit; not dependent on the letter of credit.
C. Incorrect. Although the contract of sale between the buyer and seller is independent of the letter of credit, a letter of credit is not a negotiable instrument.
D. Incorrect. Although a letter of credit is not a negotiable instrument, the contract of sale between the buyer and seller is independent of the letter of credit; not dependent on the letter of credit.

Question 10
Solution: A

A. **Correct.** The cash inflows from the corporation's assets would increase more quickly than the cash outflows. Being asset sensitive the margin would automatically increase in a rising rate environment.
B. Incorrect. An interest rate floor would not have any impact on the rising rates under this scenario.
C. Incorrect. The cash outflows for the liabilities would increase and the cash inflows would remain the same which would decrease the net interest income.
D. Incorrect. Although the net income would increase, this would not be considered a hedge for a corporation that is asset sensitive in a rising rate environment.

Question 11
Solution: C

A. Incorrect. This statement is false. Endowment policies provide a specified benefit amount whether the insured lives to the end of the term of coverage or dies during the term.
B. Incorrect. Premiums are level throughout the term of the endowment policy.
C. **Correct.** An endowment can be purchased with a single premium or with a series of premiums over a limited period of time.
D. Incorrect. Cash values build during the term of an endowment policy.

Question 12
Solution: A

A. **Correct.** Helping policy owners with requests for information, interpreting policy language, and answering questions regarding policy coverage are responsibilities of the customer service department.
B. Incorrect. Verifying that the mortality/morbidity rates of the company's insureds do not exceed the rates assumed when the premiums were calculated is a responsibility of the underwriting department.
C. Incorrect. Considering the applicant's age, weight, physical condition, personal/family history, and other factors to determine the degree of risk is a responsibility of the underwriting department.
D. Incorrect. Negotiating and managing reinsurance agreements are responsibilities of the underwriting department.

Question 13
Solution: D

A. Incorrect. I is incorrect. All option transactions must be completed by the expiration date on the option contract.
B. Incorrect. III is incorrect. All option transactions must be completed by the expiration date on the option contract.
C. Incorrect. III is incorrect. All option transactions must be completed by the expiration date on the option contract.
D. **Correct.** II is correct. A long put allows the investor to sell the underlying security at the specified strike price until the option expiration date. IV is also correct. An investor who is short a put is obligated to buy the underlying security at the specified strike price if a put option is exercised by the option expiration date.

Question 14
Solution: B

A. Incorrect. The underlying stock goes down in price.
B. **Correct.** The call expires, and the underlying stock goes down in price.
C. Incorrect. Although the underlying stock goes down in price, the stock does not split.
D. Incorrect. Although the call does expire, the underlying stock does not split and it goes down in price.

Section I
Financial Services Auditing

The Certified Financial Services Auditor® (CFSA) measures an individual's knowledge of, and proficiency in, audit principles and practices within the banking, insurance, and securities financial services industries

A. IIA Professional Practices Framework

In June 1999, The Institute of Internal Auditors' (IIA) Board of Directors voted to approve a new definition of internal auditing and a new Professional Practices Framework. Both were based on the recommendations of the Guidance Task Force, a special committee of The IIA charged with examining the adequacy of current standards and guidance for the practice of internal auditing. The Task Force concluded that a significant gap existed between available guidance and current practice and that a new framework was needed to carry the profession into the 21st century. In order to meet this goal, The IIA developed the Professional Practices Framework (PPF).

In general, a framework provides a structural blueprint of how a body of knowledge and guidance fits together. As a coherent system, it facilitates consistent development, interpretation, and application of concepts, methodologies, and techniques useful to a discipline or profession. Specifically, the purpose of the PPF is to organize the full range of internal audit guidance in a manner that is readily accessible on a timely basis. By encompassing current internal audit practice as well as allowing for future expansion, the PPF is intended to assist practitioners throughout the world in being responsive to the expanding market for high quality internal audit services.

Internal auditing is an independent, objective assurance and consulting activity designed to add value and improve an organization's operations. It helps an organization accomplish its objectives by bringing a systematic, disciplined approach to evaluate and improve the effectiveness of risk management, control, and governance processes.

Throughout the world, internal auditing is performed in diverse environments and within organizations that vary in purpose, size, and structure. In addition, the laws and customs within various countries differ from one another. These differences may affect the practice of internal auditing in each environment. The implementation of the PPF, therefore, will be governed by the environment in which the internal audit activity carries out its assigned responsibilities. No information contained within the PPF should be construed in a manner that conflicts with applicable laws or regulations. If a situation arises where information contained within the PPF may be in conflict with legislation or regulation, internal auditors are encouraged to contact The IIA or legal counsel for further guidance.

The Professional Practices Framework consists of three categories of guidance: Standards and Ethics, Practice Advisories, and Development and Practice Aids. The first category (Mandatory Guidance) consists of core materials: the Code of Ethics and the *International Standards for the Professional Practice of Internal Auditing (Standards).* All mandatory guidance has been submitted for review by the profession through the exposure draft process and is considered to be essential for the professional practice of internal auditing. Other elements of the PPF are linked to these *Standards*.

The purpose of The IIA's Code of Ethics is to promote an ethical culture in the profession of internal auditing. A code of ethics is necessary and appropriate for the profession of internal auditing, founded as it is on the trust placed in its objective assurance about risk management, control, and governance.

The *Standards*, as described within the PPF, are the criteria by which the operations of an internal audit department are evaluated and measured. They are intended to represent the practice of internal auditing as it should be. The *Standards* are meant to serve the entire profession of internal auditing in all types of organizations where internal auditors are found. Within the new framework, the Guidance Task Force called for the development of three sets of standards: Attribute, Performance, and Implementation Standards. The Attribute Standards address the attributes of organizations and individuals performing internal audit services. The Performance Standards describe the nature of internal audit services and provide quality criteria against which the performance of these services can be measured. The Attribute and Performance Standards apply to all internal audit services. The Implementation Standards expand upon the Attribute and Performance Standards, providing guidance applicable in specific types of engagements. These standards ultimately may deal with industry-specific, regional, or specialty types of audit services.

Compliance with the concepts enunciated in the mandatory guidance is essential before the responsibilities of internal auditors can be met. As stated in the Code of Ethics, internal auditors shall perform internal audit services in accordance with the *Standards*. All members of The IIA and all Certified Internal Auditors agree to abide by the *Standards* and Code of Ethics, and this guidance is intended to be applicable to all members of the internal auditing profession, whether or not they are members of The IIA.

To be widely applicable, mandatory guidance must necessarily be somewhat generic in nature. Therefore, the PPF includes two additional categories of guidance. In the second category, the Practice Advisories (formerly known as Guidelines) are strongly recommended and endorsed by The IIA. Although not mandatory, Practice Advisories represent best practices endorsed by The IIA as ways to implement *Standards*. In part, Practice Advisories may help to interpret the *Standards* or to apply them in specific internal audit environments. Many Practice Advisories are applicable to all internal auditors, while others may be developed to meet the needs of internal auditors in a specific industry, audit specialty, or geographic area. All Practice Advisories are submitted to a formal review process by The IIA's Professional Issues Committee or other group designated by the Guidance Planning Committee.

The third category of guidance (Development and Practice Aids) includes of a variety of materials that are developed and/or endorsed by The IIA. This category includes research studies, books, seminars, conferences, and other products and services related to the professional practice of internal auditing that do not meet the criteria for inclusion in mandatory guidance or Practice Advisories. Development and practice aids can help to implement the guidance offered in the Code of Ethics, *Standards*, and Practice Advisories. Development and practice aids provide internal audit practitioners with the views of various experts on techniques and processes related to the professional practice of internal auditing.

During the coming years, internal auditors can help to ensure that the Professional Practices Framework will continue to grow more robust through their active involvement in guidance development.

The Professional Practices Framework (PPF)

The PPF was approved by The IIA's Board of Directors in June 1999, and consists of the following components:

- Definition of Internal Auditing
- Code of Ethics
- *Standards*
- Practice Advisories
- Development and Practice Aids

Definition of Internal Auditing

Internal auditing is an independent, objective assurance and consulting activity designed to add value and improve an organization's operations. It helps an organization accomplish its objectives by bringing a systematic, disciplined approach to evaluate and improve the effectiveness of risk management, control, and governance processes.

Code of Ethics

The following Code of Ethics[1] was approved by The IIA in June 2000.

Introduction

The purpose of The IIA's Code of Ethics is to promote an ethical culture in the profession of internal auditing.

> *Internal auditing is an independent, objective assurance and consulting activity designed to add value and improve an organization's operations. It helps an organization accomplish its objectives by bringing a systematic, disciplined approach to evaluate and improve the effectiveness of risk management, control, and governance processes.*

A code of ethics is necessary and appropriate for the profession of internal auditing, founded as it is on the trust placed in its objective assurance about risk management, control, and governance. The IIA's Code of Ethics extends beyond the definition of internal auditing to include two essential components:

1. Principles that are relevant to the profession and practice of internal auditing
2. Rules of Conduct that describe behavior norms expected of internal auditors

These rules are an aid to interpreting the principles into practical applications and are intended to guide the ethical conduct of internal auditors.

The Code of Ethics, together with The IIA's Professional Practices Framework and other relevant IIA pronouncements, provide guidance to internal auditors serving others. "Internal auditors" refers to IIA members, recipients of or candidates for IIA professional certifications, and those who provide internal auditing services within the definition of internal auditing.

Applicability and Enforcement

This Code of Ethics applies to both individuals and entities that provide internal auditing services.

For IIA members and recipients of or candidates for IIA professional certifications, breaches of the Code of Ethics will be evaluated and administered according to The IIA's Bylaws and Administrative Guidelines. The fact that a particular conduct is not mentioned in the Rules of Conduct does not prevent it from being unacceptable or discreditable, and therefore, the member, certification holder, or candidate can be liable for disciplinary action.

Principles

Internal auditors are expected to apply and uphold the following principles:

1. *Integrity* — The integrity of internal auditors establishes trust and thus provides the basis for reliance on their judgment.

2. *Objectivity* — Internal auditors exhibit the highest level of professional objectivity in gathering, evaluating, and communicating information about the activity or process being examined. Internal auditors make a balanced assessment of all the relevant circumstances and are not unduly influenced by their own interests or by others in forming judgments.

3. *Confidentiality* — Internal auditors respect the value and ownership of information they receive and do not disclose information without appropriate authority unless there is a legal or professional obligation to do so.

4. *Competency* — Internal auditors apply the knowledge, skills, and experience needed in the performance of internal auditing services.

Rules of Conduct

1. *Integrity*

   Internal auditors:
   1.1. Shall perform their work with honesty, diligence, and responsibility.
   1.2. Shall observe the law and make disclosures expected by the law and the profession.
   1.3. Shall not knowingly be a party to any illegal activity, or engage in acts that are discreditable to the profession of internal auditing or to the organization.
   1.4. Shall respect and contribute to the legitimate and ethical objectives of the organization.

2. *Objectivity*

   Internal auditors:
   2.1. Shall not participate in any activity or relationship that may impair or be presumed to impair their unbiased assessment. This participation includes those activities or relationships that may be in conflict with the interests of the organization.
   2.2. Shall not accept anything that may impair or be presumed to impair their professional judgment.
   2.3. Shall disclose all material facts known to them that, if not disclosed, may distort the reporting of activities under review.

3. *Confidentiality*

Internal auditors:

3.1. Shall be prudent in the use and protection of information acquired in the course of their duties.

3.2. Shall not use information for any personal gain or in any manner that would be contrary to the law or detrimental to the legitimate and ethical objectives of the organization.

4. *Competency*

Internal auditors:

4.1. Shall engage only in those services for which they have the necessary knowledge, skills, and experience.

4.2. Shall perform internal auditing services in accordance with the *Standards for the Professional Practice of Internal Auditing.*

4.3. Shall continually improve their proficiency and the effectiveness and quality of their services.

Adopted by The IIA Board of Directors, June 17, 2000.

Standards

The Professional Practices Framework, as approved, includes Attribute Standards (AS), Performance Standards (PS), Implementation Standards—Assurance (ISA), and Implementation Standards—Consulting (ISC).

The text below outlines The IIA's basic philosophy for the development of standards.

International Standards for the Professional Practice of Internal Auditing [2]

Internal audit activities are performed in diverse legal and cultural environments; within organizations that vary in purpose, size, and structure; and by persons within or outside the organization. While differences may affect the practice of internal auditing in each environment, compliance with the *International Standards for the Professional Practice of Internal Auditing (Standards)* is essential if the responsibilities of internal auditors are to be met. If internal auditors are prohibited by laws or regulations from complying with certain parts of the *Standards*, they should comply with all other parts of the *Standards* and make appropriate disclosures.

Assurance services involve the internal auditor's objective assessment of evidence to provide an independent opinion or conclusions regarding a process, system, or other subject matter. The nature and scope of the assurance engagement are determined by the internal auditor. There are generally three parties involved in assurance services: (1) the person or group directly involved with the process, system, or other subject matter — the process owner, (2) the person or group making the assessment — the internal auditor, and (3) the person or group using the assessment — the user.

Consulting services are advisory in nature, and are generally performed at the specific request of an engagement client. The nature and scope of the consulting engagement are subject to agreement with the engagement client. Consulting services generally involve two parties: (1) the person or group offering the advice — the internal auditor, and (2) the person or group seeking and receiving the advice — the engagement client. When performing consulting services the internal auditor should maintain objectivity and not assume management responsibility.

The purpose of the *Standards* is to:

1. Delineate basic principles that represent the practice of internal auditing as it should be.
2. Provide a framework for performing and promoting a broad range of value-added internal audit activities.
3. Establish the basis for the evaluation of internal audit performance.
4. Foster improved organizational processes and operations.

The *Standards* consist of Attribute Standards, Performance Standards, and Implementation Standards. (See Appendix B for the complete *Standards*.) The Attribute Standards address the characteristics of organizations and parties performing internal audit activities. The Performance Standards describe the nature of internal audit activities and provide quality criteria against which the performance of these services can be evaluated. While the Attribute and Performance Standards apply to all internal audit services, the Implementation Standards apply to specific types of engagements.

There is one set of Attribute and Performance Standards; however, there are multiple sets of Implementation Standards: a set for each of the major types of internal audit activity. The Implementation Standards have been established for assurance (A) and consulting (C) activities.

The *Standards* are part of the Professional Practices Framework. The Professional Practices Framework includes the Definition of Internal Auditing, the Code of Ethics, the *Standards*, and other guidance. Guidance regarding how the *Standards* might be applied is included in Practice Advisories that are issued by the Professional Issues Committee.

The development and issuance of the *Standards* is an ongoing process. The Internal Auditing Standards Board engages in extensive consultation and discussion prior to the issuance of the *Standards*. This includes worldwide solicitation for public comment through the exposure draft process.

All exposure drafts are posted on The IIA's Web site and distributed to all IIA affiliates.

Practice Advisories

Practice Advisories (formerly Guidelines) are endorsed guidance but are non-mandatory. In part, Practice Advisories may help to interpret the *Standards* or to apply them to specific internal auditing environments. Although some Practice Advisories may be applicable to all internal auditors, others may be developed to meet the needs of a specific industry, a specific audit specialty, or a specific geographic area, including guidance on topics such as environmental issues, control self-assessment, information technology, government auditing, and guidance issued by other standard-setting bodies and adopted by appropriate committees of The IIA. Practice Advisories address topics that currently require attention. They may have a limited life or may be elevated to a standards level based upon importance, usage, and acceptance. All Practice Advisories are submitted to a formal review process by The IIA's Professional Issues Committee or other group designated by the Guidance Planning Committee.

As a part of the development of the Professional Practices Framework, significant portions of the information contained in the "Red Book" Guidelines have been converted to Practice Advisories. Omnibus Practice Advisories 1000-1 through 2600-1 are based on information previously published in the "Red Book," but have been updated to be consistent with the new *Standards* and the Professional Practices Framework. The numbering for these Practice Advisories corresponds to the numbering system for related *Standards*.

Practice Advisories are available online as a basic benefit of IIA membership. Practice Advisories will also be available for sale to nonmembers in the future. Other documents listed below the Practice Advisories Index (Professional Practices Pamphlets) are not formally approved as Practice Advisories but may be converted to Practice Advisories in the future. Additional Practice Advisories are also under development. Please visit the Guidance Update page for more information on planned future guidance.

Practice Advisories Index

Practice Advisory 1000-1: Internal Audit Charter
Practice Advisory 1000.C1-1: Principles Guiding the Performance of Consulting Activities of Internal Auditors
Practice Advisory 1000.C1-2: Additional Considerations for Formal Consulting Engagements
Practice Advisory 1000.C1-3 Additional Considerations for Consulting Engagements in Government Organizational Setting
Practice Advisory 1110-1: Organizational Independence
Practice Advisory 1110.A1-1: Disclosing Reasons for Information Requests
Practice Advisory 1110-2: Chief Audit Executive (CAE) Reporting Lines
Practice Advisory 1120-1: Individual Objectivity
Practice Advisory 1130-1: Impairments to Independence or Objectivity
Practice Advisory 1130.A1-1: Assessing Operations for Which Internal Auditors were Previously Responsible

Practice Advisory 1130.A1-2: Internal Audit Responsibility for Other (Non-audit) Functions
Practice Advisory 12001-1: Proficiency and Due Professional Care
Practice Advisory 1210-1: Proficiency
Practice Advisory 1210.A1-1: Obtaining Services to Support or Complement the Internal Audit Activity
Practice Advisory 1210.A2-1: Identification of Fraud
Practice Advisory 1210.A2-2: Responsibility for Fraud Detection
Practice Advisory 1220-1: Due Professional Care
Practice Advisory 1220-2: CAATS
Practice Advisory 1230-1: Continuing Professional Development
Practice Advisory 1300-1: Quality Assurance and Improvement Program
Practice Advisory 1310-1: Quality Program Assessments
Practice Advisory 1311-1: Internal Assessments
Practice Advisory 1311-2 Establishing Measures (Quantitative Metrics and Qualitative Assessments) to Support Reviews of Internal Audit Activity Performance
Practice Advisory 1312-1: External Assessments
Practice Advisory 1312-2: External Assessment – Self Assessment with Independent Validation
Practice Advisory 1320-1: Reporting on the Quality Program
Practice Advisory 1330-1: Use of "Conducted in Accordance with the *Standards*"
Practice Advisory 2000-1: Managing the Internal Audit Activity
Practice Advisory 2010:1: Planning
Practice Advisory 2010-2: Linking the Audit Plan to Risk and Exposures
Practice Advisory 2020-1: Communication and Approval
Practice Advisory 2030-1: Resource Management
Practice Advisory 2040-1: Policies and Procedures
Practice Advisory 2050-1: Coordination
Practice Advisory 2050-2: Acquisition of External Audit Services
Practice Advisory 2060-1: Reporting to Board and Senior Management
Practice Advisory 2060-2: Relationship with the Audit Committee
Practice Advisory 2100-1: Nature of Work
Practice Advisory 2100-2: Information Security
Practice Advisory 2100-3: Internal Audit's Role in the Risk Management Process
Practice Advisory 2100-4: Internal Audit's Role in Organizations Without a Risk Management Process
Practice Advisory 2100-5: Legal Considerations in Evaluating Regulatory Compliance Programs
Practice Advisory 2100-6: Control and Audit Implications of e-Commerce Activities
Practice Advisory 2100-7: The Internal Auditor's Role in Identifying and Reporting Environmental Risks
Practice Advisory 2100-8: The Internal Auditor's Role in Evaluating and Organization's Privacy Framework
Practice Advisory 2100-9: Application Systems Review
Practice Advisory 2100-10: Audit Sampling

Practice Advisory 2100-11: Effect of Pervasive IS Controls
Practice Advisory 2100-12: Outsourcing of IS Activities
Practice Advisory 2100-13: Effect on Third Parties on an Organization's IT Controls
Practice Advisory 2100-14: Audit Evidence Requirement
Practice Advisory 2110-1: Assessing the Adequacy of Risk Management Processes
Practice Advisory 2110-2: The Internal Auditor's Role in the Business Continuity Process
Practice Advisory 2120.A1-1: Assessing and Reporting on Control Processes
Practice Advisory 2120.A1-2: Using Control Self-assessment for Assessing the Adequacy of Control Processes
Practice Advisory 2120.A1-3: The Internal Auditor's Role in Quarterly Financial Reporting, Disclosures, and Management Certifications
Practice Advisory 2120.A1-4: Auditing the Financial Reporting Process
Practice Advisory 2120.A4-1: Control Criteria
Practice Advisory 2130-1: Role of the Internal Audit Activity and Internal Auditor in the Ethical Culture of an Organization
Practice Advisory 2200-1: Engagement Planning
Practice Advisory 2210-1: Engagement Objectives
Practice Advisory 2210.A1-1: Risk Assessment in Engagement Planning
Practice Advisory 2230-1: Engagement Resource Allocation
Practice Advisory 2240-1: Engagement Work Program
Practice Advisory 2240.A1-1: Approval of Work Programs
Practice Advisory 2300-1: The Internal Auditor's Use of Personal Information in Conducting Audits
Practice Advisory 2310-1: Identifying Information
Practice Advisory 2320-1: Analysis and Evaluation
Practice Advisory 2330-1: Recording Information
Practice Advisory 2330.A1-1: Control of Engagement Records
Practice Advisory 2330.A1-2: Legal Considerations in Granting Access to Engagement Records
Practice Advisory 2330.A2-1: Retention of Records
Practice Advisory 2340-1: Engagement Supervision
Practice Advisory 2400-1: Legal Considerations in Communicating Results
Practice Advisory 2410-1: Communication Criteria
Practice Advisory 2420-1: Quality of Communications
Practice Advisory 2440-1: Recipients of Engagement Results
Practice Advisory 2440-2: Communications Outside the Organization
Practice Advisory 2440-3: Communicating Sensitive Information Within and Outside the Chain of Command
Practice Advisory 2500-1: Monitoring Progress
Practice Advisory 2500.A1-1: Follow-up Process
Practice Advisory 2600-1: Management's Acceptance of Risks

Practice Advisory list updated as of October 2005.

International Federation of Accountants (IFAC)[3]

The International Federation of Accountants (IFAC) is the worldwide organization for the accountancy profession. Founded in 1977, its mission is to serve the public interest, strengthen the global accountancy profession, and contribute to the development of strong international economies by establishing and promoting adherence to high-quality professional standards, furthering the international convergence of such standards, and speaking out on public interest issues where the profession's expertise is most relevant. IFAC's governing bodies, staff, and volunteers are committed to the values of integrity, transparency, and expertise. IFAC also seeks to reinforce professional accountants' adherence to these values, which are reflected in the IFAC Code of Ethics for Professional Accountants.

The mission of the International Federation of Accountants (IFAC), as set out in its constitution, is "the worldwide development and enhancement of an accountancy profession with harmonized standards, able to provide services of consistently high quality in the public interest." In pursuing this mission, the IFAC Board has established the International Auditing and Assurance Standards Board (IAASB) to develop and issue, in the public interest and under its own authority, high-quality auditing and assurance standards for use around the world. The IFAC Board has determined that designation of the IAASB as the responsible body, under its own authority and within its stated terms of reference, best serves the public interest in achieving this aspect of its mission.

Introduction

1. The purpose of this International Standard on Auditing (ISA) is to establish standards and provide guidance on the objective and general principles governing an audit of financial statements. This ISA is to be read in conjunction with ISA 120, "Framework of International Standards on Auditing."

Objective of an Audit

2. The objective of an audit of financial statements is to enable the auditor to express an opinion whether the financial statements are prepared, in all material respects, in accordance with an identified financial reporting framework. The phrases used to express the auditor's opinion are "give a true and fair view" or "present fairly, in all material respects," which are equivalent terms.
3. Although the auditor's opinion enhances the credibility of the financial statements, the user cannot assume that the opinion is an assurance as to the future viability of the entity nor the efficiency or effectiveness with which management has conducted the affairs of the entity.

General Principles of an Audit

4. The auditor should comply with the Code of Ethics for Professional Accountants issued by the International Federation of Accountants. Ethical principles governing the auditor's professional responsibilities are:
   (a) Independence;

(b) Integrity;
(c) Objectivity;
(d) Professional competence and due care;
(e) Confidentiality;
(f) Professional behavior; and
(g) Technical standards.

5. The auditor should conduct an audit in accordance with ISAs. These contain basic principles and essential procedures together with related guidance in the form of explanatory and other material.

6. The auditor should plan and perform an audit with an attitude of professional skepticism recognizing that circumstances may exist that cause the financial statements to be materially misstated. An attitude of professional skepticism means the auditor makes a critical assessment, with a questioning mind, of the validity of audit evidence obtained and is alert to audit evidence that contradicts or brings into question the reliability of documents or management representations. For example, an attitude of professional skepticism is necessary throughout the audit process for the auditor to reduce the risk of overlooking suspicious circumstances, of over generalizing when drawing conclusions from audit observations, and of using faulty assumptions in determining the nature, timing, and extent of the audit procedures and evaluating the results thereof. In planning and performing an audit, the auditor neither assumes that management is dishonest nor assumes unquestioned honesty. Accordingly, representations from management are not a substitute for obtaining sufficient appropriate audit evidence to be able to draw reasonable conclusions on which to base the audit opinion.

Scope of an Audit

7. The term "scope of an audit" refers to the audit procedures deemed necessary in the circumstances to achieve the objective of the audit. The procedures required to conduct an audit in accordance with ISAs should be determined by the auditor having regard to the requirements of ISAs, relevant professional bodies, legislation, regulations, and, where appropriate, the terms of the audit engagement and reporting requirements.

Reasonable Assurance

8. An audit in accordance with ISAs is designed to provide reasonable assurance that the financial statements taken as a whole are free from material misstatement. Reasonable assurance is a concept relating to the accumulation of the audit evidence necessary for the auditor to conclude that there are no material misstatements in the financial statements taken as a whole.

Reasonable assurance relates to the whole audit process.

9. However, there are inherent limitations in an audit that affect the auditor's ability to detect material misstatements. These limitations result from factors such as:
   - The use of testing.

Paragraph 6 reflects the changes indicated in ISA 240, "The Auditor's Responsibility to Consider Fraud and Error in an Audit of Financial Statements," and is effective for audits of financial statements for periods ending on or after June 30, 2002. The original Paragraph 6 is indicated below:

The auditor should plan and perform the audit with an attitude of professional skepticism recognizing that circumstances may exist which cause the financial statements to be materially misstated. For example, the auditor would ordinarily expect to find evidence to support management representations and not assume they are necessarily correct.

- The inherent limitations of any accounting and internal control system (for example, the possibility of collusion); and
- The fact that most audit evidence is persuasive rather than conclusive.

10. Also, the work undertaken by the auditor to form an opinion is permeated by judgment, in particular regarding:
    (a) The gathering of audit evidence, for example, in deciding the nature, timing, and extent of audit procedures; and
    (b) The drawing of conclusions based on the audit evidence gathered; for example, assessing the reasonableness of the estimates made by management in preparing the financial statements.

11. Further, other limitations may affect the persuasiveness of evidence available to draw conclusions on particular financial statement assertions (for example, transactions between related parties). In these cases certain ISAs identify specified procedures which will, because of the nature of the particular assertions, provide sufficient appropriate audit evidence in the absence of:
    (a) Unusual circumstances which increase the risk of material misstatement beyond that which would ordinarily be expected; or
    (b) Any indication that a material misstatement has occurred.

Responsibility for the Financial Statements

12. While the auditor is responsible for forming and expressing an opinion on the financial statements, the responsibility for preparing and presenting the financial statements is that of the management of the entity. The audit of the financial statements does not relieve management of its responsibilities.

Public Sector Perspective

1. Irrespective of whether an audit is being conducted in the private or public sector, the basic principles of auditing remain the same. What may differ for audits carried out in the public sector is the audit objective and scope. These factors are often attributable to differences in the audit mandate and legal requirements or the form of reporting (for example, public sector entities may be required to prepare additional financial reports).

2. When carrying out audits of public sector entities, the auditor will need to take into account the specific requirements of any other relevant regulations, ordinances, or ministerial directives which affect the audit mandate and any special auditing requirements, including the need to have regard to issues of national security. Audit mandates may be more specific than those in the private sector, and often encompass a wider range of objectives and a broader scope than is ordinarily applicable for the audit of private sector financial statements. The mandates and requirements may also affect, for example, the extent of the auditor's discretion in establishing materiality, in reporting fraud and error, and in the form of the auditor's report. Differences in audit approach and style may also exist. However, these differences would not constitute a difference in the basic principles and essential procedures.

B. Internal Control/Risk Management/Governance

Management must evaluate the effectiveness of its internal control over financial reporting on a suitable and recognized control framework.

1. Internal Control Frameworks

Internal control is defined as the process effected by an entity's board of directors, management, and other personnel designed to provide reasonable assurance regarding the achievement of objectives in the following categories:

- Operations controls — relating to the effective and efficient use of the entity's resources
- Financial reporting controls — relating to the preparation of reliable published financial statements
- Compliance controls — relating to the entity's compliance with applicable laws and regulations[3.5]

The definition is broad and encompasses all aspects of an organization. Additionally, since internal controls are effected by people, there are inherent limitations and they can only provide reasonable assurance as to the achievement of control objectives.

The American Institute of Certified Public Accountants' (AICPA) professional standards identify the following internal control components:

- Control environment
- Risk assessment
- Information and communication
- Control activities
- Monitoring[4]

The control environment establishes the foundation for the rest of the internal control components. The control environment is often a function of the "organizational culture" and is usually only as strong as the ethics and attitudes of those in charge of implementing internal controls. Organizations that foster an ethical environment and promote compliance with internal controls, especially through top management, have a solid foundation.

These organizations often have effective personnel policies and a "code of conduct." A strong training program is also a key ingredient. For example, some retail organizations have found that training programs to identify instances of fraud and theft and the associated penalties have reduced the instances of fraud and theft in sales and cashier positions.

Internal auditing can also have a positive impact as it assists in preventing and detecting invalid transactions and statements. Internal audit also reviews compliance with accepted policies, procedures, and practices to ensure that basic internal controls (such as segregation of duties) are present.

Management must continually *assess business risk* and develop clearly defined control objectives. The objectives can be either operating or compliance. Operating objectives define specific organizational goals and should be reasonably obtainable and contain execution strategies. All of the basic business risks relating to economic conditions, natural catastrophes, political unrest, competition, legislation, and technology impact the fulfillment of the operating objectives. Compliance objectives relate to the observance of tax laws, industry requirements, and regulatory requirements.

Risk assessment is the process of assessing the inherent risks associated with achieving business goals. The effective management of business risk can help increase the profitability of an organization. For risk management controls to be implemented, operating objectives must be instituted and be reasonably obtainable. The risks associated with operating objectives include the business climate, competitors, technology, client requirements, and legislation.

There are also risks associated with compliance with laws and regulations. These are often more difficult to implement since compliance may actually negatively impact financial goals in the short term. For example, noncompliance with environmental regulations may seem cost effective in the current quarter; however, the fines and associated negative publicity could have severe long-term consequences.

Internal audit routinely reviews compliance risk and also should be reviewing business risk. The efforts to control both risk types will enhance the short-term and long-term profitability and viability of an organization.

An effective internal control system provides pertinent and *timely information and communication*. The information requirements should be identified and the necessary mechanisms created to disseminate the information. Without relevant and timely information, management will be unable to assess and monitor the control environment and control objectives.

Control activities are the policies and procedures that help ensure that management's objectives are followed. Control activities are designed to prevent and detect errors and omissions in the conduct of routine business functions. Some of these activities include safeguard controls such as physical and logical security controls to prevent unauthorized access to resources. They also include basic concepts such as segregation of duties.

Internal controls must be monitored to ensure that they are effective and followed. *Monitoring* needs to be conducted routinely and continually. Monitoring is the process of reviewing internal controls to ensure that they are effective. Even the best system of internal controls must be continually reviewed to ensure that the activities are being followed and continue to meet organizational needs. Beyond routine activities of monitoring (such as comparing budget to actual performance) more extensive evaluations of the internal control system should be conducted. Internal auditors generally perform these in-depth evaluations of internal control systems. The threat of monitoring generally increases compliance with controls and in effect becomes a preventive control.

The text above provides a basis for understanding an internal control system. Specific processes such as the Committee of Sponsoring Organizations of the Treadway Commission (COSO) and the Canadian Institute of Chartered Accountants' Criteria of Control (CoCo) were developed to provide an internal control framework. As will be evidenced in section 3 below, both COSO and CoCo stress the concept of self-assessment and responsibility of management in maintaining and monitoring the internal control environment. The primary goals of maintaining the effectiveness and efficiency of operations, ensuring the reliability of financial reporting and complying with applicable laws and regulations, are the same for COSO and CoCo. The basic concepts of providing management with a mechanism to achieve goals and objectives and minimize risks are the foundation for both systems.

2. Risk Management Frameworks

Risk is a concept used to express concerns about the probable effects of an uncertain environment. Because the future is unknown, any range of events could have a significant impact on an organization's goals and objectives. Organizations strive to meet goals through "opportunities" which constitute the positive possibilities. There is also the potential for negative possibilities associated with the pursuit of goals, which are called "risks."[5]

The *Standards* include the following definitions of risk (see Appendix B for the complete *Standards*):

- Risk — The possibility of an event occurring that will have an impact on the achievement of objectives. Risk is measured in terms of impact and likelihood.

- Residual Risks — The risk remaining after management takes action to reduce the impact and likelihood of an adverse event, including control activities in responding to a risk.
- Risk Management — A process to identify, assess, manage, and control potential events or situations to provide reasonable assurance regarding the achievement of the organization's objectives.

Two additional legal definitions were found in *Black's Law Dictionary*:

Risk — the element of uncertainty in an undertaking.

Assumption of risk — legally the plaintiff may not recover from an injury to which he assents. The requirements for defense include:

- Plaintiff has knowledge of facts constituting a dangerous condition.
- Plaintiff knows the condition is dangerous.
- Plaintiff appreciates the nature and extent of the danger.
- Plaintiff voluntarily exposes himself to the danger.

If you replace plaintiff with organization, the definition applies to risk management and the CSA process. This coupled with some recent legislation, such as the U.S. Sarbanes-Oxley Act of 2002, promote the concept of clearly defined management responsibilities.

Some additional descriptions of risk are:

- Risk is described in management and strategy as a continuum (risk and opportunity) with payoffs (negative or positive) and probabilities (likelihood of occurrence and consequences).
- Risk appears in the finance profession as a quantifiable element (cost) of holding assets.
- Risk in the environmental safety and occupational health industry focuses on hazards of tasks and defined probabilities of chemical properties and physical events.
- Risk in the insurance and risk management industry focuses on probability distributions of material loss events.
- Risk in the security and audit professions tends to be protective and negative, focusing on the effects of material asset loss.

Risk is inherent in all business activities and one of the best ways to illustrate the relationship between risk and reward is the basic investment philosophy which promotes the positive relationship between risk and reward. As the potential for rewards increases, so does the possibility of losses (risk). From an investment perspective, investors need to assess their investment needs and their tolerance for risk.

Although the relationship between risk and reward varies by business activity, there is some element of risk in all business activities. It is incumbent upon management to incorporate some form of risk assessment into all strategic planning activities.

Strategic planning is the process of taking a long-term view of the organization. The longer the view, the greater the uncertainty of risks and opportunities. Since the risks and opportunities change over time, management must be prepared to adapt plans and processes. An effective risk management process provides a mechanism to continually assess risks as they relate to opportunities.

The following text from *Business Risk Assessment*[6] provides an excellent overview of strategic, process, operational risk, and risk management.

Business risk assessment refers to the assessment of risks and opportunities affecting the achievement of the organization's goals and objectives. Risk is assessed at three levels:

- *Strategic: Used to guide the organization over a time period of five to 10 years. This assessment is usually performed by senior management.*
- *Process (also called program or project): Used to develop and manage the current period of organizational activity. The "process" manager is usually responsible for the initial assessment. He or she may also be responsible for monitoring project risk.*
- *Operational: Used in everyday operations, largely a health and safety issue. This assessment is usually performed at the supervisory level or by individuals or work teams tasked with a particular assignment.*

Strategic risk assessment is usually limited to assessment (the identification, measurement, and prioritization of risks). Operational risk assessment usually focuses on risk management (standard workplace risks and hazards have already been identified; the task is to manage the risk to get the job done). Project risk assessment has a blend of both: risk assessment in the planning phase and risk management in the implementation phase.

Business risk assessment at all three levels is essential to identify the threats, opportunities, and alternatives for action to achieve the organization's goals and objectives.

Strategic Risk Assessment

The process of strategic risk assessment includes these six steps:

1. *Gain an understanding of the organization's overall goals and objectives:*
    - *Examine the fundamental documents (mission statement, purpose statement, vision, or other fundamental document) for goals and objectives. There are typically three to seven of these.*

- *Classify each of the identified goals and objectives into short, medium, and long-term issues. Most mission statements will have some of each of these.*

2. *Choose the strategic risks that are likely to be of greatest importance to the organization:*
   - *Operational Risk: The risk that the entity will not meet its operational goals and objectives.*
   - *Fiscal Risk: The risk that deficiencies in expenditure control or revenues will adversely affect agreed-upon outcomes or objectives.*
   - *Reputation Risk: The risk that some action or inaction by the entity will impair the organization's ability to reach its goals and objectives.*
   - *Other strategic risks, such as Policy Risk, Regulatory Risk, etc.*

3. *Define the various environments that are important to the organization, such as:*
   - *Political/Government.*
   - *Technology.*
   - *Legal and Regulatory.*
   - *Competitors.*
   - *Clients, Constituents, and Stakeholders.*
   - *Physical.*
   - *Markets.*
   - *Suppliers.*
   - *Economic/Financial.*

Each of these "environments" represents a bundle of uncertainties generally associated with that area.

4. *Create a series of matrices, with Strategic Risk Areas put at the top axis, and Environments along the side axis. The matrices should be in a "set" of three; that is, for each issue identified in step 1 (Goals and Objectives), there should be a matrix to record the risks focusing on short-term, medium-term, and long-term issues.*

5. *Using various creative processes such as brainstorming, imagine scenarios of possible threats and opportunities for each of the cells on the matrix. It is important to think "outside of the box" as much as possible — some organizations use an outside consultant to help break through any preconceptions and bias. Use tools such as multivoting to pare the list of threats and opportunities to the most significant (a combination of most likely and those with the largest impact). Because not every environment affects every strategic risk area, not every cell will have data.*

6. *Combine the risk assessments for various goals and objectives for each of the three time horizons to get a composite strategic risk assessment. Based on the assessment of likely scenarios, managers can then plan to deal with those risks.*

Procedures (Process):

A. Identify Risk

1. *Use one or more methods to identify risk (exposure analysis, environmental analysis, or threat scenarios).*

B. Measure Risk/Develop Alternatives

2. *Read each factor and sub-criteria to familiarize yourself with the aim of each.*
3. *Consider the project, program, or process using each of the factors/criteria.*
4. *Score each factor for the project, etc. on a scale of 1 to 5 (Lowest to Highest) based on your subjective assessment of the strength/weakness or presence/absence of the criteria.*
5. *Sum the scores for each factor and divide by the number of factors to get the average score.*
6. *High-risk scores are those with an average of 4.25 or more. Low-risk scores are those with an average score of less than 2.25. These are starting figures that can be adjusted for experience.*
7. *Analyze the high-risk areas and develop alternatives (controls or other risk management techniques) to deal with each of the high-risk components.*
8. *Price out the alternatives and compare risks and costs.*

C. Control Design

9. *Choose the most cost-effective controls within reasonable prudence and organizational tolerance for accepting risk.*

D. Risk Management

10. *Monitor risks and hazards, making adjustments to the project plan as necessary to meet changing conditions.*

Operational Risk Management

Operational risk is the day-to-day mitigation of safety and health risks of employees performing their jobs. Operational risk also covers visitors and temporary workers in the workplace and risks to the general public due to operations. The focus of operational risk is on risk management. Risk assessment is usually done by a specialist involved in workplace risks:

- *Health risks, including exposure to toxins, radiation, and infectious organisms.*
- *Safety risks, including exposure to equipment, machinery, and work processes.*
- *Environmental/physical risks, including exposure to climate and terrain.*

Beyond the global strategy, risks must also be assessed from an operational perspective (day-to-day activities), and ultimately managed. The responsibility for operational risk assessment is usually at the mid-management level.

The following text from *Business Risk Assessment*[7] provides an excellent overview of risk management.

Risk management includes risk assessment and the process of acting on that assessment. Using risk assessment in the planning stages assumes (rightly or wrongly) that prudent management will take the necessary steps to manage the risk once it is assessed. Risk assessment includes a three-step process:

1. *Risk Identification: Understanding what the risks and consequences of those risks can be.*
2. *Risk Measurement: Measuring the likely consequences and their severity.*
3. *Risk Prioritization: Ranking the results to place more management effort on the highest risks.*

Risk management then closes the loop by making decisions on how to deal with the risks assessed:

- *Avoid the risk: Design the process to eliminate particular risks, minimize the risks, or change the nature of the risks to be faced.*
- *Control the risk: Institute procedures to control the process that minimize the consequences and severity of risk occurrence. This includes accepting some risk.*
- *Share the risk: Through contractual arrangements with suppliers, clients, constituents, or third parties (such as insurers), apportion some of the risk or risky activities to others and accept the remainder.*

There is always an amount of residual risk left over after all efforts have been made to avoid, control, or share the risk. If the residual risk is too high, then the task should not be done. If the residual risk is not too high, management may choose to accept this amount of risk in order to achieve objectives.

In addition to the residual risks left over from efforts of risk management, there are risks inherent in the management process known as control risks, or those risks associated with relying upon a control procedure, etc., that fails to accomplish its task. Both residual risk and control risk need to be explicitly dealt with in project management.

After a thorough assessment of risk, organizations will have determined their risk tolerance, identified residual risk and determined if exceeds their threshold, and ultimately accepted some tolerable level of risk (exposure).

One of the tasks of a board of directors is to establish and maintain the organization's governance processes and obtain assurances concerning the effectiveness of the risk management and control processes. Senior management's role is to oversee the establishment, administration, and assessment of that system of risk management and control processes. The purpose of that multifaceted system of control processes is to support people of the organization in the management of risks and the achievement of the established and communicated objectives of the enterprise. More specifically, those control processes are expected to ensure, among other things, that the following conditions exist:

- Financial and operational information is reliable and possesses integrity.
- Operations are performed efficiently and achieve effective results.
- Assets are safeguarded.
- Actions and decisions of the organization are in compliance with laws, regulations, and contracts.[8]

Risk management is a key responsibility of management. To achieve its business objectives, management should ensure that sound risk management processes are in place and functioning. Boards and audit committees have an oversight role to determine that appropriate risk management processes are in place and that these processes are adequate and effective. Internal auditors should assist both management and the audit committee by examining, evaluating, reporting, and recommending improvements on the adequacy and effectiveness of management's risk processes. Management and the board are responsible for their organization's risk management and control processes. However, internal auditors acting in a consulting role can assist the organization in identifying, evaluating, and implementing risk management methodologies and controls to address those risks.[9]

The five key objectives of a risk management process are:

1. Risks arising from business strategies and activities are identified and prioritized.
2. Management and the board have determined the level of risks acceptable to the organization, including the acceptance of risks designed to accomplish the organization's strategic plans.
3. Risk mitigation activities are designed and implemented to reduce, or otherwise manage, risk at levels that were determined to be acceptable to management and the board.
4. Ongoing monitoring activities are conducted to periodically reassess risk and the effectiveness of controls to manage risk.
5. The board and management receive periodic reports of the results of the risk management processes. The corporate governance processes of the organization should provide periodic communication of risks, risk strategies, and controls to stakeholders.[10]

Recent legislation has added some additional legal requirements that promote the need for comprehensive risk assessments.

The rules and enforcement policies outlined by Sarbanes-Oxley amend or supplement existing legislation dealing with security regulations. Some related provisions include:

- Establishment of a Public Company Accounting Oversight Board, where public companies must now be registered.
- Strict auditor regulation and control by means of auditing committees and inspecting accounting firms.
- Heightened corporate responsibility for any fraudulent actions taken.
- Stricter disclosure within company financial statements, and ethical guidelines to which senior financial officers must adhere.
- Guidelines for analyst conflicts of interest.
- Enforcement methods available for punishment of activities deemed criminal by the Act.

The efforts to reduce risk and promote management accountability are not limited to the United States. In January 2004, legislation titled the Companies (Audit, Investigations and Community Enterprise) Bill was introduced in the United Kingdom's Parliament. The bill aims to enhance the reliability of financial reporting, provide auditors with greater powers, and increase investigative powers to uncover misconduct.

3. Governance Models

COSO

COSO was a private-sector initiative started in the 1980s to address the problem of fraudulent financial reporting. In the 1970s there were a number of scandals that called into question the integrity of corporate financial reporting. For example, some corporations made significant payments to foreign entities to secure contracts and business opportunities. However, the payments were not properly recorded or disclosed in financial reports. These scandals led to the enactment of the Foreign Corrupt Practices Act of 1977.

Problems continued to persist in the 1980s and the private sector was wary of additional government intervention. As a result, five organizations banded together to form COSO:

- American Institute of Certified Public Accountants
- American Accounting Association
- Financial Executives Institute
- The Institute of Internal Auditors
- Institute of Management Accountants

COSO's mission was to improve the quality of financial reporting through a focus on corporate governance, internal controls, and ethical standards.

The initial project was the Treadway Commission Report, issued in October 1987. The Treadway Commission Report called for an adequate system of internal control. The report also recommended a public management report describing management's responsibility for a company's financial statements and internal controls, and an assessment of the internal control system. The Treadway Commission developed an internal control framework called *Internal Control – Integrated Framework*. The *Framework* defines internal control broadly and does not limit internal controls to accounting controls over financial reporting. While financial reporting is an important responsibility of the audit committee, there are other very important aspects of the business relating to resource protection, operational efficiency and economy, and compliance with rules, regulations, and policies that are also important. The *Framework* promotes the concept that effective internal control is management's responsibility and requires the participation of all persons within an organization if it is to be effective.

COSO defines internal control, describes its components, and provides criteria against which control systems can be evaluated. It offers guidance for public reporting on internal control and provides materials that management, auditors, and others can use to evaluate an internal control system.

Two major goals of COSO were to:

- Establish a common definition of internal control.
- Provide a standard against which organizations can assess their control systems.

COSO emphasizes that the internal control system is a tool of, but not a substitute for, management and that controls should be built into, rather than built onto, operating activities. Although the report defines internal control as a process, it recommends evaluating the effectiveness of internal control as of a point in time.

COSO also addresses the limitations of an internal control system and the roles and responsibilities of the parties that affect a system. Limitations include faulty human judgment, misunderstanding of instructions, errors, management override, collusion, and cost/benefit considerations.[11]

The COSO document, *Internal Control – Integrated Framework*,[12] defines internal control as:

Internal control is a process, effected by an entity's board of directors, management, and other personnel, designed to provide reasonable assurance regarding the achievement of objectives in the following categories:

- Effectiveness and efficiency of operations
- Reliability of financial reporting
- Compliance with applicable laws and regulations

This definition reflects certain fundamental concepts:

- Internal control is a *process*. It is a means to an end, not an end in itself.
- Internal control is effected by *people*. It is not merely policy manuals and forms, but people at every level of an organization.
- Internal control can be expected to provide only *reasonable assurance*, not absolute assurance, to an entity's management and board.
- Internal control is geared to the achievement of *objectives* in one or more separate but overlapping categories.

Internal controls consist of five interrelated components.[13] Note: These are the same components as the AICPA's internal control components. They are derived from the way management runs a business and are integrated with the management process. The components are:

- *Control Environment* — The core of any business is its people — their individual attributes, including integrity, ethical values, and competence — and the environment in which they operate. They are the engine that drives the entity and the foundation on which everything rests.
- *Risk Assessment* — The entity must be aware of and deal with the risks it faces. It must set objectives, integrated with the sales, production, marketing, financial, and other activities, so that the organization is operating in concert. It also must establish mechanisms to identify, analyze, and manage the related risks.
- *Control Activities* — Control policies and procedures must be established and executed to help ensure that the actions identified by management as necessary to address risks to achievement of the entity's objectives are effectively carried out.
- *Information and Communication* — Surrounding these activities are information and communication systems. These enable the entity's people to capture and exchange the information needed to conduct, manage, and control its operations.
- *Monitoring* — The entire process must be monitored and modifications made as necessary. In this way, the system can react dynamically, changing as conditions warrant.

The control environment provides an atmosphere in which people conduct their activities and carry out their control responsibilities. It serves as the foundation for the other components. Within this environment, management assesses risks to the achievement of specified objectives. Control activities are implemented to help ensure that management directives to address risks are carried out. Meanwhile, relevant information is captured and communicated throughout the organization. The entire process is monitored and modified as conditions warrant.[14]

COSO Internal Control Components

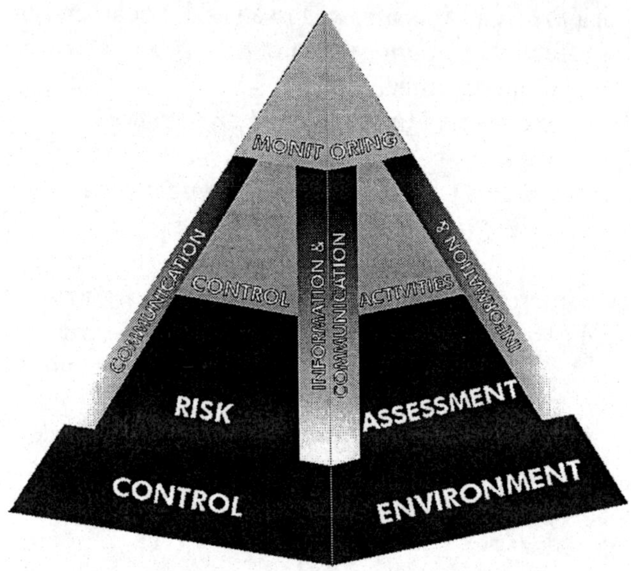

COSO Enterprise Risk Management – Integrated Framework[15]

The framework describes the essential components, principles, and concepts of enterprise risk management (ERM) for all organizations, regardless of size.

The underlying premise of enterprise risk management is that every entity exists to provide value for its stakeholders. All entities face uncertainty, and the challenge for management is to determine how much uncertainty to accept as it strives to grow stakeholder value. Uncertainty presents both risk and opportunity, with the potential to erode or enhance value. Enterprise risk management enables management to effectively deal with uncertainty and associated risk and opportunity, enhancing the capacity to build value.

Value is maximized when management sets strategy and objectives to strike an optimal balance between growth and return goals and related risks, and efficiently and effectively deploys resources in pursuit of the entity's objectives. Enterprise risk management encompasses:

- Aligning risk appetite and strategy — Management considers the entity's risk appetite in evaluating strategic alternatives, setting related objectives, and developing mechanisms to manage related risks.
- Enhancing risk response decisions — Enterprise risk management provides the rigor to identify and select among alternative risk responses — risk avoidance, reduction, sharing, and acceptance.

- Reducing operational surprises and losses — Entities gain enhanced capability to identify potential events and establish responses, reducing surprises and associated costs or losses.
- Identifying and managing multiple and cross-enterprise risks — Every enterprise faces a myriad of risks affecting different parts of the organization, and enterprise risk management facilitates effective response to the interrelated impacts, and integrated responses to multiple risks.
- Seizing opportunities — By considering a full range of potential events, management is positioned to identify and proactively realize opportunities.
- Improving deployment of capital — Obtaining robust risk information allows management to effectively assess overall capital needs and enhance capital allocation.

These capabilities inherent in enterprise risk management help management achieve the entity's performance and profitability targets and prevent loss of resources. Enterprise risk management helps ensure effective reporting and compliance with laws and regulations, and helps avoid damage to the entity's reputation and associated consequences. In sum, enterprise risk management helps an entity get to where it wants to go and avoid pitfalls and surprises along the way.

The definition of Enterprise Risk Management is:

> *Enterprise risk management is a process, effected by an entity's board of directors, management, and other personnel, applied in strategy setting and across the enterprise, designed to identify potential events that may affect the entity, and manage risk to be within its risk appetite, to provide reasonable assurance regarding the achievement of entity objectives.*

The framework is set forth in four categories: Strategic, Operations, Reporting, and Compliance. It consists of eight interrelated components, which are: internal environment, objective setting, event identification, risk assessment, risk response, control activities, information and communication, and monitoring.

Risk Management and Governance (formerly called CoCo)

The Canadian Institute of Chartered Accountants' (CICA) Board of Directors approved a change in the name and mission of the Criteria of Control (CoCo) Board at its meeting in February 2001. The new Risk Management and Governance (RMG) Board will focus on a practical, commercial approach to risk management and governance.

CoCo was developed by the CICA in the early 1990s primarily as a "control" framework. Market research conducted by the CoCo Board indicated that while the ideology of CoCo continues to have relevance for the CA profession, a greater focus needed to be placed on using the CoCo framework for corporate governance and risk management.

The new RMG Board will strive to help CAs become trusted advisors on broader issues related to risk management and governance and look at the role individuals can play in improving the quality of governance and risk management in organizations.[16]

Criteria of Control (CoCo) was an initiative of Canada's chartered accountants to strengthen control and corporate governance. In any organization of people, the essence of control is the blending of purpose, commitment, capability, and monitoring and learning. Control encompasses all the elements of an organization that, taken together, support people in the achievement of the organization's objectives. The elements include resources, systems, processes, culture, structure, and tasks. Looking at control means looking at all these elements and how they are interrelated and aligned with objectives. At the highest level, the organization's "objective" is its reason for existing, its mission. That mission is lived out through vision, strategic objectives, and plans to realize them. Objectives can be described in three general categories:

- Effectiveness and efficiency of operations includes objectives related to an organization's goals, such as client service, the safeguarding and efficient use of resources, profitability, and meeting social obligations. This includes the safeguarding of the organization's resource from inappropriate use or loss and ensuring that liabilities are identified and managed.

- Reliability of internal and external reporting includes objectives related to matters such as the maintenance of proper accounting records, the reliability of information used within the organization, and of information published for third parties. This includes the protection of records against two main types of fraud: the concealment of theft and the distortion of results.

- Compliance with applicable laws and regulations and internal policies includes objectives related to ensuring that the organization's affairs are conducted in accordance with legal and regulatory obligations and internal policies.[17]

Ultimately any system of control is the responsibility of the governing board. The Canadian Institute of Chartered Accountants' (CICA) publication, *Guidance for Directors – Governance Processes for Control,* describes six control responsibilities for boards:

- Establishing and monitoring the organization's ethical values;
- Approval and monitoring of mission, vision, and strategy;
- Overseeing external communications;
- Evaluating senior management;
- Monitoring management control system; and
- Assessing the board's effectiveness.[18]

C. Audit Process

Although every audit project is unique, the audit process is similar for most engagements and normally consists of similar stages. A detailed analysis of the basic audit process follows.

1. Audit Planning

The following performance standards from the *International Standards for the Professional Practice of Internal Auditing (Standards)* (also see Appendix B) will help provide the foundation for the audit planning section.

2010 – Planning
The chief audit executive should establish risk-based plans to determine the priorities of the internal audit activity, consistent with the organization's goals.

2010.A1 – The internal audit activity's plan of engagements should be based on a risk assessment, undertaken at least annually. The input of senior management and the board should be considered in this process.

2010.C1 – The chief audit executive should consider accepting proposed consulting engagements based on the engagement's potential to improve management of risks, add value, and improve the organization's operations. Those engagements that have been accepted should be included in the plan.

2200 – Engagement Planning
Internal auditors should develop and record a plan for each engagement, including the scope, objectives, timing, and resource allocations.

2201 – Planning Considerations
In planning the engagement, internal auditors should consider:

- The objectives of the activity being reviewed and the means by which the activity controls its performance.
- The significant risks to the activity, its objectives, resources, and operations and the means by which the potential impact of risk is kept to an acceptable level.
- The adequacy and effectiveness of the activity's risk management and control systems compared to a relevant control framework or model.
- The opportunities for making significant improvements to the activity's risk management and control systems.

2201.A1 – When planning an engagement for parties outside the organization, internal auditors should establish a written understanding with them about objectives, scope, respective responsibilities, and other expectations, including restrictions on distribution of the results of the engagement and access to engagement records.

2201.C1 – Internal auditors should establish an understanding with consulting engagement clients about objectives, scope, respective responsibilities, and other client expectations. For significant engagements, this understanding should be documented.

There are two types of audit planning. The first type involves management's role in setting up the audit function, authorizing appropriate resources, and selecting the functional areas to be audited. The second type of audit planning involves tasks associated with specific audits.

Management's Role in Planning

The audit unit's management is responsible for establishing goals and objectives for the audit function, outlining the methods to be used in achieving the goals and objectives, and developing a method to ensure that an appropriate level and type of resources are applied to the function. The plans developed for the audit function should be updated as circumstances dictate. Specific types of plans include:

- Goals for the audit unit.
- Criteria to measure progress toward achieving goals.
- Target dates.
- Audit work schedules (e.g., activities to be audited, time frames for audit, resource estimates).
- Staffing plans and financial budgets.
- Activity reports.

Audit work schedules may be based on one or more of the following factors:

- The length of time since the area was last audited
- The extent and type of findings in the last audit
- Audits prioritized based on assessment of the degree of risk of potential loss (such as potential loss of dollars, lives, or of public trust) associated with the audit area
- The occurrence of major recent changes in operations, programs, systems, or controls
- The availability of audit staff resources
- Requests by management or policy makers (such as elected officials or governing board members)
- Opportunities to achieve operating benefits

Audit department management should develop a plan describing what to audit and when to audit each selected area. In a broad sense, the audit plan describes how the audit department will carry out its responsibilities. The purpose of the plan is to enable projection of items such as work schedules, budgets, resources needs, and training needs. A risk assessment is often used to select audits to include in the audit plan.

Risk assessment involves using professional judgment to determine the critical areas for audit attention, based on the potential for adverse effects on the organization. Therefore, risk assessment begins by considering factors that may affect risk and giving the highest audit priority to audit areas that have the highest potential for adverse consequences. The risk assessment model should be updated continuously as additional information becomes available. The potential effects from risk exposures include:

- Loss of assets, errors, fraud.
- Bad decisions.
- Stakeholder or client dissatisfaction.
- Adverse publicity.
- Noncompliance with laws, rules, and regulations.
- Failure to achieve the organization's goals and objectives.

Risk is the probability that an event or action may adversely affect the organization or activity under review. In other words, risk is anything that can prevent an organization from achieving an objective. The three major components of risk are:

- An event or cause that can interfere with achieving the objective (e.g., What can go wrong?).
- A probability or likelihood of occurrence.
- The negative consequences of not achieving the objective.

Inherent risk — Risk is inherent in any activity, regardless of the existence or effectiveness of controls. For example, theft, loss, and an inaccurate recording of cash received are inherent risks in cash-handling operations. Also, inherent risks in a construction program might be noncompliance with building code, failure to meet the client's facility needs, or excessive cost growth (change orders). Thus, inherent risk is uncertainty or exposure, assuming no controls are in place. Inherent risks are the possible adverse effects based solely on the type of activity, the type of resources, amount of assets, or complexity of transactions.

Control risk — Control risk is the extent of uncertainty remaining after the mitigating effects of the control system are in place. The extent to which an organization has implemented controls to minimize the actual occurrence of the risk determines the vulnerability to the risk actually occurring, or the "control risk."

The risk analysis process involves:

- Identifying auditable activities (e.g., programs, accounts, contracts, transactions).
- Identifying relevant risk factors (e.g., complexity of program, size of program, adequacy of internal control system).
- Estimating the significance of a risk (e.g., magnitude of exposure in dollars or other type of measure, type of threat, duration, etc.).
- Estimating the likelihood that a risk will occur.
- Prioritizing risks.
- Determining how to manage the risks.

Determining the numerical degree of risk remains a matter of judgment. Therefore, Lawrence B. Sawyer suggests the following risk assessment method:[19]

> *All audit projects can be given a numerical rating from 1 to 5, based on auditor judgment and experience. An audit project rated 1 has the highest risk and deserves the highest priority. An audit project rated 5 has the lowest risk and would be carried out only when higher rated projects have been completed and time is available. Where budget restrictions require a reduction in audit staff, all or some of the 5-rated and 4-rated projects can be eliminated.*

Some types of audit organizations have less latitude in selecting the audits they perform. Many government audit units are subject to laws that stipulate a time frame in which certain agencies or programs must be audited. For example, many states statutorily require that a legislative post audit unit conduct a financial and compliance audit of each state agency on a set schedule (e.g., every two years). Performance audits or other special audits are often done at the request of some governmental authority such as Congress, a state legislature, or a city council.

Specific Audit Planning Tasks

Planning is important to help ensure the efficient use of audit resources and the fulfillment of audit objectives. Auditors should understand the area to be audited, including regulations, goals, operations, efforts, outputs, and outcomes. Specifically, the role of laws, regulations, rules, and ordinances should be considered in the planning process. While audit planning is described as the first phase of the audit process, planning activities should be performed continuously throughout the entire audit.

The major areas to consider in the audit planning process include:

- Identify what is to be audited.
- Collect and analyze background information on area to be audited.
- Assess risk and vulnerability.

- Define audit objectives.
- Define audit scope.
- Develop specific issues and questions for the audit.
- Develop audit criteria (criteria should be reasonable, attainable, and relevant).
- Develop audit methods, strategies, tests, analyses, and comparisons.
- Design data collection and measurement procedures.
- Determine resources available and needed to conduct audit.
- Communicate with management about the audit.
- Establish an audit timeline and a goal completion date.
- Develop a written audit program that incorporates the above information.
- Assign specific tasks to audit staff.
- Determine staff independence.
- Determine the need for external assistance or outsourcing.
- Estimate travel costs and other expenses.

The following sections cover some of the major aspects of the planning process in greater detail.

Collect and analyze background information on the area to be audited—Generally, auditors should obtain background information before determining the audit objectives. An exception to this guideline is when the audit objective is known at the start of the audit. The following is a list of background items auditors should review to determine their impact on audit objectives:

- The purpose and goals for a specific program or the entire organization — Purpose is defined as the result or effect that is intended or desired. The purpose of a program may be implicitly or explicitly stated in laws and regulations. On the other hand, management is responsible for defining a program's goals, which are defined as the level of desired performance. Auditors may use the purpose and goals as criteria for assessing program performance.
- The history of the program or entire organization.
- Organizational data (e.g., organizational charts, job descriptions, policy and procedure manuals, information system manuals).
- Financial data (e.g., budgets, management reports).
- Results of prior audits and their working papers.
- Applicable laws, rules, and regulations — Specific items usually set forth in laws and regulations include the following:
  - What the program is supposed to do.
  - Who is supposed to do it.
  - What population is to be served.
  - How much can be spent on what.
- Work of external audits in process.
- Correspondence files to determine potential significant audit issues.
- Authoritative technical literature related to the audit activity.

Auditors can use background information to define and modify the scope of the audit. An assessment of background information may result in the need to modify projected audit completion dates, the level or type of testing, or staffing plans.

Auditors may decide to conduct a survey to become familiar with the activities, risks, and controls associated with an audit area. A survey is a process for gathering information, without detailed verification, on the activity being examined. The main purposes are to assist with the following goals and tasks:

- Understand significant audit issues.
- Identify significant areas warranting special emphasis.
- Obtain information for use in performing the audit.
- Determine whether further auditing is necessary.
- Define audit objectives, audit procedures, and special approaches such as computer-assisted audit techniques.
- Identify potential critical control points, control deficiencies, or excessive controls.
- Identify important aspects of program operations — Program operations are the strategies, processes, and activities the client uses to convert efforts into outputs.
- Identify inputs or efforts (e.g., the amount of resources such as money, material, and personnel) that are put into a program.
- Identify output measures — Outputs are the quantity of goods and services provided. Examples of output measures are tons of solid waste processed, number of students graduated, and number of students graduated who have met a specified standard of achievement.
- Identify outcome measures — Outcomes are accomplishments or results that occur (at least partially) because of services provided. Outcomes may be intentional or unintentional, immediate (e.g., number of graduates placed in jobs) or ultimate (e.g., whether program graduates are more likely to remain employed than similar persons not in the program).
- Develop preliminary estimates of time and resource requirements.

A survey may involve:

- Discussions with the client.
- Interviews with individuals affected by the activity, e.g., users of the activity's output.
- Onsite observations.
- Review of management reports and studies.
- Analytical auditing procedures.
- Flowcharting.
- Documenting key control activities.

Define audit objectives — Audit objectives broadly define the intended accomplishments of the audit. More specifically, audit objectives are questions that need to be answered during the audit.

Auditors define audit objectives based on information gained either from knowledge they already have or from inquiries and observations. Auditors should use risk assessments to identify audit objectives. Risk is defined as the probability that an event or action may adversely affect the activity under audit. See Section II.A.4 and Section II.C.3 for information on risk assessment techniques.

The following is a list of principles for formulating well-stated audit objectives:

- Phrase objectives either as precisely worded questions or as items to determine (e.g., "To determine whether…").
- Eliminate ambiguous, abstract, or unfocused terms.
- Clearly identify the client.
- Clearly identify the type of performance to be audited and separate objectives if more than one element of performance is to be reviewed.
- Identify the specific elements of finding needed to meet the objective.
- Frame objectives that consider a realistic scope and methodology.
- Review the audit objectives with management or others requesting the audit.
- Answer the audit objectives in the report.

Carefully crafted audit objectives are important for the following reasons:

- Objectives provide direction.
- Limit collection of unneeded information.
- Control scope, methodology, timing, and nature of the audit work.
- Increase probability that questions will be answered.
- Determine how audit findings should be formulated.

Define audit scope — The scope defines the boundaries of the audit by addressing such items as the audit period or number of locations to be reviewed. Some important considerations when defining the scope of an audit include:

- Type of audit (financial, compliance, performance, etc.).
- Program or management objectives (e.g., the audit may be limited to a specific program within an organization).
- Needs of the potential users of the audit report.
- Time period to be audited.
- Specific audit requirements.
- Type and extent of problems found in prior years' audit reports.
- Preliminary judgment about materiality levels.
- Availability of staff and other resources.
- Statutory mandates.
- Risks identified (inherent and control risks), also called level of risks and extent of vulnerability to the risk/strength of control activities.

The following elements should be documented in the audit scope:

- Time period to be covered by audit tests
- Description of the audit universe
- Time allotted to conduct audit
    - Staff time
    - Reporting deadline
- Available data
    - Number of records
    - Locations
    - Need to create data
    - Form
    - Reliability
- Site selection rationale
- Sample size rationale
- Client officials, clients/requesters for audit results
- Expert advice
- Scope limitations encountered or anticipated

Determine resources needed to conduct the audit — Some considerations for determining required audit resources include:

- The time frame for the release of the audit.
- The audit objectives and scope.
- The number of audit staff needed to meet the audit objectives based on resource or time constraints.
- The experience level (e.g., knowledge and skills) needed by assigned staff.
- Training needed by audit staff to meet the audit objectives.
- Contractual assistance needed to meet the audit objectives.

Communicate with management about the audit — Client management often has a negative perception of the audit process; therefore, communication throughout the audit process is essential to alleviate some of the concerns of management. Some basic steps to communicate with the client include:

- Formal notification of the audit — The first step in the process is to formally notify the client in writing. The notification letter may include information that describes:
    - The assigned audit manager.
    - The entity to be audited.
    - The audit period.
    - The type of audit.
    - The preliminary audit scope and objectives.

    - The assigned staff.
    - A request for a formal entrance conference.

- Entrance conference — The entrance conference may be the auditor's first face-to-face contact with the client. The objectives of the entrance conference are to:
    - Explain audit processes.
    - Explain preliminary audit scope and objectives.
    - Establish mutually agreeable working relationships.
    - Present projected audit milestone dates and completion dates.
    - Introduce assigned audit staff.
    - Identify key contacts and desired communication protocols.
    - Obtain an overview of the program or activity being audited, including a description of recent changes in management or major systems.
    - Solicit and address any client questions or concerns.
    - Discuss auditor space requirements.
    - Give the client an initial written request for information and data.
    - Take a tour of facilities.
    - Discuss any types of data or information that the client may consider sensitive or confidential.

The information obtained from meetings with client management should be recorded in writing, distributed to appropriate individuals, and retained in audit working papers.

Determine appropriate audit methods and strategies — Proper planning allows audit management to make decisions about the future conduct of the audit. Audit management must determine which methodology is appropriate for which audit objective and client conditions. For example, audit management must decide whether to sample (judgment or statistical) or use the entire universe, and which specific quantitative and qualitative methodologies will provide sufficient, competent, and relevant evidence to answer the questions posed in the audit objectives.

Develop an audit program with appropriate procedures and tasks to achieve audit objectives — The form and content of the written audit program will vary depending on the size and complexity of the area audited. However, examples of information that may be included in an audit program include:

- Background information about the audit area.
- Procedures for collecting, analyzing, interpreting, and documenting information during the audit.
- Audit objectives and requirements.
- Audit scope and degree of testing required to achieve the audit objectives.
- Technical issues, risks, processes, and transactions to be considered or examined.
- Discussion of relevant legal issues.

- Specific tasks assigned to staff.
- Timeline for completing the various audit phases and the final report.

The audit program should be updated as necessary to reflect any significant changes made during the audit.

2. Audit Fieldwork

The following performance standards from the *International Standards for the Professional Practice of Internal Auditing (Standards)* (also see Appendix B) will help provide the foundation for the audit fieldwork section.

2300 – Performing the Engagement
Internal auditors should identify, analyze, evaluate, and record sufficient information to achieve the engagement's objectives.

2310 – Identifying Information
Internal auditors should identify sufficient, reliable, relevant, and useful information to achieve the engagement's objectives.

2320 – Analysis and Evaluation
Internal auditors should base conclusions and engagement results on appropriate analyses and evaluations.

2330 – Recording Information
Internal auditors should record relevant information to support the conclusions and engagement results.

2330.A1 – The chief audit executive should control access to engagement records. The chief audit executive should obtain the approval of senior management and/or legal counsel prior to releasing such records to external parties, as appropriate.

2330.A2 – The chief audit executive should develop retention requirements for engagement records. These retention requirements should be consistent with the organization's guidelines and any pertinent regulatory or other requirements.

2330.C1 – The chief audit executive should develop policies governing the custody and retention of engagement records, as well as their release to internal and external parties. These policies should be consistent with the organization's guidelines and any pertinent regulatory or other requirements.

2340 – Engagement Supervision
Engagements should be properly supervised to ensure objectives are achieved, quality is assured, and staff is developed.

The purpose of fieldwork is to gather audit evidence for use in supporting the facts, conclusions, and findings that will be contained in the audit report. The categories below describe how evidence can be used:

- *Primary or direct evidence* supports a finding with the greatest degree of certainty. This type of evidence provides direct proof of a fact without requiring additional inference or presumption. For example, a signed contract is generally considered direct evidence of the terms of a contract. However, if the authenticity of the signatures is questionable, auditors should reexamine the evidence or obtain additional supporting evidence.

- *Secondary evidence* provides less certainty than direct evidence. This type of evidence generally requires the use of additional evidence to develop and support conclusions. Examples of secondary evidence include information obtained from interviews and internally prepared documents. The way secondary evidence is used and the importance of the finding determine whether such evidence is considered primary or secondary.

- *Corroborative evidence* is additional evidence in support of primary or secondary evidence. Therefore, this type of evidence provides indirect support for a conclusion. Corroborative evidence does not have power to support a finding or conclusion by itself.

Audit evidence may be classified in the following ways:

- *Documentary evidence* includes internally or externally prepared documents such as letters, contracts, records, external reports, bank statements, and invoices. Auditors should exercise a healthy degree of professional skepticism when reviewing internally generated information. It is always possible that the evidence may have been manipulated or altered. If there is any doubt about the validity of evidence, corroborative evidence (e.g., through independent tests of the data) should be obtained.

- *Analytical evidence* is compiled from other types of evidence. It includes calculations, comparisons, and interpretations made by the auditor. If the client prepared the analysis, it is considered documentary evidence.

- *Testimonial evidence* is information obtained from individuals through oral or written statements such as interviews, surveys, and questionnaires. Important interview information should be corroborated by examining records and performing tests.

- *Physical evidence* is obtained through auditors' direct inspection or observation of people, property, or events. Physical evidence may be in the form of memos summarizing items or events observed, photographs, drawings, charts, maps, or physical samples. Findings and conclusions based on physical evidence require a substantial number of unbiased observations using a predetermined sample design and plan. Inspection and observation may be used for:
  - Documenting work flows, processes, and control.
  - Counting inventory or estimating transaction volumes.
  - Testing compliance with statutes, rules, policies, and procedures.

Auditors should base findings and conclusions on adequate evidence. The evidence should be retained in the audit working papers. The following terms are used to define the adequacy of audit evidence:

- *Sufficiency* refers to whether there is enough evidence (e.g., different sources, large sample, statistical support, number of examples) to justify a finding. Individual items of evidence, which when standing alone would be insufficient, may be combined to be sufficient to support conclusions.

- Sufficiency of evidence is a judgmental decision based on the risk the auditor is willing to assume. The risk should be held as low as practical by assuring that the evidence is complete, accurate, and reliable, and that the data acquisition, measurement, and analytical methods are appropriate.

- *Competency* refers to the validity and reliability of audit evidence. Information is valid if it measures and documents the issue being reviewed or the inference being made. For example, an incomplete or inaccurate quote from a law or from the wrong law is invalid. The reliability of audit evidence refers to its ability to be replicated. If multiple observations elicit the same results, or if another auditor finds the same evidence, the evidence can be considered reliable.

  It is necessary to determine both the validity and reliability of evidence. For example, if a clerk consistently applied an incorrect formula in calculating payroll deductions, the result would be consistent and predictable (i.e., reliable) but not valid because the result would be based on an incorrect formula. The following general guidelines apply to assessing the competency of information:
  - Independent sources generally provide more competent evidence than non-independent sources.
  - Good control systems generally provide more competent evidence than weak control systems.

    - Directly obtained evidence (e.g., through observation, examination, computation, or inspection) is generally more competent than indirectly obtained evidence (e.g., through interviews).
    - Original documents generally provide more competent evidence than copies.
    - Testimonial evidence is more competent when it is obtained from people who are unbiased, who have complete knowledge about the subject, and who are able to speak freely.

- *Relevancy* is the determination that evidence has a logical relationship to the finding. The relevancy of evidence should be considered in the context of the specific audit, issue, and finding.

d. Working papers need to be prepared, organized, and summarized in sufficient detail and with sufficient care to enable the work to be reviewed, judged, and understood by persons independent of the audit. Working papers:

- Assist the audit manager in monitoring and controlling audits.
- Assist auditors in conducting their work.
- Provide evidence to support audit findings and conclusions.
- Provide evidence to show how work was planned and performed.
- Provide evidence that audit work was performed in compliance with standards.
- Identify who performed and reviewed the work.
- Provide information for audit evaluations, including internal quality assurance reviews and external peer reviews.

Laws and regulations for some audit entities require that working papers become open to public inspection after the audit report is issued. In these cases it is important that all confidential information (e.g., social security numbers) be removed from the working papers before they are made public. Also, auditors should be advised to avoid including unsupported allegations, statements of personal bias, and unsubstantiated personal opinion in the working papers.

Complete audit findings contain the following four elements:

- *Condition* is the situation or practices found during the review. The condition can be summarized as "what is." The statement of condition should be accurate, clear, and precise, in addition to being supported by sufficient, competent, and relevant evidence. The finding statement may also indicate whether the condition is isolated or widespread.

- *Criteria* is defined as "what should be." Noting a difference between the condition and criteria is the first step in developing an audit finding. Criteria should be based on authoritative sources such as laws, rules, or policy guidelines. When auditors rely on their professional judgment as criteria, they are obligated to convince the report reader that the criteria are valid.

- *Cause* is the reason why things went wrong. Identifying the cause is important in making constructive recommendations. It is also important to identify the primary or root cause of the deficiency, instead of merely identifying contributing causes or symptoms.

- *Effect* demonstrates the importance or significance of the deficiency. Measures of effect are frequently stated in quantitative terms such as dollars, time, or number of transactions. Effects can also describe how a program or operation has resulted in changes in actual physical, social, or economic conditions. If past effects cannot be identified, potential effects may be presented.

Recommendations are not an element of a finding, but are part of the report if problems are found. Recommendations are suggestions to improve significant problems. Recommendations are most constructive when they are specific, feasible, action oriented, and cost effective.

a. Risk Assessment

The following performance standards from the *International Standards for the Professional Practice of Internal Auditing (Standards)* (also see Appendix B) will help provide the foundation for the risk assessment section.

2100 – Nature of Work
The internal audit activity should evaluate and contribute to the improvement of risk management, control, and governance processes using a systematic and disciplined approach.

2110 – Risk Management
The internal audit activity should assist the organization by identifying and evaluating significant exposures to risk and contributing to the improvement of risk management and control systems.

2110.A1 – The internal audit activity should monitor and evaluate the effectiveness of the organization's risk management system.

2110.A2 – The internal audit activity should evaluate risk exposures relating to the organization's governance, operations, and information systems regarding the:
- Reliability and integrity of financial and operational information.
- Effectiveness and efficiency of operations.
- Safeguarding of assets.
- Compliance with laws, regulations, and contracts.

2110.C1 – During consulting engagements, internal auditors should address risk consistent with the engagement's objectives and should be alert to the existence of other significant risks.

2110.C2 – Internal auditors should incorporate knowledge of risks gained from consulting engagements into the process of identifying and evaluating significant risk exposures of the organization.

Risk assessment allows organizations to identify potential effects and their significance. Management should continually monitor and assess potential risks that could keep the organization from achieving its goals in the following key areas:

- Effectiveness — Whether the organization is meeting its objectives
- Efficiency — Whether the organization is making optimal use of its resources in achieving its objectives
- Compliance — Whether the organization is meeting laws and regulations or not exceeding appropriated budgets
- Safeguarding of assets — Whether the organization is protecting its assets against integrity violations
- Reliability of financial reporting
- Reliability of operational information

Generally, risks become more difficult to manage the longer they remain undetected. Therefore, early detection of potential internal and external risks will give management more opportunity to take required preventative or corrective actions.

The questions addressed in assessing risk are the following:

- How likely is it to go wrong?
- What will happen if it goes wrong (e.g., assets lost, clients unserved, noncompliance with law, etc.)?

Risk assessment can be used in individual audits to prioritize the use of audit resources. The process involves the following:

- List potential audit areas — An audit area is a subject, unit, or system that is capable of being defined and evaluated. Auditors may identify audit areas by organizing the organization's operations, activities, and processes into major categories such as:
  - Function (e.g., purchasing, disbursement, inventory, or payroll).
  - Location.
- Identify relevant risk factors — Risk factors are the criteria used to identify the *relative significance* of conditions and/or events that could adversely affect the organization or audit unit. For example: the relative pervasiveness or complexity of a specific activity might cause it to have a larger impact on the audit unit as a whole compared to other activities. The number of risk factors used should be sufficient to provide confidence that the risk assessment is comprehensive. Risk factors may include:

    - Changes in the external operating environment (e.g., new laws or regulations, increased public scrutiny).
    - Pressure on management and staff to meet difficult or ambiguous objectives.
    - Size of unit.
    - Complexity of activities, laws, or regulations.
    - Degree that operations are decentralized.
    - Presence of cash receipts or cash-like payments (e.g., food stamps).
    - Rapid growth.
    - New programs and services.
    - Recent changes in operational, technological, or accounting systems.
    - Reliance on obsolete technology.
    - Recent changes in key personnel.
    - Numerous changes of staff in high-level or sensitive positions.
    - Functions controlled by one person.
    - Potential for public embarrassment of the organization (loss of public trust).
    - Impact from failure to accomplish objectives.
    - Amount of funding (expenditures or budget).
- Assess the relative significance of the risk — The head of the audit unit may obtain information from the following sources to assess the significance of risk factors:
    - Various members of management
    - Audit unit staff
    - External auditors
    - Applicable laws and regulations
    - Financial and operating data
    - Prior audits

Auditors must use professional judgment to determine the impact a risk factor may have on the use of audit resources. Generally, higher risk areas are assigned higher audit priorities. However, changing conditions can affect the significance of risk factors and require that the results of the risk assessment be updated.

- Assess the likelihood that a given risk will occur — The organization will generally want to focus on implementing corrective and preventative actions in areas that have the highest significance along with the highest likelihood of occurrence. See Section II.B.2.i for a description of a risk/vulnerability assessment methodology.

Auditors should obtain sufficient knowledge about how the organization's management addresses risks. Management may choose from three broad alternative courses of action to address a specific risk:

- Control the risk — Risk can be controlled by various preventative measures such as adding personnel to a function, installing burglar alarms, increasing the frequency and level of management review, or implementing tighter standards.

- Transfer the risk — Risk can be transferred by purchasing insurance policies to cover losses of several types such as cash, property, or facilities.
- Accept the risk — It is actually quite difficult to control or transfer all risk associated with an area of operation. Therefore, organizations often must decide how much loss they are willing to accept. For example, an organization might decide that the risk of fire is high so it will pay a high premium on its fire insurance policy to transfer as much risk as possible; however, the organization will still have to pay the deductible amount on the policy if a fire occurs.

The organization's control environment influences the level of risk. The control environment sets the tone of an organization and influences the control consciousness of its employees. An unfavorable control environment increases the risk of fraud, abuse, or illegal acts. The characteristics of an effective control environment are as follows:

- Management communicates the importance of internal controls to all employees.
- Employees have clearly defined responsibilities.
- Employees are held accountable for their performance.
- A system is in place to monitor controls on a regular basis.

The following factors influence the state of an organization's control environment:

- Organizational history of control weaknesses or violations
- Whether management emphasizes and values competence, integrity, and ethical behavior
- Whether the organization has a strong code of conduct
- Whether the organization has a strong ethics policy
- Whether the code of conduct and ethics policy are communicated to employees and enforced by management in a sound and consistent manner
- An inconsistent or unfair employee performance evaluation, compensation, and promotion system

The controls described below are categorized based on when they occur in the control process:

- *Preventative controls* are designed to deter undesirable events from occurring.
- *Detective controls* are designed to identify and correct undesirable events that have occurred.
- *Corrective controls* help bring performance back into compliance, or address problems that have been identified — such as the employee grievance system, employee performance appraisals, or an administrative appeals process.

Control activities are policies and procedures used by the organization to address identified risks. Some examples of control activities include:

- Internal accounting controls (e.g., segregation of duties, monitoring, reconciliation).
- Management controls (e.g., the plan, methods, and procedures adopted by management to ensure its goals are met, including systems for measuring, reporting, and monitoring program performance).
- Physical controls (e.g., security).
- Information technology controls (e.g., access security controls, data center operation controls).

There is no universal formula or mix of control activities that can be applied to all organizations. Rather, each organization should design the type and degree of control activities it needs to mitigate its own specific identified risks.

The internal and external environments of all organizations are subject to constant change. Therefore, it is necessary for organizations to monitor and reevaluate the effectiveness of their control systems. Examples of ongoing monitoring functions include:

- Management's review of performance reports and comparing them to budgets and other benchmarks.
- Feedback obtained from external parties (e.g., complaints from stakeholders).
- Direct supervision and review of work by functional-level managers.
- Internal and external audits.
- Physical inventories of assets.

b. Analytical Review

The following performance standards from the *International Standards for the Professional Practice of Internal Auditing (Standards)* (also see Appendix B) will help provide the foundation for the analytical review section.

> **2240 – Engagement Work Program**
> Internal auditors should develop work programs that achieve the engagement objectives. These work programs should be recorded.
>
> > **2240.A1** – Work programs should establish the procedures for identifying, analyzing, evaluating, and recording information during the engagement. The work program should be approved prior to the commencement of work, and any adjustments approved promptly.
> >
> > **2240.C1** – Work programs for consulting engagements may vary in form and content depending upon the nature of the engagement.

Auditors must be able to develop appropriate and supportable conclusions for the evidence they have collected. In addition, auditors are sometimes called upon to evaluate the soundness of decisions made by management, or to review the adequacy of support for conclusions developed by other auditors.

Written findings are essentially formal arguments made in support of a particular position. To develop the critical thinking skills necessary in developing findings and conclusions, auditors should be familiar with the two major categories of logical fallacies:

- *Inductive fallacies* result when evidence is used incorrectly. For example, after interviewing one dissatisfied employee of an agency, an auditor might incorrectly assume that all employees are dissatisfied with agency management or that the morale of all agency employees is low.

- *Deductive fallacies* result from a failure to follow the logic of a series of statements. Deductive arguments are based on a series of statements or premises. Deductive logic states that if a series of premises is true, then the conclusion must also be true. However, deductive arguments are valid only if a sound relationship exists between the premises. An example of an invalid deductive argument follows:

  Major Premise: All employees who are committing fraud drive luxury cars.
  Minor Premise: John Doe drives a luxury car.
  Conclusion: Therefore, John Doe is committing fraud.

Auditors should be familiar with the principles of argumentation and be able to make judgments based on available information. Auditors may exhibit illogical thinking in their own attempts to support conclusions that are not fully supported by the evidence. In addition, auditors may find flaws in the logic supporting some management decision that was not fully explored prior to being implemented. Listed below are some specific types of logical fallacies auditors may encounter.

- *Slippery Slope* — This is the argument that if a particular action is taken, it will inevitably lead to another, less desirable action. Clients often resort to slippery slope arguments in an effort to resist adopting audit recommendations. For example, a client might make the following statement: "If you make us put property tags and numbers on major equipment, next we will have to put tags on every pen, pencil, and paper clip in the place." One can easily recognize this argument as exaggerated and illogical. Auditors are also prone to these logical fallacies. For instance, an auditor might note that the lack of a standard or recommended control (based on use of an ICQ) will lead to losses. The auditor's supervisor should ascertain if the auditor has ruled out the existence of any compensating controls or other risk-reduction strategies.

- *Non Sequitur* — This means "it does not follow." Again, clients often use *non sequiturs* to oppose findings. For example, a client might make the following statement: "Our financial accounting system is well controlled — our books always balance." Before accepting this argument in favor of effective controls, determine the extent of adjusting entries that must be made to ensure that the books balance.

- *Post Hoc, Ergo Propter Hoc* — This means "after this, therefore because of this" and infers that because one event follows another event, the first event must have caused the second. For example, after implementation of a dropout recovery program, employment rates rose. Prior to concluding that the dropout recovery program is responsible for increases in employment, look for possible economic or other factors that might have contributed to the rise.

- *Hasty Generalization* — These are judgments based on limited information that often reflect a bias or prejudice. For example, a person might incorrectly attribute some negative personal characteristic to all members of a particular race, gender, or ethnic group.

- *Ad Hominem* — This means "against the man" and refers to attacks on an individual, rather than the issue being debated. For example, it would be illogical for a cat-loving manager to not recommend a qualified auditor for promotion simply because the auditor expressed a dislike of cats.

- *False Use of Authority* — An auditor might cite support for a finding from an external source such as a book or article. However, it is important to ensure that the auditor present this evidence fairly, which means presenting not only the author's view but also the opposing or alternative views of other authors. It is not acceptable to present a biased or skewed version of available research.

Auditors should base findings and recommendations on significant information. For example, one exception in 1,000 cases is probably not reason enough to recommend overhauling the entire system, although the final answer must be derived from the context and the condition of the related control system. Findings and recommendations should be based on sound logic and evidence.

Auditors should be aware that the concepts of materiality and significance take on different meanings in the public and private sectors. Issues affecting public accountability, equity, and stewardship may have a greater direct impact in the public sector. For example, a manager of a very controversial program may have stolen only $200, but the controversy and public accountability aspects may make the $200 significant, where it would not be material in the private sector financial statement opinion audit. Therefore, during the planning and reporting processes, government auditors may need to consider qualitative factors such as the visibility or sensitivity of the program under audit, or the newness of the program or changes in its condition.

c. Data Gathering and Evaluation (also see the introduction to the Fieldwork Section above)

The following performance standards from the *International Standards for the Professional Practice of Internal Auditing (Standards)* (also see Appendix B) will help provide the foundation for the data gathering and evaluation section.

2300 – Performing the Engagement
Internal auditors should identify, analyze, evaluate, and record sufficient information to achieve the engagement's objectives.

2310 – Identifying Information
Internal auditors should identify sufficient, reliable, relevant, and useful information to achieve the engagement's objectives.

2320 – Analysis and Evaluation
Internal auditors should base conclusions and engagement results on appropriate analyses and evaluations.

A primary purpose of fieldwork is to accumulate sufficient, competent, relevant, and useful evidence to reach a conclusion concerning performance expectations, and to support our audit comments and recommendations. Audit evidence is sufficient when it is factual and would convince an informed person to reach the same conclusion. Evidence is competent if it consistently produces the same outcomes. It is relevant when it is directly related to the audit comments, recommendations, and conclusions.

Throughout fieldwork, professional judgment should be used to:

- Determine whether evidence gathered is sufficient, relevant, competent, and useful to conclude on the established objectives; and
- Based on the information available, reassess the audit objectives, scope, and procedures to ensure efficient use of audit resources (e.g., should the remaining audit steps be eliminated, should the objective or scope be modified, have more efficient procedures been identified, or should additional hours be allocated to achieve an expanded audit objective).

Data gathering and evaluation includes:

- Gaining an understanding of the activity, system, or process under review and the prescribed policies and procedures, supplementing and continuing to build upon the information already obtained in the preliminary survey.
- Observing conditions or operations.
- Interviewing people.
- Examining assets and accounting, business, and other operational records.

- Analyzing data and information.
- Reviewing systems of internal control and identifying internal control points.
- Evaluating and concluding on the adequacy (effectiveness and efficiency) of internal controls.
- Conducting compliance testing.
- Conducting substantive testing.
- Determining if appropriate action has been taken in regard to significant audit concerns and corrective actions reported in prior audits.

Workpapers serve as the connecting link between the audit assignment, the auditor's fieldwork, and the final report. Most importantly, the workpapers document the auditor's conclusions and the reasons those conclusions were reached. Workpapers also provide a basis for demonstrating compliance with The IIA's *Standards*.

Among other things, workpapers may include:

- Planning documents and audit procedures;
- Controls questionnaires, flowcharts, checklists and narratives;
- Notes and minutes resulting from interviews;
- Organizational data, such as charts and job descriptions;
- Copies of important documents;
- Information about operating and financial policies;
- Results of control evaluations;
- Letters of confirmation and representation;
- Analysis and test of transactions, processes, and account balances;
- Results of analytical review procedures;
- Audit reports and management responses; and
- Audit correspondence that documents the audit conclusions reached.
- Workpapers should be clear and understandable. The auditor should keep in mind that other people will examine and refer to the workpapers. The workpapers should not need any supplementary information and should stand alone. Anyone reviewing the workpapers, without referring to documents outside of those included in the workpapers and without asking questions, should be able to tell what the auditor set out to do, what they did, what they found, and what they concluded. Conciseness is important; but clarity should not be sacrificed just to save time and space.

The following text from the Government Auditing Standards[20] confirm the need to ensure that sufficient data is gathered and sufficient evidence is available to support audit conclusions.

7.52 Evidence should be sufficient, competent, and relevant to support a sound basis for audit findings, conclusions, and recommendations:

a. Evidence should be sufficient to support the auditors' findings. In determining the sufficiency of evidence, auditors should ensure that enough evidence exists to persuade a knowledgeable person of the validity of the findings. When appropriate, statistical methods may be used to establish sufficiency.
b. Evidence is competent if it is valid, reliable, and consistent with fact. In assessing the competence of evidence, auditors should consider such factors as whether the evidence is accurate, authoritative, timely, and authentic. When appropriate, auditors may use statistical methods to derive competent evidence.
c. Evidence is relevant if it has a logical relationship with, and importance to, the issue being addressed.

d. Testing (also see the introduction to the Fieldwork Section above)

The overall objective of the audit is to gather and evaluate audit evidence of sufficient quantity and appropriate quality (i.e., appropriate relevance and reliability) in order to form and support a conclusion. Testing is the next logical step in the audit process. After (often these steps are performed simultaneously) data has been gathered, the data must be tested to develop the support for audit conclusions.

The reliability (or competence) of evidence gathered by auditors is a variable. The reliability of evidence is a key factor in the audit analysis. Relevance is also a key factor in determining the quality of evidence. Audit evidence is relevant when the evidence is relevant to the assertion about which the evidence is being gathered. Testing helps confirm the data quality and assertions regarding the reliability and relevance.

Specifically, the auditor will design test procedures for key control areas and associated activities. The testing phase usually requires the auditor to conduct interviews, examine documents, and obtain explanations. The auditor documents the results of the tests, the conclusion, and this information becomes the foundation for audit conclusions and ultimately the audit report.

The following text from the Government Auditing Standards[21] provides an excellent framework for testing principles.

7.53 The following presumptions are useful in judging the competence of evidence. However, these presumptions are not to be considered sufficient in themselves to determine competence. The amount and kinds of evidence required to support auditors' conclusions should be based on auditors' professional judgment.

a. Evidence obtained when internal controls are effective is more competent than evidence obtained when controls are weak or nonexistent. Auditors should be particularly careful in cases where controls are weak or nonexistent and should, therefore, plan alternative audit procedures to corroborate such evidence.

b. Evidence obtained through the auditors' direct physical examination, observation, computation, and inspection is more competent than evidence obtained indirectly.
c. Examination of original documents provides more competent evidence than do copies.
d. Testimonial evidence obtained under conditions where persons may speak freely is more competent than testimonial evidence obtained under compromising conditions (for example, where the persons may be intimidated).
e. Testimonial evidence obtained from an individual who is not biased or has complete knowledge about the area is more competent than testimonial evidence obtained from an individual who is biased or has only partial knowledge about the area.
f. Evidence obtained from a credible third party may in some cases be more competent than that secured from management or other officials of the audited entity.

7.54 Auditors may find it useful to obtain written representations concerning the competence and completeness of certain evidence from officials of the audited entity. Written representations ordinarily confirm oral representations given to auditors, indicate and document the continuing appropriateness of such representations, and reduce the possibility of misunderstandings concerning the matters that are the subject of the representations. Written representations can take several forms, including summary documents prepared by the auditors and signed by the entity's management. If officials of the audited entity refuse to provide a written representation that the auditors have requested, the auditors should consider the effects of the refusal on results of the audit.

7.55 The auditors' approach to determining the sufficiency, competence, and relevance of evidence depends on the source of the information that constitutes the evidence. Information sources include original data gathered by auditors and existing data gathered by either officials of the audited entity or a third party.

e. Tools and Techniques (e.g. CAATs)

As computers became integral to the performance of primary business functions, auditors needed to develop new audit techniques and tools. Auditors had a choice to either audit "around the computer" or "through the computer." Initially auditors audited around the computer and focused their efforts on the input and output from the system, not the processing. This approach assumes that the processing is accurate if the inputs and outputs are correct. As more and more primary business functions were computerized, auditors wanted additional assurances on the integrity of processing logic. As a result, audit tools were developed to permit auditors to efficiently audit through the computer. Under this approach, the program logic and edit checks are reviewed and verified. In some instances, test data is run through the system to check for processing accuracy, the enforcement of edit checks, and output accuracy.

Some specific computer-based audit tools and techniques include[22]:

- Electronic Working Papers.
- Information Retrieval and Analysis.
- Fraud Detection.
- Security Review Software.
- Network Security.
- Continuous Monitoring.
- Audit Reporting.
- Computer-based Training.

The IIA maintains a list of audit tools on its Web site. To obtain additional information on specific software tools, go to (http://www.theiia.org/itaudit/index.cfm?fuseaction=include&page=1). As indicated, there are numerous tools and techniques available and a software specialist may be needed to support audit staff.

Electronic Working Papers

Electronic workpapers automate the working paper process from preparation review to report generation. They enhance the capability to search for information in text, databases, or other audit records and provide auditors with the ability to coordinate efforts. The increased standardization for workpaper format, content, and review promote efficiencies. Some efficiencies include:

- Important information such as audit steps, audit findings, review notes, signoffs, and edit histories are contained in database tables (allows real-time team based use as well as filtering and sorting for key information).
- Concurrent and simultaneous access of the same audit file.
- Filtering and sorting tools to provide specific views of information.
- Automated report generation and referencing.
- Automated backup.
- Ability to image documents and include pictures, sound, and video in files.

Information Retrieval and Analysis *(to sample or not to sample)*

Historically, auditors have relied on samples of transactions to perform their tests. With the use of automated retrieval and analysis tools, it may be easier to assess all records than to evaluate a sample. Furthermore, auditors can set parameters in software to identify all records meeting selection criteria.

Accumulation of information about business data over a period of time may allow analysis software to identify patterns, shifts, or trends in the data indicating changes in the business, the business environment, the client base, the economy, changing competition factors, etc. More common audit data analysis routines include matching employee data to client or vendor records, duplicate payments, payroll and overtime, approvals versus authorization levels, force codes, system overrides, access authorities, telephone usage, and much, much more. Examples abound in auditing literature.

Fraud Detection

Areas most frequently identified by auditors for fraud detection include accounts payable, employee payroll, expense reporting, and inventory management. Historically, auditors have looked for typical fraud indicators such as duplicate payments for invoices or expense reports, invalid vendors, unusually high payments or payments exceeding authority levels, payroll payments to former employees, or detectable patterns in inventory "shrinkage." In recent years software has provided auditors with tools that can also identify unexpected or unexplained patterns in data that may indicate fraud.

Security Review Software

Software that assists the auditor by performing online analysis of security software and operating system parameters. Auditors frequently review global security standards such as password length and change interval. Historically, auditors would review the global system parameters and a sample of users and try to identify those that had less restrictive parameters. Security review software provides auditors with the capability to identify any user that has less restrictive parameters. For example, all users with a password of less than six characters could be identified.

Network Security and Performance

Network security software is typically used by network administrators; however, auditors have found the value to performing network security assessments. Auditors may use the same tools as those used by their network administrators or use their own specialized tools. Before performing such tests, auditors should coordinate closely with network managers and administrators since tests and scans can adversely impact network performance.

More important than the tools used by auditors for network assessments and analyses are the tools that make up the entire security environment for the organization and its networks. Network security tools include firewalls, intrusion detection systems, worm and virus protection, backup and recovery, traffic and pattern analysis, encryption, public key infrastructure (PKI) and certificate authority (CA) administration, access control and monitoring, vulnerability assessments, and much more.

Continuous Monitoring

Continuous monitoring in systems and networks is a by-product of the increasing demand for immediate and continuous access to reliable information. Advancements in information monitoring and analysis are being accelerated both by increasing demands for timely and accurate information and by advances in technology that contribute to the intelligence, capabilities, and timeliness of monitoring and analysis systems. The advances in systems and the increasing expectations of information availability will ensure that continuous monitoring and auditing systems will be the rule rather than the exception in the near future.

In September 2005, The IIA Research Foundation published a guide — *Continuous Auditing: Implications for Assurance, Monitoring, and Risk Assessment.*

Organizations are continually exposed to significant errors, frauds, or inefficiencies that can lead to financial loss and increased levels of risk. An evolving regulatory environment, increased globalization of businesses, market pressure to improve operations, and rapidly changing business conditions are creating the need for more timely and ongoing assurance that controls are working effectively and risk is being mitigated. These demands have put increased pressure on chief audit executives (CAEs) and their staffs.

Continuous auditing is a method used to automatically perform control and risk assessments more frequently. Technology is the key to enabling such an approach. Continuous auditing changes the audit paradigm from periodic reviews of a sample of transactions to ongoing audit testing of 100 percent of transactions. It becomes an integral part of modern auditing at many levels.

For more information on this Guide, go to http://www.theiia.org/bookstore.cfm

Audit Reporting
Some audit tools provide automatic linking between work performed, information gathered, auditor assessments, and information used in or supporting audit reports. Intelligent workpapers may note answers in internal control questionnaires (ICQs) that indicate actual or potential weaknesses and automatically prepare a section in the audit report to document the weakness and/or resolution of the problem. Audit reports can be distributed in electronic format via e-mail, file transfer, or audit Web site.

Computer-based Training
Embedded training and help features are included in most audit software tools today. Many software providers and other organizations offer both generic and specific training for the use of software tools. However, computer-based training (CBT) can span the broad realm of auditing, as well as activities subject to auditing, and should not be limited by previous experience. Training can be informal and self-motivated, or it can be a formal element of audit administration providing feedback to the trainee as well as to audit management.

3. Audit Communications

The following performance standards from the *International Standards for the Professional Practice of Internal Auditing (Standards)* (also see Appendix B) will help provide the foundation for the audit communications section.

2400 – Communicating Results
Internal auditors should communicate the engagement results.

2410 – Criteria for Communicating
Communications should include the engagement's objectives and scope as well as applicable conclusions, recommendations, and action plans.

2410.A1 – Final communication of engagement results should, where appropriate, contain the internal auditor's overall opinion and/or conclusions.

2410.A2 – Internal auditors are encouraged to acknowledge satisfactory performance in engagement communications.

2410.A3 – When releasing engagement results to parties outside the organization, the communication should include limitations on distribution and use of the results.

2410.C1 – Communication of the progress and results of consulting engagements will vary in form and content depending upon the nature of the engagement and the needs of the client.

2420 – Quality of Communications
Communications should be accurate, objective, clear, concise, constructive, complete, and timely.

2421 – Errors and Omissions
If a final communication contains a significant error or omission, the chief audit executive should communicate corrected information to all individuals who received the original communication.

2430 – Engagement Disclosure of Noncompliance with the *Standards*
When noncompliance with the *Standards* impacts a specific engagement, communication of the results should disclose the:
- *Standard(s)* with which full compliance was not achieved,
- Reason(s) for noncompliance, and
- Impact of noncompliance on the engagement.

2440 – Disseminating Results
The chief audit executive should communicate results to the appropriate parties.

2440.A1 – The chief audit executive is responsible for communicating the final results to parties who can ensure that the results are given due consideration.

2440.A2 – If not otherwise mandated by legal, statutory, or regulatory requirements, prior to releasing results to parties outside the organization, the chief audit executive should:

- Assess the potential risk to the organization.
- Consult with senior management and/or legal counsel as appropriate.
- Control dissemination by restricting the use of the results.

2440.C1 – The chief audit executive is responsible for communicating the final results of consulting engagements to clients.

2440.C2 – During consulting engagements, risk management, control, and governance issues may be identified. Whenever these issues are significant to the organization, they should be communicated to senior management and the board.

Obtaining feedback from client management throughout the audit is encouraged in order to ensure that appropriate information is being obtained and to alleviate problems at the conclusion of the audit.

Some specific components of continual communication to consider include:

- Keep client management informed of audit issues and concerns as they arise.
- Submit a draft audit report to ensure that accurate and appropriate information has been reported.
- Advise client management of projected audit timelines and any delays.

An exit conference should be held with the client to eliminate any factual errors in the audit report, to add clarity to findings and recommendations, and to obtain client responses. Specific objectives of an exit conference include:

Provide the client management with findings and recommendations identified during the audit.

- Allow client management to state concerns and objections to the findings and recommendations.
- Give the client management and the audit team the opportunity to identify and correct any errors or misinterpretations that may appear in the draft report.
- Provide the audit team with the formal opportunity to explain the remaining steps in the audit process prior to the release of the final report.

The format and content of audit reports will vary by organization and type of audit. Therefore, the following elements should be included in audit reports as appropriate:

- Audit reports should state the audit objectives, scope, and methodology. If appropriate, the report should describe any performance aspects examined (e.g., outputs, outcomes). The audit scope should describe, as necessary:
  - Organizations audited.
  - Geographic locations of clients.
  - Period covered.
  - Audit standards followed.
  - Management controls assessed.
  - Criteria used.
  - Assumptions made.
  - Sampling plans used.
  - The kinds and sources of evidence used.
  - The depth and coverage of work performed to accomplish the audit objectives, including a description of specific controls tested.
  - As applicable, the relationship between the universe and what was audited.
  - Significant scope impairments or data limitations.
  - Confidential information omitted from the report.

- Audit reports may include background information about the client and the programs or functions reviewed. The report may also include information about the status of prior findings and recommendations.

- Audit reports should include findings, conclusions, and recommendations for corrective actions, as well as the client's response to those recommendations. Recommendations are most constructive when they:
  - Are directed toward resolving the cause of the problems.
  - Are action-oriented and address specific organizational objectives.
  - Are addressed to parties that have the authority to take corrective action.

  - Audits reports should include all significant integrity violations. In some cases, illegal acts should be reported directly to responsible external parties. Insignificant noncompliance should be communicated to the client, preferably in a management letter that is documented in the working papers and mentioned in the report.

  - Audit reports should include a description of significant noteworthy accomplishments and issues that need further work. If significant issues warrant further work but are not directly related to the audit objectives or there is not enough time or resources, auditors should refer the issues to those responsible for planning future audits.

Practice Advisory 2020-1[23] provides the following guidance on monitoring:

The chief audit executive (CAE) should submit annually to the board for approval, and senior management as appropriate, a summary of the internal audit activity s work schedule, staffing plan, and financial budget. The CAE should also submit all significant interim changes for approval and information. Engagement work schedules, staffing plans, and financial budgets should inform senior management and the board of the scope of internal auditing work and of any limitations placed on that scope.

The approved engagement work schedule, staffing plan, and financial budget, along with all significant interim changes, should contain sufficient information to enable the board to ascertain whether the internal audit activity s objectives and plans support those of the organization and the board.

4. Monitoring Outcomes

The following performance standards from the *International Standards for the Professional Practice of Internal Auditing (Standards)* (also see Appendix B) will help provide the foundation for the monitoring outcomes section.

2500 – Monitoring Progress
The chief audit executive should establish and maintain a system to monitor the disposition of results communicated to management.

> **2500.A1** – The chief audit executive should establish a follow-up process to monitor and ensure that management actions have been effectively implemented or that senior management has accepted the risk of not taking action.
>
> **2500.C1** – The internal audit activity should monitor the disposition of results of consulting engagements to the extent agreed upon with the client.

Auditors should monitor the results from previous audit findings and recommendations to ensure that the client has taken corrective action or consciously accepted the risk of not implementing corrective measures. The corrective action taken should be timely, appropriate, and sufficient enough to achieve desired objectives.

Auditors should determine that implemented actions have corrected the underlying causes and conditions of deficiencies, not just the symptoms of the problem.

The level of appropriate follow-up on prior findings is determined by the following:

- The amount of risk and exposure involved if corrective actions fail to correct the problem.
- The amount of time management has had to correct the problem.

- The complexity of the management's corrective action plan.
- The amount and quality of interim feedback the auditor has received from the client regarding the status of correcting the finding since the prior audit.

Practice Advisory 2500-1[24] provides the following guidance on monitoring:

The chief audit executive (CAE) should establish procedures to include:

- A time frame within which management's response to the engagement observations and recommendations is required.
  - An evaluation of management's response.
  - A verification of the response (if appropriate).
  - A follow-up engagement (if appropriate).
  - A communications procedure that escalates unsatisfactory responses/actions, including the assumption of risk, to the appropriate levels of management.

- Certain reported observations and recommendations may be so significant as to require immediate action by management. These conditions should be monitored by the internal audit activity until corrected because of the effect they may have on the organization.

- Techniques used to effectively monitor progress include:
  - Addressing engagement observations and recommendations to the appropriate levels of management responsible for taking corrective action.
  - Receiving and evaluating management responses to engagement observations and recommendations during the engagement or within a reasonable time period after the engagement results are communicated. Responses are more useful if they include sufficient information for the CAE to evaluate the adequacy and timeliness of corrective action.
  - Receiving periodic updates from management in order to evaluate the status of management's efforts to correct previously communicated conditions.
  - Receiving and evaluating information from other organizational units assigned responsibility for procedures of a follow-up or corrective nature.
  - Reporting to senior management or the board on the status of responses to engagement observations and recommendations.

D. Implications of Information Technology

Organizations depend on computerized information systems to meet organizational objectives and to process, maintain, and report essential information. Auditors need to evaluate the reliability of computerized information that supports financial statements or is used to analyze programs or outcomes. Additionally, auditors may need to evaluate information system controls to help reduce the potential for fraud, errors, security breaches, and disasters that cause a loss or modification of data or that render a system unavailable.

Practice Advisory 2100-2[25] provides the following guidance on information security:

- Internal auditors should determine that management and the board have a clear understanding that information security is a management responsibility. This responsibility includes all critical information of the organization regardless of media in which the information is stored.

- The chief audit executive should determine that the internal audit activity possesses, or has access to, competent auditing resources to evaluate information security and associated risk exposures. This includes both internal and external risk exposures, including exposures relating to the organization's relationships with outside entities.

- Internal auditors should determine that the board has sought assurance from management that information security breaches and conditions that might represent a threat to the organization will promptly be made known to those performing the internal audit activity.

- Internal auditors should assess the effectiveness of preventive, detective, and mitigation measures against past attacks, as deemed appropriate, and future attempts or incidents deemed likely to occur. Internal auditors should confirm that the board has been appropriately informed of threats, incidents, vulnerabilities exploited, and corrective measures.

- Internal auditors should periodically assess the organization's information security practices and recommend, as appropriate, enhancements to, or implementation of, new controls and safeguards. Following an assessment, an assurance report should be provided to the board. Such assessments can either be conducted as separate stand-alone engagements or as multiple engagements integrated into other audits or engagements conducted as part of the approved audit plan.

The following basic terms provide the framework to understand some basic concepts and requirements for information technology and security.

Computer Security: The protection afforded to an automated information system in order to attain the applicable objectives of preserving the integrity, availability, and confidentiality of information system resources (includes hardware, software, firmware, information/data, and telecommunications).

Integrity: In general terms, information has integrity when it is timely, accurate, complete, and consistent.

- Data integrity: Data integrity is a requirement that information and programs are changed only in a specified and authorized manner.
- System integrity is a requirement that a system performs its intended function in an unimpaired manner, free from deliberate or inadvertent unauthorized manipulation of the system.

Availability: A requirement intended to assure that systems work promptly and service is not denied to authorized users.

Confidentiality: Requirement that private or confidential information not be disclosed to unauthorized individuals.

Management Controls: Address security topics that can be characterized as managerial. They are techniques and concerns that are normally addressed by management and focus on the management of the computer security program and the management of risk within the organization.

Operational Controls: Address security controls that focus on controls that are, broadly speaking, implemented and executed by people (as opposed to systems). These controls are put in place to improve the security of a particular system (or group of systems). They often require technical or specialized expertise and often rely upon management activities as well as technical controls.

Technical Controls: Focus on security controls that the computer system executes. These controls are dependent upon the proper functioning of the system for their effectiveness. The implementation of technical controls, however, always requires significant operational considerations and should be consistent with the management of security within the organization.

News about data security breaches and communication software vulnerabilities, as well as increasing demands from government regulations, are sending organizations a clear message: unmanaged electronic data and communication tools create unnecessary security and legal risks. Government regulations, such as the U.S. Health Insurance Portability and Accountability Act (HIPAA) of 1996 and the U.S. Sarbanes-Oxley Act of 2002, have changed the way organizations view security and control over data and communications.

When evaluating whether an organization understands its information needs, auditors should obtain an overview of each computer application that is significant to the financial statements or to achieving the mission and objectives. Information that an auditor should be interested in includes:

- Narrative summary of the operating environment and types of computer processing performed (stand-alone, distributed, networked, etc.).
- Overview of the computing environment (hardware, software, configurations, etc.).
- Detailed listing of hardware and software comprising the computer configuration, including:
    - The type, number, and location of central processing units.
    - The role of microcomputers and networks.
- Listing of applications, including a description of the general purpose, impact on the financial statements, and importance to organizational objectives.
- Listing of significant communication networks.
- Organizational chart.
- Disaster contingency plan.
- Computer security policies.
- Strategic plans for information technology.

This information should be reviewed and supplemented with interview information obtained from key staff members. Key personnel should have detailed understanding of the information technology infrastructure and how it supports the organization. A progressive organization that relies heavily on information systems should have a detailed disaster contingency plan (DCP). A detailed and thorough DCP will outline the organization's critical applications and provide specific information regarding the impact of technology on the organization. A review of the DCP can give the auditor insight into the degree of management's understanding of its reliance on information systems.

Information is selected, collected, classified, reported, and stored in a variety of ways. An understanding of the elements of information and process integrity can provide the auditor with the foundation to determine the adequacy of controls. The following table was included in the Systems Auditability and Control Report:[26]

Elements of Information and Process Integrity	
Element	**Definition**
Authorized	An element of information, from a transaction to an entire system, is appropriately entered, developed, changed, or used with proper authority.
Accurate	The information and associated processes are correct and may be used as intended.
Complete	No required information is missing. Conversely, information is not duplicated. Rejected transactions are identified, controlled, and reentered as appropriate.
Timely	The work (e.g., transactions, processes) is promptly processed and client service levels are maintained.
Recorded, processed, and reported in the proper time period	Appropriate accounting period and other cutoff dates are followed.
Secure	The information and processes are protected from unauthorized access, update, disclosure, or destruction.

Each of the elements in the table above has a relationship to the selection, collection, classification, reporting, and storage of information.

- Selection — With the increased processing power and significant decrease in the cost of storage, the selection of information has become a secondary issue. The emergence of data mining illustrates this point as organizations retain as much information as possible and then analyze it to identify unique relationships between data elements. The computing and storage power presently available provides cost-effective opportunities to obtain, retain, and process huge volumes of data.

- Collection — The method of data collection can have an impact on the cost and reliability of information. Although government has made great strides in the use of technology, much information (e.g., tax returns, licensing, Social Security) is still collected on manual forms. Since the majority of information will ultimately be placed on a computer, manual information must be entered into the computer system. If a data entry clerk enters the information, there is the possibility that data entry errors will reduce the reliability and integrity of the data. Even technologically advanced data entry processes, such as optical character recognition (OCR), are prone to errors. Therefore, the integrity of information often depends on the effectiveness of input controls.

- Classification — The method of classifying data helps to control risks associated with alteration and disclosure. Data classification schemes can vary from simple to extremely complex (such as the military classification system). Although a classification should be organizational specific, the following examples of information classes illustrate a reasonable classification approach:
  - *Public information* is available to everyone inside and outside the organization (e.g., information on a Web site).
  - *Unclassified information* is generally available to internal staff (e.g., benefit information, organizational policies).
  - *Classified information* is only available on a need-to-know basis based on job duties (e.g., payroll lists, audit workpapers, accounting data).
  - *Confidential information* is only available to select individuals who have a specific need for the information (e.g., medical records, personnel records).

Some organizations have information protection policies that place the burden of information protection on managers in individual organizational units. An information protection policy may include:

- Statements that define information as an asset that must be protected to different degrees based on its sensitivity, criticality, and value, regardless of the media on which it is stored, the manual or automated systems that process it, or the methods by which it is distributed.
- Statements outlining the responsibilities of information owners, custodians, and users.
- Definitions of the organization's data classification categories.
- Provisions stating that each business unit should develop an information protection program to implement these policies.[27]

A sound data classification scheme sets the foundation for the effective implementation of access controls to ensure that data is adequately protected. The elements of a sound data classification scheme are as follows:

- Reporting — Reporting methods are needed to control the dissemination of information. There are risks associated with reporting inaccurate information. For example, inaccurate information could corrupt the integrity of database applications, spreadsheets, and external reports.

- Storing — An appropriate storage method is needed to securely store information on computer systems and backup media to prevent unauthorized disclosure. The storage controls on the computer system are generally controlled by access control software and should generally correspond to the classification system discussed earlier. Additionally, backup copies of information for recovery purposes must be adequately protected to prevent disclosure.

Information technology general controls set the foundation for effective control over computerized information system assets. General controls apply to the entire computer operation, including the following:

- *Administration controls* include the procedures necessary to ensure that resources are used efficiently and in accordance with management's intentions. They encompass the overall operation of the computer facility. Administration controls also include functions that maximize organizational efficiency and productivity. Organizational efficiency can be directed through long-range planning efforts and effective personnel policies. Productivity in the computer facility is enhanced by adherence to standards. Control techniques for administration include:
    - Segregating duties to prevent the performance of incompatible functions.
    - Providing training and direction.
    - Ensuring that information system managers and end-user managers participate in long-range planning.

- *Controls over computer operations* are vital to overall data processing effectiveness. Computer operation's management must ensure that processing meets specifications by requiring the logging of all actions initiated by computer operators and actions performed by computer software. Control techniques for computer operations include:
    - Maintaining records of operator actions, system actions, and operating problems.
    - Establishing procedures for restart and recovery.
    - Controlling and monitoring system changes.
    - Controlling job schedules and magnetic tape/cartridge usage.
    - Using available error correction techniques.

- *Security controls* reduce or prevent disruption of service, loss of assets, and unauthorized access to equipment. An effective physical security program is necessary to protect the system and data. Control techniques for security include:
    - Establish control over access to and within the facility.
    - Develop an adequate equipment-servicing program.
    - Ensure that there are adequate backup power sources, alarms, and prevention equipment.
    - Implement a written and tested disaster contingency plan.

- *Security administration* is responsible for security over the computer facility, including all aspects of physical and data security. Control techniques for security administration include:
    - Ensuring that the computer security administration function is independent of computer operations.
    - Providing reports and performing reviews of attempted security violations.
    - Ensuring that users and employees are counseled on security considerations.

- *System programmers* control the operation of the computer system and are responsible for the efficient use of computer resources. Systems programming must develop a method of evaluating the performance of computer hardware and software. Criteria for measuring performance must be formalized and deviations from the performance criteria must be corrected. Control techniques for systems programming include:
  - Implementing standards, policies, and procedures for administering the systems programming function.
  - Implementing standards, policies, and procedures for measuring system performance.
  - Implementing procedures for testing and approving system software changes.

- *Telecommunications systems* control the transmission of messages between users and the computer. Through the telecommunications network, users at remote sites can access data and applications at the computer facility. The majority of devices interface with the computer facility by a telecommunications device. Control over the telecommunications network is necessary to ensure that only authorized users have access to the computer facilities. Telecommunications network controls should encompass the network's operating performance and security. Control techniques for telecommunications include:
  - Implementing procedures for testing and approving telecommunications software changes.
  - Securing dial-up lines for access to computer resources.
  - Analyzing response time, detecting problems, and documenting problem resolutions.
  - Selecting available security options built into the telecommunications software (i.e., data encryption).

- *Systems software* consists of computer programs and related routines that control computer processing. The operating system is the prime component of system software because it controls the execution of user application programs. System software products can be tailored to meet user needs. System tailoring is accomplished by setting optional system parameters and, therefore, has an impact on system performance and security. Control techniques for systems software include:
  - Setting appropriate system parameters and security options for operating systems.
  - Controlling procurement and maintenance of software licenses.
  - Using the security features of security software effectively.

Information technology application controls apply to a specific application or system such as payroll. Application controls are specific to the flow of transactions for a system and are designed to ensure accurate, authorized, and complete processing of transactions (e.g., input, processing, output). Application controls are designed to prevent, detect, and correct errors and irregularities as transactions flow through the application.[28] Unlike general controls that apply to the entire computer operation, application controls for each application must be reviewed individually. Application controls are classified into the following categories:

- *Input controls* are concerned with the accuracy and completeness of data entered into an application. Two common input controls are edit and transaction logs. Edit controls are programmed routines that check the validity and accuracy of input. With real-time systems (i.e., where information is input directly into the system without the benefit of a hard copy source document) becoming increasingly prevalent, edit routines are critical to maintaining the integrity of data. Examples of edit controls include:
  - Field tests that ensure that only numeric data are entered into numeric fields and only alphabetic data are entered alphabetic fields.
  - Validity tests that check against an existing table to ensure that a match exists (e.g., an employee number or product code number).
  - Reasonableness tests to reject any data of an abnormal amount (e.g., a check for a weekly salary over $10,000).
  - Completeness tests ensure that all required fields contain data (e.g., name, address, phone number, and Social Security number may be required fields in an employee record).
  - Check digit tests are computed using a formula to calculate an amount or digit. When data are entered into the field, the digit is recalculated and compared to the original value. If the digit differs from the original value, then an apparent error in input has occurred.
  - Transaction logs are computerized records of input activities that become an audit trail to verify the accuracy and timing of input activities. Transaction logs maintain the history of input activities and are used to recreate transactions and determine when and who entered a transaction.

- *Processing controls* are concerned with the proper processing of data entered into an application. Processing controls include:
  - Header and trailer label information to help ensure that the proper data was processed.
  - Record counts that compare input record counts to output records to ensure that all records were processed.
  - Echo checks are the sending of automated verification messages between computer systems to verify the receipt of data.

- *Output controls* are concerned with the verification and proper distribution of computer output. Output controls include:
  - Ensuring that output is only distributed to authorized parties (this includes hard copy and electronic distributions).
  - Verifying the accuracy of output through manual or automated reconciliation activities.

Controls over systems development help ensure system reliability, quality, predictability, and user satisfaction. The acceptance of a structured systems development methodology helps ensure that system designers meet the requirements of system users. A structured approach includes the use of standards for systems design, documentation, testing, and post-implementation review. It also ensures that new and enhanced computer systems meet organizational requirements. Control techniques for application systems development include:

- Appropriate standards, policies, and procedures to control systems and programming functions.
- Standards to ensure that system development activities are properly authorized, tested, reviewed, documented, implemented, and approved.
- Active user and management participation in defining, developing, testing, and reviewing systems and programming activities.

A systems development methodology should include standards on:

- Feasibility studies and cost benefits analysis.
- Approval process for initiating system development and implementation of systems developed.
- Change control procedures for new system developments and modifications to existing systems to ensure that only authorized changes are moved to production.
- Appropriate documentation required for each phase of the development life cycle, including the development of system, operations, and user manuals.
- User training.
- Software and hardware specifications.
- General and detailed design specifications.
- Testing requirements, including requirements for user and programmer testing.
- Project reviews, including periodic milestone reviews and post-implementation reviews.
- Contracting procedures that include the requirements for describing expected project deliverables such as system components and source codes, project time frames, estimated hours, and the maximum allowable expense for each phase.

An audit of systems development activities may include a review of the:

- Adequacy of systems development standards and methodology.
- Method to update and distribute the methodology.
- Adequacy and use of project management tools and techniques.
- Adherence to the methodology for systems development projects.
- Formal approval process for new and modified application systems.
- Adequacy of system, operations, program, and user documentation.
- Testing requirements for new systems and major modifications to existing systems.
- Post-implementation review activities.
- Controls associated with placing authorized programs into production.
- Adequacy of the quality assurance function.

Standards related to information technology are not as well-developed or universally accepted as standards in some other audit areas. The lack of generally accepted information systems standards has prompted many organizations to develop their own standards. However, there have been efforts to develop uniform standards for processing and audit activities. The following are three examples of information systems audit standards:

- Control Objectives for Information and Related Technology (COBIT)[29] — COBIT was released by the Information Systems Audit and Control Foundation (ISACF) in 1996 (1st Edition) and updated in 1998 (2nd Edition). COBIT 3rd Edition was released by the IT Governance Institute (http://www.itgi.org/) in 2000. Note: COBIT 4.0 is expected to be released in late 2005. The COBIT was developed as a generally applicable and accepted standard for good practices for Information Technology (IT) control. COBIT is based on existing Information Systems Audit and Control Foundation (ISACF) control objectives enhanced with existing and emerging international technical, professional, regulatory, and industry-specific standards.

  COBIT has four domains or high-level classifications:

  - *Planning and Organization (PO)* — This domain covers strategy and tactics and concerns the identification of the way information technology can best contribute to the achievement of objectives. Furthermore, the realization of the strategic vision needs to be planned, communicated, and managed for different perspectives. Finally, a proper organizational and technological infrastructure must be put in place.

  - *Acquisition and Implementation (AI)* — This domain covers the identification, development or acquisition, and integration of IT solutions into the business process. In addition, this domain covers changes to existing systems.

  - *Delivery and Support (DS)* — This domain covers the delivery of required services such as staff training. The necessary support processes required to deliver services under this domain include the actual processing of data by application systems, often classified under application controls.

  - *Monitoring (MN)* — All IT processes need to be assessed regularly to monitor their quality and compliance with control requirements.

  Detailed information on COBIT is available at the Information Systems Audit and Control Association's Web site (http://www.isaca.org/cobit.htm).

E. Auditing Financial Statement Elements

The purpose of audits of financial statements is to issue an opinion on the fairness of the financial statements and to evaluate the following assertions (explicit or implicit) by management:

- Existence or occurrence assertions address whether available information addresses actual transactions, assets, and liabilities.
- Completeness assertions address whether all material financial information is included in financial statements.
- Rights and obligations assertions address whether the entity has material rights to the assets and obligations to the liabilities disclosed on the financial statements.
- Valuation or allocation assertions address whether the financial statements show the correct amounts.
- Presentation and disclosure assertions address whether elements of the financial statements are properly organized, classified, and disclosed.

Financial statements that are fairly presented meet the following guidelines:

- Generally accepted accounting principles are used.
- Appropriate accounting principles are used.
- Financial statements address matters that may affect their use or interpretation.
- Financial statements classify and summarize information in a reasonable manner.
- Financial statements reflect underlying transactions and events in a way that facilitates the presentation of the financial position, results of operations, and cash flows.

The following addresses controls over financial reporting:

- The internal control framework developed by the Committee of Sponsoring Organizations of the Treadway Commission (COSO) recognizes financial reporting information as a major element of the control environment. Management must have complete and accurate financial information to facilitate the decision-making process. An adequate system of controls helps management rely on information about the acquisition and safeguarding of receipts and the expenditure of those resources. Categories of financial information include cash receipts, cash disbursements, accounts receivable, accounts payable, and payroll.

- Auditors need to be familiar with the client's controls related to financial reporting, safeguarding financial transactions, and compliance with laws and regulations affecting the financial statements if they plan to rely on them in order to reduce substantive testing on the financial statement audit. The following areas of financial information should be considered:

- How transactions are classified.
- How transactions are initiated.
- How accounting records are maintained.
- What accounting processes are used.
- What method is used to prepare financial statements.
- What methods are used to communicate financial information within the entity.

Materiality Concepts — Not all misstatements will be material enough to affect the fair presentation of the financial statements. A material misstatement is one that the auditor determines would change or influence the opinion of a reasonable person relying on the financial statements for information. Material misstatements may result from:

- Misapplication of accounting principles.
- Omission of necessary information.
- Inaccurate or misleading information.

Auditors must design audits to provide reasonable assurance that financial statements contain no material misstatements due to violations of relevant laws and regulations. Therefore, auditors should understand internal controls relevant to financial statement assertions affected by those laws and regulations. Auditors should use that understanding to identify types of potential misstatements, consider factors that affect the risk of material misstatement, and design substantive tests. Ultimately, auditors must exercise judgment to assess materiality based on the qualitative nature of the misstatements and their quantitative extent. Materiality is also based on the auditor's assessment of control risk levels in the organization. The following factors may influence the auditors' assessment of control risk:

- Management's awareness or lack of awareness of applicable laws and regulations
- Client policy regarding such matters as acceptable operating practices and codes of conduct
- Assignment of responsibility and delegation of authority to deal with such matters as organizational goals and objectives, operating functions, and regulatory requirements

1. Balance Sheet

The balance sheet is one of the most important financial statements. It is reported to investors at least once per year and may also be presented quarterly, semiannually, or monthly. The balance sheet provides information on what the company owns (its assets), what it owes (its liabilities), and the value of the business to its stockholders (the shareholders' equity). The name — balance sheet — denotes that the accounts must always be in balance (assets must always equal the sum of liabilities and shareholders' equity).

The balance sheet is the fundamental report of a company's financial position. An examination of a balance sheet will assist in determining:

- If the company meet its financial obligations.
- The amount of money invested in the company.
- The company's debt ration.
- The type of assets the company has purchased with its financing.

The balance sheet provides insight into a company's future performance. The concept behind the balance sheet is very simple. In order to acquire assets, a firm must pay for them with either debt (liabilities) or with the owners' capital (shareholders' equity). Therefore, the following equation holds true:

Assets = Liabilities + Shareholders' Equity

Assets are economic resources (cash, receivables, inventory, buildings, machinery, patents, copyrights, etc.) that are expected to produce economic benefits for its owners. Following is a brief overview of important asset types.

Current assets are those that are usually converted to cash within one year and include:

- Cash — In addition to currency, bank accounts without restrictions, checks, and drafts are also considered cash due to the ease with which one can turn these instruments into currency.
- Cash equivalents — are not cash but can be converted into cash so easily that they are considered equal to cash. Cash equivalents are generally highly liquid, short-term investments such as U.S. government securities and money market funds.
- Accounts receivable — represent money that clients owe to the company. Since more and more business is being done with credit instead of cash, this item is a significant component of the balance sheet.
- Inventory — is the stock of materials used to manufacture their products and the products themselves before they are sold. For example, a manufacturer will often have three different types of inventory: raw materials, works in process, and finished goods. A retail company's inventory generally will consist only of products purchased that have not yet been sold.

Long-term Assets are those that are not readily convertible to cash. Long-term assets are grouped into several categories. The following are some of the common terms that may be encountered:

- Fixed assets — are tangible assets with a useful life greater than one year. In general, fixed assets refer to items such as equipment, buildings, production plants, and property.

On the balance sheet, these are valued at their cost (depreciation is subtracted from all except land). Fixed assets represent long-term illiquid investments that a company expects to help it generate profits.

- Depreciation — is the process of allocating the original purchase price of a fixed asset over the course of its useful life. The amount appears in the balance sheet as a deduction from the original value of the fixed assets.
- Intangible assets — are non-physical assets such as copyrights, franchises, and patents. It is often difficult to estimate their value and often there is no readily available market for them. Nevertheless, for some companies, an intangible asset can be the most valuable asset it possesses.

Liabilities are obligations a company owes to outside parties. They represent rights of others to money or services of the company. Examples include bank loans, supplier debts, and debts to employees. On the balance sheet, liabilities are generally broken down into current liabilities and long-term debt.

Current liabilities are those obligations that are usually paid within the year, such as accounts payable, interest on long-term debts, taxes payable, and dividends payable. Current liabilities are usually paid with current assets, thus it is important to examine the degree to which current assets exceed current liabilities. Accounts payable is generally the most pervasive item on balance sheet and represents the debts owed to suppliers for the purchase of goods and services. Since most companies buy some or all of their goods on account, accounts payable is included on most balance sheets.

Long-term debt is a liability of a period greater than one year. It usually refers to business loans and is often paid in installments. If installment payments are used, the portion to be paid off in the current year is considered a current liability.

Shareholders' equity is the value of a business to its owners after all of its obligations have been met. This net worth belongs to the owners, and shareholders' equity generally reflects the amount of capital the owners invested plus any profits that the company generates that are subsequently reinvested (retained earnings) in the company.

Balance sheets are audited and analyzed to identify potential liquidity problems. These may signify the company's inability to meet financial obligations.

2. Statement of Cash Flows

A statement of cash flows is a financial report that shows incoming and outgoing money during a particular period (often monthly or quarterly). It does not include non-cash items such as depreciation. The statement is a useful tool for determining the short-term viability of a company, particularly its ability to pay bills.

People and groups interested in cash flow statements include:

- Accounting personnel who need to know whether the organization will be able to cover payroll and other immediate expenses.
- Potential lenders or creditors who want a clear picture of a company's ability to repay.
- Potential investors who need to judge whether the company is financially sound.
- Potential employees or contractors who need to know whether the company will be able to afford compensation.

Cash flow statements are particularly important for startup companies with limited liquid assets as these companies are vulnerable to extreme cash shortages that can impact routine operations.[30]

3. Income/Expense Statements[31]

Income statements for companies indicate how net revenue (money received from the sale of products and services before expenses are taken out — also called the "top line") is transformed into net income (the result after all revenues and expenses have been accounted for — also called the "bottom line").

Income statement should help investors and creditors:

- Evaluate the past performance of the enterprise.
- Predict future performance.
- Assess the risk of achieving future cash flows.

However, information in an income statement has several limitations. For example, items that might be relevant but cannot be reliably measured are not reported (e.g. brand recognition and loyalty). In addition, the accounting methods used to measure inventory or depreciation will have an impact of the statements.

Below is an example of simple "single-step" income statement. In the single-step statement, just two groups exist: revenues and expenses. Expenses are deducted from revenues to get net income (single step). Its main advantage is simplicity, but more and more companies choose multiple-step statements. The basic format is shown below.

Revenues	
Net sales	$3,400,000
Rent revenue	40,000
Interest revenue	12,000
Total revenue	3,452,000
Expenses	
Cost of goods sold	2,000,000
Selling expenses	450,000
Administrative expenses	350,000
Interest expense	45,000
Total expense	2,850,000
Income before taxes	602,000
Income taxes	180,600
Net income	421,400

4. Off-balance-sheet Items

Off-balance-sheet usually means an asset or debt or financing activity not on the company's balance sheet. It could involve a lease or a separate subsidiary or a contingent liability such as a letter of credit.[32]

The use of off-balance-sheet entities has been a common practice. These separate legal entities were permissible under generally accepted accounting practices and tax laws so companies could finance business ventures by transferring the risk of these ventures from the primary company to an off-balance-sheet subsidiary. After the Enron scandal, any type of off-balance-sheet item is subject to additional scrutiny.

The term off-balance-sheet often refers to separate legal entities (separate companies of which the primary company holds less than 100% ownership) or contingent liabilities such as letters of credit or loans to separate legal entities that are guaranteed by the primary company. Accepted accounting practices permits the exclusion of these items from the primary company's financial statements but usually requires a footnote disclosure.

Off-balance-sheet companies were created to help finance new ventures. Theoretically, these separate companies were used to transfer the risk of the new venture from the parent to the separate company. This way, the primary company could finance the new venture without diluting existing shareholders or adding to its debt burden. This use of off-balance-sheet entities is positive in that it transfers risk from the primary company's shareholders to others that were willing to take the business risk.

While accounting principles and tax laws allow off-balance-sheet entities for valid reasons, there can be negative consequences when economic reality differs significantly from the assumptions that were used to justify the off-balance-sheet entity. Enron exemplifies the problems associated with the misuse of off-balance-sheet items. Enron used off-balance-sheet vehicles to give the appearance of enhanced financial results rather than for legitimate business purposes.

A major problem with off-balance-sheet items is the difficulty in reading filings and financial statements to understand how they might impact short-term and long-term results. A key element is the primary company's ability to provide full disclosure in an understandable manner.[33]

References

[1]Information obtained from The Institute of Internal Auditors' (IIA) Web site in October 2005, http://www.theiia.org/.

[2]Information obtained from The Institute of Internal Auditors' (IIA) Web site in October 2005, http://www.theiia.org/index.cfm?doc_id=124.

[3]International Standards on Auditing. International Federation of Accountants. www.ifac.org.

[3.5]AICPA Professional Standards (New York: American Institute of Certified Public Accountants, 2000), Section AU 319.06.

[4]AICPA Professional Standards (New York: American Institute of Certified Public Accountants, 2000), Section AU 319.14.

[5]McNamee, David, *Audit Risk Assessment – A Special Workbook for Internal Auditors* (Altamonte Springs, FL: The Institute of Internal Auditors, 1997), p. 2.

[6]McNamee, David, *Business Risk Assessment* (Altamonte Springs, FL: The Institute of Internal Auditors, 1998), pp. 23-27.

[7]Ibid, p. 81.

[8]*Practice Advisory 2120.A1-1: Assessing and Reporting on Control Processes* (Altamonte Springs, FL: The Institute of Internal Auditors, June 2001), p. 1.

[9]*Practice Advisory 2110-1: Assessing the Adequacy of Risk Management Processes* (Altamonte Springs, FL: The Institute of Internal Auditors, March 2001), p. 1.

[10]Ibid, p. 2.

[11]Information obtained from the AICPA Web site in August 2000, http://www.aicpa.org/news/p032699b.htm.

[12]*Internal Control - Integrated Framework* (New Jersey: Committee of Sponsoring Organizations of the Treadway Commission, 1994), p. 13.

[13]Ibid., p. 16.
[14]Ibid., p. 17.
[15]Enterprise Risk Management – Integrated Framework (New Jersey: Committee of Sponsoring Organizations of the Treadway Commission, 2004), excerpts from Executive Summary.
[16]Information obtained from CICA Web site in January 2005, http://www.cica.ca/index.cfm?la_id=1&ci_id=1089&highlight_keywords=Coco
[17]Information obtained from CICA Web site in August 2000, http://www.cica.ca/cica/cicawebsite.nsf/Public/133D3A09CD3143018525694900348AE2.
[18]Information obtained from CICA Web site in January 2005, http://www.cica.ca/index.cfm?la_id=1&ci_id=3089&highlight_keywords=Coco
[19]Sawyer, Lawrence B., et al., *Sawyer's Internal Auditing: The Practice of Modern Internal Auditing, 4th Edition* (Altamonte Springs, FL: The Institute of Internal Auditors, 1996), p. 1001.
[20]*Government Auditing Standards,* Comptroller General of the United States, June 2003 (www.gao.gov), pp. 148-149.
[21]*Government Auditing Standards,* Comptroller General of the United States, June 2003 (www.gao.gov), pp. 150-153.
[22]Le Grand, Charles, *Use of Computer Assisted Audit Tools and Techniques (CAATTs),* IT Audit, Volume 4, October 2001, http://www.theiia.org/itaudit/index.cfm?fuseaction=forum&fid=320.
[23]Practice Advisory 2020-1: Communication and Approval, January 2001, The Institute of Internal Auditors.
[24]Practice Advisory 2500-1: Monitoring Progress, January 2001, The Institute of Internal Auditors.
[25]Practice Advisory 2100-2: Information Security, February 2001, The Institute of Internal Auditors.
[26]*Systems Auditability and Control, Module 1 – Executive Summary* (Altamonte Springs, FL: The Institute of Internal Auditors Research Foundation, 1991), pp. 1-14.
[27]*Executive Guide - Information Security Management - Learning From Leading Organizations,* General Accounting Office, May 1998, p. 45, GAO/AIMD-98-68 Information Security Management.
[28]*Systems Auditability and Control, Module 2 - Audit and Control Environment* (Altamonte Springs, FL: The Institute of Internal Auditors Research Foundation, 1991), pp. 2-7.
[29]*Control Objectives for Information and Related Technology (COBIT), 4th Edition,* Information Systems Audit and Control Foundation (ISACF), 2005, (http://www.isaca.org/cobit.htm).
[30]WikipediA, the Free Encyclopedia, http://en.wikipedia.org/wiki/Statement_of_cash_flows.
[31]WikipediA, the Free Encyclopedia, http://en.wikipedia.org/wiki/Income_statement.
[32]WikipediA, the Free Encyclopedia, http://en.wikipedia.org/wiki/Off-balance-sheet.
[33]Off-balance-sheet Entities: The Good, The Bad And The Ugly, Wayman, Rick, February 20, 2005, http://www.investopedia.com/printable.asp?a=/articles/analyst/022002.asp

Section II
Auditing Financial Services Products

This section introduces the key terms and audit considerations related to financial services products. Many of these topics are also described in other domains and discipline sections of this study guide.

A. Lending/Loans

The starting point for any loan audit should be the institution's loan policy manual. Loan policies typically address items such as application and approval procedures, types of loans that the institution offers, financial information required by applicants, acceptable collateral, evaluation guidelines, requirements and responsibilities of the board of directors, and loan review, collection, and charge-off procedures. Auditors should ensure that loans are granted in accordance with lending policies and that appropriate documentation is available to support loans granted and rejected.

There are restrictions on the amount banks may loan to an individual borrower and limits on specific types of loans that can be made. Regulations also govern loans to individuals closely associated with the lending institution. Auditors can select a sample of loans to employees, officers, and principal shareholders to ensure the loans comply with lending policies and that unusually favorable terms were not granted. Auditors can also review large loans to these individuals to ensure they received proper board approval. Any of these related-party transactions should be disclosed if they are material to the loan portfolio.

Each type of loan typically should have a separate general ledger control account that should be supported by subsidiary records. Depending on the type of subsidiary records used, single or multiple records may be needed to record loan information such as escrow balances or monthly payment amounts. Many banks use ancillary ledgers to post all borrowers' liability transactions.

There are three major categories of loans:

- *Commercial loans* are typically made for business purposes to sole proprietors, partnerships, and corporations. A commercial loan may be secured or unsecured. A loan is secured when the bank holds a lien against pledged collateral. Commercial loans may be written as short-term time loans, demand loans, or term loans. Some types of commercial loans include:
  - Short-term working capital loans generally finance the production needs of manufacturing companies until finished goods are sold.

- Asset-based financing involves loans that are secured by the borrower's current assets (receivables or inventories).
- Seasonal loans provide funds to businesses to carry them through off-season periods of the year.
- Term loans are extended-maturity loans that allow businesses to acquire capital assets. Because of the extended maturity dates, term loans have a greater risk of loss. For this reason, term loans are usually secured, may require amortization, and may contain other restrictive covenants.
- Agricultural loans are common in rural areas and offer alternative financing to farmers who must often wait years before new operations begin turning a profit.
- Floor-plan financing allows businesses that sell durable goods such as automobiles to finance inventories. As the business sells goods, the loan advance against those goods is repaid.

- *Residential loans* are usually secured by mortgages, deeds of trust, land contracts, or other types of real estate liens. Interest rates for residential mortgage loans may be fixed or variable. Repayment of principal may be set up for full amortization, negative amortization, or partial amortization with a balloon payment at a specified date. Lending institutions may require some borrowers to purchase credit life insurance to reduce the institution's credit risk.

- *Consumer loans* cover personal use items such as automobiles, appliances, vacations, educational expenses, and home repairs or updates. These loans are generally for smaller amounts and are repaid each month over the loan period. Two primary types of consumer loans are:
  - Installment loans allow the consumer to repay a loan over a set period. They require periodic principal and interest payments. The loan is generally secured by the item being purchased. Automobile loans or real estate mortgage loans are common types of installment loans.
  - Credit cards allow customers to make purchases up to a set dollar limit. Most credit cards are unsecured, but some secured card programs are available for customers that are a high credit risk. Many cards carry an annual fee and charge interest on balances unpaid after a specified period.

All lending institutions assume some loans will not be repaid and thus estimate the losses they expect from their loan portfolio. Management of the lending institution sets a reserve for loan losses at a given point based on factors such as the number and type of loans made, the quality of the loans made, the number of problem loans, historical loss experience, collateral value on non-performing loans, guarantor's financial strength, and the general state of the economy. If more funds than expected are needed to cover loan losses in a given period, the reserve must be increased and the difference is charged to operating expenses. Auditors should test the calculations establishing the reserve for loan losses to determine whether it appears adequate as compared to target reserves established by the institution.

Exception reports generated by the lending institution are designed to identify past-due loans. Auditors should review these exception reports to identify an unusually high number of exceptions and old or unusual exceptions that might indicate that the institution is not following up on exceptions in a timely manner. Also, when a loan becomes delinquent or when collection seems unlikely, banks often suspend accrual of interest. If principal is paid on a loan after it has been placed on non-accrual status, the bank must determine whether it should record the payment as a reduction of the loan principal amount or as interest income.

Financial institutions regularly identify uncollectible accounts and charge them off against the reserve for loan losses. Auditors should ensure that the institution has developed adequate criteria for charge-offs and select a sample of charged-off loans to determine whether they were handled properly. Another useful test is to select a sample of loans that are significantly past due to determine whether they meet the charge-off criteria and assess why they have not been charged off. Auditors should also verify that large charge-offs are appropriately approved by the loan committee and reported to the board.

Financial institutions also keep watch lists of loans that are in danger of becoming delinquent. Watch lists generally contain information such as the customer's name and account information, the loan balance outstanding, and available collateral and its estimated value. Auditors can review these watch lists to look for unusual entries that do not meet the institution's guidelines, to check whether action on these loans is being taken in a timely and appropriate manner, and to help assess whether the lending institution is using all possible methods to recover loan.

B. Deposits

Deposit accounts are either interest bearing or non-interest bearing. Interest bearing accounts include savings accounts and certificates of deposit. These types of accounts bear interest for a fixed period of time and are known as time deposits.

Some small businesses keep funds in a savings account to gain interest on liquid assets. However, savings accounts require frequent trips to the bank to make transactions, and the interest paid is generally not as high as some other options. Thus, many small businesses opt for money market deposit accounts that allow transactions by check (although the number of transactions per month may be limited) and that have historically paid a slightly higher rate of return than regular savings accounts. Most large companies do not use savings accounts as part of their money management plan.

Certificates of deposit (CDs) generally pay higher rates of interest than savings accounts or money market deposit accounts. CDs are sold with a specific maturity and rate of interest. Interest rates offered on new CDs changes daily at most banks. Bearer CDs are payable to the owner, and registered CDs are payable to a specified person or entity. Negotiable CDs are short-term instruments generally purchased in large denominations by companies and pension funds. Non-negotiable CDs are usually sold in smaller denominations. There is a penalty payable if the holder of a non-negotiable CD redeems the certificate prior to the maturity date. In general, the longer the maturity of a CD, the higher the interest rate earned. But because money has to be tied up to an extended period to achieve these higher returns, many businesses find CDs to be a less than satisfactory money management approach.

Non-interest bearing accounts include checking accounts and escrow accounts and are known as demand deposit accounts. This type of account allows customers to transfer money through the use of checks, automated teller machines (ATMs), electronic funds transfers (EFTs), or point-of-sale (POS) terminals. Owners of demand deposit accounts receive regular statements from their bank showing a record of deposits and payments during the previous period.

The financial institution's general ledger records activity on deposit accounts. Posting of time deposit transactions usually occurs on the day the transaction occurs or the next day. During the posting process, banks may reject some transactions because they lack proper endorsements or are subject to stop payment orders. A bank may also reject a transaction if it would create an overdraft.

In the United States, banks are required to report cash deposits that exceed $10,000 a day to any one account, regardless of how many branches or deposits have been used in the transactions. Banks are also required to report when cash is used to purchase cashier's checks, money orders, traveler's checks, or bank checks in excess of $3,000. In the United States, accounts are federally insured by the Federal Deposit Insurance Corporation (FDIC). An individual is limited to $100,000 in insurance coverage at each bank (including branches).

The following audit objectives and steps should be considered when performing an audit of deposit accounts:

- Assess the adequacy of policies, procedures, and internal controls regarding deposit accounts.
- Determine whether documentation exists to show that accounts are properly opened and closed in a timely manner and in accordance with establish policies. Ensure that applications and signature cards are on file. Send confirmations on a sample of accounts. If any confirmations are not received, compare the signature on recent checks or transactions to the signature card for the account.
- Determine whether deposit transactions and any accrued interest are posted properly. Verify that subsidiary records are reconciled to the general ledger on a reg-ular basis and agree with the general ledger totals.
- Ensure that there is adequate separation of duties between the posting and reconciling functions. Recalculate a sample of reconciliations to verify accuracy. Note whether any unusual transactions were properly verified and authorized.

- Determine whether applicable fees and penalties are properly assessed and posted. Ensure that any waived fees are properly authorized and processed.
- Determine whether overdrafts are properly approved and processed in accordance with established bank policies. Verify that overdraft charges are properly debited on customer account statements.
- Determine whether there are adequate controls to prevent unauthorized access and change to customer accounts.
- Determine whether dormant accounts are closed in a timely manner and in accordance with policies.

C. Trusts

Trust departments administer trusts, estates, pension accounts, profit sharing accounts, and custodian accounts. Trust departments also provide services to publicly held companies related to issuing and maintaining stock transactions. The board of directors is responsible for any trust funds the bank holds. All bank employees participating in trust operations should be bonded.

Funds held in trust accounts are not assets of the financial institution administering the trust. Therefore, records relating to trust accounts must be segregated from other bank accounts. Funds held in trust cannot be reinvested in the financial institution's own securities. Banks may transfer funds from one trust account to another unless prohibited by a trust agreement or unless it is unfair to either account.

Banks provide the following personal trust services for individuals:

- Estate Settlement — Banks serve as executors or administrators of estates. As administrator of an estate, the bank's major duties are to assemble, control, and inventory the deceased person's assets; arrange to pay applicable costs, taxes, and claims; and distribute the net remaining estate according to the terms of the will.

- Trusts — There are numerous kinds of trusts:
  - *Living trusts* are created by individuals for the purpose of owning another person's assets during that person's life and for distributing the assets after that person's death. These arrangements allow assets to be given to heirs without going through probate.
  - *Testamentary trusts* are implemented through a will after a person dies.
  - *Charitable trusts* are established by will or agreement for religious, educational, or community improvement purposes.
  - *Guardianship trusts* are designed to provide for someone who has been declared legally incompetent. In these cases a bank may be named as trustee by court order.

- Guardians of Estates — Courts may direct a bank to hold and manage the assets of a minor until he or she is of legal age. Banks may also be appointed to serve as guardians of assets for adults who are deemed incompetent or unable to manage their money.

- Co-fiduciary — Some wills specify that more than one responsible party share the trustee responsibilities of an estate. The named parties are referred to as co-fiduciaries.

- Agent — A bank serves as agent when the bank takes possession of a piece of property but the owner retains the title. Agency accounts at a bank include when the bank serves as custodian of property, escrow agent, investment advisory agent, or safekeeping agent. A bank also serves as agent when it executes any authorized powers of attorney.

A bank's corporate trust department handles the functions related to stocks and bonds. Corporations, government entities, and other organizations use banks as trustees to handle the issuance, redemption, transfer, and recordkeeping functions associated with a stock or bond issue. A trust agreement or "indenture" specifies the bank's responsibilities. Additional duties of corporate trust departments include:

- Stock Transfer Agent — The transfer agent may issue stock certificates to increase shares outstanding or reissue new certificates when ownership changes.
- Bond Registrar — The bond registrar is responsible for registering bonds at issue.
- Stock Registrar — The stock registrar checks new issues and transfers to prevent over-issuance.
- Dividend Reinvestment Agent — The dividend reinvestment agent receives a stockholder's dividends and purchases additional shares on the stockholder's behalf.

A bank may serve as the administrator, trustee, co-trustee, agent, custodian, or depository for a company's employee benefit and retirement plans. Types of retirement plans that banks may administer include:

- Pension Plans — These plans provide retirement income for employees. Pension plans that an employer establishes for retired or disabled employees, regardless of whether an employee contributes, are known as "defined benefit plans."
- Self-employed Retirement Trusts — Banks may serve as trustee or custodian for pension and profit sharing plans that self-employed individuals establish for themselves and their employees. These types of trusts are referred to as Keogh plans.
- Individual Retirement Accounts (IRAs) — Banks may administer IRA accounts in accordance with individual agreements with customers. Individuals do not have to pay taxes on deferred income, and any additional contributions are tax deductible until withdrawals begin.

Auditors conducting trust department audits should review the department's policies and procedures. Audit tests should focus on whether there are adequate internal controls over trust assets and whether reports on those assets are complete and accurate. In addition, the trust committee activities should be reviewed, such as:

- Whether regular meetings are held and documented by meeting minutes.
- Whether the trust committee contains at least one member who is not a bank officer.
- Whether the committee is performing adequate and timely reviews of accounts.
- Whether there is adequate oversight of the trust committee's activities by the board of directors.

D. Annuities

An annuity is a contract between the purchaser of the annuity (known as the *annuitant*) and an insurer, under which the annuitant makes a lump-sum payment or series of payments to the insurer. In return, the insurer agrees to invest the funds for a stated period (known as the *accumulation period*). When the maturity date of the annuity arrives, the insurer begins making a series of payments to the annuitant over a stated period (known as the *payout period*).

Annuities provide the annuitant with tax-deferred earnings. If the annuitant dies before payments begin, the insurer pays the annuity's cash value to the annuitant's beneficiaries. Annuities contain a withdrawal provision that allows the annuitant to withdraw a percentage of the annuity's accumulated value each year. There is usually a withdrawal charge only if the annuitant withdraws more than the maximum withdrawal amount stated in the contract.

An annuitant can surrender the annuity in exchange for its cash surrender value, which equals the accumulated value of the annuity minus any applicable surrender charges. Surrender charges usually apply only if the annuity has not been in force for a minimum period of time.

According to the Securities and Exchange Commission (SEC), annuities are generally classified into two categories:[1]

- Fixed annuities — Insurers guarantee a minimum rate of interest during the time that the account is growing and periodic payment amounts of a specified amount for a stated period (either a specific period of time, such as monthly for 20 years, or for an indefinite period, such as the lifetime of the annuitant and his or her spouse).

- Variable annuities — These are contractual arrangements that combine some features of an investment company's products (the contract holder assumes the risk of investment gain or loss) with certain traditional insurance features (the insurance company provides certain insurance guarantees and assumes the risk of mortality and administrative expenses).[2] The annuitant can choose to invest purchase payments from among a range of different investment options, typically mutual funds. The rate of return and the amount of the periodic payments the annuitant will eventually receive varies depending on the performance of the investment options selected.[3] The actual amounts of payments to the annuitant are based on the:

- Amount of money invested.
- Interest rate.
- Length of time the principle has been invested.
- Number of annuity payments to be made.

Fixed and variable annuities are different in that when an insurance company sponsors a fixed annuity, it assumes the risk of investment gain or loss and guarantees the contract holder a specified interest rate and monthly annuity payment. Holders of variable annuities assume the risk of investment gain or loss because the value of the account varies according to the performance of a specific securities portfolio. For both types of annuities, insurance companies generally assume the mortality risk and administrative expenses for a specified fee.[4]

Equity-indexed annuities are a special type of annuity that involve a contract between the annuitant and insurer in which insurer credits the annuity account with return amounts based on changes in an equity index, such as the S&P 500 Composite Stock Price Index. The insurer typically guarantees a minimum return, although the rates vary. After the accumulation period, the insurer makes payments to the annuitant, either periodic or lump sum as specified in the contract.[5]

Some common features used to compute an equity-indexed annuity's interest rate:[6]

- The *participation rate* determines how much of the index's increase will be used to compute the index-linked interest rate. For example, if the participation rate is 80% and the index increases 9%, the return credited to the annuity would be 7.2% (9% x 80% = 7.2%).
- Some equity-indexed annuities set a maximum rate of interest that the equity-indexed annuity can earn. If a contract has an upper limit, or *interest rate cap*, of 7% and the index linked to the annuity gained 7.2%, only 7% would be credited to the annuity.
- The index-linked interest for some annuities is determined by subtracting a percentage from any gain in the index. This fee is sometimes called the *margin*, *spread*, or *administrative fee*. In the case of an annuity with a spread of 3%, if the index gained 9%, the return credited to the annuity would be 6% (9% - 3% = 6%).

Another feature that can affect an equity-indexed annuity's return is its indexing method (or how the amount of change in the relevant index is determined). Some common indexing methods include:[7]

- The *annual reset* (or *ratchet*) method credits index-linked interest based on any increase in index value from the beginning to the end of the year.
- The *point-to-point* method credits index-linked interest based on any increase in index value from the beginning to the end of the contract's term.
- The *high water mark* method credits index-linked interest based on any increase in index value from the index level at the beginning of the contract's term to the highest index value at various points during the contract's term, often annual anniversaries of when the annuity was purchased.

Equity-indexed annuities combine features of traditional insurance products (guaranteed minimum return) and traditional securities (return linked to equity markets). Depending on the mix of features, an equity-indexed annuity may or may not be a security. The typical equity-indexed annuity is not registered with the SEC. Likewise, fixed annuities are not securities and are not regulated by the SEC. However, variable annuities are considered to be securities contracts and thus are regulated by the SEC.

The U.S. Department of the Treasury, Office of the Comptroller of the Currency (OCC), provides guidance to national banks regarding annuity sales. Auditors should be aware of this guidance when planning and conducting annuity audits. Specific guidance can be found in the Interagency Statement on Retail Sales of Nondeposit Investment Products, which include fixed and variable annuities. Under the Interagency Statement, when a bank recommends or sells these products, it should inform the customer that the products are:[8]

- Not insured by the FDIC.
- Not a deposit or other obligation of, or guaranteed by, the depository institution.
- Subject to investment risks, including possible loss of the principal amount invested.

The Interagency Statement calls for these disclosures to be provided:

- Orally during any sales presentation.
- Orally when investment advice concerning the nondeposit investment products is provided
- Orally and in writing prior to or at the time an investment account is opened to purchase these products
- In advertisement and other promotional materials, as specified in the Interagency Statement.

When accounts are opened, banks should obtain signed statements from the customers acknowledging that they have received and understand the disclosures. All written disclosures should be conspicuous and presented in a clear and concise manner.[9]

Auditors should also be aware that according to the OCC, confirmations and account statements for annuities and other nondeposit investment products should contain the minimum disclosures if they contain the name or logo of the bank or an affiliate, in addition to any other required disclosures.

If a customer's periodic deposit account statement includes account information concerning the customer's annuity or other nondeposit investment products, the information should be clearly separate from other account information. The bank should also disclose the existence of any advisory or material relationship between the bank or an affiliate of the bank and an investment company whose shares are sold by the bank and any material relationship between the bank and an affiliate involved in providing nondeposit investment products.[10]

Auditors should also note that the U.S. Securities and Exchange Commission (SEC) has stated that certain insurance company depositor or sponsor financial statements included in the registration statements of variable annuity contracts may be audited in accordance with either the auditing standards of the Public Company Accounting Oversight Board (PCAOB) or generally accepted auditing standards issued by the American Institute of Certified Public Accountants Auditing Standards Board (GAAS). According to the SEC, "this applies only to certain mutual insurance companies and other insurance company depositors whose sole nexus to the Securities Exchange Act of 1934 (Exchange Act) is as depositor of one or more separate accounts that issue variable insurance contracts and that are registered as investment companies under the Investment Company Act of 1940."[11]

The SEC also notes that "financial statements of insurance company depositors that are, in their own right, Exchange Act filers, including mutual insurance companies that issue registered market value adjustments contracts, must be audited in accordance with PCAOB standards. In addition, the financial statements of registered separate accounts that issue variable insurance contracts must be audited in accordance with PCAOB standards."[12]

E. Derivatives

A derivative is a financial instrument that derives its value from the value of other financial instruments or an underlying asset such as currency, commodities, stocks, bonds, or index or interest rate. Derivatives can be effective, low-cost tools for managing exposure to risks, although some banks may experience losses due to interest rate changes, commodity price changes, or other fluctuations. In order to manage risks, banks should have adequate oversight by senior management and the board of directors, as well as comprehensive policies and procedures governing the use of derivatives.

There are two basic categories of derivatives:[13]

- Option-type contracts — Options give buyers the right, but not the obligation, to buy or sell an asset at a preset price over a specified period. The option's price (called "premiums") is usually a small percentage of the underlying asset's value.
- Forward-type contracts — These are futures contracts in which a specified amount of a commodity or financial instrument is to be delivered at a specified future date. Normally, no money changes hands until the delivery date

Derivatives can be either exchange traded or traded over the counter:[14]

- Exchange traded securities — Offers standardized contracts, provides liquidity in the securities by matching trading partners, and guarantees performance on the contracts to both sides of the trade.
- Over-the-counter trading — Offers more flexibility to meet investor objectivity, but can have substantial credit risk and lower liquidity due to customization.

Basic controls to consider when auditing derivative strategies include:[15]

- Board-approved guidelines.
- Regular reporting to board on positions.
- Experienced personnel.
- Independent risk management.
- Valuation models suitable to activity level.
- Sensitivity analysis capabilities.
- Counterparty exposure monitoring and management.
- Master agreements.

Indicators of control weaknesses in derivative strategies include:[16]

- Management not involved.
- Lack of an internal control culture.
- Evidence of a "star manager" syndrome.
- Large concentration of a single counterparty.
- Highly volatile markets or illiquid markets.
- Poor risk management systems.
- No risk or position limits.
- Compensation based on performance.
- "Created" reports.
- Inadequate segregation of duties.
- Absence of a fiduciary mentality.

The Committee of Sponsoring Organizations of the Treadway Commission (COSO) issued a report called *Internal Control Issues in Derivatives Usage: An Information Tool for Considering the COSO Internal Control – Integrated Framework in Derivatives Applications*. The report gives guidance on applying the COSO framework to derivatives strategies. The report provides the following guidance for developing derivative audit programs:[17]

Market Risk

Ensure the entity has comprehensive, written market risk management policies and procedures for derivative activities. For example, consider whether the following are addressed:

- The types and sources of derivative market risk to which the entity is exposed.
- Board-approved limits, such as:
  - Trader limits.
  - Counterparty position limits.
  - Levels of unhedged market exposure.
  - Stop-loss limits.
  - Open positions by product type.
- Frequency of review and re-approval of policies, procedures, and limits.
- Clear definitions of market risk policies, procedures, and limits.
- Adequate distinction of limits between transactions used to risk-manage the entity's assets, liabilities, and other positions versus trading activity.
- Limits that consider bid/ask spreads for the full range of products in normal markets.
- Limits that consider bid/ask spreads in distressed markets.
- Limits appropriate for the entity and the level of derivative activity.
- Limits are in place for market exposures prior to transacting a deal.
- A methodology and documentation for one-off approvals.
- Use of dynamic hedging strategies.
- Use of appropriate hedging instruments.
- Mechanisms are in place to calculate forward rates (interest, currency, etc.) based on current market conditions.
- Appropriate accounting and pricing policies and procedures.
- An explanation of the board of directors' and senior management's philosophy regarding illiquid markets.
- Circumstances requiring additional quotes from alternative dealers before trade execution.
- Valuation of positions independent from the front office.
- New/complex/modified product reviews by front office, accounting, tax, legal, credit, insurance, risk management, and audit personnel prior to entry.
- All parties involved in approving the introduction of new products have a full understanding of the impact and potential exposure of such products before entering into the market.

Market Liquidity Risk

The entity has comprehensive, written market liquidity risk management policies and procedures for derivative activities. For example, consider whether the following are addressed:

- The types and sources of derivative market liquidity risk to which the entity is exposed.
- Board-approved market liquidity minimums.

- Limits appropriate for the entity and the level of derivative activity.
- Response to significant changes in composition of market makers or investors in the markets where the entity participates.
- Close monitoring of over-the-counter (OTC) markets in which the entity participates where a particularly high volume of transactions is concentrated among a few market makers.
- An explanation of the board of directors' and senior management's philosophy regarding illiquid markets.
- Requirements for determining the existence of liquid secondary markets for OTC contracts.
- Frequency of review and re-approval of policies, procedures, and limits.
- Contingency market liquidity risk plans.
- Limits to mitigation of market risk through offsetting OTC contracts or executing hedge transactions on exchanges.
- Response to sharp market price/rate/index changes.
- Response to trading "halts," extended wide bid/ask spreads, and other liquidity crises.
- Acceptability of derivative products that are traded only in less liquid markets, or that involve complex strategies for which market liquidity is a key requirement.
- How information regarding opportunities to unwind or liquidate positions is to be obtained.
- Limits on the size of derivative portfolios held relative to the respective markets.

Counterparty Risk

The entity has comprehensive, written credit risk management policies and procedures for derivative activities. For example, consider whether the following are addressed:

- The types and sources of derivative credit risk to which the entity is exposed.
- An explanation of the board of directors' and senior management's philosophy regarding illiquid markets and credit events (downgrades/deteriorations).
- Board-approved limits, such as:
  - Counterparty credit risk (including both on- and off-balance sheet exposures).
  - OTC transactions in particular markets or products.
- Credit guidelines to be used in setting credit risk limits.
- How credit excesses are to be handled.
- Credit administration procedures:
  - Counterparty credit conditions are analyzed and lines reviewed with adequate frequency (no less than annually).
  - Management can identify downgrades in creditworthiness between reviews.
  - Credit risk management staff has demonstrated the ability to work out positions with counter-parties whose credit quality has deteriorated.
  - Limits are in place for counterparties prior to transacting a deal.
  - The on-off approval process is as formal as for counterparty limits.
  - Credit risk policies, procedures, and limits are clearly defined.
  - Frequency of review and re-approval of policies, procedures, and limits.

- Circumstances requiring collateral or third-party guarantee credit enhancements.
- Regular, accurate credit exposure reports.
- Minimum credit standings for counterparties and/or collateral and margining requirements for counterparties under certain circumstances.
- Establishment and duties of a senior management risk policy committee.
- The credit approval process.
- Technical expertise requirements of credit risk management staff.
- Procedures for monitoring credit exposure on an entity-wide basis.
- Measuring credit risk of differing derivative products on terms of both current and potential exposure.
- Frequency of credit risk measurement updates.
- Responsibilities of credit risk management personnel for participation in validating modifications made on models to accommodate new products or variations on existing products.
- Program review flexibility to allow for comprehensive credit monitoring in step with new products use.
- Limits appropriate for the entity and its level of capital.

Legal Risk

The entity has comprehensive, written legal risk management policies and procedures for derivative activities. For example, consider whether the following are addressed:

- The types and sources of derivative-activity legal risk to which the entity is exposed.
- Derivative activities requiring the involvement of legal counsel.
- The form, content, and circumstances requiring use of master netting agreements with counterparties.
- Due diligence contract enforcement activities.
- Required minimum written documentation for OTC contracts.
- Legal capacity of the counterparty to enter into the transaction.
- Circumstances requiring written legal opinions as to the enforceability of netting arrangements.
- Reliance on communications from counterparties or other market participants is based on legal agreements indicating the counterparty has agreed to do business on that basis and that the entity has provided the counterparty with accurate and complete information regarding its financial objectives and the size, nature, and condition of its business.

Systemic or Interconnection Risk

The entity has comprehensive, written systemic or interconnection risk management policies and procedures for derivative activities. For example, consider whether the following are addressed:

- The types and sources of derivative-activity systemic or interconnection risk to which the entity is exposed.
- Risk management systems that include limits or controls on interconnection risk to which the entity is willing to expose itself.
- Provisions for monitoring systemic risk effectively.
- Contingency plans setting forth actions to be taken when system-wise market disruptions occur.

Operational Risk

The entity has comprehensive, written operational risk management policies and procedures for derivative activities. For example, consider whether the following are addressed:

- The types and sources of derivative-activity operational risk to which the entity is exposed.
- A description of the relevant business objectives to be achieved by derivative activities.
- The specific trading and hedging strategies authorized to be employed.
- A description of the types of derivatives and markets that may be used.
- Policies and procedures regarding off-premises trading, if any.
- Segregation of duties and reporting responsibilities.
- Front-office/back-office organization.
- Details of each transaction required to be captured at the time of execution.
- Appropriate review levels for information reporting to senior management.
- Error investigation and reporting.
- Required levels of expertise for back-office employees.
- Follow-up procedures for legal documentation.
- Bookkeeping for terminated or expired transactions.
- Monitoring of confirmation data against oral agreements.
- Amounts and direction of payments made under netting arrangements.
- Appropriate reconciliations are performed on a timely basis.
- Appropriate assumptions and estimates to be used in modeling valuations.
- Appropriate sources and guidelines for reevaluation data.
- Resolution, documentation, and reporting of discrepancies.
- Prohibitions on use of in-house traders for market value information.
- Periodic evaluation of the source of market-to-market valuations.
- Methodology for addressing difficult-to-value products or positions.
- A general framework for measuring portfolio risk and aggregate risk limits.
- Specific delegation of responsibility and authority in the following areas:
    - Trading
    - Recording of transactions
    - Cash movements (settlement)
    - Valuations
    - Management reporting

    - Financial reporting
    - Risk management
- Taping of trader telephone lines, facilitating the resolution of disputes, and providing a valuable source of information to auditors, managers, and examiners.
- Monitoring of broker usage, limits regarding undue concentrations of business and review of the short list of approved brokers at least annually.
- Trade tickets and blotters (or their electronic equivalents) prepared in a timely and complete manner to facilitate reconciliation and position and exposure monitoring.
- Trade tickets or input sheets include all necessary trade details.
- The entity has procedures to ensure timely processing of all transactions.
- The entity has a method with which to resolve trade discrepancies on transactions, regardless of communication medium.
- Contractual terms of transactions are confirmed prior to settlement.
- Appropriate accounting and revaluation policies and procedures.
- The entity's activities and the related balance sheet and off-balance-sheet instruments are identified and risk management reports are prepared.
- The entity has established an effective audit trail that summarizes exposures and management approvals with the appropriate frequency.
- Risk management, revaluations, and closeout valuation reserves are subject to audit.

Management Risk

- Management puts controls in place to limit the risk of unauthorized transactions or fraud. Such controls include requirements that traders obtain control numbers from the operations department before executing transactions, and that derivative managers sign all contracts, letters to dealers listing who is authorized to execute derivative transactions, and confirmations sent directly to the back office or accounting department.
- Policies, procedures, and controls are clear, unambiguous, and communicated to and understood by all relevant personnel.
- Senior management reviews the adequacy of these policies and procedures, in light of the entity's activities and market conditions, at least annually.
- Management at all levels enforces policies and procedures established by senior management.
- The entity follows its internal policies and procedures.
- Management is aware of limit excesses.
- Management takes appropriate action when necessary.
- Senior management performs, or designates an independent group or individuals to perform, a regular review of the results of the entity's derivative activities to determine whether the entity's strategies are being effectively implemented and whether they are achieving the desired business objectives.
- Such reviews are conducted with sufficient frequency by persons with appropriate experience, skill level, and authority to ensure that potential problems can be identified and

corrective actions taken in a timely manner. The oversight responsibility also includes monitoring compliance with control procedures and risk exposure limits.

- Documentation is reviewed that evidences credit management's adherence to its program.
- Written approvals for limit excesses are prepared on a timely basis and copies are maintained.
- The master agreements are appropriately signed in a timely manner. There is a chasing process to follow up on unsigned master agreements.
- There is a regularly produced derivative management report covering:
  - Commentary of derivative activities.
  - Position balances and market exposures by product type.
  - Credit balances.
  - Cash balances.
  - Unhedged positions outstanding.
  - Performance measurement (e.g., effectiveness of hedging strategies).
  - Actual compared to forecast.
- The financial statements contain sufficient information about the use of derivatives to provide an understanding of the purposes for which transactions are undertaken, the extent of the transactions, the degree of risk involved, and how the transactions have been accounted for.
- Managers regularly present a detailed analysis of derivative positions to senior management and the board of directors to review the execution of derivative transactions in the context of entity-wide objectives.
- Adequate systems for data capture; processing and management reporting are in place so that derivative transactions are conducted in an orderly and efficient manner in compliance with management policies. The size and scope of the required systems will depend on the nature and scale of an organization's derivative transactions.
- For management information systems:
  - The entity has a model validation process or uses consultants for model development and validation. Yield-curve calculations, interpolation methods, discount factors, and other parameters used are clearly documented and appropriate to the instruments utilized. Regardless of the source of the model, management ensures accurate and consistent results.
  - The system provides for different pricing conventions and accrual methods across the range of products in use.
  - The risk measurement and management system is sufficiently flexible to stress test the range of portfolios.
  - Parameter variations used for stress tests of "what if" analyses are clearly identified.
  - Management reporting relates risks undertaken to return on capital.
- For management information analyzing risk:
  - Management information and analysis are comprehensive, accurate, and sound.
  - The simulation assumptions for a normal market scenario are reasonable.

- Stress tests analyzing changes in market and credit conditions are appropriate. The market assumptions are reasonable.
- Reports are provided to the appropriate level of management.

F. Electronic Services

Electronic services can refer to Internet services provided by a financial institution, or it can refer to electronic methods of moving money, such as automated clearinghouses and wire transfers.

The Automated Clearing House (ACH) is an electronic collection and payment network that banks use to move money. The ACH receives, records, and facilitates debit and credit transactions between banks. Some of the transactions the ACH facilitates include direct deposit of employee payrolls, government and corporate payments, pension payments, dividends, direct debits, and corporate cash disbursements. The ACH allows entities to move funds to and from various locations quickly and easily. Individual consumers use the ACH to authorize debits from their accounts for a variety of payments, such as mortgage payments or other bill payments. The use of debit cards is also facilitated through the ACH.

Wire transfer systems are another method of electronic funds transfer. The transfer of funds between banks by wire is immediate and irrevocable. This method allows for the safe transfer of funds throughout the world.

Most financial institutions have Web sites that allow customers to browse for general information. Customers do not have the ability to alter any of this information, so the risk is low. However, many financial institutions also allow customers to make online transactions. The risk to customers and to the financial institution is greatly increased in these instances due to the sensitive nature of the information being exchanged. On the other hand, a properly secured and controlled Internet banking system can be less risky than paper banking because there are no written statements or documents that could fall into the wrong hands. Also, Internet banking allows customers to monitor their accounts for errors on a more frequent basis.

Electronic financial services audits should focus on whether there are adequate internal controls in place to protect customer transactions, information, and assets. Some key steps include:

- Determine whether there are effective policies for Internet banking and whether these policies and procedures are being followed.
- Determine how management addresses Internet security.
- Determine whether disaster contingency plans for the failure of Internet transactions or communications are adequate, regularly tested, and regularly updated.
- Determine whether controls are implemented to ensure user authentication, data integrity, and transaction confidentiality.

- Determine whether access is controlled by an external firewall.
- Determine whether there are adequate virus control and intrusion detection systems in place.
- Determine whether user IDs and passwords are used and controlled by encryption.
- Determine whether general security controls (e.g., access controls, physical controls, fire controls, power supply controls, maintenance controls, and backup plans) are adequate.
- Determine whether appropriate disclosures are displayed on the Web site.
- Determine whether there is an adequate audit trail for transactions.
- Determine whether there are adequate programs for customer service and support.
- Determine whether reconciliations are timely and properly reviewed.
- Determine whether there are adequate controls in place to prevent and detect duplicate transactions.
- Determine whether there are adequate controls over credit extensions.
- Determine whether customer comments and complaints are logged and resolved timely.
- Determine whether Internet accounts have the proper signed applications, signature cards, agreements, and disclosures on file.
- Determine whether the Web site contains accurate information for customers regarding items such as access procedures and hours, office locations and hours, officers and employee names and numbers, applicable fees, and security procedures.
- Determine whether the Web site displays required notices and disclosures, such as Truth in Savings disclosures, Electronic Funds Transfer Act disclosures, and Expedited Funds Availability Act disclosures.
- Determine whether management reports are sufficient to allow management to appropriately oversee Internet banking transactions.
- Determine whether any contracts with third-party service providers are adequate and properly monitored to manage Internet banking risks.

Another aspect of electronic services that auditors should be aware of is the Payment Card Industry (PCI). Credit card theft is on the rise, which creates fraud exposure risks for financial institutions, as well as for credit card companies and consumers. Visa and MasterCard have teamed up to develop Payment Card Industry Data Security Standards to govern the safekeeping of account information. Other credit card companies have also endorsed these standards. The standards consist of six major goals and 12 basic requirements:[18]

PCI Data Security Standards	
Build and Maintain a Secure Network	1. Install and maintain a firewall configuration to protect data. 2. Do not use vendor-supplied defaults for system passwords and other security parameters.
Protect Cardholder Data	3. Protect stored data. 4. Encrypt transmission of cardholder data and sensitive information across public networks.
Maintain a Vulnerability Management Program	5. Use and regularly update anti-virus software. 6. Develop and maintain secure systems and applications.
Implement Strong Access Control Measures	7. Restrict access to data by business need-to-know. 8. Assign a unique ID to each person with computer access. 9. Restrict physical access to cardholder data.
Regularly Monitor and Test Networks	10. Track and monitor all access to network resources and cardholder data. 11. Regularly test security systems and processes.
Maintain an Information Security Policy	12. Maintain a policy that addresses information security.

A business should notify the financial institution that processes or stores its credit card transactions whenever transaction data is accessed by an unauthorized entity. The financial institution can immediately place a stop on the use of the card, thereby protecting the cardholder's assets from further loss.

G. Cash Management Services

Many of the electronic services described above are used to enhance cash management services. This section discusses additional cash management tools.

The term "cash" refers both to cash and cash equivalents. Cash on hand refers to funds in the bank, either at teller windows, in the vault, in automated teller machines (ATMs), or at satellite locations. Cash equivalents are short-term investments that are readily convertible to cash. Because these are short-term investments, they are relatively insensitive to interest rate changes. Examples of cash equivalents include treasury bills, money market funds, commercial paper, returned checks, and unposted debits.

Cash due from banks are bank assets on deposit in correspondent banks that are used to collect checks. Checks are sent to the due from bank. The due from bank either credits the due to bank's account or pays the due to bank directly with a bank draft. Due from bank balances are used to ensure liquid reserves, to facilitate the transfer of funds, and to use as compensation for correspondent banking services.

A statement of cash flows reports the cash receipts, cash payments, and the net change in cash resulting from the activities of a bank during a given period. The statement reconciles beginning and ending cash balances. The statement of cash flows reports on the operating activities, investing activities, and financing activities of the bank. The function of the statement of cash flows is to show the bank's ability to generate future cash flows necessary to meet its financial obligations.

Auditors should conduct audits to ensure cash is controlled. To accomplish this, reconciliations of cash inflows and outflows should be performed by the organization and the process reviewed by auditors. Auditors should ensure that returns on any invested or deposited cash are properly credited. If a cash budget is maintained, auditors should compare the budget to actual.

Accounts receivable and accounts payable are part of cash management. Accounts receivable is the money owed to the organization by its customers. When looking at accounts receivable, auditors should ensure receipts are processed and recorded timely, collections are handled properly and timely, disbursements are made in accordance with original authorizations, and separation of duties exists in major processing functions. For payables, auditors should make sure the organization is not paying its bills sooner that necessary and thereby losing the opportunity to gain interest earnings on that money.

Inventory control and lease/buy decisions also affect cash management. Auditors should review inventory policies to ensure the organization has an optimal amount of raw materials and finished goods on hand, without having excess inventories to tie up cash flows. The organization should also have a method for recognizing and writing off old, spoiled, or otherwise useless inventory. In addition, auditors can verify that the organization has established adequate policies regarding lease or buy decisions to ensure that assets are acquired in the most cost-effective manner.

There are several other ways to improve cash management. Auditors should integrate steps into their cash management audit programs to test controls in these areas as appropriate:

- Sweep Accounts — At the end of the day all funds in a non-interest bearing checking account are cleared out and moved into a short-term investment account overnight. At the beginning of the next day, those funds are put back into the regular account for use that day. Accounts with larger banks are generally invested in the bank's own commercial paper. Repurchase agreements are often used for accounts at smaller banks. In a repurchase agreement, the money swept from the account is used to purchase securities in the bank's portfolio, with the understanding that the bank will repurchase those securities the next day.

- Lock Boxes — A lock box arrangement occurs when the organization gives the bank access to a post office box where the organization receives payment. The bank picks up the checks, deposits the funds into the organization's account, and sends the checks on through the banking system for processing. The advantage of lock boxes is that they increase the speed at which funds are available for use by the organization. Since banks charge a fee for this service, it is generally only cost-effective for organizations that receive a large volume of checks each day. Auditors should be aware of these cost-benefit issues and incorporate steps to determine the effectiveness of controls over check processing and the handling of exceptions.

- Zero-balance Accounts (ZBA) — This type of account has no balance until checks are presented for payment. When this occurs, the funds necessary to pay the checks are transferred into the account, usually from an investment account set up specifically for this purpose. The balance in the ZBA returns to zero after the checks are paid.

In addition to the steps described above, these additional steps should be considered in a cash management review:

- Document the cash management system and related controls.
- Review bank reconciliations and verify totals with canceled checks, debit memos, deposits, and credit memos.
- Confirm cash balances with third parties.
- Verify the closure of any recently closed accounts. Determine that no transactions are still taking place.
- Verify that deposits in transit are recorded on subsequent bank statements.
- Review outstanding check listing and investigate any unusual amounts (e.g., round amounts, repetitive amounts, unreasonably large amounts, etc.).

- Review canceled checks to investigate any unusual payees (e.g., checks made out to employees, related parties, cash, etc.).
- Confirm material cash funds held by employees or other custodians.

H. Stocks

Common Stock — Common stock is the term used to identify a unit (share) of ownership in a corporation. Corporations are legal entities that are chartered under the laws of the state in which they are incorporated. Common stock is the means for an individual or group to have ownership in a corporation with limited liability.

To understand the common stock principles, some basic terms must be defined:

- Authorized stock — the number of shares permitted to be issued. A limit on the number of shares is usually listed in the articles of incorporation.
- Issued stock — the number of shares sold to investors. Issued stock may not exceed the number of authorized shares.
- Unissued stock — the number of shares that have not been sold. The number of unissued shares can be determined by subtracting the number of issued shares from the number of authorized shares. Corporations often hold in reserve some shares (unissued) for future use.
- Outstanding stock — the number of shares currently held by the public.
- Treasury stock — the number of issued shares that have been reacquired by the corporation. Treasury stock does not have voting or dividend rights. The number of shares of treasury stock plus the number of outstanding shares should equal the number of issued shares. Corporations can use treasury stock to prevent against takeover by other companies or to facilitate the takeover of another company. Outstanding stock is also reacquired to meet the needs of employee stock option plans.
- Par value — a value that is printed on the stock certificate. It is usually a low number and does not have a relationship to the actual value of the stock.
- Book value — a value determined by taking the net worth of the corporation divided by the number of outstanding shares (excluding treasury stock).
- Market value — the current price of a share in the market.

Stockholders are the owners of a corporation, and as such have certain rights of ownership that include:

- Voting rights — Most corporations have an annual meeting where stockholders have the opportunity to vote on important issues. These issues include:
  - Election of the board of directors (the officers of the corporation).
  - Changes to the corporate charter.

- Reorganizations.
- Mergers and acquisitions.
- Recapitalization (to exchange stock, preferred stock, or a bond to another type of security).

Stockholders are generally allowed one vote per share held. As a result, individuals who hold large blocks of shares are more likely to be board members. The basic rights of stockholders include:

- Proxy rights — Most shareholders, particularly those with modest holdings, are unable to travel to and attend annual meetings. As a result, all corporations are required to send all shareholders a proxy, which is effectively a power of attorney. A proxy can allow the holder of the proxy to vote the shares on behalf of the shareholder. This process is often used during a hostile takeover where an external group tries to take control of a corporation by replacing the current directors with their own. A shareholder can allow the proxy holder to vote the shares as he or she wishes or provide specific voting instructions. A common practice permits the shareholder to return a proxy card with specific voting directions.
- Preemptive rights — Although these rights do not always exist, if they do, shareholders are entitled to buy any new issue of stock in proportion to their holdings. If a person owns 5% of a corporation, then he or she would have the right to buy 5% of newly issued shares.
- Inspection rights — Shareholders have the right to inspect certain records such as accounting records, shareholder meeting minutes, annual meeting minutes, and lists of all shareholders.
- Liquidation rights — If a corporation is dissolved, shareholders have the rights to any assets remaining after liabilities, bondholders, and preferred stockholders are paid.

Shareholders also have the right to receive declared dividends. Besides the potential for capital appreciation, investors also have the potential to receive dividend income. There are several types of dividends:

- Cash dividends — cash payments declared as a particular dollar amount for each share owned. Dividends may be paid quarterly, semiannually, or annually. For example, a dividend of $1.00 per share would pay $500 to a shareholder with 500 shares of stock.
- Stock dividends — Rather than giving cash to investors, corporations may provide shareholders with additional shares of stock. A stock dividend is usually declared as a percentage. For example, a 5% stock dividend for the shareholder with 500 shares would provide the investor with 25 additional shares of stock.
- Stock splits — If a corporation wants to reduce the price of a share of its stock, it may authorize a stock split. For example, an investor with 500 shares of stock selling at $50 per share would have 1,000 shares at $25 per share after a 2-for-1 stock split. As noted in the example, at the time of the split, the investor's net share value remains the same.

Preferred Stock — Preferred stock is similar to common stock in that it represents ownership in a corporation. As outlined below, preferred stockholders generally receive a fixed dividend rate. The types of preferred stock include:

- Cumulative preferred stock— Since the dividend rate is fixed, if dividends are not declared by the board of directors in a given period, preferred stockholders accumulate payment rates and must be paid in full before any dividends are paid to common stockholders.
- Non-cumulative preferred stock — If dividends are not declared, preferred stockholders lose their dividend rights for that period.
- Participating preferred stock — Additional dividends are paid to preferred stockholders (above the fixed percentage) if dividends declared to common stockholders exceed a predetermined threshold.
- Convertible preferred stock — The shares of preferred stock can be exchanged for common stock at a predetermined rate. The price of convertible preferred stock tends to mirror the price changes associated with the common stock.
- Callable preferred stock — The corporation reserves the right to purchase the stock from the shareholder at a predetermined price.

Preferred stock generally costs more than common stock because of the additional rights preferred stockholders receive, such as being paid before common stockholders in the event of a liquidation or bankruptcy.

Warrants — Warrants are similar to options as they provide the holder with the right to purchase a share of common stock at a fixed price (called the exercise price). Although generally attached to bonds or preferred stock, warrants can also be attached to other securities, such as speculative stock. Warrants allow holders to buy more stock as its value appreciates.

To understand warrants, some basic terms must be defined:

- Warrants are generally attached to a bond or preferred stock and carry the right to purchase common stock at a fixed price.
- Detached warrants can be traded and have their own value based on the current market and exercise prices. If a warrant is not detachable, it has no individual market value.
- Warrants typically expire after a number of years.
- When exercised, a warrant is relinquished in return for shares of common stock at the exercise price.

The Comptroller of the Currency restricts the types of security investments that national banks can make. For this purpose, securities are divided into five types:[19]

- Type I Securities — This category of security is backed by the full faith and credit of the U.S. government.

- Type II Securities — This category of security includes obligations issued by a state, or a political subdivision or agency of a state, for housing, university, or dormitory purposes that would not satisfy the definition of Type I securities. These securities include obligations of international and multilateral development banks and organizations such as the World Bank, Inter-American Development Bank, Inter-American Investment Corporation, African Development Bank, and Tennessee Valley Authority. Banks are limited and allowed to purchase no more than 10 percent of their capital and surplus from one source of Type II security.
- Type III Securities — These are investment securities that do not fall under one of the other four types of securities. Examples of Type III securities include corporate bonds and municipal bonds that do not satisfy the definition of Type I securities.
- Type IV Securities — These are securities that fit the following definitions:
    - A small business-related security that is rated investment grade or is the credit equivalent thereof, and that is fully secured by interests in a pool of loans to numerous obligors.
    - A commercial mortgage-related security that is rated investment grade or is the credit equivalent thereof, or a commercial mortgage-related security that is rated investment grade in one of the two highest investment grade rating categories, and that represents ownership of a promissory note or certificate of interest or participation that is directly secured by a first lien on one or more parcels of real estate upon which one or more commercial structures are located and that is fully secured by interests in a pool of loans to numerous obligors.
    - A residential mortgage-related security that is rated investment grade or is the credit equivalent thereof, or a residential mortgage-related security that is rated investment grade in one of the two highest investment grade rating categories, and that does not otherwise qualify as a Type I security.
- Type V Securities — These are marketable investment grade securities that are not Type IV. They are fully secured by interests in a pool of loans to numerous obligors and in which a national bank could invest directly.

Options — The options market provides an opportunity to enter into a contract to buy or sell securities for a set price until a specified date. The individual who buys a contract is not required to finalize the trade, but has the option to do so. If the buyer exercises the option, the securities must be sold or bought at the specified price, called the *strike price.*

A *call* is an option contract that gives the owner the right to buy the underlying security at the strike price for a certain fixed period of time (until its expiration). For the writer of a call option, the contract represents an obligation to sell the underlying stock if the option is assigned.[20]

A *put* is an option contract that gives the owner the right to sell the underlying stock at the strike price for a certain period of time (until its expiration). For the writer of a put option, the contract represents an obligation to buy the underlying stock from the option if the option is assigned.[21]

Index options are based on stock indexes (which are weighted averages of groups of stocks). Investor may trade index options for broad indexes like the S&P 500 or more narrow indexes such as stocks in a single field such as health care. Index options provide the opportunity to mitigate risk through diversification.

Interest rate options are used to speculate on the direction of interest rates. The trading of these contracts is limited. The futures market is the main trading market for securities based on interest rate movements.

Foreign currency options are used to exchange currencies at specified exchange rates. The interbank market involves currency exchanges among commercial banks. This market operates 24 hours a day, is self-regulated, and is dominated by major banks and corporations. Foreign currency options are traded in fixed contract sizes. Some of the common currencies traded are Deutsche marks, British pounds, European Currency units, Canadian dollars, Swiss francs, and Japanese yen. Trading of options on the U.S. dollar in the United States is prohibited.

Option contracts traded on the exchanges are standardized under rules set by the Options Clearing Corporation, which operates under the jurisdiction of both the Securities and Exchange Commission (SEC) and the Commodities Futures Trading Commission (CFTC). Under its SEC jurisdiction, the Options Clearing Corporation clears transactions for put and call options on common stocks and other equity issues, stock indexes, foreign currencies, interest rate composites, and single-stock futures. As a registered Derivatives Clearing Organization (DCO) under CFTC jurisdiction, the Options Clearing Corporation offers clearing and settlement services for transactions in futures and options on futures.[22]

The Options Clearing Corporation is equally owned by the five exchanges that trade options:[23]

- American Stock Exchange
- Chicago Board Options Exchange
- International Securities Exchange
- Pacific Stock Exchange
- Philadelphia Stock Exchange

The Options Clearing Corporation also has a set of rules by which customers and registered representatives must abide. Along with detailed rules for settlement, maintenance of records, and position limits, the registered representative must give the customer an Options Disclosure document that explains basic option strategies, their risks, and uses.

Options are quoted daily in the newspapers. The listing provides the name of the underlying stock and its closing price that day, the strike price of the option, the closing prices (premiums) of the 3 call, and 3 put contracts trading closest to expiration. Listings can be divided into two categories:

- Option Class — Contracts of one type on an underlying issue (e.g., all calls on IBM constitute a class).
- Option Series — Contracts of the same class with the same strike price and expiration (e.g., all calls on IBM with September expiration and 90 premiums constitute a series). Note: any contract followed by an "r" indicates an option that is not traded.

Trading Securities — Trading securities are securities that a bank intends to sell within a short period, usually less than one month. Commercial banks can underwrite and initiate securities transactions. How banks record securities transactions on their financial statements depends on whether the securities are purchased for trading purposes or for inclusion in the bank's own investment account. Management should approve whether purchased securities belong in the trading account or the investment account. The decision on how to record the securities in the financial statement should be immediate. It is not advisable to record purchased securities in a suspense account and then later decide whether the securities are for trading or investment.

Banks generally record securities transactions as of the trade date. However, it is acceptable to record the transactions as of the settlement date if the difference between the settlement date and trade date is not materially different.

Banks should account for trading securities at market value. Any changes in cost should be regarded as an unrealized gain or loss within net income. The total unrealized gain or loss is the difference between the total cost of the securities and their total fair value. Also, banks should use market value to transfer securities from a trading account to an investment account, with any resulting gain or loss regarded as trading income.

Banks can record interest earned on trading securities as either interest income or trading income. However, the recommended method is to report interest income separately from trading income if the amount is material. Also, it may be necessary to include a note to the financial statements that discloses the major categories of securities in the trading portfolio.

Securities Available for Resale — Banks hold some securities with the intent of selling them in the future. Any securities intended for sale in the next year or operating cycle are classified as current assets on the balance sheet. Otherwise, they are classified as long-term assets in the investments portion of the balance sheet. Securities available for resale should be reported at current market value. When this type of security has an unrealized gain or loss, it is not reported on the income statement. Rather, it is reported as a separate component of stockholders' equity. Also, for securities available for resale, unrealized gains or losses are carried forward to future periods and adjusted based on the current fair value.

Securities Investment Audits — When conducting an audit of securities investments, the following objectives and audit steps should be considered:

- Determine whether policies, procedures, practices, and internal controls over security investments are adequate and being followed.
- Determine whether transactions are properly authorized and recorded. Verify that dividend or interest income is accurately calculated and recorded in the general ledger.
- Determine that the institution has an adequate process for reconciling subsidiary records to the general ledger on a regular basis.
- Determine whether the institution's security holdings meet established guidelines for risk diversification.
- Determine whether the institution is generating a favorable return on investments.
- Determine whether any required investment committee and board of director approvals have been obtained regarding selection and approval of securities dealers or firms the institution may do business with.
- Determine whether the institution has developed adequate policies, procedures, practices, and internal controls to comply with the Financial Accounting Standards Board's (FASB) Statement 115 (Accounting for Certain Investments in Debt and Equity Securities - Issued 5/93). FASB Statement 115 addresses accounting and reporting for investments in equity securities that have readily determinable fair values and for all investments in debt securities.[24]
- Determine whether the bank is in compliance with the Office of the Comptroller of the Currency's In-vestment Securities Regulations (12 CFR 1). These regulations prescribe standards under which national banks may purchase, sell, deal in, underwrite, and hold securities, consistent with the authority contained in 12 U.S.C. 24 and sound banking practices.[25]
- Determine whether the institution adequately control and records securities on hand.
- Determine whether adequate policies, procedures, and internal controls exist over securities held by correspondent banks or custodians. Verify via mail confirmation that such securities on the institution's inventory lists are accounted for.
- Determine whether any gains or losses on sold securities are accurately calculated and recorded on the general ledger.

Specific steps for auditing short-term investments include:[26]

- Ensure that policies and procedures for short-term trading activities exist, are periodically reviewed for changes, and are properly approved.
- Review to ensure that trading policies include allowed and restricted trading instruments, approved traders or brokers, trading limits, required documentation on trades, approval requirements, reporting requirements, regulatory compliance procedures, error correction procedures, and other internal control procedures.
- Review the short-term trading activity to ensure compliance with trading policies and procedures and applicable regulatory requirements.

- Determine if short-term trading transaction charges are reasonable and properly recorded.
- Determine if proper diversification exists in short-term investments and credit exposures are aggregated with other markets (i.e., equity, fixed income, and derivative markets).
- Review cash receipts and disbursement procedures to determine efficient management of cash within the organization:
    - Review lock box arrangements for applicability and/or proper utilization.
    - Determine if cash collections are timely.
    - Review overnight "idle" cash to determine if sweep accounts or earnings credits are being properly utilized.

I. Bonds

Long-term debt includes notes and bonds. Notes are debt instruments issued to a single investor. Bonds are long-term, fixed-interest debt instruments issued to multiple investors. Both notes and bonds have written agreements that describe the principal and interest payable.

Long-term debt instruments are sold at discount when the market rate exceeds the stated interest rate. An instrument is sold at a premium when the stated rate exceeds the market rate. An instrument is sold at face value when the market rate and stated rate are equal.

Debt Securities — Debt securities are a major category of investment securities. Debt securities differ from equity securities in that the investor in debt securities becomes a creditor of the company; the investor in equity securities becomes a part owner of the company. Some basic terms related to debt securities include:

- Bond — A contract between the issuer and investor that provides the issuer with immediate capital in return for a promise to pay back a given amount at given date and to pay interest at a stated rate throughout the life of the bond.
- Coupon bonds — have actual coupons attached to them that must be "clipped" and sent to the paying agent for interest payments. Coupon bonds are generally clipped twice a year. These bonds must be kept in a safe place since the certificate and coupon are the only proof of ownership.
- Bearer bonds — similar to coupon bonds in that ownership is based on possession. Bearer bonds have not been issued for the last couple of decades; however, those previously issued will continue to exist until they reach maturity.
- Registered bonds — are registered in the owner's name on the issuer's records. Interest payments are sent directly to the owner. If a registered bond is sold, the seller must endorse the certificate and send it to a transfer agent who cancels the old certificate and issues a new one. The transfer is completed when the new holder is listed on the bond issuer's records.
- Book-entry bonds — No certificate is issued and computer-based records of ownership are retained. This is currently the most common form of bond since it reduces costs.

- Callable bonds — are bonds that have "call provisions" that give the issuer the option of calling (redeeming) the bond before the maturity date. The call provisions outline the possible date of the call and the price. Issuers usually call bonds when interest rates significantly decrease or to change the bond maturity date.
- Putable bonds — similar to callable bonds except the owner has the right to redeem a bond before the bond maturity date.
- Bond pricing — similar to stocks, bonds have a par value (normally $1,000) and a market value that fluctuates based on market conditions. The price of previously issued bonds has an inverse relationship to market interest rate changes. Bond prices fall as interest rates rise, and bond prices rise as interest rates fall.
- Bond yields — the return on a bond. The following terms apply to bond yields:
    - Nominal yield — the rate of return stated on the bond. This is also called the coupon rate. For example, a $1,000 par value bond with a nominal yield of 10% would return $100 per year.
    - Current yield — Since bond prices fluctuate based on market conditions, the current yield is based on the current price of the bond. For example, a bond currently priced at $1,250 with a 10% nominal yield of $100 would have a current yield of 8%. The same bond priced at $800 would have a current yield of 12.5%.
    - Yield to maturity — the return on the bond if it is held to maturity. If at maturity a bond were selling for par ($1,000), then the yield to maturity would equal the nominal yield. However, if at maturity a bond were selling for less than par value, the investor would also receive the difference. An investor would lose the difference on a bond selling for over par value.
- Bond quotations — Bonds are generally quoted on yield to maturity to make it easier to compare bonds with the same maturity date.

Corporate Debt — Corporations issue debt (bonds) to obtain capital for long-term use. Unlike stockholders, bondholders are not owners and have no voice or vote in management decisions. However, interest on bonds must be paid before any stock dividends are paid. In addition, if corporate assets are liquidated, the claims of bondholders receive priority over the claims of stockholders. Some basic terms related to corporate bonds include:

- Bond certificate — shows the name of the issuing firm, face value of the bond, interest rate, interest payment dates, maturity date, special features, and the paying agent (either the corporation or a trustee).
- Trust indenture — a contract that defines corporation and bondholders responsibilities and is designed to protect the rights of bondholders. A trustee (most often a commercial bank) is generally appointed to ensure that the obligations defined in the agreement are carried out. A copy of the trust indenture must be filed with the SEC.
- Secured bonds — bonds that are backed by real or tangible assets. These include:
    - 1st mortgage bonds — give bondholders claim against real property. This is the most secure type of corporate bond since it is has priority for claims on assets.

  - 2nd mortgage bonds — are also backed by real property but are second in priority for claims on assets.
  - Collateral trust bonds — are backed by marketable securities held by a trustee. These are often stocks and/or bonds of corporations other than the bond issuer.
- Unsecured bonds — bonds that are not backed by assets and provide no claim on assets for bondholders. These include:
  - Debentures — a long-term debt instrument used by governments and large corporations. Debentures are not secured by specific assets. Instead, debentures are backed by the "good faith and credit" of the issuing corporation.
  - Subordinated debenture — similar to debentures except they are honored after debentures on asset claims.

U.S. Government Debt — The U.S. government is the largest borrower in the world and has a variety of debt instruments. These government obligations or issues are a safe form of debt security, and there has never been a default. The "full faith and credit of the government" back these issues. Some terms and definitions include:

- Negotiable securities — are traded continuously and are considered very liquid and safe. In general these government obligations are exempt from state and local taxes. Some specific types include:
  - Treasury bills (T-bills) — are short-term instruments that are sold at a discount at auctions. The auction winner is the bidder offering the highest dollar price, which is in effect the lowest interest rate for the issue. For tax purposes the difference in price is considered interest income rather than a capital gain.
  - Treasury notes — are instruments with maturities from two to 10 years with amounts from $1,000 to $100,000. They are redeemable at maturity and pay interest twice a year. They are also sold at auction; however, the interest rate is fixed and bids are either at a premium or discount from par.
  - Treasury bonds — are instruments with maturities of 30 years for new issues (10- to 30-year issues were allowed in the past). The amounts range from $1,000 to $1,000,000 and are sold at auction in a manner similar to that for treasury notes.
  - Treasury receipts (strips) — were created in the 1980s. The interest payments on treasury bonds were removed (stripped) from the bonds. The coupons (interest payment) from bonds with the same maturity date were then sold independently by the U.S. Treasury.
- Non-negotiable securities — are not transferable and can be redeemed only by the purchaser. Since they are not transferable, securities firms generally do not sell them; however, they are a very common investment among individual investors. Two types of U.S. savings bonds are classified as non-negotiable securities:
  - Series EE bonds — are registered bonds that are sold at a 50% discount of the face value. These bonds are available in denominations from $50 to $10,000. Maturity varies depending on the interest rate and can be redeemed anytime after being held

for six months. For tax purposes, gains are treated as ordinary income and can be deferred until redemption for tax purposes.

- Series HH bonds — are registered bonds that are sold at par value with semiannual interest payments. EE bonds must be used to purchase HH bonds which mature in 20 years. They must be purchased at U.S. Treasury offices or Federal Reserve banks.

Municipal Debt — These government obligations are issued by state and local governments, U.S. territories, and non-federal public agencies such as school districts, cities, and airport authorities. Municipal debt is considered the second safest form of debt security after U.S. government obligations. However, the safety of an issue depends on the financial condition of the entity backing it. Most municipal bonds are issued to raise funds for infrastructure improvements and although default is rare, it can happen. Interest is generally paid semiannually and the most attractive feature is the exemption from federal tax requirements. Investors that are concerned about tax issues generally hold these issues. Some types of municipal bonds include:

- General obligation bonds — are backed by the full faith and credit and taxing power of the issuer. General obligation bonds are generally used to finance non-revenue-producing projects. An unlimited tax general obligation bond is backed by the issuer's unlimited taxing power and is considered a safe investment. Limited bonds generally have higher yields and are considered riskier investments because they are backed by issuers that have a taxing limit.
- Revenue bonds — are the most common type of municipal bonds and are backed by projected revenue streams from the infrastructure built by the bond. These revenues can be in the form of rental or user fees for facilities or even tolls for road improvements. Revenue bonds generally have higher yields than general obligation bonds and are intended to be self-supporting.
- Special tax bonds — are repayable from the proceeds from a special tax. Special tax bonds are also often used to fund infrastructure projects. If these bonds are backed by the full faith and credit of the issuer, they are then considered general obligation bonds. Some examples of special taxes are taxes on liquor and cigarettes or special assessments for a group affected by an improvement.
- Double barreled bonds — are bonds that are backed by two sources of revenue. For example, a special tax bond that is also backed by the full faith and credit of the issuer is a double barrel bond.
- Moral obligation bonds — are bonds that are backed by the projected revenue from a project. If sufficient revenue is not generated, then the issuer is morally (but not legally) obligated to repay the bonds.

Money Market Debt — These are highly liquid, short-term debt obligations with a maturity of less than one year. These include treasury bills, treasury notes, certificates of deposit, and bonds that mature in less than one year. These are highly liquid instruments and a common investment form is a money market fund. Some terms and definitions include:

- Repurchase agreements — occur when a security is sold with an agreement to buy it back. The repurchase date is usually very short term, often one day. Dealers sell a portion of their securities to entities with cash reserves and agree to buy them back for the principal plus interest. If the market price of the instrument rises more than the interest paid, the dealer realizes a profit, and conversely if the interest paid is more than the rise in the instrument price, the dealer suffers a loss.
- Federal Reserve requirements — The Federal Reserve requires banks to hold a portion of its funds in reserve. As a result, banks may need to borrow funds in the short term to comply with this requirement. Banks often enter into overnight borrowing with other banks or the Federal Reserve itself. The daily interest rate paid varies depending on the demand for funds.
- Commercial paper — are instruments issued by corporations with good credit ratings and are in effect an unsecured promissory note. These instruments are issued at a discount of the face value and have become a substitute for bank borrowing for qualified corporations. Mutual fund companies, insurance companies, and banks often buy these instruments.
- Negotiable certificates of deposit — are tradable certificates issued by commercial banks in exchange for time deposits. The maturity date is generally one year; however, maturity can be as short as seven days.
- Money market fund — a mutual fund that invests in short-term liquid securities. Interest is often calculated daily and reinvested in the investor's account at a specified interval. These accounts are very liquid and often provide limited check writing capability as a means to redeem shares.

Eurodollar Debt — is U.S. currency deposited in banks outside the United States. The interest rate is the interbank interest that is generally slightly higher than the rate of treasury bills. The higher interest rate compensates for the increased risk associated with depositing funds in a foreign bank.

Effect of Interest Rates on Bond Prices — As interest rates change, the price of an issued bond also changes. The change in prices has an inverse relationship to changes in interest rates (if one rises, the other falls). If new bond issues are paying a higher interest rate than existing bonds, investors will not purchase existing bonds unless the bond is discounted (sold at a lower price) to align itself with the current interest rate. The discounted bond is in effect being sold with the same total return as the new issue. The opposite is true if a new issue has a lower interest rate than an existing issue. In this case, the existing bond can be sold at a premium (sold at a higher price). The basic relationship between interest rates and bond prices is as follows:

- If interest rates rise, existing bond prices fall.
- If interest rates fall, existing bond prices rise.

Bond Ratings — Most municipal and corporate bonds are rated by an independent rating firm such as Standard & Poor's (S&P) or Moody's. These ratings provide investors with information regarding the risk of default on the bond issue. The higher rated bonds (S&P—AAA, AA, A, and BBB; Moody's—Aaa, Aa, A, Baa) are considered investment grade bonds. These bonds are less risky and as result have a lower yield. Lower rated bonds (S&P — BB and below; Moody's — BA and below) are considered junk bonds due to their speculative nature and thus are more risky and have higher yields to attract investors. Banks are less likely to lend against bonds with low ratings.

Bond Audits — Objectives and audit steps to consider in bond audits include:

- Determine whether policies, procedures, practices, and internal controls over bond investments are adequate and being followed.
- Determine whether transactions are properly authorized and recorded. Verify that interest income is accurately calculated and recorded in the general ledger.
- Determine that the institution has an adequate process for reconciling subsidiary records to the general ledger on a regular basis.
- Determine whether the institution's bond holdings meet established guidelines for risk diversification.
- Determine whether the institution is generating a favorable return on investments.
- Determine whether any required investment committee and board of director approvals have been obtained regarding bond investments.
- Determine whether the institution has developed adequate policies, procedures, practices, and internal controls to comply with the Financial Accounting Standards Board's (FASB) Statement 115 (Accounting for Certain Investments in Debt and Equity Securities - Issued 5/93). FASB Statement 115 addresses accounting and reporting for investments in equity securities that have readily determinable fair values and for all investments in debt securities.[27]
- Determine whether the institution has developed adequate control and safeguards bonds on hand (e.g., vault security, separation of duties).
- Determine whether adequate records of bond transactions are maintained.

Some of the organizations that provide additional information about bonds and bond audits are the Municipal Securities Rulemaking Board (MSRB), the National Association of Bond Lawyers (NABL), the Council of Infrastructure Financing Authorities (CIFA), the Internal Revenue Service (IRS), the Department of Treasury, and the Securities and Exchange Commission (SEC).

J. Commodities

Commodities include bulk goods such as grains, metals, foods, and financial instruments (e.g., U.S. and foreign currencies). A futures contract is an agreement to buy or sell a specific quantity of a commodity or financial instrument at a specified price on a particular date in the future. All firms and individuals who trade futures with the public or give advice about futures trading must be registered with the National Futures Association (NFA). The Commodity Futures Trading Commission (CFTC) is the federal agency that regulates futures trading.

The CFTC provides some guidance for designated self-regulatory organizations (DSROs) to enforce rules that provide minimum financial standards and related reporting requirements for member-futures commission merchants (FCMs). The following is a list of examination procedures from CFTC Letter No. 99-32:[28]

1. Each DSRO must ensure that all FCMs that carry customer accounts are subject to periodic examination by the DSRO. An examination must be conducted within nine to 18 months of the "as of" date of the previous examination. Only FCMs that have an adequate financial position and who have demonstrated a history of strong compliance and risk management procedures may be considered for an examination cycle that exceeds 15 months from the "as of" date of the previous examination. In making this determination, a DSRO may consider, among other things, whether an FCM has ever breached the net capital early warning level, reported a material inadequacy in internal controls, failed to maintain books and records on a current basis, or violated the segregation requirements. While in most circumstances FCMs must be subject to an examination at least once every 15 months, DSROs will be permitted to extend the cycle to a total of 18 months in order to provide flexibility for unexpected events or to vary examination dates.

2. Each examination must be of a sufficient scope as to satisfy the DSRO that the FCM is in compliance with applicable capital, segregation, recordkeeping, and reporting rules. The scope of the review of other audit areas may vary between examinations; however, each financial and sales practice/compliance audit area must be subject to a detailed examination pursuant to the Joint Audit Program of the Joint Audit Committee (JAC) at least once every three examination cycles. The initial examination of newly registered FCMs must be a full scope audit.

3. In the first phase of each examination and as part of the review and evaluation of internal controls, sufficient testing must be carried out to permit the DSRO to conclude whether the FCM's records are current with regard to: daily segregation calculations; monthly net capital computations; daily reconciliations of open commodity positions and the settlement account; monthly reconciliations of other control accounts; and posting of transactions and adjustments to account balances. These tests must normally be performed on a surprise basis, since advance notice may impair the effectiveness of the examination in determining that the records are prepared on a current basis. The DSRO's assessment of the timeliness of the preparation of the above records, as well as the promptness of the resolution of reconciling items, must be taken into consideration in setting the scope of the examination.

4. For each examination, the areas selected for detailed review must be tested in accordance with the uniform audit guide developed by the JAC. The JAC audit programs must be used

unless other audit programs have been filed with division staff that provide the same coverage. SRO rules that are related, directly or indirectly, to Commission regulations must be addressed by audit procedures subject to this guidance. SRO rules not directly or indirectly related to or required by Commission regulations are not subject to this guidance (e.g., collection of registered futures association fees).

5. DSROs must carry out in-field examinations of FCMs as of the most recent month-end for which a net capital computation should have been available at the time fieldwork commences. A DSRO must notify the division of any examinations that are not completed within five months of the inception of fieldwork.

6. DSROs must strive to vary the examination dates. At a minimum, a DSRO must vary the "as of" date of a member-FCM after two consecutive "as of" dates are the same. Furthermore, an FCM's examination date must not be its fiscal year-end date except in unusual circumstances or where the objective of the examination is to ascertain the quality of the certified public accountant's examination. DSROs also must vary "as of" dates to ensure that they do not always coincide with quarterly reporting dates.

7. DSROs that have incorporated the Commission's segregation rules into their own rules (either directly or by reference) and discover serious apparent violations of those rules must take appropriate remedial and/or punitive action against the FCM and must promptly notify the Commission of such violations and the actions taken. DSROs that do not have their own segregation rules must promptly notify the FCM and Commission whenever it discovers that a member-FCM committed an apparent violation of the Commission's segregation rules.

8. Complete documentation of the scope-setting process must be included in the DSRO's examination workpapers in the form of a scope memorandum and appropriate supporting documentation. The scope of each examination must initially be determined after taking into consideration all information available on the FCM, including particularly that obtained pursuant to the procedures specified in the Joint Audit Program Risk Based Scope Rationale. If material weaknesses or apparent violations of SRO or Commission rules are discovered during the course of the examination, the DSRO must modify the scope of the examination, where appropriate.

9. The scope of each examination may vary depending on the nature and extent of the FCM's proprietary business, the nature and extent of its customer business, and the strength of its internal controls as identified through ongoing oversight by the DSRO and through the scope-setting process. The examination should focus on those areas identified as potential exposures or weaknesses, and possible violations of SRO or Commission rules identified during the scope-setting process, and should only defer detailed examinations of those areas identified during the scope-setting process as unlikely to have exposures or weaknesses. The assessment of internal controls must include a review and evaluation of the procedures followed by an FCM

in evaluating and minimizing the financial risk to the FCM and its customers. The assessment must take into account the types, size, and concentration of customer, non-customer, and proprietary transactions, positions, and commitments the FCM carries, on exchange and off-exchange, both domestic and foreign. Each examination must be of sufficient scope to satisfy the DSRO that the member FCM is complying with the applicable capital, segregation, recordkeeping, and reporting requirements, and that the DSRO has carefully examined those areas identified during the scope-setting process as potential weaknesses.

K. Mutual Funds

Mutual funds are companies that pool money from shareholders and invest it in group of assets, in accordance with a stated set of objectives. Mutual funds sell shares to the public and invest in a portfolio of stocks, bonds, and money-market instruments. Mutual funds are often quoted as bid and ask prices. The bid price is the price at which the fund will redeem its shares (Net Asset Value). The ask price is the price at which the fund will sell its shares (Public Offering Price).

Shareholders own a portion of the mutual fund portfolio and may sell their shares at any time by selling them back to the fund at their net asset value minus any fees (such as deferred sales loads or redemption fees). (29) The value of the shares redeemed will be based on the value of the investments held by the mutual fund. Mutual funds provide investment diversification and professional management.

Auditors should be aware that the investment objectives of a mutual fund are usually based on a risk profile outlined in the fund prospectus. For example, an aggressive growth fund may invest in highly volatile stock issues and a money market fund may invest in low-risk money market instruments. Other funds have investment objectives based on the type or location of companies they invest in, such as funds that invest only in environmentally conscious companies or international companies. The Securities and Exchange Commission provides the following information about the various types of funds and their investment objectives:[30]

- *Index funds* try to achieve the same return as a particular market index, such as the S&P 500 Composite Stock Price Index, the Russell 2000 Index, or the Wilshire 5000 Total Market Index. These funds invest primarily in the securities (stocks or bonds) of companies that are included in a selected index. Some index funds may also use derivatives (such as options or futures) to help achieve their investment objective. Some index funds invest in all of the companies included in an index; other index funds invest in a representative sample of the companies included in an index. The management of index funds is more "passive" than the management of non-index funds, because an index fund manager only needs to track a relatively fixed index of securities. This usually translates into less trading of the fund's portfolio, more favorable income tax consequences (lower realized capital gains), and lower fees and expenses than more actively managed funds.

- *Stock funds* invest primarily in stocks or *equities*. The types of stocks in which a stock fund will invest will depend upon the fund's investment objectives, policies, and strategies. For example, one stock fund may invest in mostly established, "blue chip" companies that pay regular dividends. Another stock fund may invest in newer, technology companies that pay no dividends but that may have more potential for growth. The prices of the stocks of companies the funds invest in may fluctuate based on changes in the companies' financial condition and on overall market and economic conditions. This can affect the performance of a stock fund. Some stock funds attempt to minimize these risks by spreading out ("diversifying") their investments among different companies, industries, and markets.

- *Bond funds* or *income funds* invest primarily in income-producing securities such as bonds or other types of debt securities. Depending on its investment objectives and policies, a bond fund may concentrate its investments in a particular type of bond or debt security — such as government bonds, municipal bonds, corporate bonds, convertible bonds, mortgage-backed securities, zero-coupon bonds — or a mixture of types. The securities that bond funds hold will vary in terms of risk, return, duration, volatility, and other features. The primary objective of an income fund is to produce a steady stream of income for the investor rather than an appreciation in the value of shares. A mutual fund that invested primarily in utility companies and bonds would be an example of an income mutual fund. Risks associated with bond funds include:

    - *Credit risk* is the risk that the issuers of the bonds owned by a fund may default (fail to pay the debt that they owe on the bonds that they have issued). This risk may be minimal for funds that invest in insured or U.S. government bonds.

    - *Prepayment risk* is the risk that the issuers of the bonds owned by a fund will prepay them at a time when interest rates have declined. Because interest rates have declined, the fund may have to reinvest the proceeds in bonds with lower interest rates, which can reduce the fund's return. (Not all bonds, however, can be prepaid.)

    - *Interest rate risk* is the risk that the market value of the bonds owned by a fund will fluctuate as interest rates go up and down. Nearly all bond funds are subject to this type of risk, but funds holding bonds with longer maturities are more subject to this risk than funds holding bonds with shorter maturities. Because of this type of risk, you can lose money in a bond fund, including those that invest only in insured bonds or government bonds.

  A bond fund's prospectus should disclose these and any other risks. Also, many bond funds invest in tax-exempt municipal bonds of a particular state. Bonds of some states may be exempt from state as well as federal income tax. The fund's prospectus will describe any of its tax-exempt features.

- *Money market funds* are a type of mutual fund that is required by law to invest in highly liquid and low-risk securities such as certificates of deposit or government securities. These funds pay dividends that generally reflect short-term interest rates and are not federally insured. Due to the low-risk nature of the investments, money market funds rarely lose money. Money market funds are regulated primarily under the Investment Company Act of 1940 and the rules adopted under that Act, particularly Rule 2a-7 under the Act.

Mutual funds are considered "open-ended" because they can issue an unlimited number of new shares and have an unlimited number of shareholders. Open-end mutual fund shares are not traded on exchanges; rather, investors purchase shares from the fund itself or from one of its agents. The price of a share is calculated by adding the fund's per share net asset value and any shareholder fees (such as sales loads). The total annual fund operating expense is the total of a fund's annual fund operating expenses, expressed as a percentage of the fund's average net assets. The net asset value is the company's total assets minus its total liabilities.[31]

All mutual funds change operating fees. In addition, according to the Securities and Exchange Commission, some funds also charge "12b-1 fees." These fees are authorized by SEC rule 12b-1 and are paid by the fund out of fund assets to cover distribution expenses and sometimes shareholder service expenses. A fund may only pay these fees out of fund assets only if the fund has adopted a plan (12b-1 plan) authorizing their payment. "Distribution fees" include fees paid for marketing and selling fund shares, such as compensating brokers and others who sell fund shares, and paying for advertising, the printing and mailing of prospectuses to new investors, and the printing and mailing of sales literature. The SEC does not limit the size of 12b-1 fees that funds may pay. But under National Association of Securities Dealers, Inc. (NASD) rules, 12b-1 fees that are used to pay marketing and distribution expenses (as opposed to shareholder service expenses) cannot exceed 0.75 percent of a fund's average net assets per year. Some 12b-1 plans also authorize and include "shareholder service fees," which are fees paid to persons to respond to investor inquiries and provide investors with information about their investments. Unlike distribution fees, a fund may pay shareholder service fees without adopting a 12b-1 plan. If shareholder service fees are part of a fund's 12b-1 plan, these fees will be included in this category of the fee table. If shareholder service fees are paid outside a 12b-1 plan, then they will be included in the "other expenses" category, discussed below. The NASD imposes an annual .25% cap on shareholder service fees (regardless of whether these fees are authorized as part of a 12b-1 plan).[32]

Other possible mutual fund fees, in addition to management fees and 12b-1 fees, include shareholder service expenses that are not included in the "Distribution [and/or Service] (12b-1) Fees" category, custodial expenses, brokerage fees, marketing and distribution expenses, legal expenses, accounting expenses, transfer agent expenses, and other administrative expenses. The Securities and Exchange Commission does not impose limits on the size of fees a fund may charge, except that it does limit redemption fees to 2% in most situations. The NASD does impose limits on some fees.[33]

The fund prospectus is the document that provides a general overview and description of the fund. The intent is to provide a potential investor with enough information to make a sound financial decision. The following information is generally placed in a prospectus:

- General description of the fund
- Condensed financial information (including annual rate of return and fees)
- Portfolio turnover rate
- Key management personnel
- Synopsis of the investment objectives and restraints
- How to purchase and redeem shares
- Pending legal proceedings
- Operating fees and expenses

Mutual funds are subject to SEC registration and regulation, and are subject to numerous requirements imposed for the protection of investors. Mutual funds are regulated primarily under the Investment Company Act of 1940 and the rules and registration forms adopted under that Act. Mutual funds are also subject to the Securities Act of 1933 and the Securities Exchange Act of 1934.[34]

Auditors testing mutual funds transactions will typically focus on whether customer purchases and redemptions are accounted properly. In cases where brokers are used to maintain customer accounts, auditors may need to confirm the number of shares held by the broker. Auditors may also test whether fees are properly accounted for and whether deferred sales charges are properly deferred and amortized.[35]

L. Employee Benefits

Employee benefits or fringe benefits can be a significant source of financial risk for many organizations. Auditors should become familiar with the characteristics of the major categories of employee benefits such as group insurance, leave time (e.g., vacation, sick leave, maternity leave), stock options, profit-sharing plans, 401(k) plans, and pensions. Other types of employee benefits that some organizations offer include daycare services, health club facilities, and free use of special equipment (e.g., car, computer, or mobile phone).

Employee benefits are generally considered non-wage compensations designed to enhance any employee's salary compensation. However, it should be noted that payroll is one of the largest operating expenses in many banks. Losses can occur if a bank does not have adequate controls over this function. The largest risks banks face in this function are making salary payments to employees no longer on the payroll; paying employees for unearned overtime, sick time, or vacation time; entering improper or unauthorized salary increases into the system; and miscalculating Social Security or income tax deductions. Additional risks include failing to monitor employee benefit providers and compliance with federal regulations.

1. Types of Employee Benefits

Insurance that employers provide to employees is known as *group insurance*. All members of a group insurance plan (group *insureds*) are covered under a single contract, known as a *master group insurance contract*. The employer or entity purchasing the group insurance is known as the *group policyholder*. In a *noncontributory plan*, group insureds do not pay any premium for the coverage. In a *contributory plan*, group insureds pay a premium in order to receive coverage under the plan, typically through a payroll deduction. The types of group insurance include:

- Life insurance — Just like individual life insurance policies, group life insurance policies usually include provisions for eligibility requirements, termination clauses, and a benefit schedule. The coverage amounts may be determined by a formula, such as a multiple of the employee's salary, or it may be set in the policy (e.g., a particular amount for all group insureds or for those individuals in a specific job classification). A group policy cannot describe coverage amounts for specific individuals. Each group insured can name beneficiaries who will receive benefits payable when the insured dies. Employees have the right to convert to individual coverage without evidence of insurability if the group policy terminates. The amount of individual coverage the individual can purchase may be limited to the amount of insurance held under the group policy. Insurance companies must charge the standard premium rate that any individual of the insured's sex and age would normally pay for the type of policy being issued. Most group insurance policies are *yearly renewable term (YRT) insurance plans*. These policies do not require insureds to provide evidence of insurability when the policy is renewed each year. Also, YRT policies do not build cash values.

- Health insurance — A group heath insurance policy is a contract between an insurance company and the employer or other group purchasing the policy. Employees or other individuals receive specific benefits covered in the policy, but they are not issued individual policies. Optional dependent coverage is usually available through group policies for an additional fee.

  Group policies typically include a *preexisting condition provision* that excludes coverage for conditions that the individual received treatment for during specified period prior to the effective date of coverage. Some policies include exceptions to the preexisting condition provision which allow for coverage if the individual was not treated for the condition for a specified period or if the individual has been covered under the group plan for a specified period. Most policies also waive the preexisting condition provision if the group switches carriers and the member was covered under the previous group policy.

  Most group health policies contain a *coordination of benefits (COB) provision* to prevent individuals covered under more than one plan from receiving benefits greater than the expense incurred. The COB provision defines the group plan that will serve as a primary provider and the one that will be the secondary provider. The primary provider is usually the one that covers the individual as an employee rather than as a dependent. After the primary provider pays all claims payable, the individual can submit any unpaid bills to the secondary provider.

Most group health policies contain a *conversion provision* that allows an individual leaving the group to purchase individual insurance without providing evidence of insurability. An exception to the conversion provision applies to individuals who are changing jobs and are being covered under another group policy. In these cases, purchasing individual insurance in addition to the new group policy coverage may result in the individual being overinsured.

The cost of most group health insurance plans depends on the type of business in which the members work, the ages of the group members, and the number of males and females in the group. However, *consumer-driven health* plans provide employees with a specified amount of money to pay for medical expenses. After those funds are used, a deductible applies and when it is met, a traditional plan takes over. These plans have high deductibles and employees pay higher premiums, which reduces the cost employers pay. The theory behind consumer-driven health plans is that employees will make wiser health care choices if they have to spend more of their own money. However, opponents are concerned that these plans may hurt low-income workers or individuals with significant health bills who may struggle with high deductibles and delay necessary health care.[36]

- Accidental death and dismemberment — These policies pay stated benefit amounts if the insured dies as the result of an accident or loses limbs or eyesight. They are usually low in cost and some only cover accidents that occur while an employee is traveling on the job.

- Disability income — Disability income insurance is designed to provide income replacement for individuals who become unable to work because of an illness or accidental injury. These policies usually provide an incentive for the insured to return to work by providing less income than the insured received before becoming disabled. The actual amount payable is either based on a percentage of the insureds pre-disability earnings or on a flat rate determined when the policy is purchased. Disability income policies typically do not cover injuries that are intentionally self-inflicted or those that are caused by active participation in a war or riot.

  In order to receive benefits, the insured must generally be totally disabled (although some disability income policies pay for partial disabilities). Most policies initially define total disability as the inability of the insured to perform the duties of his or her regular occupation. However, after a specified period following the incident that caused the disability, insureds may be considered disabled only if they cannot work in any occupation that they are reasonably fitted for by education, training, or experience. Disability income payments made through group policies usually cease when the insured returns to work in any gainful occupation.

Presumptive disability provisions allow the insured to be considered totally disabled if certain conditions arise. Presumptive disability conditions typically include permanent blindness, speech loss, or hearing loss. Insureds disabled in these ways receive full benefits even if they resume employment in their former occupation.

Many disability income policies include a *waiting period.* The waiting period is a specified time that must pass after a person becomes disabled before the insurance company begins making benefit payments. The purpose of waiting periods is to reduce the need to pay for disabilities that last only for a short period.

Most group disability income policies contain a physical examination provision that requires a doctor to examine a claimant before a claim is paid. The insurer may also require the claimant to undergo periodic examinations to verify that the disability still exists. The insurer bears the cost of these examinations.

- Dental — Most dental insurance is provided through group policies. Very few individual dental policies are written. Group dental policies emphasize preventative care such as examinations and x-rays. Most group dental policies provide full coverage for examinations and preventative treatments, but deductibles or co-payments generally apply to specific corrective procedures.

- Workers' compensation — This is a type of insurance that employers provide for employees. Injured employees must file claims with the agency that administers workers' compensation in their state and notify their employer. Workers' compensation pays:
  - Medical expenses for employees who are injured or who contract an occupational disease through work.
  - Disability income and rehabilitation benefits for employees who become disabled through work.
  - Death benefits for survivors of employees who die because of an occupational injury of disease.

  Each state has its own workers' compensation laws. Premium amounts that employers pay are based on the class rating for the type of business being covered. There are several hundred class ratings used to calculate workers' compensation rates. The classifications reflect the risk associated with each type of occupation. A company's premium can also vary based on the number of claims during a given period. This process of adjusting rates either up or down is known as an *experience modification.*

Another type of employee benefit is the *employee stock option plan.* These plans are contracts between the organization and its employees. The contract allows employees to buy a specific number of the company's shares at a fixed price within a set time period. Naturally, employees hope the value of their shares will grow until they are redeemed. Employee stock option plans are not retirement plans. Because company stock is bought and sold, the Securities and Exchange Commission oversees employee stock option plans.

Employee stock options plans are not the same as *employee stock ownership plans* (ESOPs). An ESOP is a retirement plan in which the company contributes its stock to the plan for the benefit of the company's employees. The U.S. Department of Labor's Employee Benefits Security Administration oversees ESOPs.

Profit sharing plans are based on the performance of the organization. There is no mandatory contribution into the plan by the employer. Periodically the employer will decide whether to contribute into the plan based on the organization's performance and profitability over the past period. These plans provide an incentive for employees to perform well and to contribute to the organization's growth and success.

Many employers establish *pension plans* to provide employees with a monthly income benefit when they retire. Many pension plans are funded at least in part by employee contributions. Individuals can also establish their own retirement plans through products such as the *individual retirement account* (IRA). *HR-10 plans* (also known as *Keogh plans*) are individual retirement accounts that are specifically for self-employed persons. *401(k) plans* allow participants to invest pretax dollars, in many cases with a predefined percentage matched by the employer and contributed into the employee's account. The principle and interest in IRA, HR-10, or 401(k) plans are not taxed until the funds are withdrawn.

The Employee Retirement Income Security Act (ERISA) regulates retirement plans in the United States. ERISA imposes restrictions on certain investment transactions involving the assets of a qualified plan. A primary goal of these restrictions is to ensure the safety of participants' investments. An insurance company or a designated trustee is typically responsible for investing the assets of qualified plans. Individuals who administer qualified plans are considered to be *fiduciaries* or persons in positions of trust. ERISA requires that fiduciaries act in the best interest of the plan. Fiduciaries may be held criminally liable for any losses that occur because they did not adequately perform their fiduciary duties. Plan administrators must establish a minimum time in which an employee must be employed before being vested in the plan. *Vested employees* are entitled to receive benefits even if they terminate employment before retiring.

Federal income tax laws provide tax benefits to employers that provide retirement plans to their employees. Employees who contribute to qualified pension plans do not pay tax on the contributions until the funds are withdrawn from the plan. Any retirement plan that is legally authorized to receive these tax benefits is known as a qualified plan. The Internal Revenue Service approves qualified plans entitled to receive favorable tax treatment. Qualified retirement plans have a *nondiscrimination requirement* that prohibits plan administrators from discriminating in favor of highly paid employees.

2. Administration of Group Insurance

Organizations may administer group insurance through managed care plans that require insureds to receive care only from physicians or providers that participate in the managed care network. Managed care plans have fee arrangements that encourage providers to deliver the most cost-effective care possible and discourage patients' overuse of medical services.

Health Maintenance Organizations (HMOs) have many characteristics of managed care plans. HMOs are governed by the HMO Act of 1973. An HMO is both an insurer and a provider of health care services. In other words, HMOs serve two functions:

- To pay insured's medical expenses.
- To provide a medical network (e.g., doctors and hospitals) for medical care to plan insureds, commonly known as HMO subscribers.

Subscribers must receive their medical care from within their HMO's network of providers. HMOs pay for preventative care as well as medical treatments. Providers within the HMO network are typically reimbursed a set fee for each service they provide, although some physicians receive a salary. Additionally, HMOs often require subscribers to pay a co-payment for some services.

Subscribers are usually required to select a *primary care physician*. The primary care physician serves as the subscriber's personal physician and refers the subscriber to any specialists that are needed. *Open panel HMOs* allow any qualified physician or provider to provide services to the HMO members. *Closed panel HMOs* require physicians to belong to the group under contract with the HMO before providing services to members.

Another type of managed care is a *Preferred Provider Organization* (PPO), which is similar to an HMO in that they contract with health care providers to deliver medical services. *Traditional PPOs* offer coverage to subscribers who use out-of-network providers. However, traditional PPOs typically reimburse at a lower rate when the subscriber uses an out-of-network provider. *Gatekeeper PPOs* require subscribers to choose a primary care physician from within the PPOs network and reimburse at a higher rate if subscribers coordinate their care through their primary care physician. Traditional PPOs pay providers on a fee-for-service basis, whereas gatekeeper PPOs pay providers a flat amount for each subscriber the provider serves (called a *capitation rate*).

Some employers allow outside parties to administer their group insurance plans. Administrative-service-only contracts allow an insurer or other third-party administrator to assume the administrative responsibilities of a group benefit plan. Fees paid for administrative-service-only contracts are not subject to state premium taxes.

Insurance companies and managed care plans use utilization management to ensure that services provided to patients are appropriate and cost effective. The specific process of reviewing a patient's care is called a *utilization review*. Utilization reviews begin with a *preadmission certification*. Except in cases of emergency, insureds must have approval from their insurance company or care plan before being admitted to a hospital. In emergency situations, insureds must make notification within 48 hours of admission or face reduced or lost benefits. *Utilization* reviewers monitor the appropriateness of care while a patient is hospitalized. This is known as a *concurrent review*. After a patient is released, a *retrospective review* takes place. This review is designed to catch billing errors and identify excessive costs.

M. Capital Market Products

Capital markets include the stock market and bond market. Stocks and bonds are discussed in greater detail in Sections II.H and II.I, as well as in Securities Disciplines A.4 and A.5. This section briefly explains the specific markets and their operation.

The *primary market* refers to capital markets involved in issuing initial public offerings (IPOs) of new stock issues. The *secondary market* refers to the trading of securities that were previously issued in an IPO.

The *stock market* is the mechanism for trading stock. The stock of publicly held companies is listed on a stock exchange such as the New York Stock Exchange (NYSE), the American Stock Exchange (AMEX), or NASDAQ. The Securities and Exchange Commission regulates capital markets in the U.S. Oversight of capital markets in the UK is performed by the Financial Services Authority. The value of stocks in the market is measured by market indices, such as the S&P 500 (index based on 500 U.S. companies and maintained by Standard and Poor's) or the FTSE (index of the 100 largest companies on the London Stock Exchange).

The *bond market* refers collectively to the individuals, governments, and private institutions that buy and sell bonds. The bond market is also referred to as the credit market or debt market.

The *derivatives market* is the market for derivatives, which were discussed earlier in this section. A derivative is a financial instrument that derives its value from the value of other financial instruments or an underlying asset such as currency, commodities, stocks, or bonds. Derivatives can be either traded in a futures exchange, such as the Chicago Mercantile or Euronex, or traded over the counter. See Section II.E and Securities Discipline A.2 for more information about derivatives.

N. Securities Lending

Securities lending refers to the practice of temporarily transferring securities to a borrower with the intent that the lender will buy them back at a future date. The borrower is required to return the securities to the lender, either on demand or at a specified time. The lender receives a fee for providing this service. In addition, the lender is protected because the borrower has to put up collateral to secure the transaction. The collateral can be cash, other securities, or other assets.

During a securities lending transaction, the title over both the securities on loan and the collateral received are transferred between parties. However, although the borrower is technically entitled to receive any economic benefits associated with ownership (e.g., dividends or coupons), the borrower is required to make equivalent payments to the lender.

The international organization for the securities lending industry is the International Securities Lending Association. Securities lenders are usually large securities holders, such as large banks that act as custodians by holding the securities of third parties.

A major reason for securities lending is to facilitate a *short sale* of a stock or bond. A short sale occurs when a security is sold prior to owning it, with the intent to buy it later at a lower price. Thus, the security is borrowed from the lender and held by the buyer, until it is sold back to the lender. Short sales are undertaken when the price of a security is expected to decline. If this occurs, the profit the borrower receives is the difference between the sales price of the securities borrowed and the purchase price when an equivalent security is bought back by the lender.

In a *repurchase agreement* transaction, a bank sells U.S. government securities one day and repurchases them for the same price plus interest on a specified date (usually the next day). In a *reverse repurchase agreement*, the purchaser of the securities agrees to resell them to the seller (lender) at a stated price plus interest at a specified date. These types of federal funds transactions do not involve a physical transfer of funds. The Federal Reserve facilitates these transactions by making the appropriate credits or charges to the reserve accounts of the banks involved. The banks then make the appropriate credits or charges to their federal funds purchased or sold accounts. Any federal funds transactions exceeding one business day should be treated as a loan.

Auditors should be aware of the following control and monitoring activities typically associated with securities lending:[37]

- Reviewing counterparties for creditworthiness and obtaining master trade agreements and credit approval for counterparties before entering into a stock-loan or stock-borrow transaction.
- Establishing transaction limits by counterparty.

- Listing those securities in excess of SEC rule 15c3-3 possession or control requirements as available to be loaned for any given day. Recalling those securities in deficits within the time frames required.
- Obtaining physical possession or control of all collateral.
- Ensuring that borrows are made in accordance with the requirements of Federal Reserve Regulation T.
- Marking to market all collateral daily and, if a deficit (within established guidelines) exists, obtaining additional collateral from the counterparty.
- Reconciling the stock-loan and stock-borrow subsidiary ledgers to the stock record and general ledger daily. Out-of-balances are recorded as suspense items and researched immediately.
- Confirming transactions periodically on a basis that, at a minimum, complies with SEC rule 17a-13 regarding the quarterly verification of securities.
- Listing transactions with unusually high or low rebate terms on an exception report for review by management.

Whenever reviewing situations where brokers-dealers finance proprietary or customer activity through collateralized bank loans, auditors should consider the flowing review activities:[38]

- Ensuring that customer, noncustomer, and firm bank loans are separately maintained and that procedures are in place to prevent commingling of collateral.
- Maintaining separate accounts in the general ledger for each loan, with separate positions being maintained on the stock record for the securities collateralizing each loan.
- Ensuring that securities used to collateralize bank loans for customers are not fully paid or excess-margin securities, because such securities are required to be segregated pursuant to SEC rule 15c3-3 possession or control requirements.
- Periodically confirming bank loan collateral on a basis that, at a minimum, complies with SEC rule 17a-13 regarding the quarterly verification of securities.

Control and monitoring activities related to repurchase agreements and reverse repurchase agreements include:[39]

- Reviewing counterparties for creditworthiness and obtaining master trade agreements and credit approval for counterparties before entering into a repurchase or reverse repurchase agreement.
- Establishing position and credit limits by counterparty.
- Obtaining collateral from the counterparty.
- Marking to market all collateral daily; if a deficit (within established guidelines) exists, additional collateral may be obtained from the counterparty.
- Reconciling the repurchase and reverse repurchase subsidiary ledgers to the stock record and general ledger daily. Out-of-balances are recorded as suspense items and researched immediately.

- Periodically confirming transactions on a basis that, at a minimum, complies with SEC rule 17a-13 regarding quarterly verification of securities.
- Listing transactions with unusually high or low interest terms on an exception report for review by management.

The International Securities Lending Association (ISLA) is a trade association established in 1989 to represent the common interests of the securities lending industry. More information about the securities lending industry can be found at the ISLA's Web site (www.isla.co.uk).

O. Insurance Policies

Insurance is a method of transferring, for a fee, the financial responsibility for the risk to another party. The concept of insurance is based on the fact that there is risk that the thing being insured will be lost, destroyed, damaged, injured, or adversely affected in some other way.

Insurance policies are legal contracts. There are four elements that constitute a legal, binding contract:

- *Agreement*: A valid contract involves one party making an offer and the other party accepting that offer. The contract is not considered valid if fraud, undue influence, or duress are used in securing the agreement of another party.
- *Consideration*: A valid contract involves each party giving something of value. This exchange of value, or consideration, may take the form of money, action, or promise. For insurance contracts, the insured's consideration is the payment of premiums and a promise to fulfill the conditions of the contract, and the insurer's consideration is the promise to pay after a loss occurs.
- *Competent Parties*: A valid contract must involve legally competent parties. Types of parties typically considered not legally competent to enter into contracts include minors, people with mental impairments, and people under the influence of alcohol or drugs. An adult parent or guardian is usually required to sign a minor's insurance application in order to avoid any legal confusion.
- *Legal Purpose*: A valid contract must have a legal purpose, and every insured must have a valid insurable interest. For example, insurers cannot issue polices to cover intentional or criminal actions.

Some of the major sections of a typical insurance policy include:

- Definitions — Defines key terms used throughout the contract.
- Agreement — States in a legally binding way that the insurer will pay the insured for covered losses as long as the policy is in force.

- Declarations — Defines specifically what is covered (e.g., which address for homeowner's insurance, which car for automobile insurance, etc.).
- Exclusions — Defines what the policy does not cover.

Other characteristics of insurance policies are that they are:

- Unilateral — The insured decides whether on not to pay the premium to be covered by the policy. If the insured pays the premium, the insurance company is obligated to make payments as stated in the policy.
- Aleatory — The term aleatory means random or pertaining to luck. Thus, the amounts paid by either the insurer or insured throughout the life of an insurance policy is not predetermined, but will instead be based on as yet unknown future events.
- Incontestable — Most insurance policies are incontestable after they have been in force for two years. Even if the insurance company identifies an unknown risk in the insured after two years, the company must still pay benefits; however, if the insurance company can prove that the insured intentionally defrauded the company, the benefits may be denied.

Insurance contracts are also considered *contracts of adhesion* in that they are legal documents that require the insurer to pay if covered events occur. Because the insurance company creates the contract, it is liable if there are any ambiguities in the contract language.

Insurance companies assist individuals in managing personal risk through *risk pooling*. Risk pooling is based on fact that the probability of any one type of loss occurring for a given individual is small. Therefore, insurers can insure a large number of people against a given peril, based on the knowledge that only a small percentage of those insured will ever file a claim for that particular peril. For example, of the many people who buy earthquake insurance, only a small percentage will suffer earthquake damage to their property. However, earthquake insurance will cost more in high-risk areas. Underwriters and actuaries help insurance companies assess risks. These functions are discussed elsewhere in this *CFSA Study Guide*.

P. Insurance Products

Section II.E discussed employee benefits, including group insurance. However, some people do not qualify for group insurance policies. These individuals must purchase individual insurance policies. In an individual insurance policy, the contract between the insurer and the insured describes applicable coverage, exclusions, and benefits that are specific to the individual policy. This section discusses several types of individual insurance: whole life, term life, universal life, endowments, and property and casualty products.

Whole Life Insurance — Whole life policies offer lifetime coverage at a level premium rate that does not increase as the insured ages. Whole life policies accrue a *cash value* that the insurer must surrender to the policyholder if the policy does not remain in force until the policyholder's death. The actual cash value payable to the policyholder in this circumstance would be less any surrender charges or policy loan repayments outstanding. The cash value usually does not equal the face amount of the policy until the policyholder reaches the age at the end of the mortality table used to calculate the premiums for the policy, usually age 99 or 100. At that time, the insurance company usually pays the policyholder the full face amount of the policy, even if the policyholder is still living.

Whole life policies are classified as *continuous premium policies* (or *straight life policies*), *limited payment policies*, or *single premium policies*. Premiums are payable under continuous premium policies until the death of the insured. Because premiums are payable for a longer period, each premium payment is lower than for limited payment policies. Premiums for limited payment policies are payable for a stated period (for example, 20 years from the policy's inception or until the insured reaches a certain age) or until the death of the insured, whichever comes first. Single premium policies require only one premium payment.

Modified premium whole life policies have premium payments that change during the life of the policy. Typically, premium payments increase at specified intervals (for example, every five years) during the life of the policy. This allows young policyholders to purchase a higher level of coverage than they may otherwise be able to afford.

Joint whole life policies (or *first-to-die policies*) insure two lives under one policy. Death benefits are paid to the surviving insured. The surviving insured usually has the option of purchasing an individual whole life policy of the same face amount without providing evidence of insurability.

Last survivor life insurance policies (or *second-to-die policies*) pay benefits only after both insureds covered by the policy have died. Married couples typically use this type of policy to pay estate taxes after they die.

Term Life Insurance — Term life policies provide a death benefit when the insured dies during a specified period. The term of this type of policy is usually not less than one year, but may be up to 40 years or more. Term life provides only temporary protection because coverage ends at the end of the term of coverage stated in the policy.

Level term life insurance policies provide the same level of death benefit throughout the term of the policy. The premium for a level term policy usually stays the same throughout the term of coverage.

Decreasing term life insurance policies provide decreasing policy benefits over the term of coverage. The policy's death benefit begins at a set value and gradually decreases to a level stated in the policy. For example, a $50,000 five-year policy might decrease to $40,000 in benefits payable the second year, to $30,000 the third year, to $20,000 the fourth year, and to $10,000 in the final year. At the end of the fifth year, the policy expires. Premiums for decreasing term policies usually remain level throughout the term of coverage.

Increasing term life insurance policies provide an increasing amount of death benefit throughout the life of the policy. Premiums for increasing term life policies usually increase during the term of coverage.

Term policies often contain provisions that allow the policyholder to keep life insurance coverage after the policy expires. *Renewable term insurance policies* contain a renewal provision that allows the policyholder to renew the term policy at the end of the term. However, the premium rate increases when the policy is renewed. *Convertible term life insurance policies* contain a conversion privilege that allows the policyholder to convert the term policy to permanent coverage without providing evidence of insurability. Therefore, an increase in the premium for the permanent coverage cannot be based on level of the insured's health, even if the insured has serious health problems. Some insurers reduce their risk by not permitting conversions after a specific age. When term policies are converted under an *attained age conversion*, the renewal premium is based on the insured's age at the time of conversion. On the other hand, *original age conversions* base the premium for permanent coverage on the insured's age at the time the original term policy was purchased.

Universal Life Insurance — Universal life policies are a form of permanent life insurance that has flexible premiums, flexible face amounts, and separate pricing for the three major pricing categories:

- Mortality charges based on the insurer's risk classification
- Interest rate paid on the cash value
- Expenses associated with administering the policy

Purchasers of universal life policies specify the policy's face amount and whether the death benefit will be level or vary as the policy's cash value changes. Under *level death benefit policies* the death benefit payable equals the policy's face amount. Under *variable level death benefit policies* the death benefit is equal to the policy's face amount plus any accumulated cash value.

Within limits, universal life policyholders can choose how much to pay for initial and subsequent premiums. Insurance companies set maximum payment amounts to maintain the policy's status as a contract, as well as minimum initial payment amounts. However, the policy will remain in force, even if no premiums are paid, as long as the cash value is large enough to pay the periodic charges assessed by the insurer. Universal life insurance policies accumulate cash values that are tax deferred.

Endowment Insurance — Endowment insurance provides a specified benefit amount in either of the following cases:

- If the insured survives to the maturity date of the policy
- If the insured dies before the maturity date of the policy is reached

Policy maturity dates may be set either when the insured reaches a certain age (e.g., age 65) or after a stated period of time has elapsed (e.g., 20 years) from the date the policy is issued.

Endowment policies are similar to permanent life insurance policies in that premiums are usually level throughout the term of the policy and the policies build cash values. However, an endowment policy builds cash value more rapidly than a comparable whole life policy. This is because the reserve and cash value of an endowment policy usually equals the policy's face amount on the policy's maturity date, which is typically for a much shorter period than for a whole life policy. Whole life policies do not accrue a reserve and cash value equal to the face amount until the insured reaches the age at the end of the mortality table used to calculate the policy's premium (usually age 99 or 100).

Property and Casualty Products — Property and casualty insurance policies protect individuals and businesses from financial loss. Workers compensation policies protect an employer from financial loss resulting from an employee's injury on the job. General liability policies provide additional liability coverage for businesses. Individuals are protected by automobile and homeowner policies. Umbrella policies provide the most extensive liability coverage for individuals and businesses.

General liability insurance covers the major liability exposures of a business, including lawsuits against an organization's facilities or products. General liability insurance does not cover liabilities that a business incurs through the use of its automobiles. Therefore, businesses must buy separate automobile coverage for its rolling fleet. General liability also does not cover damage to property not owned by the business, even if that property is left in the care of the business.

Products liability coverage covers damages caused by products sold by a business. *Completed products liability coverage* covers damages that result from work (such as repair work) done by a business.

Medical payments liability coverage covers injuries to the public that occur on the premises of a business.

Automobile Insurance — Personal automobile policies typically provide the following types of coverage:

- *Liability coverage* pays benefits to parties the insured injures in an automobile accident. The liability section also covers property damage. Coverage usually applies to autos mentioned in the policy's declaration, as well as autos temporally used by the insured (such as rental cars or a borrowed car). The insured's car is also covered when other people drive it. Personal auto policies typically do not cover autos used for regular business purposes. Business auto policies are used to extend coverage to a company's rolling fleet.

- *Medical coverage* pays benefits to all passengers in a vehicle involved in an accident, not only the insured, even if the insured was not legally responsible. Benefits are usually limited, with the dollar amount of the limit set according to the premium paid.

- *Auto coverage* pays benefits in cases where the auto is stolen, damaged, or destroyed. *Collision insurance* provides coverage when the auto strikes another vehicle or object. *Other than collision insurance* or *comprehensive coverage* covers incidents other than collision. These incidents may include theft, fire and hail damage, or broken glass.

- *Uninsured motorist coverage* pays damages incurred by the insured and the insured's passengers when injured in an auto accident caused by a motorist without liability insurance. This coverage also covers accidents caused by hit-and-run drivers.

Auto policies do not cover damage that is intentionally inflicted. Coverage is also excluded for individuals who use the car without believing they were authorized to do so. In cases when an accident occurs in another state with higher liability limits, most auto policies will protect the insured by raising the level of benefits payable to the higher level.

Homeowners Insurance — Homeowner policies combine property and casualty coverage into the same policy (known as *multi-line policies*). Homeowner policies provide four major types of property coverage:

- *Dwelling* — covers the house and attached structures, such as an attached garage or carport.
- *Other buildings or structures* — covers unattached structures such as a tool shed, a swimming pool, or a fence.
- *Personal property* — covers the contents of the house and other items, such as patio furniture. Automobiles are not covered as personal property under a homeowner policy. Limits are usually set on jewelry, furs, fine art, and other items likely to be stolen. Homeowners have the option of buying additional coverage on valuable personal items.
- *Loss of use* — provides additional living expenses when the home is unlivable so homeowners can continue to live comfortably. While the home is being made livable, the homeowner policy will pay for items such as rented rooms at a hotel, restaurant meals, and laundry expenses.

Homeowner policies provide two major types of liability coverage:

- *Personal liability* — covers claims for bodily injury or property damage caused by the insured. For example, the policy would cover an incident where someone is injured by tripping on a crack in the sidewalk in front of the insured's home.
- *Medical payments* — provides a low level of medical payment to help avoid legal action between the insured and the injured party, regardless of whether or not the insured is legally liable for the incident. For example, if the insured's dog bit a neighbor, the policy would cover the cost of the emergency room visit (usually up to about $1,000) without the need to establish fault.

Broad form policies provide coverage for loss due to causes such as fire, lightening, wind, hail, explosion, riot, vandalism, theft, and volcanic eruption. Common exclusions from homeowner policies include intentional acts, negligence, flood, earthquake, and war.

Umbrella Coverage — *Personal umbrella policies* are designed to provide coverage if losses exceed the limits of a basic homeowner or automobile policy. The liability limit for an umbrella policy is usually high — often $1 million or more. A small deductible, known as a *self-insured retention*, may apply.

Commercial umbrella policies are similar to personal umbrella policies. However, the self-insured retention is usually higher for a commercial umbrella policy — often $10,000 or more.

Q. Foreign Exchange

The foreign exchange market (known as "Forex") is an international market where financial institutions and corporations buy and sell one currency (such as dollars, euros, or yen) for another. International companies often need to acquire the currency of a particular country in order to transact business there. Individuals traveling in foreign countries also need to acquire the currency used in the country they are visiting.

The forex is the largest financial market in the world and currencies are traded around the clock. There is no central headquarters for the foreign exchange market. All transactions are done by phone or via computer. Sometimes participants in the foreign exchange markets conduct the transactions themselves, but in some cases brokers are used to search for the most favorable exchange rates.

Foreign currency futures contracts may be legitimately traded either on a recognized futures exchange or in the *interbank market*, which generally involves trading between large institutions such as banks and corporations. The interbank market does not typically include individual or retail customers. Individuals trading in the foreign exchange market typically use a broker. These brokers are not regulated by the Securities and Exchange Commission since they do not sell securities.[40]

In general, there is less government supervision and regulation of stock exchanges, brokers, and companies in foreign countries than in the United States. Also, foreign companies may not be subject to the uniform accounting, auditing, and financial reporting standards that apply to U.S. companies.[41]

There are two different types of foreign exchange transactions:[42]

- *Spot transactions* occur when two parties trade currencies at a mutually agreed upon exchange rate. One trader calls another trader asking for the price of a particular currency, and the second trader quotes both buying and selling prices for that currency. When the price is agreed upon, the currencies are exchanged. The "ask" or "offer" is the price currency is offered to be sold, and the "bid" price is the price at which the customer will buy.

- *Forward transactions* occur when a buyer and seller agree on an exchange rate for a future date, and the transactions occur on that date at the prevailing market rates at that time. The most common type of currency transaction is a currency *swap*, in which two parties exchange currencies for a certain period of time and then reverse the transaction at a later date. A related type of transaction is an *option*, in which a market participant buys the right to buy or sell a specified amount of a currency at a fixed price at any time up to a specified expiration date.

The *exchange rate* is the price on one currency compared to another. Currency traders attempt to make a profit by speculating on changes in the exchange rates, either purchasing currency and selling it at a higher price, or in anticipation of a falling price, selling at a high price and buying back later at a lower price. Fluctuation in exchange rates, or *exchange rate risk*, is an important consideration in any overseas investment decision.

Numerous factors can influence foreign exchange rates, including:[43]

- Business cycles.
- Balance of payment statistics.
- Political developments.
- New tax laws.
- Stock market news.
- Inflationary expectations.
- International investment patterns.
- Governmental and central bank policies.

A stronger U.S. dollar implies that the U.S. can buy foreign goods more cheaply, and foreign countries find U.S. goods more expensive and demand falls. Conversely, a weaker U.S. dollar implies that foreign countries can buy more U.S. goods and products from foreign countries become more expensive.[44]

Audits of foreign exchange transactions may include the following objectives and tasks:

- Determine whether internal controls over the authorization of transactions are adequate.
- Determine whether the valuation of transactions is properly calculated.
- Determine whether net assets, dividends, interest, and taxes are properly calculated and recorded.
- Determine whether adequate documentation is maintained to substantiate transactions.
- Determine whether all electronic systems that facilitate foreign exchange transactions have adequate general and application controls.
- Determine that transactions are properly recorded on financial statements.

Auditors of financial statements of investment companies should consider the risk implications of any investment in foreign securities. Auditors should consider whether management has considered all factors relevant to the valuation of such securities.[45]

Registered investment companies may keep their foreign securities with eligible foreign custodians. In order to protect the safekeeping of fund assets held in other countries, banks and trust companies generally enter into specific custodial or subcustodial agreements that outline the custodian's responsibilities.

Additional information about the foreign exchange market is available from the following sources:

- The Web site of the Financial Markets Association is www.aciforex.com. This is an industry association based in Paris, France. Their Model Code has many additional details about the foreign exchange market.
- The Web site of the London FX Ltd is http://londonfx.co.uk.
- The Web site of the Federal Reserve of New York is http://www.ny.frb.org.

R. Asset Management

Assets are anything that can produce a future economic benefit for its owner. In business, something has asset value if it can contribute directly or indirectly to an entity's cash flow. The term *asset management* is defined as the business of providing financial products or services to a third party for a fee or commission. Asset management services that banks provide may include personal trust and estate administration, retirement plan services, brokerage services, and investment company services.[46]

Current assets typically include those assets an entity expects to convert into cash or be sold within one year. The amount of net current assets is the total of current assets minus current liabilities. Net current assets are also referred to as working capital. Types of current assets include:

- Cash — a liquid asset that includes currency, funds available on deposit at the bank, or negotiable instruments such as checks and money orders.
- Short-term investments — securities bought and held for sale in the near future.

Long-term investments are those that are to be held for more than one year. Long-term investments include investments in securities, investments in affiliated companies, or fixed assets not used in current operations (e.g., investment property).

Asset/liability management (ALM) is a planning tool designed to maximize earnings. ALM tries to create optimal risk/reward decisions and focuses on creating prices that achieve a desired spread. A sound ALM policy must manage many types of risks:

- Credit Risk — Loans are more profitable than most investments, but loans are also riskier.
- Liquidity Risk — Banks must maintain some liquid assets, but not too much because liquid assets typically draw little or no interest.
- Interest-rate Risk — Earnings and capital can fluctuate due to changes in interest rates.
- Capital Risk — Banks must maintain adequate capital levels. However, retaining too much capital can reduce the bank's growth potential.

Risks related to asset/liability management that auditors should be aware of include:[47]

- Deficient information processing, accounting, reconcilement, and reporting systems in relation to transaction volume and complexity.
- Deficient operating processes and internal controls over information systems and accounting records, particularly during system conversions.
- Inadequate disaster contingency planning for information systems.
- Failure to effectively manage third-party vendors.
- Deficient account acceptance and review processes.
- Deficiencies in the ethical culture and expertise of management and supporting personnel.
- Weak internal compliance systems and training programs.
- Failure to use legal counsel effectively.
- Failure to adopt and implement an asset management strategic planning process.
- Failure to provide adequate financial, technological, and human resources to asset management business lines and control functions.
- Weaknesses in the administration of acquisitions, mergers, and alliances.
- Lack of a strong and enforced ethical culture and risk control environment.
- Lack of a clearly defined and consistently applied investment management philosophy.
- Deficiencies in the integration of sales-oriented businesses with the responsibilities associated with fiduciary relationships.
- Marginal or poor customer service and product performance.
- Adverse regulatory enforcement actions.
- Liability for damages or restitution as a result of litigation.

Banks should develop policies related to ALM, including specific guidelines regarding risk/reward tradeoffs. The goal is to manage risks while achieving acceptable returns on investments. In developing these policies bank officials analyze cash flows and liabilities by reviewing historical financial reports, ratio reports, the balance sheet, the income statement, liquidity reports, and other available information.

The following is a list of audit steps for use in audits of ALM:[48]

- Observe and review the ALM process to ensure it is an integral part of the management process.
- Ensure that the ALM process has the support of senior management and that the importance of ALM responsibilities is communicated through the organization.
- Often the ALM process is assigned to a team rather than a specific unit. The responsibility should be assigned with dedicated staffing in order for the process to be efficient, effective, and timely.
- Review policies and procedures to assess compliance with internal policies and outside regulatory or rating agency requirements.
- Observe the measurement and assessment of risk activities and ensure these functions are performed routinely.
- Ensure good communication between investment and product areas so they work closely together toward a common goal.
- Ensure investment and liability strategies are integrated to ensure data integrity and timely analysis.
- Verify ALM models used to quantify risk are accurate and data uploaded to systems is of the highest integrity.
- Ensure that models provide real-time analysis to support management decision-making.
- Review minutes and reports from the ALM committee to ensure complete information is presented to foster good decision-making.
- Test a sample of ALM system data on assets and liabilities to ensure validity of information.
- Review backup and recovery procedures on ALM systems.

Although the term "asset management" in the context of this study guide and the CFSA exam refers to the provision of financial products or services to a third party for a fee, it is important to be aware that this term can also refer to how an organization manages its non-financial assets. Listed below are a brief definition of asset types and related terms.

Fixed assets are the capital assets used in the operation of the organization. Fixed assets include property, plant, and equipment owned by the organization. They are usually reported on the balance sheet either at historical cost or fair market value, whichever is lower. Fixed assets are tangible assets. The following guidelines apply to fixed assets held by banks:

- Banks own fixed assets, such as buildings, land, and equipment for use in business operations. However, regulations set limits on the amount of fixed assets a bank may own. A bank's holdings of real estate must not exceed a stated percentage of the bank's capital and surplus, unless approved by regulatory authorities.
- Banks should use fair market value to record assets acquired through foreclosure. However, the fair market value amount should not exceed the amount at which the investment was recorded. If the recorded investment amount exceeds the fair market value of the real estate, then the bank should record a loss.
- Banks should use Generally Accepted Accounting Principles (GAAP) to capitalize and depreciate their fixed assets.
- The cost of a fixed asset should include all acquisition and construction costs (e.g., transportation costs, installation costs, excavation costs, and architect fees).

Intangible Assets do not physically exist. Rather, they are the ideas, expertise, capacities, and privileges that belong to an entity. Common types of intangible assets are:

- *Copyrights* prevent others from violating an entity's proprietary rights to writings, designs, or processes. Research and development costs associated with copyrights are treated as expenses. Legal expenses necessary to defend a copyright may be capitalized. Amortization of a copyright usually is done in five years or less.
- *Patents* give owners exclusive rights to unique products or processes. The U.S. government issues patents for a 17-year period. Patents may be purchased or developed individually. Purchased patents are recorded at cost and developed patents are recorded at cost minus any costs for research and development.
- *Franchises* allow a franchisee to provide a company's products or services. Franchise fees paid in advance are capitalized and amortized over the useful life of this intangible asset.
- *Trademarks* are symbols that allow the public to easily recognize a product or company name. Trademark development costs, except for associated research and development, are capitalized. Amortization of a trademark must be completed in less than 40 years.
- *Goodwill* is the establishment of a reputation and the perception among stakeholders and customers regarding quality of service.
- *Leases* allow one party to use another party's property for a fee. Lease payments paid in advance are capitalized in the leasehold account. A leasehold improvements account is set up to record any improvements made by the lessee. Leaseholds are amortized over the life of the lease. Leasehold improvements are amortized over the remaining life of the lease or over the useful life of the improvement, whichever is less.

S. Money Market Products

The money market is distinguished from the capital market (see Section II.M) in that the money market generally refers to short-term borrowing and lending for periods of less than a year. Banks use the money market to lend and borrow from other banks. Money market instruments are considered to be low risk for investors. They may be bought at face value or at a discount from face value.

Major types of money market instruments include:

- Certificates of deposit (CDs) — CDs are time deposits with specific dates of maturity and either a fixed or variable interest rate. Customers receive more favorable interest rates by investing larger principal amounts or by investing for longer periods. CDs from banks are insured by the Federal Deposit Insurance Corporation (FDIC) and from credit unions by the National Credit Union Administration (NCUA). There are usually substantial penalties for early withdrawal prior to maturity of the CD.

- Commercial paper — Unsecured promissory notes issued by large banks and corporations with fixed maturities of up to nine months. Commercial paper is usually considered to be low risk, low return investments.

- Banker's acceptance — A time draft drawn on and accepted by a bank. Before acceptance, the draft is not the bank's obligation; it is merely an order by the drawer to the bank to pay a specified sum of money on a specified date to a named person or the bearer of the draft. Upon acceptance, the draft becomes the bank's liability.[49]

- Repurchase agreements — These are short-term loans in which a bank sells securities one day and repurchases them for the same price plus interest on a specified date (usually the next day).

The amortized cost of money market instruments with relatively short-term maturities usually approximates market value. However, if the credit standing of the issuer is impaired, or if there are significant changes in interest rates, the market value of short-term investments can be affected. In these cases, amortized cost may not approximate the market value of such investments.[50]

Money market funds are a type of mutual fund that is required by law to invest in highly liquid and low-risk securities such as certificates of deposit or government securities. These funds pay dividends that generally reflect short-term interest rates and are not federally insured. Due to the low-risk nature of the investments, money market funds rarely lose money. Money market funds are regulated primarily under the Investment Company Act of 1940 and the rules adopted under that Act, particularly Rule 2a-7 under the Act.

References

[1]Securities and Exchange Commission Web site – http://www.sec.gov/answers/annuity.htm
[2]"Audits of Investment Companies" (New York: American Institute of Certified Public Accountants, 1998), p. 127.
[3]Securities and Exchange Commission Web site – www.sec.gov
[4]"Audits of Investment Companies" (New York: American Institute of Certified Public Accountants, 1998), p. 127.
[5]Securities and Exchange Commission Web site – www.sec.gov
[6]Ibid.
[7]Ibid.
[8]U.S. Department of the Treasury, Office of the Comptroller of the Currency Web site, www.occ.treas.gov/ftp/advisory/96-8.htm
[9]Ibid.
[10]Ibid.
[11]Securities and Exchange Commission Web site, www.sec.gov/divisions/investment/letters030805.htm
[12]Ibid.
[13]Davison, Barbara, *Auditing Derivative Strategies* (Altamonte Springs, FL: The Institute of Internal Auditors, 2000), p. 2.
[14]Ibid., p. 2.
[15]Ibid., p. 101.
[16]Ibid., p. 102.
[17]*Internal Control Issues in Derivatives Usage: An Information Tool for Considering the COSO Internal Control – Integrated Framework in Derivatives Applications*, Committee of Sponsoring Organizations of the Treadway Commission, 1996. Excerpted in *Auditing Derivative Strategies*, published by the Institute of Internal Auditors, Altamonte Springs, FL.
[18]Visa Web site,
http://usa.visa.com/business/accepting_visa/ops_risk_management/cisp.html?ep=v_sym_cisp
[19]Code of Federal Regulations, Title 12, Part 1.2, obtained from Internet at www.gpoaccess.gov
[20]888options.com Web site, http://www.888options.com/basics/whatis/default.jsp
[21]Ibid.
[22]Options Clearing Corporation Web site, http://www.optionsclearing.com/about/who_we_are/who_we_are.jsp
[23]Ibid.
[24]Federal Accounting Standards Board Web site, http://www.fasb.org/st/summary/stsum115.shtml
[25]U.S. Treasury, Office of the Comptroller of the Currency's Web site, http://www.occ.treas.gov/fr/cfr.htm
[26]Davison, Barbara, *Auditing Investments* (Altamonte Springs, FL: The Institute of Internal Auditors, 1999), pp. 7-8.
[27]Federal Accounting Standards Board Web site, http://www.fasb.org/st/summary/stsum115.shtml

[28]Commodity Futures Trading Commission Web site, http://www.cftc.gov/tm/letters/99letters/tm99-32.htm)
[29]Securities and Exchange Commission Web site, www.sec.gov.
[30]Ibid.
[31]Ibid.
[32]Ibid.
[33]Ibid.
[34]Ibid.
[35]"Brokers and Dealers in Securities" (New York: American Institute of Certified Public Accountants, 1999), p. 151.
[36]Agovino, Theresa, "Consumer driven health plans don't work for everyone," Associated Press article printed in *The State Journal-Register*, Springfield, Illinois, December 4, 2005, p. 43
[37]"Audits of Investment Companies" (New York: American Institute of Certified Public Accountants, 1998), p. 187.
[38]Ibid, p. 187.
[39]Ibid, p. 188.
[40]Securities and Exchange Commission Web site, www.sec.gov.
[41]"Audits of Investment Companies" (New York: American Institute of Certified Public Accountants, 1998), p. 31.
[42]Federal Reserve of New York Web site, http://www.ny.frb.org/education/fx/foreign.html#types
[43]Ibid.
[44]Ibid.
[45]"Audits of Investment Companies" (New York: American Institute of Certified Public Accountants, 1998), p. 32.
[46]"Asset management" (Comptroller of the Currency, Administrator of National Banks, Comptroller's Handbook, December 2000), pp. 1-4.
[47]Ibid, p. 19-21.
[48]Davison, Barbara, *Auditing Investments* (Altamonte Springs, FL: The Institute of Internal Auditors, 1999), pp. 58-59.
[49]LaRoche, Robert K., *Banker's Acceptances* (Federal Reserve Bank of Richmond *Economic Quarterly*, Volume 79/1, Winter 1993), pp. 75-76. Obtained from the Federal Reserve Bank of Richmond's web site: http://www.richmondfed.org/publications/economic_research/economic_quarterly/pdfs/winter1993/laroche.pdf
[50]"Audits of Investment Companies" (New York: American Institute of Certified Public Accountants, 1998), p. 20.

Section III
Auditing Financial Services Processes

Introduction

The Certified Financial Services Auditor® (CFSA) is one of The Institute of Internal Auditors' (IIA) specialty certifications that measures an individual's knowledge of, and proficiency in, audit principles and practices within the banking, insurance, and securities financial services industries. The exam format offers candidates a choice of three financial services disciplines — banking, insurance, and securities.

This section of the *CFSA Examination Study Guide* focuses on a review of the general concepts involved in auditing financial services.

The examination addressing the audit of financial services covers the following material, and the study material is presented in roughly the same order in this guide.

A. Risk Management
   1. Asset/Liability Management
   2. Trading Market Risk
   3. Credit, Liquidity, Operational Risk
   4. Allowance for Loan and Lease Losses
   5. Reserves
B. Underwriting
   1. Loans
   2. Securities
   3. Insurance
   4. Private Placement
   5. Initial Public Offerings
C. Securitizations
D. Treasury Operations (e.g., Cash Management)
E. Back-office Operations
F. Marketing Sales and Distribution (e.g., Insurance Agencies, Bank Sales Departments and Branches, Brokers)
G. Claims
H. Investments
I. Broker-dealer Activities

J. Rating Advisory Service
K. Mergers and Acquisitions
L. Loan Operations (e.g., Collateral Issues, Perfecting Liens)

The candidate is advised that the materials included in this section are not all inclusive and that there are other materials which the candidate may find useful and beneficial in preparing to take the examination. The candidate is encouraged to seek out these resources and not to rely solely on this study guide as a single source of preparation.

Exactly What Is/Are Financial Services?

There are four main areas within Financial Services: Banking, Insurance, Investment Management, and Operations.

Financial services includes insurance (property, casualty, and life), financial planning, banking, capital markets, and investment banking. Organizations ensure the financial health and security of their companies and customers through asset management and protection, capital allocation management, financial risk analysis and management. They strive to improve customer acquisition, service, and retention through the use of market analysis, performance management, and customer relationship management. Fraud prevention and anti-money laundering processes protect not only customers, but the financial institution itself. Regulatory reporting requirements (such as Sarbanes-Oxley and Basel II) require specialized data collection and reporting.

Financial services organizations are challenged to provide responsible fiduciary management while increasing profitability and competitive differentiators. These organizations must make performance improvements, reduce administrative costs, and increase customer satisfaction while mitigating risk.[1]

Financial services represent the largest industry (or category of industries) in the world in terms of earnings 20 percent of market cap in the S&P 500 in 2004. Banks, insurance companies, investment banks, and brokerages are just some examples of the different types of firms found in this industry "segment." Financial service firms provide money and investment and related services. Financial services, therefore, are those services that would be commonly associated with the supply of financial instruments such as debt securities, equity securities, and insurance policies.

Therefore, financial services is the term used to describe those organizations that deal with the management of money. Financial services include banking, insurance, credit card companies, etc. Companies involved in financial services need to hold a lot of information about individuals. Basically, the umbrella market segmentation term for banking, insurance, and securities (www.primode.com/glossary.html).

The term financial services became more prevalent in the United States partly as a result of the Gramm-Leach-Bliley Act of the late 1990s which enabled different types of companies in the U.S. financial services industry to merge. Critics of this act say the term financial services attempts to make the unison of these operations sound natural, ignoring the possible problems from combining them, such as conflicts of interest and monopolization. Others, noting that many of the restrictions abolished by the Gramm-Leach-Bliley Act had never existed in other countries or had been abolished earlier than in the U.S., say the term financial services is a natural one in long-term use which means nothing more than its constituent words.

In the United States, most companies that previously described themselves as a bank, insurance company, or brokerage house now describe themselves in some way as a financial services institution. Allstate Insurance, for example, now provides CDs and investment brokerage services. Bank of America offers full-featured brokerage products, while E-trade has expanded into offering bank accounts and loans. Companies usually have two distinct approaches to this new type of business. One approach would be a bank which simply buys an insurance company or an investment bank; keeps its original brands; and adds it to its holding company simply to diversify its earnings. Outside the United States (for example, in Japan), it is also permitted to have non-financial services companies within the holding company. In this scenario, each company still looks independent, has its own customers, etc. This is essentially the style of Citigroup and JP Morgan Chase.

In the other style, a bank would simply create its own brokerage division or insurance division and attempt to sell those products to its own existing customers, with incentives for combining all things with one company. This is the style of Washington Mutual and Wells Fargo.[2]

Financial Services Examination — A Global Reach

The International Financial Reporting Standards (IFRS), along with International Accounting Standards (IAS), are accounting standards currently issued by the International Accounting Standards Board (IASB).

IASs were issued between 1973 and 2001 by the Board of the International Accounting Standards Committee (IASC). In April 2001 the IASB adopted all IASs and continued the development, calling new standards IFRSs. Although IASs are no longer produced, they are still in effect unless replaced by an IFRS, whether in its entirety or in part.

IFRSs are considered a "principles-based" set of standards in that they establish broad rules rather than dictate specific treatments. As of 2002 a number of IFRSs offer the preparer choices of treatments; the IASB's Improvements Project is seeking to reduce these choices (http://en.wikipedia.org/wiki/Ifrs).

IASC has no authority to require compliance with its accounting standards. However, many countries require the financial statements of publicly traded companies to be prepared in accordance with IAS.

Other countries do not permit companies to use IAS without a reconciliation to domestic generally accepted accounting principles. Most notable among these countries are Canada, Hong Kong, Japan, and the United States.

The interconnectedness of banks, and therefore their shared risk, led to the formation of the 1988 Capital Accord, which focused on the overall amount of capital available to each bank, as this is crucial for limiting a bank's insolvency risk and the potential costs for depositors if the bank fails.

Building on this foundation, Basel II aims to improve the security and long-term viability of the financial system by focusing on banks' internal control systems and management, supervisory scrutiny, and market discipline.

Basel II's mandate was initially limited to banks that trade internationally; subsequently it has been acknowledged that its principles are also valid at other banks.

At the heart of Basel II is the issue of aligning banks' capital requirements with existing and potential, possibly unidentified, economic risk. Basel II lays out a framework for identifying credit and operational risk, and rewards banks that measure risk stringently.

This is good, but not good enough. What of a bank's risk/return profile and the ability to control and manage the risks it has embarked upon? Basel II seeks to improve both banks' internal management systems and the regulatory review process.[3]

Governance: From Compliance to Strategic Advantage, [www.pwcglobal.com/images/gx/eng/fs/0404eiugov.pdf] a study carried out by PricewaterhouseCoopers in partnership with the Economist Intelligence Unit (March 2004), found that the adequacy of internal controls is now the most critical priority for boards of financial services organizations. However, the PricewaterhouseCoopers 8th Annual Global CEO Survey indicated that only 25 percent of chief executives believe they were managing governance, risk management, and compliance effectively.

Effective enterprise-wide risk management underpins sound governance and related compliance requirements by providing a comprehensive framework of internal controls and reporting procedures. The enterprise-wide approach focuses both on familiar financial risks and harder-to-measure — though equally important — strategic, operational, and reputational risks. The result: enhanced stakeholder confidence and sustainable value creation (www.pwcglobal.com/extweb/industry.nsf/docid/DD536AA67A8C9C768525701300569DD8)

European Union

IFRS was given a boost in 2002 when the European Commission issued a regulation that all listed companies in Europe must adopt IFRS by 2005 for their consolidated accounts (as opposed to the firm's individual accounts). Many member countries within the European Union have made the accounting regulation more restrictive by requiring private companies to comply with IFRS. Prior to 2005 there were approximately 350 publicly listed companies using IFRS. In 2005 the figure will be around 7000.

United Kingdom

The Financial Services Authority (FSA) is an independent non-governmental body, given statutory powers by the Financial Services and Markets Act 2000.

> "The creation of the FSA has been a work in progress since 1997 when the functions of banking supervision and investment services regulation were merged into the Securities and Investments Board (SIB) which subsequently changed its name to the Financial Services Authority. Following this, the most significant event in our history was the implementation of the Financial Services and Markets Act in November 2001 which brought a number of other organizations within our remit. These organizations included the Building Societies Commission, the Personal Investment Authority, and the Securities and Futures Authority. We are also the Competent Authority for Listing in the UK, a function which we inherited from the London Stock Exchange, and most recently we have taken on the regulation of mortgages and general insurance."[4]

Statutory auditors of firms in the financial services industry have additional responsibilities over and above those contained in the Companies Act 1985. For instance, under s.39 Banking Act 1987, the Bank of England (BoE) was responsible for the supervision of banks and had powers inter alia to call for reports on a bank by 'reporting accountants,' normally the auditors, on certain matters. Under s.342 FSMA 2000 statutory auditors are required to report certain matters to the FSA. Under s.166 FSMA 2000, the FSA may call for reports on a firm by 'skilled persons' on various matters. Skilled persons may include accountants, lawyers, and actuaries, and the statutory auditors of financial services firms may be appointed as skilled persons.[5]

Scotland

Financial services makes a major contribution to the life and economy of Scotland and generates £5 billion (nearly six percent) of Scottish GDP (measured as Gross Value Added). The industry accounts for 10 percent of Scottish jobs, employing over 108,000 people directly and over 100,000 more in support services.

In the six years to 2003, the yearly average direct employment in financial services in Scotland rose by 30.4 percent compared with 6.3 percent for the economy as a whole.

Financial services is the fastest growing sector of the Scottish economy. In the last five years (2000 Q1 to 2005 Q1) financial services in Scotland grew by 34.4 percent while the overall Scottish economy grew by 8.8 percent and the whole of the UK financial services industry grew by 16.2 percent.

Russia

By any measure, Russia's financial services sector is in an early stage of development, especially on the consumer side. The ratio of bank assets to GDP is barely 40 percent, compared with 80-120 percent in the U.S. and EU. Although many Russians own their own home, only 1.5 percent of house sales are funded by mortgages.

The ratio of mortgage lending to GDP is just 0.007 percent, compared with around 40 percent in the EU and more than 50 percent in the U.S. Similarly, while workers can now invest their retirement savings with private fund managers, less than two percent have opted to do so. The take-up of life assurance is also relatively low in comparison with many other countries.

A recent relaxation of the rules governing trading and foreign ownership in insurance suggest that the government's commitment to liberalization is genuine. Although the ceiling has only been lifted from 15 percent to 25 percent, this could still allow considerable foreign capital into the insurance sector. Short-term growth in the insurance market has been boosted by the introduction of mandatory car insurance.

Russia is now firmly on the radar of overseas financial institutions. At the beginning of 2005, there were 33 foreign-owned banks, up from 20 at the beginning of the decade. Overseas firms had a stake of 50 percent or more in a further 42 institutions.[6]

Candidates interested in further reading on the future global outlook for financial services may wish to examine "Piecing the Jigsaw: The Future of Financial Services," a 2005 PricewaterhouseCoopers paper focusing on the future of the financial services industry over the next three years. The paper considers the drivers, risks, and opportunities, as well as the impact and responses for existing and potential players in the industry. The study identifies five principal drivers that will affect all financial institutions: Politics, Demographics, The Economic Cycle, Regulation and Reporting, and Technology. The paper can be found at www.pwcglobal.com/Extweb/pwcpublications.nsf/docid/FC5C75152FCFFB438525702E0055C734/$File/futurefssum.pdf

New Zealand

The desire for a common global accounting language has been in place for some time. However, the various stock market crashes of the 1980s and the Asian Economic Crisis of 1997-1998 heightened the push for international standards. The International Financial Reporting Standards ("IFRS") promulgated by the International Accounting Standards Board ("the IASB") are gaining almost worldwide acceptance, and many of New Zealand's major trading partners are in the process of adopting, or have already adopted, these international standards. This includes Australia, Singapore, Hong Kong, and the European Union, although there are some notable exceptions, particularly the United States, Canada, and Japan.

In New Zealand, the Accounting Standards Review Board ("the ASRB"), the statutory body established by the Financial Reporting Act 1993 ("the FRA") and charged with setting New Zealand's accounting standards, has announced that New Zealand should adopt international standards for periods commencing January 1, 2007, with the option to adopt for periods commencing January 1, 2005. Adopting such standards can bring considerable benefits, particularly the ability to more readily attract international investment.

The fundamental shift of emphasis from being an accounting standards setter to an accounting standards taker and influencer means that there is a need to change the accounting standards framework, including aspects of the FRA.

The report "International Financial Reporting Standards - Cabinet Paper 19 November 2003," (www.med.govt.nz/buslt/bus_pol/bus_law/corporate-governance/financial-reporting/cabinet/20031119/index.html) proposes a strategy to further implement the introduction of international standards. This strategy will include preparing a discussion document outlining, and seeking submissions on, the various issues that surround the introduction of IFRS, including:

- The application of the FRA;
- Institutional arrangements;
- Enforcement issues; and
- The particular role of Australia in New Zealand considerations and the possibility of a joint trans-Tasman standards body.

As a 2005 adoption of IFRS requires comparative information to be prepared from 2004, it is important that these issues are considered relatively urgently.

Australia

The Australian Accounting standards, previous to January 1, 2005, were based around accounting standards developed by the Australian Accounting Standards Board (AASB). As a result of pressure toward international harmonization, the AASB had been working toward a convergence between the Australian Standards and the IFRS.

From January 1, 2005, the Australian equivalent of IFRS has been fully implemented as AASB 101 - 141. It is a requirement that all reporting entities adopt the standards as they have replaced the previous Australian generally accepted accounting principles. Due to the accounting standards operating halfway through the year, the requirements can be summarized as follows:

- Year ended 30 June 2004 — Prepare under pre-IFRS standards and state in notes the expected effect of the adoption of IFRS.
- Year ended 30 June 2005 — Prepare under pre-IFRS standards and prepare a reconciliation to IFRS standards.
- Year ended 30 June 2005 — Prepare under Australian Equivalents to IFRS standards (http://en.wikipedia.org/wiki/Ifrs).

Hong Kong

In Hong Kong, HK GAAP is more restrictive than IFRS due to regulatory laws. HK GAAP only deviates from IFRS in minor instances. Therefore, many companies complying with HK GAAP are already IFRS compliant. HK GAAP is moving toward full convergence with IFRS in 2005.

People's Republic of China

In the People's Republic of China, the standard used for accounting is PRC GAAP, which is required by law. The accounting requirements for publicly traded companies in China differ based on the type of company:

- A-share companies are companies trade in Renminbi and inaccessible to foreigners.
- B-share companies are companies trade in a foreign currency and accessible to foreigners.

Because foreign investors have access to B-share companies, all B-share companies are required to file also in IFRS. This requirement is also extended to A-share financial companies.

United States

The accounting standard in the United States has been the U.S. Generally Accepted Accounting Principles created by the U.S. Financial Accounting Standards Board. In late 2002, IASB and US FASB issued a joint statement saying that they will work toward the eventual convergence of two standards. The Securities and Exchange Commission is in the process of analyzing differences between IFRS and U.S. GAAP (www.answers.com/topic/international-financial-reporting-standards).

EU Savings Directive

The EU Savings Directive requires paying agents making cross-border interest payments to EU individuals to report information about the interest payment to their domestic tax authorities or, for paying agents in Austria, Belgium, and Luxembourg (and certain other non-EU territories), to levy a withholding tax on such payments. These measures are to apply from July 1, 2005.

The directive is aimed at ensuring effective taxation of savings income in the form of interest payments which are generally included in the taxable income of resident individuals in all member states. The directive applies to interest payments made by a paying agent within the EU member states, regardless of the place of establishment of the issuer of the debt claim giving rise to interest.

Paying agent has a wide definition and is likely to include payments made by banks and deposit takers, brokers, custodians, transfer agents, registrars, and investments funds. Interest will also include distributions and redemption proceeds from certain investment funds to the extent that the fund invests in a required level of debt securities. The reporting information that is required to be furnished broadly relates to the identity of the beneficial owner of the interest receipt and the amount of the interest receipt.

The directive has profound implications for financial services organizations. The directive cuts across many different areas of an organization, from account opening and accounting, to customer communication and IT, to compliance. (www.savingsdirective.com/eusd/index.html).

2005 Global Financial Services Industry Outlook

Deloitte & Touche Tohmatsu's Global Financial Services Industry (GFSI) practice examines the Top 10 Issues for 2005 for each industry sector. The complete study results can be found at www.deloitte.com/dtt/article/0,1002,sid%253D1013%2526cid%253D72248,00.html.

Following are summaries of the top 10 issues by industry.

2005 Global Asset Management Industry Outlook

1. Regulatory Onslaught
2. Distribution Becomes More Transparent
3. Focus on Fund Governance
4. "Alternative" Investments Becoming Mainstream
5. The Rush to Wrap Accounts
6. Product Rationalization
7. The Off-shoring Decision
8. Investing in Efficiency

9. Making Top Talent a Top Priority
10. Global Asset Managers: An Exclusive Club

2005 Global Banking Industry Outlook

1. Consolidation: Achieving Strategic Balance
2. Retail Renaissance: Bonding with Customers
3. Grooming the Next Generation of Talent
4. The Off-shoring Decision
5. Transforming the Finance Function
6. Monitoring Credit Quality
7. Achieving Comprehensive Governance of Risk Management
8. Basel II: Driving Enterprise-wide Change
9. Corporate Governance: Boards in the Spotlight
10. The Last Stretch for IAS 39 Implementation: Will You Be Ready?

2005 Global Insurance Industry Outlook

1. Restoring Confidence
2. Regulatory Ripples
3. Pursuing Global Growth
4. Emerging Opportunities in the Retirement Market
5. Unlocking Profits in Closed Books of Business
6. Driving Performance Through Embedded Value
7. The Off-shoring Decision
8. Developing Creative HR Strategies
9. Enterprise-wide Approach to Risk Management
10. The Challenge of International Accounting Standards

2005 Global Securities Industry Outlook

1. Rethinking Strategy
2. Hedge Funds Take Center Stage
3. Transparency Comes to Retail Brokerage
4. Technology: The Need for Speed
5. Building a New Operating Model
6. Holistic Approach to Compliance
7. Enterprise-wide Approach to Risk Management
8. Corporate Governance: Boards in the Spotlight
9. Talent Search
10. The Last Stretch for IAS 39 Implementation: Will You Be Ready?

National Organizations for Financial Reporting Standards	
Country	**Name**
Austria	Kammer der Wirtschaftstreuänder (KWT)
Belgium	Commission des Normes Comptables (CNC)Commissie voor boekhoudkundige normen (CBN)
Denmark	Foreningen af Statsautoriserede Revisore (FSR)
Estonia	The Estonian national standard setter
Finland	Kirjanpitolautakunta (KILA) Bokföringsnämnden
France	Conseil national de la Comptabilité (CNC)
Germany	Deutsches Rechnungslegungs Standards Committee (DRSC) (German Accounting Standards Committee)
Hungary	The Hungarian Ministry of Finance
Iceland	Félag Löggiltra Endurskodenda (FLE)
Ireland	Institute of Chartered Accountants in Ireland (ICAI)
Italy	Organismo Italiano di Contabilità
Latvia	Latvian Accounting board
Lithuania	Lithuanian national accounting standard setter
Luxembourg	Commission de Surveillance du Secteur Financier
The Netherlands	Raad voor de Jaarverslaggeving (RJ)
Norway	Regnskapsstiftelsen (NRS)
Poland	The Polish Accounting Standards Committee
Portugal	Comissão do Mercado de Valores Mobiliários Comissão de Normalização Contabilística (CNC)
Slovenia	The Slovenian Institute of Auditors
Spain	Instituto de Contabilidad y Auditoría de Cuentas (ICAC)
Sweden	Bokföringsnämnden (BN) Swedish Financial Accounting Standards Board (Redovisningsrådet)
United Kingdom	Accounting Standards Board (ASB)
United States of America	Financial Accounting Standards Board (FASB) Securities and Exchange Commission (SEC)

Table 1.0

International Standard Bodies
Name
Committee of European Securities Regulators (CESR)
European Accounting Association (EAA)
European Financial Reporting Advisory Group (EFRAG)
Fédération des Experts-Comptables Européens (FEE) (European Federation of Accountants)
International Accounting Standards Board (IASB)

Table 2.0

A. Risk Management

Risk assessment is the process of assessing the inherent risks associated with achieving business goals. The effective management of business risk can help increase the profitability of an organization. For risk management controls to be implemented, operating objectives must be instituted and be reasonably obtainable. The risks associated with operating objectives include the business climate, competitors, technology, customer requirements, and legislation.

There are also risks associated with compliance with laws and regulations. These are often more difficult to implement since compliance may actually negatively impact financial goals in the short term. For example, noncompliance with environmental regulations may seem cost-effective in the current quarter; however, the fines and associated negative publicity could have severe long-term consequences.

Internal audit routinely reviews compliance risk and should also review business risk. The efforts to control both risk types will enhance the short-term and long- term profitability and viability of an organization.[7]

Risk management, on the other hand, is inherently a process of assembling relevant information upon which the leadership of an organization can make considered judgments about strategic direction, investments, acquisitions, divestitures, etc. Certainly identifying hazards or weaknesses in the operating environments of companies contributes to the risk profile of an organization and has impact on its ability to achieve business objectives, but these weaknesses are but one component of assessing risks.

Risk management is about assessing, both quantitatively and qualitatively, the opportunity for success of business initiatives. It is composed of methodologies and processes that are designed to develop information critical to achieving the strategic objectives of the organization. The compliance function is essential to ensure that those methodologies and processes are being followed in the manner intended. Merging the two together essentially means that there is no oversight of the risk management function. Losing the compliance function in an activity that has become as complex as risk management is not an acceptable outcome.[8]

Risk management explores strategies to assess an organization's susceptibility to risk. Minimize adverse impacts of operational risk, market risk, and credit risk on resources, earnings, and cash flows through risk analysis.

Every business unit and every manager's tactical activity is, of course, essential to the organization as a whole. Strategy seeks to understand, harmonize, and harness these activities to ensure that they are all directed toward common objectives. An intelligent risk management platform approaches risk from this higher level.

Rather than simply addressing one particular aspect of risk management, it builds a platform on existing technology investments to deliver high quality information to everyone who needs it, adding value at every step of the way. It delivers information that meets the requirements of individual managers, but it does so within the framework of a single version of the truth.

The business benefits of a strategic approach to enterprise-wide risk intelligence are clear and compelling:

- Removes disputes about whose information is "correct."
- Improves cross-function, enterprise-level analysis.
- Provides a reusable enterprise intelligence platform, able to address new needs.
- Reduces integration costs — lowering total cost of ownership. Scales to meet changing needs, irrespective of underlying technology.[9]

Enterprise-wide risk management has been defined as the uniform and integrated approach of a financial services organization to identify and manage risks across the enterprise. Basically, there are four key risks that an organization encounters — credit risk, market risk, operational risk, and liquidity risk. Operational risk is a new effort put forward by the Basel Accord II, which the industry will now have to include in its current risk portfolio.

Traditionally all these risks were treated independently by companies through different departments with independent specialists to manage them. Ultimately, as days passed, more and more complexities arose in the market, and there evolved an atmosphere where sharing of information and strategy between these independent departments became a difficult task. Even senior management members found it difficult to understand the risks to which their firms were really exposed. Thus, the need for enterprise-wide risk management was realized by the financial services industry. Gartner predicts that by 2006, enterprise risk management will be a best practice for financial institutions of all sizes.[10]

The relationship and roles of internal audit and risk management

> "In firms, risks can arise from a number of sources from the obvious such as the type of business, the type or the effectiveness of the strategy adopted or the type of customer, to the less obvious such as the firms' inability to identify, monitor, manage or respond to business and operational risks. These "control" risks can mitigate or magnify the firm's business risk."[11]

Asset/Liability Management (ALM)

Asset management is the term usually given to describe companies that run mutual funds. The largest are those who provide passive, ETF, or index funds. Exchange Traded Funds (ETFs) represent a basket of securities that are traded on an exchange. As with all investment products, exchange traded funds have their share of advantages and disadvantages.[12]

Index funds are mutual funds that attempt to copy the performance of a stock market index. The most common index fund tries to track the S&P 500 by purchasing all 500 stocks using the same percentages as the index. Other indices that mutual funds try to copy include: Russell 2000, Wilshire 5000, MCSI-EAFE, Lehman-Brothers Aggregate Bond, and NASDAQ 100.[13]

For a more detailed discussion and review of ALM, refer to the Insurance Discipline section of this study guide.

Trading Market Risk

Market risk is the risk that changes in the level of interest rates, the levels of exchange between currencies, or the price of securities and other financial contracts, including derivatives, will have an adverse financial impact. Trading market risk arises from changes in market rates such as interest rates, foreign exchange rates, equity prices, and credit spreads, as well as in their correlation and implied volatilities.

The primary mechanism for estimating potential losses is a mathematical methodology, Value at Risk ("VaR") which estimates the exposure to market risk within a given level of confidence, over a defined time period [VAR summarizes the predicted maximum loss (or worst loss) over a target horizon within a given confidence interval].

Known limitations of the VaR methodology include the fact that changes in market rates may not tend to a normal distribution (specifically, that very large movements are more likely than predicted by the normal distribution assumption), that correlations between market rate movements can vary (especially during periods of stress in the markets), that the changes in present values are not perfectly linearly related to changes in market rates, and that the use of a one-day time horizon does not fully capture the market risk of positions that cannot be liquidated in one day. Additionally, the models are based on past movements and may not be indicative of future market conditions, irrespective of the historical time period selected.

Other risk management controls used to manage trading market risk include more detailed limits and individual trader mandates designed to supplement the VaR framework. This enables market risk exposure to be monitored at a detailed, disaggregated level and on a consolidated basis.

How to Calculate VaR

The official definition of VaR is the level of loss that we are X% confident will not be exceeded in some time period, T. For the determination of bank capital, X is 1% and T is 10 days. Thus, if the VaR for some bank portfolio is $5 million, there is less than a one-percent chance that more than $5 million will be lost in the next 10 trading days. The VaR calculation is highly idealized and should be interpreted with caution.

There are three ways that it is commonly misinterpreted:

1. The VaR calculation is based on an assumption that the portfolio is held constant over the time interval. In practice, portfolios are actively managed so that as adverse conditions develop, actions will be taken to mitigate losses. As a result the true probability of a loss as large as that predicted may be much less than forecast.

2. The VaR forecast is based on what has happened in the past. If the future is not like the past, the realized losses may be larger (or smaller) than predicted.

3. There is a tendency to interpret VaR as the largest loss that will occur. This is incorrect. It is just the level of loss that has an X percent probability of being exceeded. The largest loss depends on the nature of the portfolio. For many portfolios the largest loss that may occur will not be too much larger than the VaR, while for other portfolios (particularly those including highly levered derivatives), it may be many times greater than the VaR.

There are two ways that VaR is calculated. Both are based on historical data and are illustrated with an example of the calculation of a one-day, 1% VaR for a portfolio containing a single share of stock.

A. The first method is called historical simulation. In this approach, a set of historical daily returns is accumulated for the stock. Typically from one to five years of returns are accumulated. In this example, we have 500 days of realized returns on our stock.

   The most recent 500 realized returns are sorted from lowest to highest (most negative to most positive) and the five worst returns (1% of all the returns considered) are applied to the current stock price to determine the losses that would occur if these returns occurred tomorrow. The least negative of these is considered to be the VaR since no more than 1% of all the losses reached or exceeded this level in the last 500 days.

B. The alternative method used to calculate VaR is known as the model-based approach. In this approach it is assumed that some statistical model is driving the returns on our stock. In order to calculate the VaR we first determine the parameters of the model from the historical returns and then use the model to predict the future returns that might occur. Usually the statistical models used are very simple. In our example we will assume that the daily stock returns are drawn from a normal distribution with a constant mean and variance. The mean and variance are estimated from the last 500 days of stock returns and then the 1-percentile point of the distribution is calculated. In our example the average of the last 500 returns is 0.073% and the standard deviation is 1.963%. For a normal distribution the 1-percentile level is about 2.33 standard deviations below the mean; in our case a return 4.49% below the mean return.

   Applying these values to the $30 stock price yields an expected stock price of $30.02, and a 4.49% decline of -$1.35 to $28.67. This gives a VaR of - $1.33 ($30.00 - 28.67). If we assume a mean return of zero the expected price is $30, the 4.49% decline is $28.65 and the VaR is -$1.35.[14]

Credit, Liquidity, Operational Risk

Credit risk (or default risk) management analyzes credit risk and credit exposure to determine the value of credit transactions, and proactively implements risk mitigation strategies.

Liquidity risk is financial risk due to uncertain liquidity. An institution might lose liquidity if its credit rating falls, it experiences sudden unexpected cash outflows, or some other event causes counterparties to avoid trading with or lending to the institution. A firm is also exposed to liquidity risk if markets on which it depends are subject to loss of liquidity.

The term liquidity is used in various ways, all relating to availability of, access to, or convertibility into cash.

- An institution is said to have liquidity if it can easily meet its needs for cash either because it has cash on hand or can otherwise raise or borrow cash.
- A market is said to be liquid if the instruments it trades can easily be bought or sold in quantity with little impact on market prices.
- An asset is said to be liquid if the market for that asset is liquid (www.riskglossary.com/link/liquidity_risk.htm).

The Basel Committee (2004) defines *operational risk* as the risk of loss resulting from inadequate or failed internal processes, people, and systems, or from external events.

Operational risk management analyzes and manages the firm's risk of monetary loss resulting from inadequate or failed internal processes, people, and systems, or from external events.

Understanding risk is critical for all businesses. This is particularly true in the financial services industry, where banks and insurance companies comprehend the need for enterprise risk management. It has to be an integral part of their overall strategy to manage credit risk, operational risk, and compliance in order to predict and minimize unexpected losses and increase overall profitability.[15]

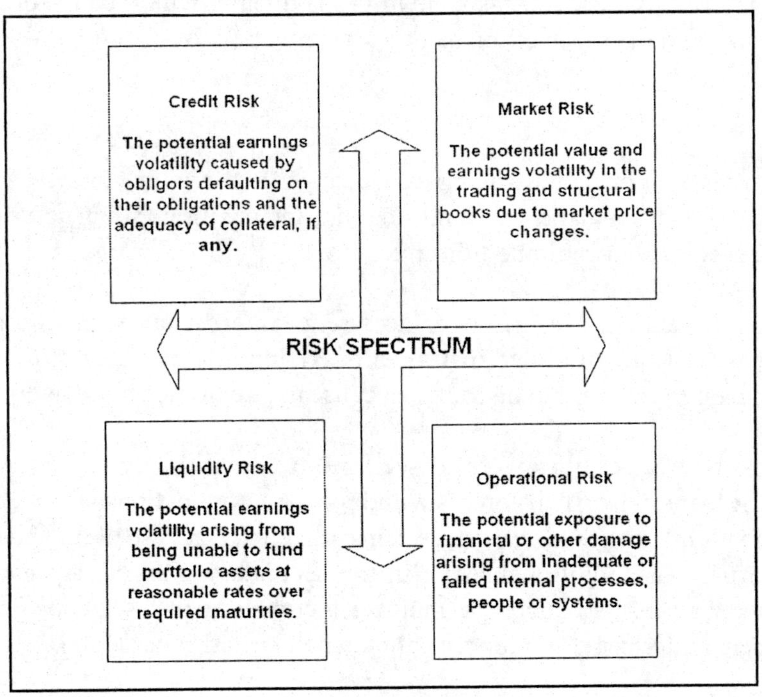

Figure 1.0

Interest Rate Risk

Interest rate risk is the risk to earnings or capital arising from movements in interest rates. The economic perspective focuses on the value of the bank in today's interest rate environment and the sensitivity of that value to changes in interest rates. Interest rate risk arises from differences between the timing of rate changes and the timing of cash flows (repricing risk); from changing rate relationships among different yield curves affecting bank activities (basis risk); from changing rate relationships across the spectrum of maturities (yield curve risk); and from interest-related options embedded in bank products (options risk). The evaluation of interest rate risk must consider the impact of complex, illiquid hedging strategies or products, and also the potential impact on fee income which is sensitive to changes in interest rates. In those situations where trading is separately managed, this refers to structural positions and not trading positions.

Changes in interest rates pose significant risks to mortgage banking activities in several ways. Accordingly, effective risk management practices and oversight by the Asset/Liability Committee, or a similar committee, are essential elements of a well-managed mortgage banking operation.

Higher interest rates can reduce homebuyers' willingness or ability to finance a real estate loan and, thereby, can adversely affect a bank that needs a minimum level of loan originations to remain profitable. Rising interest rates, however, can increase the cash flows expected from the servicing rights portfolio and, thus, increase both projected income and the value of the servicing rights. Falling interest rates normally result in faster loan prepayments, which can reduce cash flows expected from the rights and the value of the bank's servicing portfolio.

Price Risk

Price risk is the risk to earnings or capital arising from changes in the value of portfolios of financial instruments. This risk arises from market-making, dealing, and position-taking activities in interest rate, foreign exchange, equity, and commodities markets.

Price risk focuses on the changes in market factors (e.g., interest rates, market liquidity, and volatilities) that affect the value of traded instruments. Rising interest rates reduce the value of warehouse loans and pipeline commitments, and can cause market losses if not adequately hedged.

Falling interest rates may cause borrowers to seek more favorable terms and withdraw loan applications before the loans close. If customers withdraw their applications, a bank may be unable to originate enough loans to meet its forward sales commitments. Because of this kind of "fallout," a bank may have to purchase additional loans in the secondary market at prices higher than anticipated. Alternatively, a bank may choose to liquidate its commitment to sell and deliver mortgages by paying a fee to the counterparty, commonly called a pair-off arrangement.

Transaction Risk

Transaction risk is the risk to earnings or capital arising from problems with service or product delivery. This risk is a function of internal controls, information systems, employee integrity, and operating processes. Transaction risk exists in all products and services.

To be successful, a mortgage banking operation must be able to originate, sell, and service large volumes of loans efficiently. Transaction risks that are not controlled can cause the company substantial losses.

To manage transaction risk, a mortgage banking operation should employ competent management and staff, maintain effective internal controls, and use comprehensive management information systems. To limit transaction risk, a bank's information and recordkeeping systems must be able to accurately and efficiently process large volumes of data.

Because of the large number of documents involved and the high volume of transactions, detailed subsidiary ledgers must support all general ledger accounts. Similarly, accounts should be reconciled at least monthly and be supported by effective supervisory controls.

Excessive levels of missing collateral documents are another source of transaction risk. If the bank has a large number of undocumented loans in its servicing portfolio, purchasers will not be willing to pay as high a price for the portfolio. To limit this risk, management should establish and maintain control systems that properly identify and manage this exposure.

Mortgage servicers are exposed to considerable transaction risk when they perform escrow administration and document custodian activities. As the escrow account administrator, the servicer must protect borrowers' funds and make timely payments on their behalf to taxing authorities, hazard insurance providers, and other parties. The servicer also must ensure that escrow accounts are maintained within legal limits. As document custodian, the institution must obtain, track, and safe keep loan documentation for investors.

Compliance Risk

Compliance risk is the risk to earnings or capital arising from violations of, or non-conformance with, laws, rules, regulations, prescribed practices, or ethical standards. Compliance risk also arises in situations where the laws or rules governing certain bank products or activities of the bank's clients may be ambiguous or untested. Compliance risk exposes the institution to fines, civil money penalties, payment of damages, and the voiding of contracts. Compliance risk can lead to a diminished reputation, reduced franchise value, limited business opportunities, lessened expansion potential, and lack of contract enforceability.

A bank that originates and/or services mortgages is responsible for complying with applicable federal and state laws. For example, when a bank or its agent fails to comply with laws requiring servicers to pay interest on a borrower's escrow account balance, the bank may become involved in, and possibly incur losses from, litigation. In addition, failure to comply with disclosure requirements, such as those imposed under the Truth-in-Lending Act, could make the bank a target of class-action litigation.

Mortgage banking managers must be aware of fair lending requirements and implement effective procedures and controls to help them identify practices that could result in discriminatory treatment of any class of borrowers. For example, selectively increasing the price of a mortgage loan above the bank's established rate to certain customers ("overages") may have the effect of discriminating against those customers. This practice, left undetected and not properly controlled, may raise the possibility of litigation or regulatory action.

Strategic Risk

Strategic risk is the risk to earnings or capital arising from adverse business decisions or improper implementation of those decisions. This risk is a function of the compatibility of an organization's strategic goals, the business strategies developed to achieve those goals, the resources deployed against those goals, and the quality of implementation. The resources needed to carry out business strategies are both tangible and intangible. They include communication channels, operating systems, delivery networks, and managerial capacities and capabilities.

In mortgage banking activities, strategic risk can expose the bank to financial losses caused by changes in the quantity or quality of products, services, operating controls, management supervision, hedging decisions, acquisitions, competition, and technology. If these risks are not adequately understood, measured, and controlled, they may result in high earnings volatility and significant capital pressures. A bank's strategic direction is often difficult to reverse on a short-term basis, and changes usually result in significant costs.

To limit strategic risk, management should understand the economic dynamics and market conditions of the industry, including the cost structure and profitability of each major segment of mortgage banking operations, to ensure initiatives are based upon sound information. Management should consider this information before offering new products and services, altering its pricing strategies, encouraging growth, or pursuing acquisitions. Additionally, management should ensure a proper balance exists between the mortgage company's willingness to accept risk and its supporting resources and controls. The structure and managerial talent of the organization must support its strategies and degree of innovation.

Reputation Risk

Reputation risk is the risk to earnings or capital arising from negative public opinion. This affects the institution's ability to establish new relationships or services, or continue servicing existing relationships. This risk can expose the institution to litigation, financial loss, or damage to its reputation. Reputation risk exposure is present throughout the organization and is why banks have the responsibility to exercise an abundance of caution in dealing with its customers and community. This risk is present in activities such as asset management and agency transactions.

An operational breakdown or general weakness in any part of its mortgage banking activities can harm a bank's reputation. For example, a mortgage bank that services loans for third-party investors bears operational and administrative responsibilities to act prudently on behalf of investors and borrowers. Misrepresentations, breaches of duty, administrative lapses, and conflicts of interest can result in lawsuits, financial loss, and/or damage to the company's reputation. In addition, a bank that originates and sells loans into the secondary market should follow effective underwriting and documentation standards to protect its reputation in the market to support future loan sales (www.occ.treas.gov/handbook/mortgage.pdf).

Allowance for Loans and Lease Losses (ALLL)

The allowance for loan and lease losses, which was originally referred to as the "reserve for bad debts," is a valuation reserve established and maintained by charges against the bank's operating income. As a valuation reserve, it is an estimate of uncollectible amounts that is used to reduce the book value of loans and leases to the amount that is expected to be collected.

Few banks provided reserves for bad debts until the Internal Revenue Service (IRS) allowed the additions to such reserves to be deducted on a bank's tax return. Although such deductions have been allowed since the passage of the Revenue Act of 1921, no clear-cut guidelines for the amount to be deducted were established until 1965, when the IRS issued Revenue Ruling 65-92.

Under this ruling, a bank could make tax-deductible additions to its loan loss reserve until the reserve totaled 2.4 percent of eligible outstanding loans (as defined). In 1969, the OCC issued regulations requiring a provision for possible loan losses to be included in operating expenses. The regulations provided that the minimum provision charged to operating expense could not be less than the amount computed under one of three permissible methods to be selected by the bank and followed consistently beginning in 1969. Under the 1969 regulation, a bank's loan loss reserve balance consisted of three distinct elements: the valuation portion, a contingency portion, and a deferred tax portion.

Beginning with the reports of condition and income for December 31, 1976, the valuation portion of the bank's reserve was required to be reported as a deduction from total loans. The deferred tax portion was to be included with other liabilities, and the contingency portion was to be included in the equity capital section of the balance sheet. In addition, the provision for possible loan losses could no longer be based on a minimum amount as computed under one of the three methods established in 1969. Instead, all banks with more than $25 million total assets were required to provide, through charges to income, the amount considered necessary by management to bring the valuation portion of the reserve to an adequate level to absorb expected loan losses based on its knowledge of the bank's loan portfolio.

Since 1976, the Office of the Comptroller of the Currency's (OCC) guidance to banks and examiners on the determination of an adequate level for the allowance for loan and lease losses has been updated several times. Banking Circular 201 on the allowance, which was first issued in May 1985, was substantially expanded and refined in February 1992 (www.occ.treas.gov/handbook/alll.pdf).

The financial health of banks depends not only on the magnitude of their problem loans, but also on the capacity of the banks to absorb loan losses.

When a bank charges off a loan as a loss, it reduces its loans and reduces an account called the "allowance for loan and lease losses" by the amount of the loan that was charged off as a loss. The bank increases the dollar amount of its allowance for loan and lease losses by incurring an expense called "provision for loan and lease losses."

In other words, the allowance for loan and lease losses represents the accumulation of all provisions for loan and lease losses less all charge-offs to the account. Since provisions are expenses, increases in provisions reduce net income. As with any expense, provisions for loan and lease losses reduce a bank's equity.

Under the principles of bank accounting, loans reported as nonperforming have not yet been charged off as losses. When a bank charges a nonperforming loan off as a loss, it no longer reports the loan as nonperforming. An increase in nonperforming loans increases the chances that a bank will have larger charges against its allowance for loan and lease losses in the future.

Banks often increase their allowances for loan and lease losses through larger provisions when they anticipate future losses on nonperforming loans. A measure of the adequacy of a bank's allowance to absorb future loan losses is the ratio of the allowance to the amount of nonperforming loans, commonly called the "coverage ratio."

An allowance greater than nonperforming loans suggests that even if all of a bank's nonperforming loans were charged off as losses, its allowance would be adequate to absorb the charge-offs. In addition, banks with coverage ratios above unity are less likely to need relatively large provisions for loan and lease losses in the future, to offset losses charged against their allowance, than banks with coverage ratios below unity.

The capacity of banks to absorb losses also depends on the amount of equity those banks hold.[16]

Purpose of the Allowance

The allowance is a valuation reserve maintained to cover losses that are probable and estimable on the date of the evaluation. The allowance is not a cushion against possible future losses; that protection is provided by capital. Although in establishing its allowance a bank considers the inherent losses in individual loans and categories of similar loans, the allowance is a general reserve available to absorb all credit losses in the portfolio. No part of the allowance is segregated for, or allocated to, any particular asset or group of assets (www.occ.treas.gov/handbook/alll.pdf).

Calculation of the ALLL for Financial Institutions

The calculation of the ALLL for financial institutions is rooted in generally accepted accounting principles (GAAP) and not, for the most part, in regulatory theory. There are two accounting rules that apply to most situations — Financial Accounting Standards Board (FASB) Statement (FAS) No. 5, Accounting for Contingencies (FAS-5), and FAS No. 114, Accounting by Creditors for Impairment of a Loan, an amendment of FASB Statements Nos. 5 and 15 (FAS-114).

FAS-5 deals with like pools of loans, that is, loans that can be segregated with like characteristics into different groups. Those like characteristics most often will be product types, such as home equity line of credit (HELOC), unsecured consumer lines of credit, direct auto, indirect auto, and so on. Under FAS-5, commercial loans also can be segregated by type — commercial real estate, commercial and industrial loans, and so forth — when it is difficult to identify a specific allowance for individual loans.

FAS-114 impairment methodology is used when it is practical to examine each loan individually. In most banks, some set of loan ratings would establish the parameters for what loans to examine for impairment and, correspondingly, for a specific reserve. For example, many banks that use a one-through-eight grading system would segregate the six- and seven-rated loans to determine if they are impaired and need a specific allocation.

For those banks using a more stratified grading system, determination would need to be made on what loans ratings would qualify as "impaired." A loan is impaired if it is determined that all principal and interest cannot likely be repaid under the original agreed-upon terms.[17]

Reserves

Reserves are savings or funds set aside to finance future spending pressures and unknown contingencies. Bank reserves are banks' holdings of deposits in accounts with their central bank (for instance the European Central Bank or the Federal Reserve, in the later case called federal funds), plus currency that is physically held in banks' vaults (vault cash). The central bank sets minimum reserve requirements. The Bank of England uses the term "rest" to describe the same concept (http://en.wikipedia.org/wiki/Bank_reserves).

Reserves can also be defined by the specific industry in which one works. For example:

Insurance

- An amount placed on an individual claim to cover expected future payments for that claim.
- An amount representing an insurer's estimate of its liabilities on future commitments under policies outstanding. An amount allocated for a special purpose.
- Amount required to be carried as a liability in the financial statements of an insurer or reinsurer to provide for future commitments under outstanding policies and contracts.
- Reserves-case. An estimated liability from outstanding claims for losses and allocated loss adjustment expenses. Established by the claims department, the estimate provides the initial basis for evaluating statutory reserves; a statistical review measures redundancies (excess estimates) or deficiencies (shortfall in estimates) and adjust for other factors including reinsurance and recoveries.
- Reserve Deficiency (also compare to Case Reserves). The opposite of a reserve redundancy. Reserves are established based upon individual claims and a deficiency indicates that there may be a trend to "underestimate" the actual or ultimate paid claim.
- Reserve Redundancy (also compare to Case Reserves). The opposite of a reserve deficiency. Reserves are established based upon individual claims and a redundancy indicates that there may be a trend to "overestimate" the actual or ultimate paid claim.
- Reserves-statutory. The amount established under statutory accounting to pay current claims. The amount is established based upon historical trends and analysis that includes adjustments or reductions for any reinsurance ceding or other recoveries. This will be the amount recorded at period end for statutory accounting.
- Reserves-ultimate. Using statistical measures and models to evaluate claim and insurance policy data actuaries are able to predict what the "ultimate" or best forecast of claim

payments will be. Usually, the data is developed by reporting period and treaty year and provides the basis for recording the amount of liability for statutory reserves. The more developed the data the greater the confidence level in this projection (www.apmc.us/?id=52#r).

- Liabilities established by insurers and reinsurers to reflect the estimated cost of claims payments, benefits payments, and the related expenses that the insurer or reinsurer will ultimately be required to pay in accordance with the insurance or reinsurance it has written (www.converium.com/520.asp#Marine%20&).

Banking

- A depository institution's vault cash (up to the level of its required reserves) plus balances in its reserve account (not including funds applied to its required clearing balance) (www.tgbr.com/tgbr/terms.html#r).

International Economics

- The assets denominated in foreign currency, plus gold, held by a central bank, sometimes for the purpose of intervening in the exchange market to influence or peg the exchange rate. Usually includes foreign currencies themselves (especially U.S. dollars), other assets denominated in foreign currencies, gold, and a small amount of special drawing rights (SDRs) (www.personal.umich.edu/~alandear/glossary/i.html#InternationalReserves).

Managed Health Care

- Monies earmarked by health plans to cover anticipated claims and operating expenses. A fiscal method of withholding a certain percentage of premium to provide a fund for committed but undelivered health care and such uncertainties as: longer hospital utilization levels than expected, over-utilization of referrals, accidental catastrophes, and the like. The fiscal method of providing a fund for committed but undelivered health services or other financial liabilities. A percentage of the premiums support this fund. Businesses other than health plans also manage reserves. For example, hospitals document reserves as that portion of the accounts receivables that they hope to collect but have some doubt about its collectability. Rather than book these amounts as income, hospitals will "reserve" these amounts until paid.

International Financial Reporting Standard and Reserves

Reserves, together with share capital and own equity instruments, make up the shareholder's equity section of an entity's balance sheet. Reserves are not specifically defined in IFRS, but should not be treated as a type of provision.

Reserves include fair value reserves, hedging reserves, asset revaluation reserves, a foreign currency translation reserve, and retained earnings. These reserves result from fair value and foreign currency translation adjustments, required by IFRS to be reflected in equity rather than income.

Reserves are not re-measured, but they may be restated where an entity is reporting in the currency of a hyperinflationary economy.

Fair Value Reserve

Unrealized gains/losses (net of tax) on investments classified as available-for-sale may be recognized in equity (within a fair value reserve) or in the income statement. These gains/losses are recycled to the income statement on disposal or when the asset becomes impaired

Hedging Reserve

IFRS require that gains and losses (net of tax) arising from the revaluation of a financial instrument designated as a cash flow hedge be deferred in a separate component of equity. The reserve is usually described as a hedging reserve.

These deferred gains and losses are subsequently released to the income statement in the periods when the hedged item affects the income statement. Hedging gains and losses relating to forecast transactions are transferred from reserves and incorporated into the initial measurement of the hedged item.

To the extent that the hedged relationship ceases to be effective, the hedging instrument's gains/losses should be transferred from the reserve and recognized in income.

Asset Revaluation reserve

Subsequent to initial recognition, an item of property, plant, and equipment may be revalued to fair value. The revaluation surplus is recognized in equity. A subsequent revaluation decrement must in certain circumstances be charged against this reserve property.

The revaluation surplus is transferred to retained earnings periodically, net of the tax effect. The amount realized is the difference between depreciation based on the revalued carrying amount of the asset and depreciation based upon the asset's original cost. When the asset is sold or scrapped, the balance in the reserve is transferred to retained earnings as a realized gain and does not pass through the income statement

Foreign Currency Translation Reserve

Where a subsidiary is deemed a foreign entity, its financial statements are translated in accordance with IFRS. Foreign currency translation differences should be recognized in equity in a foreign currency reserve.

Translation adjustments must be separately tracked in equity. On disposal of a foreign entity, the cumulative translation difference relating to the entity is transferred to the income statement and included in the gain or loss on sale.[18]

B. Underwriting

1. The process by which investment bankers raise investment capital from investors on behalf of corporations and governments that are issuing securities (both equity and debt).
2. The process of purchasing all or any part of a new issue of municipal securities from the issuer and offering such securities for sale to investors.

Underwriters in finance are investment banks or individuals that guarantee prices on securities to corporations and then sell the securities to the public. They also provide insurance and re-insurance. A leading underwriter is Lloyds of London.

The primary market is the financial market for the initial issue and placement of securities. Unlike in the secondary market, no organized stock exchanges are necessary. An organization that needs funds contacts their investment banker who typically assembles a syndicate of securities dealers that will sell the new stock issue.

Securities dealers see this as the wholesale part of their business. This process of selling the new stock issues to prospective investors in the primary market is called underwriting. The securities that they sell are called initial public offerings (IPOs). Dealers usually earn a commission that is built into the price of the security offering; that is, it is not apparent unless you read the prospectus in detail.

Loans

Once an individual's loan file has been submitted, it will be underwritten. This is when an underwriter will review the individual's file and render a loan decision. The type of information requested by the underwriter may vary depending on the type of loan sought (mortgage, small business, educational, etc.) by the individual.

The underwriter will review the information provided by the individual and make sure that it conforms to the investment entity's guidelines. The underwriter will review all of the following aspects of the file (this is a representative sample of documentation reviewed; an underwriter may require additional documentation beyond those shown here):

- Income and debt ratios
- Employment history
- Credit history

For refinancing, home and mortgage loans for example, the underwriter may request additional documentation such as:

- Savings/source of money for down payment
- Appraisal

Once the underwriter has reviewed all of the file documentation provided, he or she will issue a written decision. The decision may be one of the following:

1. Approved — Everything in the individual's file meets the entity's guidelines for final approval.
2. Suspended — Additional documentation is needed to issue final approval.
3. Denied — Aspects of the file do not conform to the entity's guidelines for loan approval.

Securities

This is contrasted with the retail part of the business, which is acting as an intermediary between buyers and sellers of securities in the secondary market (www.bambooweb.com/articles/p/r/Primary_market.html).

Securities are tradeable interests representing financial value. They are often represented by a certificate. They include shares of corporate stock or mutual funds, bonds issued by corporations or governmental agencies, stock options or other options, other derivative securities, limited partnership units, and various other formal "investment instruments." Banknotes, checks, and some bills of exchange do not fall into this category.

Secondary markets often consist of what is called an exchange to facilitate the meeting of buyers and sellers. They are often referred to as stock exchanges, even though there are exchanges such as the Chicago Board of Options Exchange where no stocks are traded.

In the United States, securities are registered with the Securities and Exchange Commission (SEC), though some may never trade on an exchange and some are exempt from registration. Dealing in securities is heavily regulated by both the federal authorities (chiefly the SEC) and state authorities.

In addition, the industry is heavily self-policed by self-regulatory organizations (SROs), such as the NASD or the MSRB.

Due to the difficulty of creating a general definition that covers all securities, the SEC attempts to define "securities" exhaustively (and not very precisely) as: "any note, stock, treasury stock, security future, bond, debenture, certificate of interest or participation in any profit-sharing agreement or in any oil, gas, or other mineral royalty or lease, any collateral-trust certificate, preorganization certificate or subscription, transferable share, investment contract, voting-trust certificate, certificate of deposit for a security, any put, call, straddle, option, or privilege on any security, certificate of deposit, or group or index of securities (including any interest therein or based on the value thereof), or any put, call, straddle, option, or privilege entered into on a national securities exchange relating to foreign currency, or in general, any instrument commonly known as a "security"; or any certificate of interest or participation in, temporary or interim certificate for, receipt for, or warrant or right to subscribe to or purchase, any of the foregoing; but shall not include currency or any note, draft, bill of exchange, or banker's acceptance which has a maturity at the time of issuance of not exceeding nine months, exclusive of days of grace, or any renewal thereof the maturity of which is likewise limited."—Section 3a item 10 of the 1934 Act (www.bambooweb.com/articles/s/e/Securities.html).

Insurance

Historically, insurance underwriters analyzing directors' and officers' liability risks related to investment banks, commercial banks, broker-dealers, investment advisers, and mutual funds have not had a comprehensive understanding of the financial services industry and its pertinent issues.

Neither has the insurance underwriting community kept pace with the increasing complexity resulting from consolidation and integration of financial institutions. As a result of the alleged malfeasance by some firms and an aggressive plaintiffs' bar, insurers of directors and officers of financial institutions face a crisis in the form of an unprecedented number of claims and expensive settlements.

This has led to a revolution in the insurance underwriting process. In the past, a brief meeting or phone call with a company's risk manager and insurance broker would be the extent of underwriting analysis. However, this is no longer the case. The insurance industry, generally, has realized that simply attempting to increase premium rates and deductibles will not cure the problems plaguing the financial institutions' D&O insurance market.

Insurers, often with the support of the insurance brokerage community, now require initial meetings with senior executives of the particular financial institution being analyzed. Typical client attendees at underwriting meetings include the chief financial officer, treasurer, and general counsel.

Executives, such as the chief compliance officer in the mutual fund industry, or board members, such as the chair of the audit committee, may be obligated to meet with the insurer as part of the insurance underwriting process. After the initial meeting, the insurance underwriting team usually requests one or several follow-up meetings or conference calls with members of the financial institution's executive team to discuss any open items and confirm salient information.

In addition to ensuring the attendance of senior financial institution executives at underwriting meetings, brokers are providing insurers with detailed financial information. The cooperation of the insurance brokerage community is essential to achieving best practices underwriting, and most brokers fulfill their responsibility to provide useful information and client personnel to underwriters.

In addition, it is important for brokers to support reasoned and responsible underwriting and explain its long-term benefits to their clients. Since the financial statements of financial institutions are very different from those of non-financial commercial organizations, some insurance companies have recruited underwriters with special skills to analyze these companies.

To effectively underwrite these kinds of risk, an underwriter needs a strong expertise in accounting, tax, legal, finance, and corporate governance. Certain insurance companies have even used third-party consultants to augment the complicated underwriting process, and this cost is borne by either the insurer or the insured.[19]

Private Placement

1. The sale of securities directly to institutional investors, such as banks, mutual funds, insurance companies, pension funds, and foundations. Does not require SEC registration, provided the securities are bought for investment purposes rather than resale, as specified in the investment letter (www.investorwords.com/3859/private_placement.html).

2. A negotiated offering in which a new issue of municipal securities is sold on an agency basis by a placement agent directly to institutional or private investors rather than through an offering to the general investing public.

Investors purchasing privately placed securities often are required to agree to restrictions as to resale and are sometimes requested or required to provide a private placement letter to that effect (www.msrb.org/msrb1/glossary/glossary_db.asp?sel=p).

Regulation D

Regulation D, an SEC rule governing the limited offer and sale of securities without registration under the Securities Act Of 1933, regulates private placement exemptions. Regulation D:

- Allows usually smaller companies to raise capital through the sale of equity or debt securities without having to register their securities with the SEC.
- Offerings are advantageous to any private company or entrepreneur because they allow an entity to obtain funding faster and to avoid the costs associated with a public offering.

- Allows for the issuance and sale of securities to purchasers if they qualify as accredited investors.

Even if the transaction only involves one or two investors, the company or entrepreneur wanting to raise capital still needs to provide the proper framework and disclosure documentation; however, these requirements are significantly less than what is required for a public offering (www.investopedia.com/terms/r/regulationd.asp).

Initial Public Offerings (IPO)

This is the first sale of stock by a company to the public. A company can raise money by issuing either debt (bonds) or equity. If the company has never issued equity to the public, it is known as an IPO.

New issues of securities, including what is commonly known as an IPO, or Initial Public Offering, for new stock issues are offered on the primary market. Securities that have already been issued may also be traded; this trading is called the aftermarket or secondary market.

When a company decides to go public, management will meet with bankers from Wall Street brokerage houses to discuss how the IPO will be marketed to the public. This rite of passage is called a "beauty contest" because each of the bankers is competing for the business. The bankers will try to entice the management with promises of a high IPO price and ongoing research coverage. Sometimes the expertise of the underwriter's capital markets group, the people who will sell the deal to investors, wins the day. Sometimes the prospect of having a well-respected Wall Street analyst write research on the company after the IPO is the deal clincher. Remember, the companies know that an essential part of the deal is that the research is always positive.

Brokerage houses develop special strengths through their research analysts or a specialized banking team that seeks potential IPOs. Large brokerage houses like Morgan Stanley Dean Witter, Goldman Sachs, Salomon Smith Barney, CS First Boston, UBS Warburg, and Merrill Lynch have deep benches. Because they have much experience taking companies public, they and other established firms usually apply certain standards of quality to the companies they are willing to underwrite. The operative word here is usually. Usually, the internal investment banking committees conduct due diligence (asking questions about the management and finances of the company). There are many on Wall Street who think that the Internet gold rush has led to a decline in standards.

Again, usually, the biggest, best-known underwriters get the best IPOs. Companies that are in the process of deciding who is going to do their IPO are concerned with how well the deal will be distributed, and they want to have ongoing research by the brokerage house's analyst. Every large brokerage house mans a research department with analysts who toil away issuing research and investment opinions on stocks. Brokerage houses compete for star analysts who are on the "II" team (an annual survey conducted by the industry journal *Institutional Investor*, a magazine that ranks analysts in many industries).

It is a simple fact that underwriting IPOs is one of the most profitable businesses for Wall Street. On a $100 million technology IPO, an underwriter would gross about $8 million. Faced with getting stock commissions of three to five cents a share on institutional trades and with the competitive pressure on the retail side from discount brokers, IPOs are critical to continued profitability and fat bonuses. Underwriting decisions are more influenced by what underwriters think they can sell to the public than by the quality of the company.

Although it is time-consuming, individuals should pay attention to what is called the "league tables" — the lists of leading underwriters published at the end of every quarter in *The Wall Street Journal* and *The New York Times*. These tables will give you a good idea of how active a particular underwriter is and, more important, how well its deals have done. Beware of underwriters with bad track records. Bad track records mean the bankers have poor judgment in picking IPOs or fail to do their due diligence.

Also, a bad track record can mean the underwriter is too small to get a crack at the good deals. IPOs that are underwritten by small or regional brokerage firms should be looked at very cautiously. Often, an IPO that is underwritten by a small brokerage firm was rejected by the more established players.

An IPO should have at least two underwriters. If a small brokerage firm solely manages the deal, the IPO is suspect for two reasons. First of all, the offering may not be a genuine distribution to the public. There are occasions when an IPO like this is simply traded among that underwriter's brokers, who artificially boost the price with each trade. This is called a "house stock." Second, with only one underwriter, no other underwriter has any incentive to provide ongoing research.[20]

Canada

The Canadian securities are the financial products traded in Canada by the properly licensed investment dealers on behalf of private and public investors in an open financial market. This trading is regulated by the two levels of government, the Federal and the Provincial, and has particular rules in the Province of Quebec.

The Canadian securities industry is as well a self-regulated activity by the IDA (Investment Dealers Association), the CBA (Canadian Bankers Association or Association des banquiers canadiens, in Quebec), the CAIFA (Canadian Association of Insurance and Financial Advisors), and Advocis (Financial Advisors Associatons of Canada) (www.bambooweb.com/articles/c/a/Canadian_securities.html).

C. Securitizations

This is a term used to describe the process of raising funds through the sale of securities. It usually creates a new financial instrument representing an undivided interest in a segregated pool of assets such as commercial mortgages. The ownership of the assets is usually transferred to a legal trust or special purpose, bankruptcy-remote corporation to protect the interests of the security holders (www.mccarystevens.com/cssa_intro.pdf).

Securitization and Sale

Some subprime lenders have increased their loan production and servicing income by securitizing and selling the loans they originate in the asset-backed securities market. Strong demand from investors and favorable accounting rules often allow securitization pools to be sold at a gain, providing further incentive for lenders to expand their subprime lending program.

However, the securitization of subprime loans carries inherent risks, including interim credit risk and liquidity risk that are potentially greater than those for securitizing prime loans. Accounting for the sale of subprime pools requires assumptions that can be difficult to quantify, and erroneous assumptions could lead to the significant overstatement of an institution's assets.

Moreover, the practice of providing support and substituting performing loans for nonperforming loans to maintain the desired level of performance on securitized pools has the effect of masking credit quality problems.

Recent turmoil in the financial markets illustrates the volatility of the secondary market for subprime loans and the significant liquidity risk incurred when originating a large volume of loans intended for securitization and sale. Investors can quickly lose their appetite for risk in an economic downturn or when financial markets become volatile.

As a result, institutions that have originated, but have not yet sold, pools of subprime loans may be forced to sell the pools at deep discounts. If an institution lacks adequate personnel, risk management procedures, or capital support to hold subprime loans originally intended for sale, these loans may strain an institution's liquidity, asset quality, earnings, and capital.

Consequently, institutions actively involved in the securitization and sale of subprime loans should develop a contingency plan that addresses backup purchasers of the securities or the attendant servicing functions, alternate funding sources, and measures for raising additional capital.

Readers may wish to refer to the Statement of Financial Accounting Standards No. 125 (FAS 125), "Accounting for Transfers and Servicing of Financial Assets and Extinguishments of Liabilities," for guidance on accounting for these transactions.

If a securitization transaction meets FAS 125 sale or servicing criteria, the seller must recognize any gain or loss on the sale of the pool immediately and carry any retained interests in the assets sold (including servicing rights/obligations and interest-only strips) at fair value. Management should ensure that the key assumptions used to value these retained interests are reasonable and well supported, both for the initial valuation and for subsequent quarterly revaluations.

In particular, management should consider the appropriate discount rates, credit loss rates, and prepayment rates associated with subprime pools when valuing these assets. Since the relative importance of each assumption varies with the underlying characteristics of the product types, management should segment securitized assets by specific pool, as well as predominant risk and cash flow characteristics, when making the underlying valuation assumptions.

In all cases, however, institutions should take a conservative approach when developing securitization assumptions and capitalizing expected future income from subprime lending pools. Institutions should also consult with their auditors as necessary to ensure their accounting for securitizations is accurate.[21]

The Securitization Process [Refer to Figure 2.0]

(1) Production-Origination Underwriting

The production of commercial mortgage loans that serve as the underlying collateral for the commercial mortgage-backed securities (CMBS) may come from traditional portfolio holders who originate mortgages for their own portfolio or from conduits who originate mortgages solely for securitization; these loans may or may not have been originated with the expectation of being securitized. The underwriting of a commercial mortgage loan assesses, among other things, real estate risk, borrower quality, tenant quality, existing lease terms, property condition, and potential for environmental liability in order to determine whether to originate a loan on the subject property, and if so, the appropriate loan amount and terms. The underwriter will analyze whether the proposed loan-to-value is prudent, as well as whether the debt-service coverage ratio is acceptable, given the anticipated cash flows. It is the quality of the initial underwriting that will in large part drive the rest of the securitization process, for the quality of the underlying loans will dictate the amount of necessary credit enhancement and the ultimate pricing of the certificates.

(2) Mortgages

These are the underlying collateral for the CMBS. The quality of the documentation is as important as the quality of the underwriting of the loans. Each component of the mortgage loan, such as its prepayment structure, interest rate provision (floating vs. fixed), borrower reporting requirements (for rent rolls and operating statements), exculpation carve-outs, representations and warranties, indemnification of environmental liability, borrower organization, and cross-collateralization, has a direct impact upon the pricing of the mortgage loan in the securitization process. In short, a mortgage that does not contain necessary provisions to ensure an uninterrupted cash flow will be priced at the worst case scenario when securitized.

(3) Underwriting

As opposed to the loan specific underwriting of step (1), this underwriting step is concerned with whole pool issues such as geographic concentration, industry concentration, borrower concentration, weighted average coupon, weighted average life, weighted average maturity, and modified duration.

This is the step where the pool of individual mortgages begins the transformation from several distinct instruments evidencing indebtedness to being, in the aggregate, the underlying collateral for the CMBS. The underwriter will solicit input from the rating agencies as to any issues (such as the concentration issues referred to above) which may necessitate an increase in the credit enhancement. An underwriter may determine that it is advantageous to remove certain mortgage loans from the contemplated securitization.

(4) Accumulation-Warehousing-Aggregation

The mortgage loans in the post-originated but pre-securitized stage of the securitization process are said to be warehoused. If the mortgages have been originated by a portfolio lender, the portfolio lender will likely hold the loans in its own portfolio until the securitization closing. If the mortgages have been originated by a conduit, the loans will be placed with a depository.

(5) Structuring

This is the process of experimenting with various combinations of mortgages and security classes to achieve the highest price for a CMBS based upon capital market forces at that moment.

(6) Credit Enhancement

This includes provisions provided by issuers to reduce default risk in CMBS. A third party may provide this by issuing a standby letter of credit, a surety bond, or a corporate guarantee, or the structure itself may provide the enhancement through reserve accounts, cross-collateralization, cross-default, advance payment agreements, loan replacement provisions, and creating separate senior and subordinated classes of securities.

(7) Closing

Closing is the period where all legal documents, such as the Pooling and Servicing Agreement, and all necessary opinions are finalized, the ratings letters are received, and the funding is authorized.

(8) Collateral Pool

This is the pool of mortgages that now serves as the underlying collateral for the CMBS, and which is owned by the trustee for the benefit of all class holders (tranches) of the certificates.

[Tranche — one of a set of classes or risk maturities that comprise a multiple-class security, such as a Collateralized Mortgage Obligation (CMO) or Real Estate Mortgage Investment Conduit (REMIC); an investment-grade mortgage bond that separates mortgage pools into different maturity and risk classes.]

(9) Distribution

Simultaneous with closing, the loans are transferred from the depository or portfolio holder to the trustee in exchange for the requisite money, and the trustee issues certificates of beneficial ownership, which are undivided interests in a trust that owns the collateral pool. The certificates, if publicly offered, have to be distributed by a registered broker-dealer (usually an investment bank) and are distributed according to the trust indenture.

(10) Trustee

The trustee represents the trust that holds the legal title to the collateral for the benefit of all class holders (tranches) of the certificates. The trustee's duties include, among other things:

1. Holding the mortgage collateral;
2. Passing all funds collected by the master servicer to the certificate holders;
3. Acting as a supervisor to the master servicer and special servicer;
4. Ensuring that the servicers act in accordance with the terms of the Pooling and Servicing Agreement; and
5. Appointing a new servicer if the terms of the agreement are violated.

(11) Master Servicer

The master servicer is required to service the mortgage loans which collateralize the CMBS on behalf of and for the benefit of the certificate holders. Responsibilities vary according to the Pooling and Servicing Agreement. Common responsibilities include:

1. Collection of mortgage payments and passing the funds to the trustee;
2. Advancing any late payments to the trustee;
3. Providing mortgage performance reports to certificate holders; and
4. Passing all loans to the special servicer that go into REO or non-performing status.

(12) Special Servicer

A special servicer is the servicer who assumes servicing responsibilities when a loan goes into default and conducts the "work-out" or foreclosure process. There are various scenarios typical for determining special servicers:

1. Those seller/issuers retaining the first-loss piece;
2. Those investing in "B" pieces in return for special services rights; and
3. Those appointed solely because of asset-management expertise.

(13) Sub-servicer/Primary servicer

The master servicer and the special servicer may each subcontract their duties to a sub-servicer or primary servicer. The master servicer or the special servicer remains responsible for the performance of the duties that are delegated.

(14) Securities Instrument Servicing

Most certificates are held by the Depository Trust Company as custodians for the trustee for the benefit of the certificate holders, and the notice of book entry is made to the certificate holders simultaneously with the distribution. This notice shows the certificate holders their ownership and where the security is held for safekeeping. In other words, the certificate holders rarely possess the actual certificates, but instead only possess a record of where they are. The Depository Trust Company performs this service for nearly all public securities and the majority of private placements.

(15) Securities Administration

The master servicer collects all money, including their advances of principal and interest and other property protection and preservation funds, to an account controlled by the trustee. The trustee then issues wiring or check instructions to the certificate holders of record. Sometimes the trustee physically performs this service, and other times it is contracted out to paying agents who actually manage the cash flows. The trustee also submits reports to the certificate holders in accordance with the Pooling and Servicing Agreement. In some transactions, these reports are submitted directly to the certificate holders by the master servicer and/or the special servicer, but in all cases the trustee has the responsibility for these operations or functions.

(16) Securities

Securities are the certificates of beneficial ownership that are undivided interests in the trust which owns the collateral pool. The rights of the certificate holder are as provided in the trust indenture, with the servicing and administration functions of the trust performed for the benefit of the certificate holder as spelled out in the Pooling and Servicing Agreement.

(17) Investors

In the category of the investment-grade tranches, the primary investors have been life insurance companies, pension funds, and commercial banks; it is estimated that life insurance companies now own at least 50 percent of the outstanding investment-grade CMBS. For the below-investment grade tranches, the securities are placed pursuant to Rule 144(a), and thus must be sold to a Qualified Institutional Buyer (QIB); the core demand for the below-investment-grade tranches has come from prominent real estate investment funds or CMBS servicing entities, both of whom have the real estate sophistication necessary to properly underwrite the real estate risk inherent in these tranches.

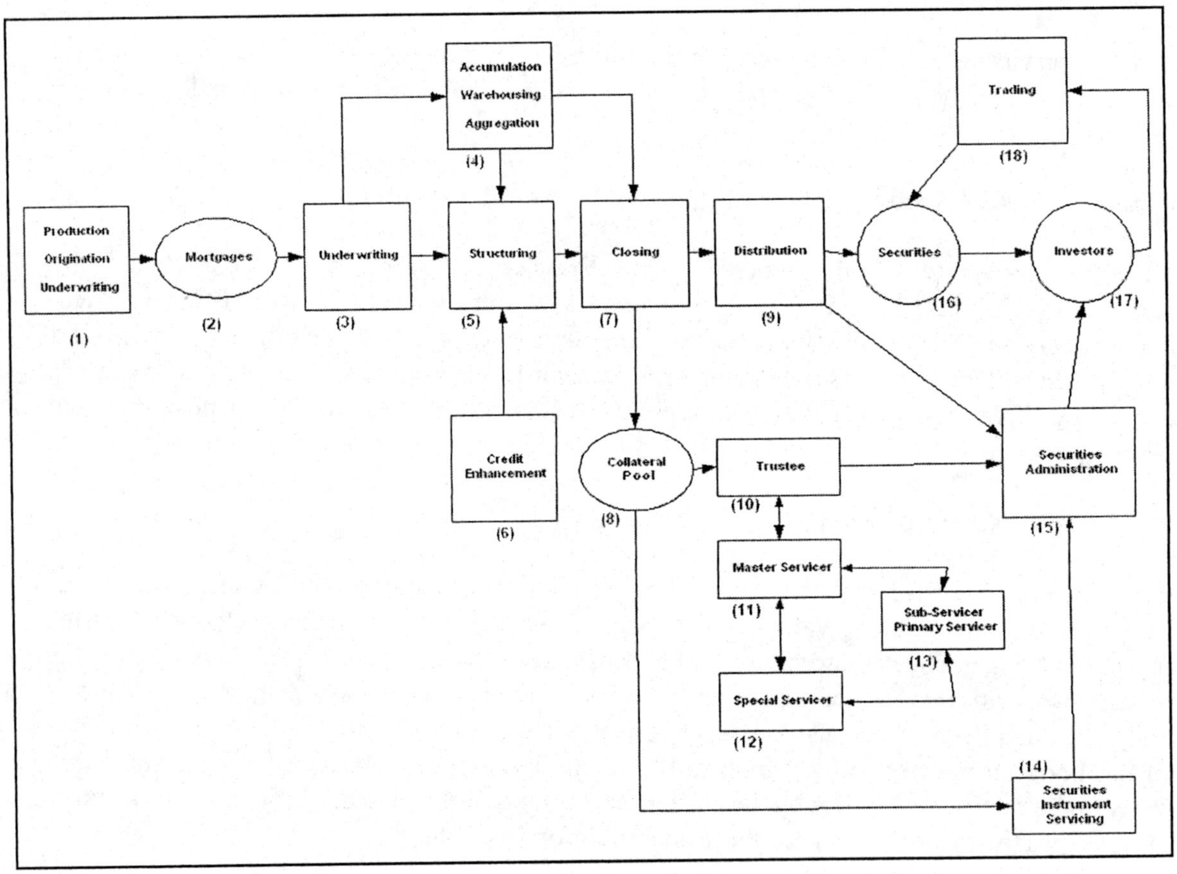

The Securitization Process[22]
Figure 2.0

(18) Trading

CMBS certificates are liquid instruments, but in reality, the higher the credit rating, the more trading actually occurs. Mid-level ratings and below tend to be a buy-and-hold market; note that the lower the credit rating of the tranche purchased, the more due diligence is typically performed by investors prior to purchase; it follows that the below-investment-grade CMBS is a relatively illiquid market due to the high amount of due diligence typically performed. However, for all certificates other than residuals, there has been marketability demonstrated in actual sales and purchases.[23]

D. Treasury Operations (e.g., Cash Management)

With the passage of the U.S. Sarbanes-Oxley Act of 2002, treasurers are faced with new responsibilities and opportunities. While some organizations will strive to simply comply with the law, others will use the Act as an opportunity to further promote Treasury best practices. Specific areas of opportunity include:

- Identifying control points/issues.
- Improving control processes.
- Improving financial reporting and support processes.
- Strengthening global governance activities.

For firms subject to Sarbanes-Oxley, the impact will vary depending on characteristics such as industry, organizational structure, banking structure, technology usage, existing processes, existing controls, and composition and experience of staff. Notwithstanding this, Treasury is greatly impacted by the two new attestation requirements faced by CEOs and CFOs:

1. Certification that financial reports reflect no untrue or misleading statements, or material omissions, and
2. Maintenance and evaluation of sound internal controls, and disclosure of any and all material deficiencies in controls to the auditors and the audit committee.[24]

Auditing financial services processes and the relationship to Treasury operations is discussed in greater depth and specific detail in the Insurance Discipline, Section B – Processes, of this study guide. The candidate is encouraged to turn to this discipline section and to read in its entirety the examination of Treasury operations for a better understanding of this critical financial services function.

E. Back-office Operations

Back-office operations refer to the offsite delivery of a range of non-core service functions, including routine administrative tasks, customer service, and technical support. Back-office operations manage an activity or function on a turnkey basis for their clients. Any aspect of service operations that involves high-volume transactions is an opportunity for back-office delivery.

Over the past 25 years, the types of service activities being outsourced have changed considerably. Outsourcing, as we know it today, began in the 1980s, when organizations began contracting out specialized functions that were not part of their core business. The availability of more cost efficient telecommunications supported corporate decisions to scan globally for the technical skills they need and hence optimize their use of talent.

The growth of the Internet and online connectivity made possible the provision of technical support and problem resolution for customers from remote locations. Contact center activity began to accelerate.

Finally, this was followed by entire support processes getting outsourced (business process outsourcing [BPO]), as corporations began to focus primarily or exclusively on their core business. Some of the earliest examples were payroll processing and credit card processing.

BPO involves turning over an entire function or business process to a back office supplier (for instance, the resource management of an organization which may involve payroll and finance; information technology; human resources; inventory management). As corporations merge and consolidate operations, this trend toward outsourcing basic business processes is becoming a new business model for international corporations.

Initially, back-office operations were created as captives of parent companies and treated as cost centers. Over time, these have evolved from cost centers to profit centers due to:

1. The emergence of third-party back-office facilities, making it possible for corporations to avail of their services on a flexible or "as required" basis.
2. Corporations are increasingly converting captive back-office operations into profit centers by accepting external clients.

Today, back-office services cover the following:

Administration

- Tax processing
- Claims processing
- Asset management

- Transcription and translation
- Document management
- Other administration

Finance
- Billing services
- Accounting transactions
- General accounting
- Tax consulting and compliance
- Risk management
- Financial reporting
- Financial analysis
- Financial management
- Other finance services

HR
- Benefits administration
- Education and training
- Recruiting and staffing
- Payroll services
- Hiring administration
- Records management
- Other HR services

Payment services
- Credit/debit card services
- Check processing
- EDI

Other transaction processing.[25]

Back-office operations provide a range of corporate, non-core services, usually at a distance. Routine administrative tasks, customer service, and technical support functions are examples of back-office operations. (Back-office operations are not the same as offshore operations, which establish business entities in tax-free export zones or offshore centers.)

Services here include loan processing, claims processing, application processing, credit and collections, reconciliations, accounts payable, time and expense reimbursement, vendor payments, benefits administration, payroll, and other industry-specific functions.

F. Marketing Sales and Distribution (e.g., Insurance Agencies, Bank Branches, Brokers)

Marketing is the process of identifying customers and developing products and processes to meet their needs. Sales is the process of agents addressing potential customers and writing applications for new policies.

An insurance company is considered authorized or admitted if it holds a valid certificate of authority from the insurance department in the state in which it does business. An unauthorized or non-admitted insurance company does not qualify for a certificate of authority.

Agents are insurance company representatives with the authority to sell the company's products. Agents must be licensed in the state in which they do business. Most agents conduct business through authorized companies. Captive agents, also known as exclusive agents, represent one company exclusively. Independent agents represent more than one company. Captive agents who work out of a field office are known as a company's field force. However, some agents, known as detached agents, work out of a private office or their home.

Insurance brokers work for insureds rather than for a specific company. The function of an insurance broker is to choose the best coverage available to meet a client's needs.

The following are examples of illegal sales practices:

- Misrepresentation occurs when agents make false or misleading statements in an attempt to encourage an individual to buy a policy. Agents are also forbidden from guaranteeing policy dividends.
- Twisting occurs when an agent purposefully misguides an individual into canceling one policy and purchasing a new one.
- Rebating occurs when an agent agrees to give an individual a share of the commission as an incentive to buy a policy.

A distribution system is the network of individuals and organizations that perform the marketing activities required to convey the insurer's products to its customers. There are two commonly used distribution systems in the insurance industry:

1. Personal selling distribution systems market products by using sales representatives to make face-to-face presentations with prospective clients. Sales representatives working in personal selling distribution systems are paid by commission or salary or a combination of both. A major type of personal selling distribution system is the agency-building distribution system. Two common agency-building distribution systems include ordinary and multiple-line:

a. The ordinary agency system (also known as the career agency system) uses agents usually working out of a company's branch offices to sell policies.
b. The multiple-line (or all-lines) agency system uses agents who sell the policies of a group of affiliated companies.

2. Direct response distribution systems use telemarketing, direct mailings, and other advertisements to solicit potential customers. Clients purchase policies and file claims directly with the company rather than through a sales representative.[26]

G. Claims

The claims function is concerned with ensuring that claims are paid promptly and correctly to the claimant (e.g., the insured or its beneficiaries). Claim specialists (commonly referred to as claim examiners or claim analysts) consider information related to the approval or denial of a claim. Claim specialists should be trained to recognize instances of insurance fraud or improper claims.

The insured is generally responsible for notifying the insurer in writing when a loss occurs. Most policies outline the proper procedures for filing a claim. There may be time limits regarding when a claim can be filed. Depending on the type of claim, the insured may be required to file a signed proof of loss statement. Insurers may also require additional evidence, such as a death certificate or a physician's statement, before approving a claim. Some property insurance policies may require the insured to have an appraisal of the property before a claim is paid. Arbitration is often used to settle claims when the insured or insurer cannot agree on the amount of loss.

The claims department considers the following questions when reviewing claims:

- Did a loss occur?
- Was the loss covered by the policy?
- Was the policy in force when the loss occurred?
- Was the insured covered by the policy?
- How much is payable to the insured or beneficiaries?
- Who are the beneficiaries?

Questionable claims may be subject to a claim investigation. The purpose of a claim investigation is to gather additional information related to the claim. Insurance companies decide on a case-by-case basis whether an investigation is necessary. Risk factors that may signal a need for an investigation include the amount of the claim, the nature of the loss, the presence of conflicting information, and the length of time the policy was in force.[27]

A further discussion of claims can be found in the Insurance Discipline, Section B – Processes, of this study guide.

H. Investments

In the late 1970s, insurance regulatory changes and high interest rates made companies develop new "investment-related" products such as universal life insurance. Agents started to sell life insurance as an investment. Policyholders began to consider permanent life insurance products as part of their investment portfolios.[28]

Insurance is an attractive option for investment. While most people recognize the risk hedging and tax saving potential of insurance, many are not aware of its advantages as an investment option as well. Insurance products yield more compared to regular investment options, and this is besides the added incentives (read bonuses) offered by insurers.

You cannot compare an insurance product with other investment schemes for the simple reason that it offers financial protection from risks, something that is missing in non-insurance products.

In fact, the premium you pay for an insurance policy is an investment against risk. Thus, before comparing with other schemes, you must accept that a part of the total amount invested in life insurance goes toward providing for the risk cover, while the rest is used for savings.

In life insurance, unlike non-life products, you get maturity benefits on survival at the end of the term. In other words, if you take a life insurance policy for 20 years and survive the term, the amount invested as premium in the policy will come back to you with added returns. In the unfortunate event of death within the tenure of the policy, the family of the deceased will receive the sum assured (www.kotaklifeinsurance.com/omkm3/insuranceguide/roleoflife.htm).

Whole life insurance policies that accumulate cash value should not be considered an investment vehicle. Insurance policies are good for insurance needs; however, as a main investment vehicle, they have considerable downsides:

1. A majority of a premium payment is "part of commission"; a small percent of your money goes toward the investment avenue.
2. The guaranteed cash value, or accumulation value of your investment is normally such a low percentage, typically one to three percent

You would be much better off using a traditional investment vehicle than an insurance policy as an investment. If you are looking for secure and guaranteed investments, consider government T-bills, government bonds, etc. The majority of your money is invested, unlike a "premium payment." If you no longer have a 401K, you should consider an IRA or Roth IRA.

Never buy life insurance as an investment without understanding that some of your "investment" is paying for your coverage. Life insurance provides protection against economic loss resulting from death.

The tax implications are to be considered as well:

Whole life — if you take the CSV (cash surrender value, which is usually less than the accumulation value) before your death, it is fully taxable as ordinary income. Once the policy is surrendered, you assume the WHOLE lump sum tax burden.

401K — you can take out in chunks to supplement income, and minimize tax burden, while keeping the majority still under the tax deferred status (not to mention the benefit of a Roth IRA). So the end result of what you have for disposable income is once again better with the 401k (when comparing investment vehicles).

Life insurance does not accumulate fast enough because of high commissions.

Whole life commissions are high. There is also expense in underwriting and certain portions of premiums that are set aside and invested to pay a permanent and increasing death benefit, whenever that may be. If life insurance were to gain cash value too quickly it would become a (MEC) modified endowment contract and would be taxable. The power in whole life insurance cash value is not just the cash value, it is also the death benefit and how it is used in one's estate plan that can make it one of the most powerful investment vehicles you own.

Does a 401K have a death benefit? No. Does it have a waiver of premium disability to continue vesting? No. Can you borrow monies if needed for an emergency? Yes, but it is penalized, taxed, and limited. Most whole life policies allow for access to monies any time there is cash value. Loans are not subject to tax or penalized. Policy loans are given by the insurance company and they can charge an interest rate like a bank. However, in most cases the interest is offset by dividends that you are earning in the policy cash value.

Note that mutual companies may pay a lower dividend while policy loans are outstanding. This is typically known as direct recognition, as apposed to a stock-held company. Can a 401K offset estate taxes? No. Life insurance is a tax deferred vehicle but never taxed as long as the life policy is in force, and death benefits are paid tax free. Unless, for example, you were using an executive bonus plan through a business and tax deducting premiums, then the premiums would be taxed upon death but not the additional death benefit.

Premiums also do not have to be paid for the life of the policy; excess dividends can also pay premiums in an established life policy so at some point, depending on the health of the insured, it can fund itself. A whole life policy gives us the freedom to spend down our estate without disinheriting the family. Another benefit is that the policy is not subject to liability or creditors.

Mutual life companies may apply direct recognition to policy loans, which means lower dividends when cash is borrowed from the policy, as opposed to stock-held companies that do not have direct recognition. The cost or interest charged by the insurance company to use your own money through a policy loan will be offset by dividends earned. This also depends on the company's policy on loan provisions.

Mutual companies have different rules or procedures than stock-held companies and it is up to the client to understand the different benefits or rules that apply to these companies.

Can life insurance be an investment? The estate bond concept is interesting. It takes life insurance and turns it into a potentially lucrative investment. The estate bond is an old life insurance concept that uses the tax benefits of life insurance to maximize your estate. The estate bond can multiply your savings by two, three, and sometimes four or five times so that you can provide a larger legacy tax free for those you care about most.[29]

Candidates interested in learning more about the pros and cons of investments and the options of utilizing insurance as an investment are directed to the Insurance Discipline section of this study guide, specifically Section B, Processes, sub-section B.1.d, Investments.

I. Broker-dealer Activities

Investment banking is the first step in the process of underwriting newly offered securities. The objective of the investment banker is to raise capital for clients at the most advantageous rate possible.

The investment banking function is crucial to the underwriting process because it brings the issuer and the investing public together.

The duties of an investment banker include:

- Advising organizations on money management issues.
- Packaging and marketing corporate securities to the public.
- Mergers and acquisitions advice.
- Reviewing corporate financial statements and advising clients on their financial condition.

Investment bankers are contracted because it is usually more efficient to use them than for organizations to issue securities directly to the investing public. Bankers have well-organized sales forces and contacts with other broker-dealers and the investing public.

Types of Offerings

Typically the investment banker or groups of investment bankers will purchase securities outright from the issuer and sell them to other investment bankers or investors. There are three types of arrangements between bankers and issuers:

1. Firm Commitment

A firm commitment underwriting is when the investment banker pledges to buy all of the securities offered by the issuer and sell them to other broker-dealers and investors. If the investment banker cannot sell the entire offering, the securities will be kept in his or her own inventory. The issuing company will receive full payment for the offering when the securities are delivered to the investment banker. The full responsibility for selling the issue rests with the banker and the issuer will not have to buy any of the offering back regardless of the performance of the offering.

2. Standby Commitment

Under a standby commitment, the issuing company will sell its own securities and the investment banker or group of investment bankers agrees to stand by, take up, and sell any part of the offering the issuing company has been unable to sell. Thus, the investment banker has a firm commitment to the extent that any of the securities cannot be sold by the issuer. This type of commitment is usually made when the company attempts to sell securities to its existing stockholders, or execute an exchange of new securities for existing securities.

3. Best-efforts Commitment

Under the best-efforts commitment, the investment bankers do not guarantee to purchase any of the unsold portions of the offering. They agree that they will use their best efforts to sell as many of the securities as possible. Thus, they are really only acting as agents in selling the company's securities. This type of arrangement is typically used in speculative common stock offerings where the successful sale of the securities is under doubt. Under this arrangement, the bankers are only paid a commission on the securities they manage to sell.

Legislation Affecting the Broker-dealer Function

The Securities Act of 1933 requires every new offering of securities to be filed with the SEC via a registration statement. A registration statement sets forth all relevant information pertaining to the specific offering.

The 1933 Act has two basic objectives:

1. Require that investors receive significant (or "material") information concerning securities being offered for public sale; and
2. Prohibit deceit, misrepresentations, and other fraud in the sale of securities.

Underlying the 1933 Act is the idea that a company (i.e., an "issuer") offering securities should provide potential investors with sufficient information about the issuer to make an informed decision.

Congress intended the law to empower investors, not the government, to make informed investment decisions.

To assist with its objectives of informing potential investors and fair dealing in the marketplace, the 1933 Act requires issuers to disclose significant information about themselves. Disclosure also has the added benefit of discouraging bad behavior. Supreme Court Justice Louis Brandeis coined the phrase "sunlight is the best disinfectant," which also is part of the philosophy underlying the 1933 Act.

Disclosure of relevant information is accomplished through the registration of securities with the SEC. The SEC is the principle federal agency responsible for oversight of the securities market and enforcement of the federal securities laws.[30]

Securities Exchange Act of 1934

The Securities Exchange Act of 1934 (the "1934 Act") extended federal regulation to trading in securities, which are already issued and outstanding. The 1934 Act is a more comprehensive statute and regulates the secondary markets and many market participants. Provisions of the 1934 Act provide for the creation of (i) the Securities and Exchange Commission ("SEC" or the "Commission"); (ii) a system for regulating the markets themselves and those who trade in those markets; (iii) a continuous disclosure system for issuers; and (iv) antifraud provisions.

Broker-dealers engage in a broad range of securities activities. For example, they may help a small investor sell 100 shares of common stock or underwrite millions of dollars worth of securities across the globe for an international corporation. The 1934 Act requires broker-dealers to register with the SEC and comply with its rules. Regulation of broker-dealers serves a number of purposes, which include:

- Ensuring basic competency of registered broker-dealers and their employees;
- Promoting financial solvency of broker-dealers;
- Requiring broker-dealers to maintain accurate books and records; and
- Preparing audited financial statements

The SEC coordinates its regulation of broker-dealers with the Self Regulating Organizations (SROs). Both the SEC and SROs inspect broker-dealers for compliance with the laws and may bring enforcement actions for wrongdoing.[31]

The Trust Indenture Act of 1939

The Trust Indenture Act of 1939 is an amendment to the Securities Act of 1939. It gives additional protection to investors in new offerings of corporate debt securities. Basically, the law states that issuers of debt subject to the law must appoint one or more trustees who will ensure that the terms of the indenture are kept by all parties to the agreement. The appointed trustees cannot have conflicting interests and reaffirm their qualifications to be trustees with SEC annually.

Many corporate debt issuers satisfy the Trust Indenture Act of 1939 by making a full disclosure in a formal registration statement that is submitted to the SEC. Debt offerings exempt from registration will comply with the 1939 Act by filing an indenture qualification statement with the SEC. This allows the offerings indenture to be registered with the SEC on the effective date.

Investment Company Act of 1940

The Investment Company Act of 1940 ("1940 Act") regulates companies that engage primarily in investing in securities of other companies. A mutual fund, one type of investment company, is a corporation (or business trust) that invests in other companies. Investors buy shares in the mutual fund, which in turn invests in other securities, called "portfolio securities." An investment adviser makes day-to-day decisions about which portfolio securities the mutual fund should buy or sell. Congress enacted the 1940 Act to address abuses in the investment company industry and is designed to help minimize conflicts of interest that arise in the operation of these companies.

The 1940 Act seeks to prevent abuses through mandating disclosure regarding the investment company's structure, operations, financial condition, and investment policies when shares of the investment company are initially offered to the public and, thereafter, on a regular periodic bases. Investment companies register with the SEC under the 1940 Act and typically register their securities under the 1933 Act. The provisions in the 1940 Act govern, among other things:

- Registration of investment companies;
- Transactions between the investment company and an affiliate (e.g., the investment adviser to the investment company");
- Purchases and sales of investment company shares; and
- Responsibilities of the investment company's directors or trustees.[32]

Private Securities Litigation Reform Act

Congress enacted the Private Securities Litigation Reform Act ("PSLRA") in 1995. The PSLRA is intended to stop abusive litigation in which trial lawyers would file suit to extract settlements from issuers and others. It made a series of very technical changes to the law.

Before the PSLRA, a trial lawyer (i.e., plaintiff's counsel) could file a lawsuit with the flimsiest claim and demand that the defendant company (i.e., the issuer), along with its investment bank and accountants, produce millions of documents. The lawyer's goal would be to make the cost of defending the case so expensive as to force the defendants to settle, even if there was no merit to the case. To stop this abuse, the PSLRA made a number of changes to the procedures for bringing a private lawsuit.[33]

Securities Litigation Uniform Standards Act

Congress enacted the Securities Litigation Uniform Standards Act ("SLUSA") in 1998 to prevent evasion of the PSLRA. After the PSLRA's enactment, trial lawyers brought an increasing number of securities class actions in state court. Trial lawyers wanted to be able to continue bringing frivolous lawsuits and extracting settlements, and moved their tactics to state court. Congress enacted SLUSA to plug that loophole. SLUSA provides that large securities class actions must proceed in federal court, where they will be governed by the PSLRA.[34]

National Securities Markets Improvement Act

The National Securities Markets Improvement Act of 1996 ("NSMIA") made substantial changes to the dual system of federal-state regulation while preserving state antifraud authority. For the first time since the New Deal, Congress modernized the relationship between federal and state securities regulators. Congress sought to make the SEC the regulator of nationally based activities, while preserving the role of states over activities that were truly local in nature. At the same time, NSMIA preserved the right of state regulators to prosecute fraud.

NSMIA also preempted to a limited extent state laws that addressed broker-dealer licensing, capital, custody, financial responsibility, and record-keeping requirements to the extent such conflicts differed from SEC requirements. This provision, for example, avoided the nightmare that would have occurred if every state securities authority had imposed its own unique book and records requirement on brokerage firms operating in all 50 states.[35]

Glass-Steagall Act

In 1933 in the aftermath of the Great Depression and its widespread bank failures, Congress enacted the Banking Act of 1933. Four sections of the Banking Act of 1933 are referred to as the Glass-Steagall Act. Many critics believed that banks had engaged in inappropriate securities activities that harmed investors. In particular, critics charged that if a bank had a bad loan to a failing company or even a country, it would sell securities to pay off the loan and leave investors with the poor investment. The Glass-Steagall Act addressed that concern in a very broad way:

- Section 16 — restricted commercial national banks from engaging in most investment banking;
- Section 20 — prohibited any member bank from affiliating in specific ways with an investment bank;
- Section 21 — restricted investment banks from engaging in any commercial banking; and
- Section 32 — prohibited investment bank directors, officers, employees, or principals from serving in those capacities at a commercial member bank of the Federal Reserve System.[36]

Regulation A

Regulation A under the Securities Act of 1933 allows the filing of a limited registration statement.

The value of the securities offered by the issuer in the previous year cannot exceed $1,500,000. In addition, offerings by a person affiliated to the issuer cannot exceed $100,000. Regulation A requires an offering circular that details most of the same information that a prospectus would. However, it is still less expensive for a company to issue securities under Regulation A.

Regulation D

SEC Rules 504 through 506, under the auspices of Regulation D, allows issuers to offer unregistered securities in specific quantities to a specific number or "type" of investor. These rules were specifically designed to facilitate the private placement of securities. These rules help issuers avoid the time, cost, and paperwork involved with a public offering.

SEC Rule 504

Any issuer who is a non-investment company (e.g., a mutual fund) or who is not subject to the public financial reporting requirements of the 1934 Act is eligible to issue securities without registering the offering. The issuer who met these requirements can publicly sell to any number of investors' unregistered securities up to $500,000 during any 12-month period. In addition, there are no information disclosures under SEC Rule 504.

SEC Rule 505

An issuer who is not an investment company or is not eligible to issue securities under Regulation A can use SEC Rule 505 to offer unregistered securities up to $5 million in any 12-month period. The distribution cannot be made to more than 35 non-accredited investors. There is no limit on the number of accredited investors. Regulation D defines "accredited investors" as any of the following:

- Individuals with net worth over $1 million
- Individuals with income in excess of $200,000 in each of the last two years, with reasonable expectation of having income in excess of $200,000 in the year of the purchase
- Purchasers of at least $150,000 of the securities being offered, with the purchase price not exceeding 20% of the purchaser's net worth at the time of the sale
- Corporate or partnership insiders
- Financial institutions, such as banks and insurance companies
- Private business development companies
- Colleges or university endowment funds and other not-for-profit organizations with assets of $5 million or more
- Any entity owned by an accredited investor

SEC Rule 506

Any issuer who is allowed to issue private placements under the Securities Act of 1933 can use SEC Rule 506 to issue non-registered securities. Issuers can offer any amount of securities for any period of time to up to 35 non-accredited investors. There is no limit on the number of accredited investors. The issuers must assure themselves that these non-accredited persons understand the merits and risks of the investment prior to purchase.

The SEC does not guarantee the adequacy or accuracy of any of the offerings registered under the Act. However, the investing public can find protection under the civil liability provisions of the 1993 Act. This law gives an investor the opportunity to bring suit for reimbursement for financial losses sustained from investing. However, the purchasers must be prepared to prove that they lost money on their investment because of incomplete or distorted material information presented in the registration statement. Omission of material facts and/or misrepresentation of fact are the two bases under which investors in a public offering can recoup their original investment.

SEC Rule 10(b)-6

When an investment banker accepts an invitation to join a syndicate, he or she becomes subject to SEC Rule 10(b)-6. Section 10(b) of the Securities and Exchange Act of 1934 is onc of thc "antifraud" provisions of the Act. These provisions are generally prohibitions against "fraud," "deceit," or "manipulative or deceptive devices or contrivances" in the offer of securities. SEC Rule 10(b)-6 makes it unlawful for any underwriter or other person participating in a distribution to bid for or purchase any units of the security being distributed, with certain specified exceptions.

At this point, the investment bankers will also begin soliciting indications of purchase interest from institutional and select individual investors. This process consists solely of giving the potential investors some overall information regarding the issuer and does not involve any type commitment whatsoever.

SEC Rule 10(b)-7 (the Securities and Exchange Act of 1934) prohibits broker-dealers from soliciting orders or accepting unsolicited orders for new issuers prior to effective date. This step is designed to determine how much initial demand there is for the offering. This process is crucial in determining the public offering price ("POP").

Regulation T — Credit by Brokers and Dealers

Regulation T is issued by the Board of Governors of the Federal Reserve System pursuant to the Securities Exchange Act of 1934 (15 U.S.C.78a et seq.). Its principal purpose is to regulate extensions of credit by brokers and dealers; it also covers related transactions within the Board's authority under the Act. It imposes, among other obligations, initial margin requirements and payment rules on certain securities transactions.

Key Risks

Management Authorization

Senior management approval must be obtained before entering into any investment banking relationship or commitment of the firm's capital. Senior management will have a broader knowledge of client relationships, capital constraints, and regulatory implications than any individual banker or department within the company.

Insider Trading

Investment bankers and syndicate traders may misuse material inside information obtained while performing their regular duties. Inside information may be passed to others or used for their own personal gain.

Broker-dealer Sales Desk

Sales desks within a broker-dealer are typically divided into two types: Retail and Institutional.

Retail sales desks may reside within a broker-dealer's headquarters or in a remote site better known as a branch office. Retail desks focus on serving individual investors, usually with accounts under $10 million U.S. in assets. Retail salespeople (also known as account representatives) are responsible for assisting their customers in determining their risk profile, designing an investment strategy, and helping to select the most appropriate investments for them based upon their particular risk profile and strategy. Account representatives with "discretionary authority" are allowed to select the customer's investments for them without prior approval from the customer.

The retail account representatives are also responsible for monitoring the performance of the portfolio and advising the customer as to the appropriate times to buy or sell securities within the customer's portfolio.

Institutional sales desks usually operate out of a broker-dealer's headquarters or out of regional offices located in major business centers, such as New York, Chicago, Los Angeles, Atlanta, or Dallas.

Institutional sales reps serve corporations, pension plans, mutual funds, foundations, and other large investors. These types of investors usually have in-house professionals or outside advisors to help them assess their risk tolerance and investment objectives. In some cases, the institutional sales rep may almost act as an order taker, providing very little input into the client's investment selections. In many cases, however, the institutional sales rep is a valuable part of the client's investment analysis team, helping the client assess potential investments and recommending various investment strategies.

Risks

1. Strategic Plan and Objectives

Every sales desk should have a plan outlining the unit's strategy and objectives for the year. The plan should include:

- An analysis of the current market situation (strategic profile).
- An identification of the targeted customer base.
- The strategy for reaching the targeted customer and the resources that will be used to reach the targeted customer.
- Plan objectives and specific strategies to achieve these objectives, including marketing, new products, financial, and personnel plans.
- Budgets.

2. Policies and Procedures

Every sales desk should have written policies and procedures that detail the process flow of the desk and all of the internal and external rules and regulations of the desk. At minimum, policies and procedures should contain:

- The scope and nature of the firm's business activities and method of operation.
- A description of the principal supervisory steps to be taken in carrying out the supervisory duties, the frequency of such efforts, and the method of documenting completed supervisory reviews.
- A designation of one or more principals to be responsible for a periodic review of the adequacy of the firm's overall supervisory system.
- A designation of the principal to be responsible for overall supervision of each type of business the firm conducts.
- A listing of supervisory personnel who are qualified for their assigned areas.
- Each employee assigned to a specific supervisor.
- A designation of one or more principals to review periodically all securities transactions in the manner and frequency described in the firm's written procedures.
- A designation of one or more principals to review sales literature, advertisements, correspondence of registered representatives and customer complaints, and a documentation of the review.

3. Management Supervision

Desk activity should be closely monitored and actively supervised by management. Management should vigorously monitor and enforce the policies and procedures of the desk through team meetings and visual and audio surveillance.

Customer correspondence (incoming and outgoing) and customer complaints must be vigorously reviewed, investigated, and resolved by management in conjunction with compliance. In addition, management should use automated software and MIS reports to closely monitor the activities of desk personal. In particular, sales commissions charged to customers must be reviewed to ensure compliance with National Association of Securities Dealers (NASD) guidelines.

4. Marketing Tactics

Management should clearly communicate the firm's marketing guidelines to sales representatives. Management and compliance should review and approve all presentations and sales pitches used for prospective customers. In addition, all marketing materials and advertisements must be reviewed and pre-approved by management and compliance.

5. Customer Suitability

Sales reps must ensure that investment recommendations are suitable for customers and that proper due diligence has been performed in determining a customer's investor profile.

Order Processing Transactions

There are two types of transactions that can be posted to the books and records of a broker-dealer: principal and agency.

Principal Transactions

A principal transaction involves the purchase or sale of a security to or from the proprietary account of the broker-dealer. For instance, a customer wants to purchase 100 shares of XYZ. In a principal trade, the broker-dealer will sell the customer the 100 shares of XYZ from its own inventory account. The broker-dealer's profit will come from marking up the security a fraction of a point above the current market price (ask price). In the case of a customer's sell transaction, the broker-dealer will mark down the security a fraction of a point below the current market price (bid price). The markup/markdown is compensation for the market risk and financing costs the broker-dealer incurs by holding the position in its inventory.

Agency Transactions

An agency transaction involves the purchase or sale of a security between a customer and another financial institution, with the broker-dealer acting as the middleman or agent. The financial institution may be trading for itself or acting on behalf of one of its customers. The broker-dealer's profit will come from the charging of a commission to the customer for finding a counterparty for the transaction.

Purchase and Sales (P&S) Department

The P&S department is responsible for four functions:

1. Recording
2. Figuration
3. Comparison
4. Booking

Recording

Every transaction in a broker-dealer is assigned a CUSIP number, or in-house security number, and a unique transaction number. All of the trade details may be recorded manually or via systems. Many firms will perform an additional comparison between the trade tickets from the order room and the P&S records to ensure the accurate recording of the trade on the books and records.

Figuration

When a trade is processed by a broker-dealer there are several computations that must be performed to determine the final settlement balance. These calculations include the amount due to the broker-dealer, the amount of money/securities due the customer, and the amount of money/securities due the counterparty. Also, in regard to bond transactions, the accrued interest, if any, must be determined. The customer or broker-dealer who has been holding an interest-paying bond is due the interest earned on the bond from the time the last interest payment was made.

Comparison

The comparison process consists of the reconciliation of customer trades against the trade of the opposing or contra-broker. Manual comparison consists of trades being separated by the exchanges on which they were executed, i.e., NYSE, AMEX, OTC, etc. The trades are coded, dated, and then sent to the computer center for processing. The P&S department will produce trading runs that will be sent out to the appropriate clearinghouse of each of the exchanges for additional processing.

Booking

Once a transaction has been processed and balanced, it must be entered onto the broker-dealer's records, or booked. Most firms have automated accounting systems that are fed information from their P&S systems and updated automatically. Most of the manual work in booking trades involves trade corrections.

Continuous Net Settlement

The Continuous Net Settlement System operated by NSCC was developed in recognition of the need for complete automation in the area of processing securities transactions.

Incorporated in CNS are functions that allow for the consolidation of transactions and automated book-entry movement of securities in a centralized and controlled environment. Compared transactions enter CNS through various front-end systems, such as NSCC's comparison and trade recording services, Depository Trust Company's Institutional Delivery System (ID), and interfaces of compared trades from other clearing corporations. As these compared transactions are processed through CNS, reports are generated, providing a complete audit trail.

The key features of CNS include the following:

- All trades in CNS eligible securities may be included in the system, regardless of size.
- Continuous recycling permits securities received by participants on settlement day to be turned around for delivery on a same-day basis.
- Deliveries between CNS and participants' depository positions are automatic.
- All deliveries are made through the Depository Trust Company by book-entry procedures, allowing CNS to operate in a certificateless environment.
- Closing positions are marked-to-market daily, giving protection to all participants in the event of a failure of any individual firm.

The CNS Process

The CNS process is designed to be completely automatic and minimize manual intervention by the participating broker-dealer. On settlement date, all transactions in each security are combined to produce a net position representing the number of shares or bonds to be settled by the participants. Once transactions are recorded in CNS, NSCC becomes the opposite side to all long and short positions, eliminating any need for participants to maintain street-side records on a trade-for-trade basis.[37]

J. Rating Advisory Service

As a consequence of Basel II, banks are becoming increasingly reluctant to grant loans. Small and medium-sized companies looking for a way out of the credit squeeze need to adopt a new approach. While debt capital alternatives such as note loans and corporate bonds are available to larger companies with annual sales of at least € 200 million, strict rules apply in the international capital market, requiring institutional investors to invest only in officially rated notes and bonds. This means that a rating is indispensable for any company wishing to raise capital in the capital market.

Alternative forms of finance for which a rating is not necessarily required are available to small and medium-sized companies in the form of syndicated loans and note loans (a scaled-down type of bond). However, these products do not fully exploit all possibilities of debt finance. Companies planning to access the capital market and wishing to issue bonds in the future simply cannot do without a rating. While obtaining an external rating (e.g. from renowned agencies such as Moody's or Standard & Poor's) initially ties down management capacities and causes incremental costs, it offers important benefits for a company in the long term.

Rating an Important Element of the Capital Market Strategy

Many institutional investors base their investments on strict criteria which restrict their investments in non-rated instruments. A rating enables a company to target this group of investors as well. A larger group of investors increases demand, which will reduce the funding costs in the capital market in the medium term. At the same time, a rating increases the liquidity of a bond and helps reduce costs. Moreover, a rating gives the issuer visibility in the global capital market. All this makes the rating an important financial marketing instrument that can be used to improve access to new investors. Apart from the image-building effect, companies also benefit from an expanded funding base, which offers new strategic flexibility and independence.

The Rating Advisory Service primarily focuses on developing solutions to complex rating issues such as:

- Identifying and weighting the relevant rating factors.
- Peer benchmarking.
- Capital structure advice.
- Effective presentation of the credit story.
- Management coaching.
- Strategies for improving the rating (in strategic, operational, and accounting terms).

A rating agency's assessment of a company's credit standing is a complex process that needs to take numerous different factors into account and may quickly test the limits of a financial department's internal resources. This makes rating advisory an integral element of the rating process that is necessary to make sure that a company secures the best possible rating. So-called Chinese Walls ensure that the information made available to the bank is treated absolutely confidentially; there is no exchange of information within the bank.[38]

Long-term Ratings

Long-term ratings are an evaluation of the degree of certainty of interest and principal payments against long-term obligation. Analysis of the default risk — i.e., the likelihood of default — is the central element of the evaluation, but it also takes account of recovery risk — i.e., the extent to which the loss may occur in the event of default. The main task lies in the credit risk analysis and sees the repayment ability of an issuer's total financial obligation. This evaluation embraces many factors of a company's credit quality and is called "Issuer Rating." The next step takes into account the recovery risk of individual debts.

The major source of funds for meeting the interest and principal payments on bonds and other financial obligations is the cash flow generated from the company's core business activities. The more copious and stable a company's cash flow, the greater the certainty that it will be able to meet its interest and principal payments.

Companies that invest aggressively in plant and equipment and in affiliated companies are aiming for long-term growth. Furthermore, companies that are highly motivated in the field of research and development (R&D) may find their cash flow reduced by R&D related costs. In such cases, the rating evaluation needs to examine a range of factors including the effectiveness of this advance investment and its impact on the company's finances.[39]

Key Financial Indicators Considered Rating Assessments

Return on Assets (ROA)

ROA is a useful indicator of how profitable a company is relative to its total assets. Calculated by dividing a company's annual earnings by its total assets, ROA is displayed as a percentage. Sometimes this is referred to as "return on investment" (www.answers.com/topic/return-on-assets).

Return on Business Assets (ROBA)

Earnings before interest and tax (EBIT) divided by business assets (working capital requirement plus net fixed assets). A measure of operating profitability (www.asba.com/capital-resource/glossaryoffinancialterms.aspx#R).

Net Debt Ratio

Debt management ratios (solvency ratios) are also called the gearing ratios. These are mostly used by providers of finance to assess the finance risk of the business. A business with a large proportion of debt capital to equity capital is said to be high geared.

Long-term solvency has to do with the business's ability to survive for many years. The aim of long-term solvency analysis is to point out early that a business is on the road to bankruptcy. Declining profitability and liquidity ratios are key signs of possible business failure. As indicated earlier on, the ratios on their own carries less business meaning unless interpreted together with other non-financial indicators, such as loss of key suppliers, threatened litigation against the business, failure to settle liabilities, and failure to adapt to new technologies.

Increasing amounts of debt in a business's capital structure mean that the business is becoming heavily geared. This condition negatively affects long-term solvency because it represents increasing legal obligations to pay interest periodically and principal at maturity. Failure to make these payments can result in bankruptcy.

Business still require debt capital. In spite of its riskiness, debt is a flexible means of financing a certain business operation. Interest on debt is allowed for tax purposes as opposed to equity dividends paid. Debt capital avoids dilution of ownership for original members of the business as opposed to issuing new shares. Also because debt usually carries a fixed interest charge, the cost of financing can be limited and the gearing can be used to advantage. If a business can earn a return on assets greater than the cost of debt (interest), it makes overall profit. However, it runs the risk of not earning a return on assets equal to the cost of financing those assets, thus incurring a loss.

The business with relatively high gearing ratios have a high expected return when the economy is normal as debt offers a cheaper source of capital. When the economy goes into recession these businesses will be exposed to loss as the interest rates increases not matching with the expected return on business assets (http://cbdd.wsu.edu/kewlcontent/cdoutput/TOM505/page25.htm).

In practice, analysts use both gross debt and net debt to compute debt ratios. Gross debt refers to all debt outstanding in a firm. Net debt is the difference between gross debt and the cash balance of the firm. For instance, a firm with $1.25 billion in interest-bearing debt outstanding and a cash balance of $1 billion has a net debt balance of $250 million. The practice of netting cash against debt is common in both Latin America and Europe and the debt ratios are usually estimated using net debt.

It is generally safer to value a firm based upon gross debt outstanding and to add the cash balance outstanding to the value of operating assets to arrive at the firm value. The interest payment on total debt is then entitled to the tax benefits of debt and we can assess the effect of whether the company invests its cash balances efficiently on value (http://pages.stern.nyu.edu/~adamodar/New_Home_Page/valquestions/whatisdebt.htm).

Ratio of Debt to Operating Cash Flow

Total liabilities divided by operating cash flow. The percentage of cash flow to total liabilities, current and long-term (www.ammbit.com/CPA/HelpDocs/HelpDefinitions.asp?Definition=).

Interest Coverage Ratio

If a business is highly geared it will be paying more interest. The ratio measures the ability of the business to pay interest to its lenders. Low interest cover is associated with high gearing. The interest cover ratio shows whether a company is earning enough profits before interest and tax to pay its interest cost comfortably, or whether its interest cost are high in relation to the size of its profit, so that a fall in profit before interest and taxation (PBIT) would then have a significant effect on profits available for ordinary shareholders (http://cbdd.wsu.edu/kewlcontent/cdoutput/TOM505/page25.htm).

K. Mergers and Acquisitions

Across the financial services sector, growth in all forms is firmly back on the agenda. As margins continue to tighten, the impetus for further consolidation is likely to strengthen as organizations seek to build scale, improve volume, and exploit opportunities for cost-saving synergies.

Focus On Restructuring: The Drivers Shaping The Financial Services Sector [www.pwcglobal.com/images/gx/eng/fs/1103eiubrief.pdf], a study carried out by PricewaterhouseCoopers in partnership with the Economist Intelligence Unit (October 2003), found that more than 90 percent of financial services executives believed that restructuring would be "important, very important, or integral" in helping them meet their goals.

However, there is unlikely to be a return to the freewheeling mega deal-making that transformed the sector in the 1990s. Winning investor backing for large-scale "visionary" acquisitions continues to prove difficult in today's risk-sensitive market environment. As a result, many institutions are looking to expand incrementally or focusing on particular products and services.

Securing investor support is likely to require exacting valuation, due diligence, and communication. Investor scrutiny will only be heightened by the move to International Financial Reporting Standards which will make it easier for the market to judge the relative success or failure of any particular deal (www.pwcglobal.com/extweb/industry.nsf/docid/CB8103D46FD04B5D85257013005CEA23).

The Financial Services M&A: Review of and Outlook for Mergers and Acquisitions in the European Financial Services Market – 2005 report analyzes the deals and trends in the financial services sector across Europe in 2004 and provides insight into some of the factors that may shape European Financial Services M&A going forward. The PricewaterhouseCoopers report can be read in further detail at www.pwcglobal.com/extweb/pwcpublications.nsf/docid/B993A106FA5E760B8525702D0048230C/$File/fsma.pdf

Some of the key findings in this report include:

1. 2004 saw deal values increase for the second year running with c. €45 billion of financial services deals announced in the year, an increase of c. €11 billion from 2003;
2. 2004 saw an increase in the value of financial services deal activity across all sectors (banking, insurance, asset management, and other) when compared to 2003;

3. Cross-border deals accounted for over 60 percent of all financial services M&A (measured by value) announced in 2004;
4. 2004 saw an increased appetite from Private Equity investors (www.pwcglobal.com/extweb/pwcpublications.nsf/docid/b993a106fa5e760b8525702d0048230c).

Steps in the typical mergers and acquisitions process are outlined in Figure 3.0.[40]

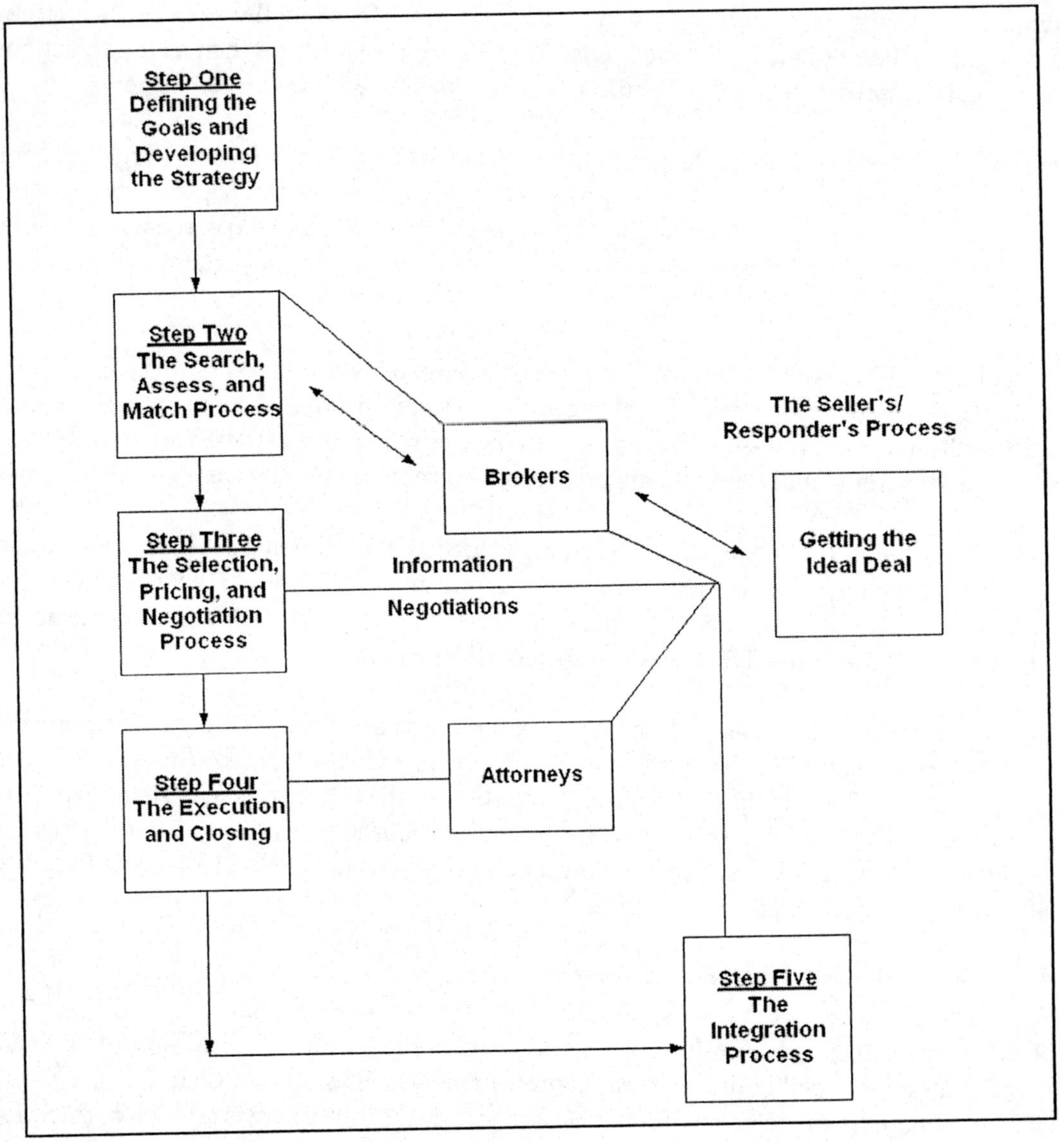

Figure 3.0

According to Joseph Bower, in his article, "Not All M&As Are Alike – And That Matters," the general public knows very little about the essence of M&As. In fact, for the majority of individuals, the collective total knowledge of M&As can be summarized as such:

- Acquirers usually pay too much.
- Friendly deals done using stock often perform well.
- CEOs fall in love with deals and don't walk away when they should.
- Integration is hard to pull off, but a few companies do it well, consistently.

Bower explains further that acquisitions occur for five reasons:

1. To deal with overcapacity through consolidation in mature industries;
2. To roll up competitors in geographically fragmented industries;
3. To extend into new products or markets;
4. As a substitute for R&D; and
5. To exploit eroding industry boundaries by inventing an industry.[41]

A further examination of the topic — mergers and acquisitions is addressed in the Insurance Discipline, Section B - Processes. The candidate is strongly encouraged to read and to review this additional in-depth study of mergers and acquisitions in preparation for this certification exam.

L. Loan Operations (e.g., Collateral Issues, Perfecting Liens)

"The examiner's evaluation of the loan portfolio involves much more than merely appraising individual loans. Prudent management and administration of the overall loan account, including establishment of sound lending and collection policies, are of vital importance if the bank is to be continuously operated in an acceptable manner. Lending policies should be clearly defined and set forth in such a manner as to provide effective supervision by the directors and senior officers.

The board of directors of every bank has the legal responsibility to formulate lending policies and to supervise their implementation. Therefore examiners should encourage establishment and maintenance of written, up-to-date lending policies which have been approved by the board of directors. A lending policy should not be a static document, but must be reviewed periodically and revised in light of changing circumstances surrounding the borrowing needs of the bank's customers as well as changes that may occur within the bank itself.

To a large extent, the economy of the community served by the bank dictates the composition of the loan portfolio. The widely divergent circumstances of regional economies and the considerable variance in characteristics of individual loans preclude establishment of standard or universal lending policies (from DSC Risk Management Manual of Examination Policies, Federal Deposit Insurance Corporation, LOANS, section 3.2.1, www.fdic.gov/regulations/safety/manual/section3-2.pdf)

Collateral — The property which is subject to a lien. A creditor with rights in collateral is a secured creditor and has additional protections in the Bankruptcy Code for the claim secured by collateral. The measure of the secured claim is the value of the collateral available to secure the claim: it is possible to have a lien on property that is subject to a senior lien or liens such that the security available to pay the claim is really without value to the junior creditor. The general rule with respect to liens is "First in time, first in right.[42]

The International Swaps and Derivatives Association, Inc. ("ISDA") is the global trade association representing participants in the privately negotiated derivatives industry, a business covering swaps and options across all asset classes (interest rate, currency, commodity, energy, credit and equity). ISDA was chartered in 1985, and today numbers over 600 member institutions from 46 countries on six continents. These members include most of the world's major institutions who deal in, as well as leading end-users of, privately negotiated derivatives. The membership also includes associated service providers and consultants.

Since its inception, ISDA has pioneered efforts to identify and reduce the sources of risk in the derivatives and risk management business. Among its most notable accomplishments are: developing the ISDA Master Agreement; publishing a wide range of related documentation materials and instruments covering a variety of transaction types; producing legal opinions on the enforceability of netting and collateral arrangements (available only to ISDA members); securing recognition of the risk reducing effects of netting in determining capital requirements; promoting sound risk management practices, and advancing the understanding and treatment of derivatives and risk management from public policy and regulatory capital perspectives.

The word "collateral" comes from the Latin collateralis, which means something that is to the side, or not direct. In the case of a privately negotiated derivatives transaction, the essential mechanism by which collateralization works is to provide an asset of value that is to the side of the primary transaction; in the event of default on the primary transaction, the collateral receiver has recourse to the collateral asset and can thus indirectly make good any loss suffered.

In 2005, the ISDA produced the ISDA Collateral Guidelines. The 2005 ISDA Collateral Guidelines (the "2005 Guidelines") update and considerably expand upon the themes of the 1998 ISDA Guidelines for Collateral Practitioners.

The objectives of the document are to:

- Document the current state of collateral management in the privately negotiated derivatives market;
- Discuss the nature and mechanics of collateralization;
- Describe how the collateral management function operates and interacts with other parts of the firm;
- Identify the benefits and risks of collateralization; and
- Outline current trends and possible future developments in the field.

Collateralization in the privately negotiated derivatives market has grown at a sustained, rapid pace over the past decade. At the end of 2003 (the date of the last published ISDA Margin Survey), in excess of US$1 trillion in collateral was reported to be in circulation, across more than 54,000 collateral agreements.

Collateral is a form of credit risk mitigation. Coupled with other techniques such as traditional credit analysis, capital reserving strategies, netting, selective termination, and credit derivatives, collateralization is part of an ever more sophisticated toolset available to credit risk managers.

Collateralization operates through improving the recovery rate in a post-default situation, and thus decreases the loss given default. This leads to lower expected losses in a collateralized portfolio, and thus allows both economic and regulatory capital reserves to be reduced. Where firms explicitly or implicitly charge for credit risk when pricing deals, this can improve deal pricing.

However, collateralization introduces other risks, principally legal and operational, in exchange for the beneficial effects on credit risk. These other forms of risk need to be carefully weighed against the benefits and appropriate risk measurement and management strategies put in place.

The collateral management function performs a range of important and unique roles within a firm. The function is most often located organizationally within operations or credit, but regardless of organization it must interface with sales and marketing, corporate treasury, legal, credit, operations, and controlling functions.

This cross-functional role places special demands upon collateral practitioners. Even as certain commoditized parts of the collateral management function are outsourced by some firms, the importance of the staff performing more value-added and risk-oriented roles are being increased.

Collateral agreements for the privately negotiated derivatives market are most often documented using the several available forms of ISDA credit support document.

Through the work of ISDA and individual firms, the legal risk issues relating to collateralization have been well characterized. Effective risk mitigation or avoidance strategies exist for most legal risk issues. Extensive research into this area continues and multinational efforts are underway to clarify or improve certain key points of law in this field.

The process of making calls for collateral (or "margin calls") has become a well-defined and operationally sophisticated procedure at most firms. In those firms, it starts with active involvement by collateral practitioners in the design, negotiation, and setup of new collateral agreements.

The day-to-day processes of portfolio reconciliation, collateral adequacy computation (i.e., computing whether the amount of collateral currently held is adequate as compared to the amount required to be held under the collateral agreement), calling for margin, and the subsequent settlement cycles are well established and consistent across the market.

The timing of margin calls has typically been accelerated over recent years, especially in the case of collateralized relationships between banks and hedge funds. This acceleration has reduced risk in this segment of the market, and also led to operational simplification, because margin calls are made often and settled within the same business day. The penalty has been increased operational tempo, which has been addressed through staffing and technology investments.

The selection of collateral assets is a critical factor in the overall success of a collateral agreement. There is a wide range of selection criteria that should be considered, including the price volatility, liquidity, and credit quality of the assets.

Valuing transactions and collateral assets is a necessary part of the collateralization process. This is a complex area with some diversity of practice across the market. It is, however, an area where firms are focusing considerable energy because of the synergies with the broader need to provide client valuation statements.

A clear trend across the market is the move toward greater automation between firms. Whereas great investments have been made in the technology used within firms to manage privately negotiated derivatives and the related collateral process, the technological links between firms are now receiving attention. Key to this is the emergence of data standards, which permit all firms to communicate in a common language. The Financial Products Mark-up Language ("FpML") initiative managed by ISDA and the related Electronic Data Interchange standard sponsored by the ISDA Collateral Committee have led to some advances in this field.

An emerging trend is the convergence seen between certain parts of collateral management, prime brokerage, exchange-traded derivatives, and client service. Driven very much from the client perspective, some firms recognize the reporting, operational, risk management, and client service synergies that exist between these different disciplines, and moving to capitalize on them.[43]

Candidates interested in reading the complete 2005 report should point their browsers to www.isda.org/publications/pdf/2005isdacollateralguidelines.pdf.

A tax depositary is required to hold collateral with the local Federal Reserve Bank equal to the depositary's main account balance to ensure that the Treasury's funds are secured.

Pledged collateral consists of the following:

Book-entry

Book-entry securities, both Treasury and government agency securities, can be deposited in a collateral account at the local Federal Reserve Bank, through the National Book-Entry System (NBES). The National Book-entry System is the central securities application of the Federal Reserve System. NBES was designed to standardize services to depository institutions regardless of district and to facilitate centralized computer processing at a single site.

Definitive

Definitive collateral consists of securities represented by actual (physical) documents. This can include securities in bearer or registered form or customer notes, which can be held by the local Federal Reserve Bank.

Third/Fourth Party

In certain cases, definitive collateral may be held off-premises by designated third- or fourth-party custodians. These custodians, authorized by the Federal Reserve, can hold collateral on behalf of the depositary through a custody agreement.[44]

The Treasury Tax and Loan (TT&L) Service enables a financial institution to collect federal tax payments from its customers and retain these funds at a competitive rate of interest. These funds can provide an institution with a ready source of liquidity.

Two systems, the Treasury Investment Program (TIP) and the Paper Tax System (PATAX), assist in the tax collection and investment process for both financial institutions and the Treasury.

The Treasury Investment Program (TIP)

The Treasury Investment Program (TIP), invests excess Treasury funds for federal tax payments, as well as other unused funds that reside in the treasurer's general account, by placing them with participating financial institutions. The financial institutions are charged interest for the use of invested funds and return the funds when the Treasury needs money to meet its financial obligations.

TIP receives summarized tax deposit information from the three electronic tax payment mechanisms: the Federal Reserve Electronic Tax Application (FR-ETA), the Electronic Federal Tax Payment

System (EFTPS), and the Paper Tax System (PATAX). This information is stored in TIP and used to provide near-real-time balances and capacity data to the Treasury. The Treasury uses this information to project the funds needed to maintain its daily working balance — projections that also help it decide whether to invest or withdraw funds from participating financial institutions' TIP accounts.

Using collateral information received from the National Book Entry System (NBES) and the Collateral Management System (CMS), TIP also prevents collateral deficiencies by monitoring the collateral pledged for the various TIP investment accounts. TIP provides similar collateral-monitoring capabilities for 31 CFR Part 202 and 31 CFR Part 225 accounts.[45]

Electronic Federal Tax Payment System

To facilitate the collection and reporting of federal tax payments, the Treasury and IRS created the Electronic Federal Tax Payment System (EFTPS). This system has been specifically designed to interface with the Treasury Tax and Loan (TT&L) Service, making it a convenient and efficient way for banks to report and pay federal taxes for its clients/customers.

Federal tax payments can be processed through EFTPS by future-day or same-day mechanisms.

Future-day Payments

The majority of taxpayers should use ACH Debit or ACH Credit to report and pay their taxes.

ACH Debit

At least one day prior to the tax due date, taxpayers access EFTPS through the Internet, a touch-tone telephone or PC software. Based upon this input, an ACH Debit is originated to the banking institution. As a retainer or investor institution, the bank will receive a credit to its TT&L account on the ACH settlement date. Collector and non-TT&L institutions' reserve accounts are debited on the ACH settlement data.

ACH Credit

At a taxpayer's request, the institution would originate an ACH credit to the U.S. Treasury at least one business day before the tax due date. As a retainer or investor institution, the institution will receive a credit to its TT&L account on the ACH settlement date. Collector and non-TT&L institutions' reserve accounts are debited on the ACH settlement data.

Same-day Payments

A same-day reporting mechanism, via Fedwire®, is available for taxpayers who cannot report their tax liability one day in advance of the tax due date via ACH. Two same-day methods exist:

Fedwire Value

Like other Fedwire funds transfers, this option settles immediately by debiting the institution and crediting the Treasury. Summary transaction information is passed to TT&L. For retainer and investor institutions, assuming that the institution has sufficient capacity, TT&L will increase the balance in the institution's TT&L account, credit the institution or the institution's correspondent's reserve account, and debit the Treasury.

Fedwire Non-value

This option settles the tax deposit through the TT&L system at the end of the day. For retainer and investor institutions, assuming that the institution has sufficient capacity, TT&L will increase the balance in the institution's TT&L account and the Treasury receives a notification of credit for the tax payment. A collector or non-TT&L institution receives a debit to its reserve account or to the designated correspondent's reserve account and the Treasury receives the credit.[46]

Treasury Tax and Loan Service (PATAX)

The Paper Tax System (PATAX) is used to collect, adjust, and report all paper-based federal tax deposits (FTDs). Upon receipt of FTDs from taxpayers, a financial institution enters its Advices of Credit (AOCs) via FedLine or the PATAX National Voice Response System. After the AOCs are submitted and verified, PATAX processes and transmits the information to the Treasury Investment Program (TIP) application. Ultimately, TIP collects the funds through charges to the financial institution and transmits the information to the Internal Revenue Service (IRS).

PATAX also processes adjustment requests from financial institutions and the IRS for paper tax payments and monitors the collateral pledged for in-transit balances.

PATAX Primary Functions

Processes Advices of Credit (AOCs)

- Processes AOCs and sends summarized information to TIP hourly
- Sends AOC information to all IRS service centers
- Creates totals (vouchers) for each IRS service center and sends to TIP during end-of-day processing
- Produces daily AOC processing reports
- Calculates late fees for AOCs
- Charges financial institutions for stale/undated FTDs
- Processes compensation payments to financial institutions
- Processes missing deposits and replacement cards

Processes Adjustments

- Requests and receives adjustments from IRS
- Processes adjustments/reconciles with IRS and financial institutions
- Sends hourly increase/decrease adjustments to TIP

Monitors Collateral for In-transit Balances

- Receives main account and collateral balances from TIP
- Considers eligible insurance
- Calculates and report collateral deficiencies[47]

Counterparty Risk Management

Counterparty risk management has been materially assisted by the widespread use of master agreements for derivatives transactions. In the event of a counterparty's default, such agreements permit the termination of all transactions with the counterparty and the netting of the resulting gains and losses. For many years, market participants have been putting such master agreements in place and working with legislatures to ensure that national laws support the enforceability of netting. Data reported by U.S. banks indicate that, on average, netting now reduces counterparty exposures by almost three-fourths.

Even with wider use of netting, however, the outsized growth of derivatives markets has resulted in ever-larger counterparty exposures. Market participants have increasingly responded by entering into collateral agreements to further mitigate counterparty credit risks. Such agreements typically permit counterparties to derivatives transactions to demand collateral if their net credit exposure exceeds a negotiated threshold amount. The threshold often varies with the credit rating of the counterparty: The lower a counterparty's credit rating, the smaller the threshold. If its credit rating falls below investment grade, a counterparty is often required to over-collateralize its counterparties' exposures. In effect, it becomes obligated to meet a margin requirement.

Collateral agreements are a very effective means of limiting counterparty credit risks. At the same time, they increase market participants' exposures to other types of risk, especially funding-liquidity risks. Once a counterparty has agreed to collateralize its derivatives contracts, day-to-day declines in the value of those contracts expose it to immediate demands for more collateral. Furthermore, the practice of tying the size of thresholds and margin requirements to credit ratings exposes a counterparty to extraordinary demands for collateral if its rating is downgraded. Collateral demands arising from rating downgrades may be especially costly to meet because a downgrade would reduce the availability of funding and increase its costs at the same time.[48]

Key Collateral Issues

Federal Agency Securities Market

Federal agency debt is issued by various government-sponsored enterprises (GSEs) which were created by Congress to fund loans to borrowers such as homeowners, farmers, and students. Through the creation of GSEs, the government addressed various public policy concerns about the ability of members of these groups to borrow sufficient funds at affordable rates. Most GSEs rely primarily on debt financing for their day-to-day operations. Among the most active issuers of agency debt securities are: Federal Farm Credit System Banks, Federal Home Loan Banks, Federal Home Loan Mortgage Corporation (Freddie Mac), Federal National Mortgage Association (Fannie Mae), Student Loan Marketing Association (Sallie Mae), and Tennessee Valley Authority (TVA). There is an estimated $2.3 trillion in agency debt currently outstanding.[49]

Mortgage-backed Securities

Mortgage-backed securities (MBS) are debt obligations that represent claims to the cash flows from pools of mortgage loans, most commonly on residential property. Mortgage loans are purchased from banks, mortgage companies, and other originators and then assembled into pools by a governmental, quasi-governmental, or private entity. The entity then issues securities that represent claims on the principal and interest payments made by borrowers on the loans in the pool, a process known as securitization.

Most MBSs are issued by the Government National Mortgage Association (Ginnie Mae), a U.S. government agency, or the Federal National Mortgage Association (Fannie Mae) and the Federal Home Loan Mortgage Corporation (Freddie Mac), U.S. government-sponsored enterprises. Ginnie Mae, backed by the full faith and credit of the U.S. government, guarantees that investors receive timely payments. Fannie Mae and Freddie Mac also provide certain guarantees and, while not backed by the full faith and credit of the U.S. government, have special authority to borrow from the U.S. Treasury. Some private institutions, such as brokerage firms, banks, and homebuilders, also securitize mortgages, known as "private-label" mortgage securities.

Mortgage-backed securities exhibit a variety of structures. The most basic types are pass-through participation certificates, which entitle the holder to a pro-rata share of all principal and interest payments made on the pool of loan assets. More complicated MBSs, known as collaterized mortgage obligations or mortgage derivatives, may be designed to protect investors from or expose investors to various types of risk. An important risk with regard to residential mortgages involves prepayments, typically because homeowners refinance when interest rates fall. Absent protection, such prepayments would return principal to investors precisely when their options for reinvesting those funds may be relatively unattractive.[50]

Valuation Date and Valuation Time

Valuation in the context of collateral management generally refers not only to the aggregation of value of exposure-bearing trades but also to the mitigating collateral positions and movements and the agreement terms and conditions that contribute to the production of credit support obligations.

Valuation Agent

The valuation agent is the institution responsible for the publication of credit support obligations (delivery and return amounts) relating to collateralized arrangements. Commonly, whichever party to an agreement is the collateral taker on the valuation date and valuation time will also become the valuation agent. In some circumstances, this role is always taken by one party and not the other, and in other circumstances, the responsibility will lie with a third party. In extremiis, for example during dispute resolution or when processing a default, a third party will be instructed to provide valuations for all relevant trades.[51]

Rehypothecation

Rehypothecation refers to when a broker pledges hypothecated client-owned securities in a margin account to secure a bank loan. This is also known as a margin loan. Pledging to banks by securities brokers of the amount in customers' margin account as collateral for broker loans, which are used to cover margin loans to customers for margin purchases and selling short.[52]

Hypothecation is the posting of collateral to secure an obligation. Rehypothecation is the reuse of posted collateral. For example, if an institution receives collateral from a counterparty to secure an obligation, that institution may rehypothecate the collateral by lending it, repoing it, or posting it as collateral for one of its own obligations to a third party.

Rehypothecation is not permitted in some jurisdictions. It is common practice in the United States. Any collateral agreement should explicitly permit or not permit rehypothecation.

Repurchase Agreement (Repo)

A repurchase agreement (or repo) is an agreement between two parties whereby one party sells the other a security at a specified price with a commitment to buy the security back at a later date for another specified price.

Most repos are overnight transactions, with the sale taking place one day and being reversed the next day. Long-term repos — called term repos — can extend for a month or more. Usually, repos are for a fixed period of time, but open-ended deals are also possible. Reverse repo is a term used to describe the opposite side of a repo transaction. The party who sells and later repurchases a security is said to perform a repo. The other party — who purchases and later resells the security — is said to perform a reverse repo.

While a repo is legally the sale and subsequent repurchase of a security, its economic effect is that of a secured loan. Economically, the party purchasing the security makes funds available to the seller and holds the security as collateral. If the repoed security pays a dividend, coupon or partial redemptions during the repo, this is returned to the original owner. The difference between the sale and repurchase prices paid for the security represent interest on the loan. Indeed, repos are quoted as interest rates.

Securities dealers use repos to finance their securities inventories. They repo their inventories, rolling the repos from one day to the next. Counterparties may be institutions, such as money market funds, who have short-term funds to invest, or they may be parties who wish to briefly obtain use of a particular security. For example, a party may want to sell the security short, or they may need to deliver the security to settle a trade with another party.

Accordingly, there are two possible motives for entering into a reverse repo:

1. Short-term investment of funds, or
2. To obtain temporary use of a particular security.

In the latter case, the security is called a special security. In the former case, it is called general collateral or GC.

Interest rates payable on special repos tend to be lower than those payable on GC repos. This is because a party reverse repoing a special security will accept a reduced interest rate on its funds in exchange for receiving the special security it requires. Economically, the transaction is no different from cash collateralized securities lending. Pricing of either type of deal depends upon demand for the desired security.

Because repos are essentially secured loans, their interest rates do not depend upon the respective counterparties' credit qualities. For GC repos, the same rates apply for all counterparties. Accordingly, GC repo rates — or simply repo rates — are benchmark short-term interest rates that are widely quoted in the marketplace. They differ from Libor rates in that they are for secured loans whereas Libor rates are for unsecured loans.

Libor stands for London interbank offered rate. It refers to any of a number of short-term indicative interest rates compiled by the British Bankers Association (BBA) at 11:00 A.M. London time each business day. For a given currency and maturity, Libor represents the simple interest rate at which banks are willing to lend to each other. As a practical matter, it is the rate other banks must pay to borrow.[53]

Glossary

Advances — Payments made by the servicer on delinquent loans. In addition to principal and interest, administration rate advances can be required for property protection, taxes, insurance, and foreclosure costs. The servicer has a proxy claim to subsequent collections and foreclosure proceeds as reimbursement for advances up to an amount that was determined "recoverable." Servicers do not have to advance fees that are deemed "non-recoverable" by the trustee or an officer of the servicers. Servicers are usually paid prime plus 1% for their advances (www.mccarystevens.com/cssa_intro.pdf).

Amortization — The process of paying off a loan by gradually reducing the balance through a series of installment payments, or the process of writing off mortgage servicing assets on a bank's balance sheet.

Appraisal Reduction — Upon certain events based on loan delinquency, an appraisal will be made to determine if the property value justifies any further advances by the master servicer. If the value is reduced below the loan balance plus authorized advances, the master servicer will stop or reduce principal and interest payments on that loan to the trustee. The trustee will then reduce principal and interest payments to the certificate holders in order of their priority, beginning with the first-loss security (www.mccarystevens.com/cssa_intro.pdf).

Basis Risk — Refers to the risk of the underlying mortgage loans and offered certificates tied to different indices. It is the possibility of the certificate accruing interest at higher interest rates than the underlying mortgage loans. When the aggregate amount of interest on the certificates is greater than the collateral, the amount is known as the basis risk shortfall (www.mccarystevens.com/cssa_intro.pdf).

Broker — (1) An individual or a firm that charges a fee or commission for executing buy and sell orders submitted by another individual or firm. (2) The role of a brokerage firm when it acts as an agent for a customer and charges the customer for its services (www.sia.com/capitol_hill/html/glossary.html).

Broker-dealer — A securities firm that is acting as a broker or intermediary and/or a dealer or principal in a transaction. Most securities firms act in both capacities (www.sia.com/capitol_hill/html/glossary.html).

Capitalize — Converting a series of anticipated cash flows into present value by discounting them at an established rate of return.

CESR — Committee of European Securities Regulators, formerly known as FESCO.

Clearinghouse Interbank Payments System (CHIPS) — An automated clearing system used primarily for international payments. This system is owned and operated by the New York Clearinghouse banks and engages Fedwire for settlement.

Collateral-dependent — A collateral-dependent loan relies solely on the operation or sale of the collateral for repayment. In evaluating the overall risk associated with a loan, examiners consider a number of factors, including the character, overall financial condition and resources, and payment record of the borrower; the prospects for support from any financially responsible guarantors; and the nature and degree of protection provided by the cash flow and value of any underlying collateral. However, as other sources of repayment become inadequate over time, the importance of the collateral's value necessarily increases and the loan may become collateral dependent.

COMC — Code of Market Conduct gives guidance to market participants to help determine whether or not their behavior amounts to market abuse. (Broadly speaking, market abuse is defined as the misuse of information, the giving of false or misleading impressions, and market distortion.) (www.fsa.gov.uk/pages/Doing/UKLA/pdf/members.pdf).

Comptroller of the Currency — An officer of the Treasury Department responsible for chartering national banks and has primary supervisory authority over them. All national banks are required to be members of the Federal Reserve System and are insured by the Federal Deposit Insurance Corporation (www.tgbr.com/tgbr/terms.html#r).

Conditional Prepayment Rate (CPR) — A standard of measurement of the projected annual rate of prepayment for amortgage loan or pool of loans. Although the standard CPR is 6% per year, it can be quoted at any percentage. For example, a 10.5% CPR assumes that 10.5% of the outstanding balance of a mortgage pool will prepay each year.

Dealer — The role of a securities firm when it acts as a principal in a trade. A firm acts as a dealer when it buys or sells a security for its own account and at its own risk and then charges the customer a markup or markdown. Any person who is engaged in the business of buying and selling securities for his or her own account either directly or through a broker is considered a dealer (www.sia.com/capitol_hill/html/glossary.html).

Debt Service Coverage Ratio (DSCR) — Measures a mortgaged property's ability to cover monthly payments, defined as the ratio of net operating income over the mortgage payments. A DSCR less than 1.0 means that there is insufficient cash flow by the property to cover debt payments (www.mccarystevens.com/cssa_intro.pdf).

Depository Institution — A financial institution that obtains its funds mainly through deposits from the public. This includes commercial banks, savings and loan associations, savings banks, and credit unions. Although historically they have specialized in certain types of credit, non-bank depository institutions have broadened their powers in recent years. For example, NOW accounts, credit union share drafts, and other services similar to checking accounts may be offered by thrift institutions.

Discount Rate — The time value of money can be interpreted as the rate at which individuals are willing to trade present for future consumption, or the opportunity cost of capital. Mathematically, the discount rate represents the rate at which future dollars are converted into present value. This rate can be used to calculate the present value of future cash flow streams generated by mortgage servicing rights.

Due Diligence — The legal definition: due diligence is a measure of prudence, activity, or assiduity, as is properly to be expected from, and ordinarily exercised by, a reasonable and prudent person under the particular circumstances; not measured by any absolute standard but depends on the relative facts of the special case. In commercial mortgage-backed security(ies) [CMBS], due diligence is the foundation of the process because of the reliance securities investors must place on the specific expertise of the professionals involved in the transaction. It is physically and financially impossible for most CMBS investors to perform the many duties required to prepare, analyze, deliver, and service commercial mortgages. Due diligence protects these investors from unethical improprieties and unprofessional practices. Prevailing industry standards are used as the primary benchmark from which prudence is judged. Due diligence is said to be the cornerstone of securities law (www.mccarystevens.com/cssa_intro.pdf).

Effective Interest Rate — Under FAS 114, a loan's "effective interest rate" is the contractual rate of interest adjusted for any net deferred loan fees, costs, premium, or discount existing at the origination or acquisition of the loan. For a loan that has been restructured in accordance with FAS 15, the Financial Accounting Standards Board has concluded that it is appropriate to use the effective interest rate in the original loan agreement to discount the expected future cash flows.

Escrow — The portion of the borrower's monthly payments held by the servicer to pay taxes, insurance, mortgage insurance (if required), and other related expenses as they become due. In some parts of the U.S., escrows are also called impounds or reserves.

Excess Reserves — Amount of reserves held by an institution in excess of its reserve requirement and required clearing balance.

Fair Value — FAS 15 defines the fair value of assets transferred to a creditor as the amount that the debtor could reasonably expect to receive for them in a current sale between a willing buyer and a willing seller, that is, other than in a forced or liquidation sale. Fair value of assets shall be measured by their market value if an active market for them exists. If no active market exists for the assets transferred but exists for similar assets, the selling price in that market may be helpful in estimating the fair value of the assets transferred. If no market price is available, a forecast of expected cash flows may aid in estimating the fair value of assets transferred, provided the expected cash flows are discounted at a rate commensurate with the risk involved.

Federal Reserve System — The central bank of the United States, created by Congress and made up of a seven-member Board of Governors in Washington, D.C., 12 regional Federal Reserve Banks, and their 25 branches (www.tgbr.com/tgbr/terms.html#r).

Fedwire — Electronic funds transfer network operated by the Federal Reserve. Fedwire is usually used to transfer large amounts of funds and U.S. government securities from one institution's account at the Federal Reserve to another institution's account. It is also used by the U.S. Department of the Treasury and other federal agencies to collect and disburse funds (www.tgbr.com/tgbr/terms.html#r).

Financial Institution — An institution that uses its funds chiefly to purchase financial assets (loans, securities) as opposed to tangible property. Financial institutions can be classified according to the nature of the principal claims they issue (www.tgbr.com/tgbr/terms.html#r).

Float — In mortgage servicing, the period of time between receipt of a borrower's loan payment and remittance of funds to investors.

Gross Spread — The difference between what the issuing company gets from the bankers for the securities and what the investors pay to the banker is called the "gross spread." The gross spread or spread represents the gross income from underwriting and selling. Out of this income the bankers would have to pay all of the expenses associated with the purchase and sale of the securities and their other expenses.

Government-sponsored Enterprise (GSE) — A private organization with a government charter and backing. The Federal Home Loan Mortgage Corporation and the Federal National Mortgage Association are GSEs.

Hurdle Rate — A break-even debt service calculation that establishes the maximum interest rate a mortgaged property can handle at maturity if the property must be refinanced. It is calculated using current net operating income and an interest-only mortgage with a reasonably short maturity of less than five years. (also called "Break Even Debt Service Analysis"). Usually calculated to answer the question, "Can all loans be refinanced at maturity, if interest rates are at a 'Disaster Rate?'" (www.mccarystevens.com/cssa_intro.pdf).

Incurred But Not Reported ("IBNR") Reserves — Reserves for estimated losses and loss adjustment expenses which have been incurred but not reported to the insurer or reinsurer, including future development of claims that have been reported to the insurer or reinsurer but where the established reserves may ultimately prove to be inadequate (www.converium.com/520.asp#Incurred%20But%20Not%20Reported%20).

I/O Strip (Interest Only Strip) — When a mortgage interest rate exceeds the interest rate paid on the security backed by the mortgage, the excess interest is "stripped" and sold as an I/O strip. The "strip" is usually described in the (notional) amount of the original security classes it was stripped from and then sold for pennies on the dollar basis. These are very volatile securities. As an example, if several loans prepay earlier than expected, there many not be an interest stream to pay the interest on the "strips" (www.mccarystevens.com/cssa_intro.pdf).

International Bank Account Number (IBAN) — The IBAN concept was developed by the European Committee for Banking Standards (ECBS) and the International Standards Organization (ISO) and is an internationally agreed standard ISO 13616: 1997. It was created as a viable and practical international bank identifier, used internationally to uniquely identify the account of a customer at a financial institution, to assist error-free cross-border payments and to improve the potential for payments STP (www.tgbr.com/tgbr/terms.html#r).

Liquidity — Quality that makes an asset easily convertible into cash with relatively little loss of value in the conversion process. Sometimes used more broadly to encompass credit in hand and promises of credit to meet needs for cash (www.tgbr.com/tgbr/terms.html#r).

Loan-to-value Ratio (LTV) — The ratio of the mortgage amount to the appraised value of the underlying property. Most mortgage lenders and secondary market participants set a maximum LTV for acceptable loans.

Loss Reserves — Reserves established by an insurer or reinsurer and recorded on its balance sheet to reflect the estimated cost of future payments for claims for which the insurer or reinsurer ultimately will be required to indemnify insureds or reinsureds in the future. Reserves are held in respect of losses occurred on or prior to the balance sheet date on insurance or reinsurance written and earned. Loss reserves are generally composed of individual case reserves for reported claims and IBNR reserves.

Master Servicer — Required to service to mortgage loans collateralizing a CMBS on behalf of and for the benefit of the certificate holders. Responsibilities vary according to the servicing agreement. Common responsibilities include (a) collection of mortgage payments and passing the funds to the trustee; (b) advancing any late payments to the trustee; (c) providing mortgage performance reports to bond holders; and (d) passing all loans to the special servicer that go into REO or non-performing (www.mccarystevens.com/cssa_intro.pdf).

Money Laundering — To move illegally acquired cash through financial systems so that it appears to be legally acquired (www.tgbr.com/tgbr/terms.html#r).

Mortgage Banker — An individual or firm that originates, purchases, sells, and/or services loans secured by mortgages on real property.

Mortgage Broker — An individual or firm that receives a commission for matching mortgage borrowers with lenders. Mortgage brokers typically do not fund the loans they help originate.

Negative Carry (also called Negative Spread) — In warehousing, the expense incurred when the interest rate paid for short-term warehouse financing is greater than the interest rate earned on the mortgages held in the warehouse.

OAS (Option Adjusted Spreads) — A technique first applied to residential MBS to price the prepayment risk an investor assumes in residential mortgage-backed securities. In residential MBS, borrowers have a legal "option" to pay off their loans when interest rates decline, thereby causing a reinvestment loss for the investor (www.mccarystevens.com/cssa_intro.pdf).

Originated Mortgage Servicing Rights (OMSR) — The right to service a mortgage loan acquired through loan origination activities. The servicer receives an income stream in the form of a contractual servicing fee every period until the maturity of the mortgage, prepayment, or default.

Pair-off Arrangement — A method to offset a commitment to sell and deliver mortgages. In this transaction, the seller liquidates its commitment to sell (forward sales contract) by paying the counterparty a fee. The amount of this pair-off fee equals the impact of the market movement on the price of mortgages covered under the commitment.

Participation Certificate (PC) — A mortgage pass-through security issued by the Federal Home Loan Mortgage Corporation that is backed by a pool of conventional mortgages purchased from a seller and in which the seller retains a 5% to 10% interest.

Pass-through Rate — The interest rate paid to the investors who purchase mortgage loans or mortgage-backed securities. Typically, the pass-through rate is less than the coupon rate of the underlying mortgage(s).

Pledged Account Mortgage (PAM) — A graduated payment loan in which part of the borrower's down payment is deposited into a savings account. Funds drawn from the account supplement the borrower's monthly payments during the early years of the mortgage.

Price Level Adjusted Mortgage (PLAM) — A mortgage loan in which the interest rate remains fixed, but the outstanding balance is adjusted for inflation periodically using an appropriate index such as the Consumer Price Index or Cost-of-Living Index. At the end of each period, the outstanding balance is adjusted for inflation and monthly payments are recomputed based on the new balance.

Principal Only Strips (POs) — A security that pays only the principal distributions from a pool of underlying loans. The interest cash flows from the underlying loans are paid to a separate interest only (IO) security. The cash flows from the underlying loans are thus "stripped" into two separate securities.Because the PO holder receives only principal distributions, the value of the PO rises when prepayments on the underlying loans increase, since a fixed amount of cash flow is received sooner than anticipated. As a result, mortgage bankers often use POs to hedge the value of servicing rights, which have cash flow risks similar to IO securities.

Private Placement — Securities or bonds that are sold to institutional investors who meet specific criteria of net worth and/or income and who are deemed to be sophisticated investors, e.g., insurance companies. Private placement securities are generally exempt from registration requirements of the Securities Act of 1933 (www.mccarystevens.com/cssa_intro.pdf).

Purchased Mortgage Servicing Rights (PMSR) — The rights to service a mortgage loan acquired by purchase. The servicer receives an income stream in the form of a contractual servicing fee for every period until the mortgage matures, is prepaid, or goes into default.

REIT (Real Estate Investment Trust) — A corporation formed to invest in real estate, mortgages, and/or securities backed by real estate. REITs are required to pass through 95% of taxable income to their investors and are not taxed at the corporate level. The three major types of REITs are equity, mortgage, and hybrid, with equity being the dominant type (www.mccarystevens.com/cssa_intro.pdf).

Reverse Annuity Mortgage (RAM) — A mortgage loan in which the lender makes periodic payments to the borrower in return for an increasing equity interest in the underlying property. RAMs are frequently made to retirees who own their residences outright.

Securities — The generic term applied to Certificates of Ownership of the funds or assets of a trust fund. These undivided interests are issued by the trustee in amounts of $100,000 until less than $100,000 is sold, then in amounts of $1000. The certificates are usually issued in lettered classes starting with Class A. There can be many classes if there are many different rated branches in a CMBS. Each class is risk-rated by a rating agency such as Standard & Poor's. If the higher risk first-loss class is included in the security and is sold instead of being held by the seller, the class is rated as "NR" (not rated). The "not rated" risk-rating is used for securities not qualifying for the minimum risk rate of B- (www.mccarystevens.com/cssa_intro.pdf).

Securities and Exchange Commission (SEC) — An independent, nonpartisan, quasi-judicial regulatory agency with responsibility for administering the federal securities laws. The purpose of these laws is to protect investors and to ensure that investors have access to disclosure of all material information concerning publicly traded securities. The Commission also regulates firms engaged in the purchase or sale of securities, people who provide investment advice, and investment companies.

Securitization — A term used to describe the process of raising funds through the sale of securities. It usually creates a new financial instrument representing an undivided interest in a segregated pool of assets such as commercial mortgages. The ownership of the assets is usually transferred to a legal trust or special purpose, bankruptcy-remote corporation to protect the interests of the security holders. (www.mccarystevens.com/cssa_intro.pdf).

Servicer — Institution acting for the benefit of the certificate holders in the administration of mortgage loans. Functions include collection of payments from borrowers, advancing funds for delinquent loans, and taking defaulted properties through the foreclosure process (www.mccarystevens.com/cssa_intro.pdf).

Servicing Runoff — Reduction in the principal of a servicing portfolio resulting from monthly payments, mortgage prepayments, and foreclosures. Runoff reduces future servicing fee income and other related cash flows as well as the current market value of the servicing portfolio.

Shared Appreciation Mortgage (SAM) — A mortgage loan in which the lender offers the borrower a below-market interest rate in exchange for a portion of the profit earned when the property is sold.

Short Sale — An arrangement entered into between a loan servicer and a delinquent borrower. The servicer allows the borrower to sell the property to a third party at less than the outstanding balance. This saves the servicer the time and expense involved in a foreclosure action. The servicer must normally obtain the approval of the investor before entering into a short sale agreement.

Special Servicer — Some transactions have a separate special servicer who assumes servicing responsibilities when a loan goes into default and conducts the "work-out" or foreclosure process. There are various types of special servicers: (1) those retaining first-loss pieces; (2) those investing in "B" pieces in return for special services rights and (3) those appointed solely because of asset-management expertise (www.mccarystevens.com/cssa_intro.pdf).

Sub-servicer — A servicer(s) who contracts with master and special servicers to perform some of the real estate services required under pool and servicing agreements, such as property inspections and individual loan administration. The master or special servicer is legally responsible for the activities of their sub-servicers (www.mccarystevens.com/cssa_intro.pdf).

Survival Ratio — An industry measure of the number of years it would take a company to exhaust its asbestos and environmental reserves for losses and loss expenses based on that company's current level of asbestos and environmental claims payments. The ratio is derived by dividing the current ending losses and loss expense reserves by the average annual payments for the prior three years. The ratio is computed based on the ending reserves for losses and loss expenses over the respective claims settlements during the fiscal year.

Society for Worldwide Interbank Financial Telecommunications (S.W.I.F.T.) — A message-writing system that connects worldwide participating banks, primarily for the purpose of communicating payment information. Frequently, the S.W.I.F.T. message is only part of an international payment (www.tgbr.com/tgbr/terms.html#r).

Table Funding — A method of acquiring mortgage loans from a non-affiliated source, usually a correspondent. The acquiring party funds the mortgage at closing. If certain conditions are met, the right to service table funded loans may be capitalized as purchased mortgage servicing rights.

Trustee — Holds the mortgage collateral, issues the Certificates of Beneficial Ownership (securities) and passes all funds collected by the master servicer to the bondholders. Distributes statements on distributions and status reports on the collateral. Acts as a supervisor to the master servicer and special servicer. Ensures that the servicers act in accordance with the terms of the Pooling and Servicing Agreement. If there is a violation of the agreement, the trustee has the right to assume the authority of or appoint a new servicer. The trustee represents the trust that holds the legal title to the collateral for the benefit of all class holders of the security. He must carry out his duties according to the indentures established within the Trust Indenture. Some trustees actually collect the proceeds from the master servicer and distribute them to the security holders, while others subcontract the distribution to "paying agents." This subcontract does not release the trustee from his legal obligations to protect the interests of the security holders (www.mccarystevens.com/cssa_intro.pdf).

Underwriter — A broker-dealer that purchases a new issue of municipal securities from the issuer for resale in a primary offering. The underwriter may acquire the securities either by negotiation with the issuer or by award on the basis of competitive bidding (www.msrb.org/msrb1/glossary/glossary_db.asp?sel=u).

Underwriter's Counsel — An attorney or law firm retained to represent the interests of an underwriter in connection with the purchase of a new issue of municipal securities. The duties of underwriter's counsel may include review of the issuer's bond resolution and documentation on behalf of the underwriter; review of the accuracy and adequacy of disclosure in the official statement; preparation of the agreement among underwriters, purchase contract, and/or the official statement; assisting the underwriter in meeting the underwriter's due diligence obligation; and delivery of a due diligence opinion (www.msrb.org/msrb1/glossary/glossary_db.asp?sel=u)

Underwriting Period — For purposes of MSRB rules and SEC Rule 15c2-12, the period during which an underwriting syndicate is considered to be engaged in the underwriting process. During this period, certain special underwriting rules apply. The underwriting period commences upon the earlier of the first submission to the syndicate of an order for the securities or the purchase of the new issue from the issuer. The underwriting period usually ends upon the later of the closing of the underwriting or the sale of the last of the securities by the syndicate. If the new issue is underwritten by a sole underwriter, the underwriting period is considered ended for purposes of MSRB rules by the later of the closing or the 21st calendar day after the date of the first submission of an order. However, in the case of municipal fund securities, sales generally are considered to be made in a continuous offering with a continuous underwriting period for purposes of MSRB rules and SEC Rule 15c2-12. (www.msrb.org/msrb1/glossary/glossary_db.asp?sel=u)

Velocity — The rate at which money balances turn over in a period for expenditures on goods and services (often measured as the ratio of GNP — gross national product — to the money stock). A larger velocity means that a given quantity of money is associated with a greater dollar volume of transactions.

Warehouse (Loan) — In mortgage lending, loans that are funded and awaiting sale or delivery to an investor.

Weighted Average Coupon (WAC) — The weighted average of the gross interest rates of the mortgages in a mortgage pool. The balance of each mortgage is used as the weighting factor.

Weighted Average Maturity (WAM) — The weighted average of the remaining terms to maturity of the mortgages in a mortgage pool as of the security issue date.

Weighted Average Remaining Maturity (WARM) — The weighted average of the remaining terms to maturity of the mortgages in a mortgage pool subsequent to the security issue date. The difference between the weighted average maturity and the weighted average remaining maturity is known as the weighted average loan age (WALA).

References

[1]"Financial Services," www.bettermanagement.com/topic/whatis.aspx?f=695, BetterManagement .com, Inc., 1915 NW. AmberGlen Parkway, Suite 400, Beaverton, OR 97006, USA, retrieved November 2005.

[2]Wikipedia contributors (2005). Financial services. Wikipedia, The Free Encyclopedia. Retrieved 21:03, January 9, 2006 from http://en.wikipedia.org/w/index.php?title=Financial_services&oldid=34446385. Permission is granted to copy, distribute and/or modify this passage, under the terms of the GNU Free Documentation License, Version 1.2 , or any later version published by the Free Software Foundation; with no Invariant Sections, no Front-Cover Texts, and no Back-Cover Texts. A copy of the license is included in the section entitled "GNU Free Documentation License," retrieved December 2005.

[3]Leonard, R., "Basel II: How Will You Deal with It?," Global Technology Associates, Inc., 3505 Lake Lynda Drive, Suite 109, Orlando, FL 32817 USA, itnews@itweb.co.za, www.bettermanagement.com/Library/Library.aspx?LibraryID=6916, retrieved November 2005.

[4]Tiner, J., (September 22, 2005), "Financial services sector regulation and internal audit," Speech by John Tiner, Chief Executive, Institute of Internal Auditors Risk Conference, www.fsa.gov.uk/pages/Library/Communication/Speeches/2005/0922_jt.shtml, retrieved November 2005.

[5]Dewing, I., Russell, P. (2000), "The Role of Auditors, Reporting Accountants and Skilled Persons in UK Financial Services Supervision, Executive Summary," ISBN 1 904574 13 0, www.icas.org.uk/site/cms/contentviewarticle.asp?article=4096, retrieved November 2005.

[6]PricewaterhouseCoopers, (June 2005), "Russian Financial Services M&A: Focus on Restructuring," www.pwcglobal.com/extweb/pwcpublications.nsf/docid/EDBA83EDEE1E2CDE85257089004D93B2/$file/fsmarussia.pdf, retrieved November 2005.

[7]Marcella, A., Sampias, W., and Kincaid, J., (2001). Study Guide for the Certified Financial Services Auditor Professional Examination, The Institute of Internal Auditors, www.theiia.org.

[8]Sharon, B., "The Difference Between Risk Management & Compliance," Strategic Operational Risk Management Solutions (SORMS), bsharon@sorms.com, (212) 280-8202, or (917) 848-1672, www.bettermanagement.com/library/library.aspx?libraryid=12810&pagenumber=3, retrieved November 2005.

[9]Metschian, P., "From Tactics to Strategy," SAS Institute Inc., 100 SAS Campus Drive, Cary, NC 27513-2414, (919) 677-8000, www.bettermanagement.com/library/library.aspx?libraryid=9850&pagenumber=1, retrieved November 2005.

[10]Kalita, M., "Enterprise-wide Risk Management: Myth or Reality?" Pinnacle Systems, Inc., www.pinnacle-sys.com, www.bettermanagement.com/library/library.aspx?libraryid=8329&pagenumber=2, retrieved November 2005.

[11]Tiner, J., (September 22, 2005), "Financial services sector regulation and internal audit," Speech by John Tiner, Chief Executive, Institute of Internal Auditors Risk Conference, www.fsa.gov.uk/pages/Library/Communication/Speeches/2005/0922_jt.shtml, retrieved November 2005.

[12]Woodword, D., "What are Exchange Traded Funds (ETFs)?", http://mutualfunds.about.com/cs/etfs/a/exchangetraded.htm, retrieved November 2005.

[13]Woodword, D., "What are Index Funds?", http://mutualfunds.about.com/cs/indexfunds/a/index_funds.htm, retrieved November 2005.
[14]White, A., "What is VaR? Value at Risk," www.investmentreview.com/archives/1999/summer/whatisvar.html, retrieved November 2005.
[15]Byram, P., (September 2, 2005), "Risk Management: Understanding the Warning Signs," www.bettermanagement.com/library/library.aspx?l=12983, peter.byram@bettermanagement.com, retrieved November 2005.
[16]Gilbert, R. A., and Sierra, G. (January/February 2003), 'The Financial Condition of U.S. Banks: How Different Are Community Banks?" The Federal Reserve Bank of St. Louis, http://research.stlouisfed.org/publications/review/03/01/GilbertSierra.pdf, retrieved November 2005.
[17]Miller, S. (January 2004), "Responding to Regulatory Scrutiny of Loan-Loss Reserves," Commercial Lending Review, Volume 19, Number 1, Pages 38-41, www.crowechizek.com/NR/rdonlyres/eo3rkdqrfandmlfycy3s4hxabhtseiamytmu247fkz3p5xoeuyqufvl4ii7lg4kwjtjs7mc25irqny4kfginvvss6md/Scott+Miller+Commercial+Lending.pdf, CCH INCORPORATED. All rights reserved. Reprinted with permission from Commercial Lending Review A WoltersKluwer Company, New York, NY, 1-800-638-8437, www.aspenpublishers.com.
[18]PricewaterhouseCoopers, (2002), "Reserves", www.pwcglobal.com/Extweb/service.nsf/docid/4603E9E1F5CA9B5680256C77004C8FCC, retrieved November 2005.
[19]Markel, G., Meyer, S., "Risk & Insurance," (March, 2005), www.findarticles.com/p/articles/mi_m0BJK/is_3_16/ai_n13454907, retrieved December 2005.
[20]Killian, L., Smith, K., and Smith, W., (2001), "How the IPO Market Works," IPOs for Everyone, www.ipohome.com/newcomer/book_chap1.asp, retrieved December 2005.
[21]FDIC Financial Institutions Letter (FIL—20—99), dated March 4, 1999], FDIC Statements of Policy, {{4-30-99 p.5479}}, Interagency Guidance on Subprime Lending, March 1, 1999.
[22]Securities Industry Association, Primer on Securities, www.sia.com/capitol_hill/html/glass-steagall_act.html, retrieved December 2005.
[23]Wratten, T. (!996), "Introduction To Commercial Real Estate Secondary And Securitization Market," Principal Commercial Advisors, Inc., 11050 Roe Avenue, Suite 200, Overland Park, Kansas 66211, (913)339-6162, www.mccarystevens.com/cssa_intro.pdf, correspondence with author, reprinted with permission, December 2005.
[24]Gallanis, M. (2005), "The Sarbanes-Oxley Act: A Treasury Obligation or Opportunity?" www.treasurystrategies.com/resources/default.htm, Treasury Strategies, Inc., 309 West Washington Street, 13th Floor, Chicago, IL 60606, www.TreasuryStrategies.com, 312.443.0840, mike_gallanis@treasurystrategies.com, reprinted with permission, retrieved November 2005.
[25]Avaya, 2005, "Back Office Operations," Avaya Global Connect Limited, and NASSCOM www.avayaglobalconnect.com/experienceindia/MSegment/backoffice.asp, retrieved November 2005, reprinted with permission.
[26]Marcella, A., Sampias, W., and Kincaid, J., (2001). Study Guide for the Certified Financial Service Auditor Professional Examination, The Institute of Internal Auditors, www.theiia.org.
[27]Ibid.
[28]Applegarth, G. (2005), "Spot unethical sales practices," MSN Money, http://moneycentral.msn.com/content/Insurance/Avoidripoffs/P35851.asp, retrieved November 2005.

[29]Yih, J. (May 4, 2004), "Estate bonds explained," Money Sense, www.moneysense.ca/planning/retirement_living/article.jsp?content=20040504_125110_3212, retrieved November 2005.
[30]Securities Industry Association, Primer on Securities, www.sia.com/capitol_hill/html/securities_act_of_1933.html, retrieved December 2005.
[31]Securities Industry Association, Primer on Securities, www.sia.com/capitol_hill/html/sec_exchange_act_of_1934.html, retrieved December 2005.
[32]Securities Industry Association, Primer on Securities, www.sia.com/capitol_hill/html/invstmt_comp_act_of_1940.html, retrieved December 2005.
[33]Securities Industry Association, Primer on Securities, www.sia.com/capitol_hill/html/private_sec_lit_reform_act.html, retrieved December 2005.
[34]Securities Industry Association, Primer on Securities, www.sia.com/capitol_hill/html/sec_lit_unfrm_stnds_act.html, retrieved December 2005.
[35]Securities Industry Association, Primer on Securities, www.sia.com/capitol_hill/html/natl_sec_mkts_impvmt_act.html, retrieved December 2005.
[36]Securities Industry Association, Primer on Securities, www.sia.com/capitol_hill/html/glass-steagall_act.html, retrieved December 2005.
[37]Ross, R. (2001), The Broker-dealer Audit Guide, The Institute of Internal Auditors, Altamonte Springs, FL, www.theiia.org, ISBN 0-89413-459-0. All of the material in this section (Broker-dealer Activities) except for citation numbers 23 through 29, were taken from Ross's The Broker-Dealer Audit Guide, and reprinted with permission.
[38]"Rating Advisory Helps Secure the Best Possible Rating," www.westlb.de/cms/sitecontent/westlb/ui/en/aktuelle_themen/archiv_20012003/rating_advisory__104710.standard.gid-N2FkNDZmMzU4OWFmYTIyMWM3N2Q2N2Q0YmU1NmI0OGU_.html, WestLB AG, Postfach, 40199 Düsseldorf, Herzogstraße 15, 40217 Düsseldorf, Tel.: 49 211 826 01, retrieved December 2005, reprinted with permission.
[39]"Overview of Long-term Ratings," Rating and Investment Information, Inc., 1325 Avenue of the Americas, Suite 2405, New York, NY 10019, 212-261-6280 Fax. 212-261-6281, www.r-i.co.jp/eng/rating/rating/framework.html, retrieved December 2005, reprinted with permission.
[40]Ferguson, S. (2003), Financial Analysis of M&A Integration, McGraw Hill, page 14, ISBN 007140211X.
[41]Bower, J., (April 2, 2001), "Not All M&As Are Alike — and That Matters," http://workingknowledge.hbs.edu/item.jhtml?id=2123&t=finance, retrieved November 2005.
[42]Moran Law Group, 1674 N. Shoreline Blvd. Suite 140 Mt. View CA, 650-694 4700, lawyers@moranlaw.net, www.moranlaw.net/glossary.htm, retrieved December 2005.
[43]"2005 ISDA Collateral Guidelines," International Swaps And Derivatives Association, Inc., 360 Madison Avenue, 16th Floor, New York, NY 10017, www.isda.org, isda@isda.org, (212) 901-6000, www.isda.org/publications/pdf/2005isdacollateralguidelines.pdf, retrieved December 2005, reprinted with permission.
[44]"Collateral Issues," Financial Services, Treasury Services Information, www.frbservices.org/Treasury/CollateralIssues.html, retrieved December 2005.

[45]"Treasury Tax and Loan Service (TIP)," www.frbservices.org/Treasury/TIP.html, retrieved December 2005.

[46]"Electronic Federal Tax Payment System," Financial Services, Treasury Services Information, www.frbservices.org/Treasury/ElectFedTax.html, retrieved December 2005.

[47]"Treasury Tax and Loan Service (PATAX)," Financial Services, Treasury Services Information, www.frbservices.org/Treasury/PATAX.html, retrieved December 2005.

[48]Remarks by Chairman Alan Greenspan, "Corporate Governance," At the 2003 Conference on Bank Structure and Competition, Chicago, Illinois, (via satellite), May 8, 2003, Federal Reserve, www.federalreserve.gov/boarddocs/speeches/2003/20030508/default.htm, retrieved December 2005.

[49]"Federal Agency Securities Market," Bond Markets & Prices, Bond Markets Defined, The Bond Market Association, www.investinginbonds.com/marketataglance.asp?catid=31, retrieved December 2005.

[50]"Mortgage-Backed Securities," The Securities and Exchange Commission, www.sec.gov/answers/mortgagesecurities.htm, retrieved December 2005.

[51]"21st century collateral management," Allustra, Glossary of terms, www.allustra.com/home/h-glossary-u.html, retrieved December 2005.

[52]Investing Glossary, Rehypothecation, www.marketvolume.com/glossary/r0140.asp, retrieved December 2005.

[53]"Repurchase Agreement," www.riskglossary.com/link/hypothecation.htm, Contingency Analysis, www.contingencyanalysis.com, retrieved December 2005.

Section IV
The Regulatory Environment

The banking, insurance, and securities industries are heavily regulated, and compliance with the intent of laws and regulations helps the system function effectively and protects the interests of consumers and shareholders. There are thousands of laws and regulations that affect these industries, and this section will provide a snapshot of a small sample of these regulations. To facilitate the review of current laws and regulations, excerpts from the actual text of some laws and regulations have been included. In addition, Web sites that provide current and detailed information have been included throughout the section.

Note: The primary focus of this section is on the laws and regulations in the United States.

A. Overview of the Regulatory Environment

Anyone involved in business activities is keenly aware of the many regulations that drive business operations. The following provides an overview of the regulatory environment in the financial services industry.

1. Function of Central Bank

Federal Reserve System[1] — The Federal Reserve, the central bank of the United States, was founded by Congress in 1913 to provide the nation with a safer, more flexible, and more stable monetary and financial system. Today the Federal Reserve's duties fall into four general areas:

- Conducting the nation's monetary policy
- Supervising and regulating banking institutions and protecting the credit rights of consumers
- Maintaining the stability of the financial system
- Providing certain financial services to the U.S. government, the public, financial institutions, and foreign official institutions

Appointments to the Board — The seven members of the Board of Governors are appointed by the president and confirmed by the Senate to serve 14-year terms of office. Members may serve only one full term, but a member who has been appointed to complete an unexpired term may be reappointed to a full term. The president designates, and the Senate confirms, two members of the board to be chairman and vice chairman for four-year terms.

Representation — Only one member of the board may be selected from any one of the 12 Federal Reserve districts. In making appointments, the president is directed by law to select a "fair representation of the financial, agricultural, industrial, and commercial interests and geographical divisions of the country." These aspects of selection are intended to ensure representation of regional interests and the interests of various sectors of the public.

Responsibilities — The primary responsibility of the board members is the formulation of monetary policy. The seven board members constitute a majority of the 12-member Federal Open Market Committee (FOMC), the group that makes the key decisions affecting the cost and availability of money and credit in the economy. The other five members of the FOMC are reserve bank presidents, one of whom is the president of the Federal Reserve Bank of New York. The other bank presidents serve one-year terms on a rotating basis. By statute the FOMC determines its own organization, and by tradition it elects the chairman of the Board of Governors as its chairman and the president of the New York Bank as its vice chairman.

The board sets reserve requirements and shares the responsibility with the reserve banks for discount rate policy. These two functions plus open market operations constitute the monetary policy tools of the Federal Reserve System.

In addition to monetary policy responsibilities, the Federal Reserve Board has supervisory and regulatory responsibilities over banks that are members of the system, bank holding companies, international banking facilities in the United States, Edge Act and agreement corporations, foreign activities of member banks, and the U.S. activities of foreign-owned banks. The board also sets margin requirements which limit the use of credit for purchasing or carrying securities. In addition, the board plays a key role in assuring the smooth functioning and continued development of the nation's vast payments system. Another area of board responsibility is the development and administration of regulations that implement major federal laws governing consumer credit such as the Truth in Lending Act, the Equal Credit Opportunity Act, the Home Mortgage Disclosure Act, and the Truth in Savings Act.

Meetings — The board usually meets several times a week. Meetings are conducted in compliance with the Government in the Sunshine Act, and many meetings are open to the public. If the board has convened to consider confidential financial information, however, the sessions are closed to public observation.

Contacts within Government — As they carry out their duties, members of the board routinely confer with officials of other government agencies, representatives of banking industry groups, officials of the central banks of other countries, members of Congress, and academicians. For example, they meet frequently with Treasury officials and the Council of Economic Advisers to help evaluate the economic climate and to discuss objectives for the nation's economy. Governors also discuss the international monetary system with central bankers of other countries and are in close contact with the heads of the U.S. agencies that make foreign loans and conduct.

The Federal Reserve System interacts with foreign central banks. Two major foreign central banks include:

- Bank for International Settlements (BIS)
- European Central Bank (ECB)

The Bank for International Settlements[2] (BIS) is an international organization that fosters cooperation among central banks and other agencies in pursuit of monetary and financial stability. Its banking services are provided exclusively to central banks and international organizations and serves as a bank for central banks.

The BIS fulfills this mandate by acting as:

- A forum to promote discussion and facilitate decision-making processes among central banks and within the international financial community.
- A center for economic and monetary research.
- A prime counterparty for central banks in their financial transactions.
- Agent or trustee in connection with international financial operations.

The head office is in Basel, Switzerland, and there are two representative offices: in the Hong Kong Special Administrative Region of the People's Republic of China and in Mexico City. Established on May 17, 1930, the BIS is the world's oldest international financial organization.

The European Central Bank (ECB)[3] is the central bank for Europe's single currency, the euro. The ECB's main task is to maintain the euro's purchasing power and thus price stability in the euro area. The euro area comprises the 12 European Union countries that have introduced the euro since 1999.

Twelve member states of the European Union are participating in the single currency:

- Belgium
- Germany
- Greece
- Spain
- France
- Ireland
- Italy
- Luxembourg
- The Netherlands
- Austria
- Portugal
- Finland

On January 1, 1999, the European Central Bank assumed responsibility for monetary policy in the euro area — the second largest economic area in the world after the United States. The transfer of responsibility for monetary policy from 11 national central banks — which became 12 with the participation of Greece on January 1, 2001 — to a new supranational institution represented a milestone in a long and complex process of integration among European countries.

The objectives of the ECB[4] are:

- The primary objective is to maintain price stability.
- To support the general economic policies in the community with a view to contributing to the achievement of the objectives of the community.
- To achieve a high level of employment and sustainable and non-inflationary growth.

The basic tasks of the ECB include:

- Defining and implementing monetary policy for the euro area.
- Conducting foreign exchange operations.
- Holding and management of the official foreign reserves of the euro area countries (portfolio management).
- Promoting the smooth operation of payment systems.
- Authorizing and issuing banknotes within the euro area.
- Collecting statistical information necessary for fulfilling the tasks, either from national authorities or directly from economic agents.
- Promoting the stability of the financial system.
- Maintaining working relations with relevant institutions, within the EU and internationally in respect of tasks entrusted to the Eurosystem.

2. Function of Insurance Regulators

The insurance industry is regulated by state governments, the federal government, and non-governmental entities. The major regulations and regulatory entities affecting the insurance industry are described below.

The McCarran-Ferguson Act was adopted in 1945 after extended controversy over the jurisdiction of state and federal governments in regulating the business of insurance. The principal objective of the Act was to establish the primacy of the states in regulating the industry. The purpose clause of the Act states that the continued regulation and taxation of the business of insurance by states are in the public's best interest.

The primary components of the McCarran-Ferguson Act (Public Law 15) are:

- To allow states to retain the right to regulate the insurance industry.
- To allow the federal government to assume regulation of the insurance industry if Congress feels that state regulation is inadequate or does not serve the public interest.

The Act allows insurers to share related information that lowers costs of doing business. This includes joint development of insurance forms and the sharing of loss data to help with policy pricing. It provides insurers with a narrow and limited exemption from federal antitrust laws as long as the activity is state regulated. It explicitly empowers states to regulate and tax insurance.

State Insurance Commissions

Because the states regulate the insurance industry:

- Each state must have an insurance commission.
- Each state's insurance commission holds legal authority over insurance company operations.
- Each state's insurance commission is directed by a state insurance commissioner, superintendent, or director.

The responsibilities of state insurance commissions include:

- Making the state's insurance rules and regulations.
- Authorizing companies to operate in the state thorough the issuance of licenses and certificates of authority.
- Issuing licenses to insurance agents.
- Holding hearings and suspending or revoking licenses or certificates of authority.
- Reviewing insurance companies' financial statements.
- Verifying that policy forms meet all requirements and contain all provisions and disclosures.
- Ensuring insurance company compliance with reserve requirements and investment guidelines.
- Receiving and following up on consumer complaints.

The National Association of Insurance Commissioners (NAIC)[5]

The NAIC is a nongovernmental organization comprised of the various state insurance commissioners, superintendents, or directors. State insurance regulators created the NAIC in 1871 to address the need to coordinate regulation of multistate insurers. The mission of the NAIC is to assist state insurance regulators, individually and collectively, in serving the public interest and achieving the following fundamental insurance regulatory goals in a responsive, efficient, and cost effective manner, consistent with the wishes of its members:

- Protect the public interest.
- Promote competitive markets.
- Facilitate the fair and equitable treatment of insurance consumers.
- Promote the reliability, solvency, and financial solidity of insurance institutions.
- Support and improve state regulation of insurance.

The NAIC is the organization of insurance regulators from the 50 states, the District of Columbia, and the four U.S. territories. The NAIC provides a forum for the development of uniform policy when uniformity is appropriate. A state regulator's primary responsibility is to protect the interests of insurance consumers, and the NAIC helps regulators fulfill that obligation. That assistance is related to the regulators' shared objectives of financial and market conduct regulation.

A major function of the NAIC is to encourage uniformity among state insurance departments through the development of model bills and regulations. However, the NAIC has no direct regulatory authority.

- The NAIC Financial Regulation Standards recommend minimum levels of resources and authority necessary for effective solvency regulation.
- The NAIC Financial Regulation Standards and Accreditation Program set up a system of peer review among state insurance commissions.
- The NAIC created a zone system to streamline the financial examination of companies operating in more than one state. The NAIC divided the United States into four zones (western, midwestern, northeastern, southeastern). Each zone has a pool of examiners supplied by each state's insurance commission within the zone. The following guidelines apply to insurance company examinations:
    - The examiner-in-charge must be from the company's home state.
    - Examiners from other states in the zone may also participate in the examination.
    - A zone examiner may be assigned from any zone in which a company receives as much as $1 million premiums or more than 20 percent of its total premiums.
    - Insurance companies are usually examined once every three to five years.
    - A written report of the examination must be issued.
    - The home-state commissioner is responsible for resolving any disagreements that arise between the examiners and the company regarding the content of the final report.
    - The final report of the examination is a matter of public record.

The Securities and Exchange Commission (SEC)

The SEC has regulatory authority over investment products. Investment-based life insurance products or variable insurance products include annuities, variable life insurance, and variable universal life insurance. These products, which are also known as non-guaranteed products, are considered speculative because the cash value or benefit level can change relative to the performance of the insurer's investments. Thus, some insurance products fall under the regulatory authority of the SEC.

- Insurers that sell investment-based insurance products must comply with federal laws that govern securities.
- Agents selling investment-based insurance products must be certified by the SEC, licensed as a broker-dealer with the National Association of Securities Dealers (NASD), and licensed as a state insurance agent.

3. Function of Securities Regulators

To help ensure that investors receive equitable treatment from companies and investors, regulations have been developed by federal and state governments, and governing bodies for brokers.

The following topics will be outlined in this section:

- Securities Act of 1933
- Securities Exchange Act of 1934
- Investment Company Act and Advisors Act of 1940
- National Association of Securities Dealers Rules
- Municipal Securities Rule Making Board
- Margin Lending

Securities Act of 1933

The Securities Act of 1933 was the first legislation designed to regulate the sale of securities and associated activities. The Act was designed to ensure that potential investors receive accurate and complete information. The primary purpose of the Act is to require full and fair public disclosure of important elements in stock issues and to prevent fraud. The Act is administered and enforced by the SEC.

Some requirements of the Act follow.

Registration Requirements — applies to all new securities sold through interstate commerce and requires registration with the SEC. Registration is accomplished by filing a S-1 statement and a prospectus. The prospectus is an abbreviated version of the registration. There are severe penalties associated with false or misleading information on S-1 statement, including criminal and civil penalties. The S-1 statement includes:

- Information on corporate officers and directors.
- The nature of the business.

- Financial information for the last three years.
- A description of how the proceeds from the issue will be used.
- Amount of corporate holdings for all officers and directors and a list of all owners holding more than 10 percent of the securities.
- Legal opinion.
- Description of any legal actions pending against the company.
- Articles of incorporation.
- Fees for the underwriter of the issue.

SEC Review Process — Before issues can be sold to the public, the SEC must review the registration. The SEC has 20 days (called the cooling-off period) to review the materials; however, the period is often longer than 20 days as the SEC may request additional information from the issuer. Note: the SEC may lengthen or shorten the cooling-off period. The SEC has the power to issue the following:

- Deficiency letters — letters that ask the issuer for more information or specific amendments to the registration. Once the new information is received the SEC has additional time to review the information.
- Stop orders — if the SEC believes that the registration statement contains false or misleading information or that pertinent information has been omitted, it can suspend the process with a stop order.
- Effective date — after the SEC is satisfied, the effective date is established and sales may begin. The SEC never actually approves an issue or judges the quality of the issue; its primary objective is to review the statements for completeness.

Preliminary Prospectus — while the SEC review is in progress, the issuer can circulate a preliminary prospectus to determine the interest in the issue. The preliminary prospectus must include the following:

- Statement that the registration is filed but not effective.
- Statement that information is subject to change.
- Statement that it is not an offer to buy or a solicitation to sell.
- Red ink to distinguish it from a final prospectus. Preliminary prospectuses are often called "red herrings."

Exempt Securities — The Act specifically exempts certain securities from the registration requirements: These include:

- Securities issues by the U.S. government or agencies.
- Obligations issued by state or other political subdivisions.
- Commercial paper that matures in less than 270 days.

- Instruments that are covered by the Interstate Commerce Act (railroads and airlines for example).
- Nonprofit groups.
- Fixed annuity contracts and insurance policies.
- Issues of $1.5 million or less (Regulation A small-scale offerings that do not exceed $5 million for a 12-month period and must be filed with the SEC at least 10 days prior to the issue).
- Intrastate issues (Rule 147) — securities are sold only to residents of the state where the issuer resides.
- Private placements (regulation D) — securities that are sold to selected investors and are not sold to the public.

Securities Exchange Act of 1934

The Securities Exchange Act of 1934 was enacted to help prevent unfair trade practices on previously issued securities. In other words, the 1934 Act regulated trading in secondary markets while the 1933 Act regulated new issues. The 1934 Act created the SEC.

The SEC is the enforcing authority for the securities industry and is comprised of commissioners. The commissioners are appointed by the president and approved by the Senate. They serve five-year terms and are prohibited from any business or stock activity during their term. The SEC establishes rules to regulate the securities industry.

Some specific requirements of the Act include.

Registration Requirements — National securities exchanges must register with the SEC, agree to abide by the law, and provide information regarding internal rules and regulations. Individuals who are firm members and are engaged in securities transactions and interstate commerce must also register with the SEC. There are some exceptions to the registration requirements, such as small local exchanges and brokers that do not do business with the public. It should also be noted that all securities must be registered with the SEC.

Credit Regulations — Members of exchanges or broker-dealers are prohibited from borrowing on any listed security, except through a Federal Reserve bank. In addition, they are prohibited from having a total debt that is in excess of 15 times their net capital. It should be noted that these regulations do not apply to exempt securities such as federal government obligations.

Manipulation and Deception — Fraud and/or the manipulation of securities' prices is prohibited by SEC regulations. It is unlawful to generate false trading activities to give the impression that an issue is being actively traded or to provide misleading information to generate sales. Other activities that are prohibited include short sales (preventing an investor from continually driving the price down by selling short only to eventually buy the securities back at reduced prices) and solicitations (soliciting purchases on an exchange).

Insider Rules — Insiders are not allowed to profit from their information by trading a stock before that information is public. Insiders must file a personal statement with the SEC and report all personal security transactions in their corporation no later than 10 days after the end of the calendar month in which they occur. Insiders are generally barred form short-selling. Insiders include the officers or directors of a corporation, anyone with 10 percent or more of the shares, and anyone who has information on the corporation not available to the public.

Proxies — Regulations state that companies that solicit proxies from shareholders must provide detailed and accurate information regarding proposals to shareholders. A copy of this information must also be submitted to the SEC.

If a firm is trying to acquire another company (a proxy contest), then all participants in the proxy contest must register with the SEC. There are possible criminal penalties for those who fail to register.

Investment Company Act of 1940

The Investment Company Act (ICA) of 1940 was instituted to ensure that investors are fully informed and are treated fairly. All firms that are bound to abide by this Act are also subject to SEC regulations. The Act specifically defines three types of investment companies:

- Unit investment trust company issues securities that represent an interest in a specified security. The shares are redeemable and the holdings can be a mutual fund portfolio.
- Face amount certificate companies promise to pay an amount at a future date in return for periodic payments from the investor. The payment amount is the face value at maturity or a surrender value if it is redeemed prior to maturity.
- Management companies are investment companies that do not fit either one of the categories listed above.

Some of the requirements of the ICA are:

- Sponsors must invest at least $100,000 prior to offering an investment to the public.
- Changes to investment objectives or policies require a majority vote of the shareholders.
- Fund managers can not exceed 60 percent of the board. In other words, at least 40 percent of the board must be outsiders.
- A contract that specifies the management fees must be developed and the fees should be reasonable and based on performance.
- Board members must be elected by shareholders.

National Association of Securities Dealers (NASD) Rules

The NASD was established as part of the 1934 Act with the primary objective of regulating the over-the-counter (OTC) market. Broker-dealers involved with interstate commerce or transactions with national exchanges must register with the NASD. Some specific regulations under this portion of the Act include:

- Recommendations for a particular security to a customer by a broker-dealer must be determined to be reasonable and suitable for the customer.
- Supervision of all employees of a firm is required. Written procedures to promote adequate supervision must be developed and reviews of customer accounts, transactions, correspondence, and customer complaints must be conducted.
- Account documentation must be maintained for all customers. This includes developing a consistent method to open a new account and to maintain current and accurate records of customer accounts. In addition, all customer complaints must be maintained.

In general all broker-dealers must maintain detailed records to ensure that investors are protected. This includes maintaining accounting records and having a review by an independent accountant. Summary accounting information must be distributed to customers annually and the SEC has the right to examine these records at any time.

Registered Representative Rules — NASD considers any person who solicits or conducts business in securities to be a registered representative. NASD has established some specific rules for registered representatives. The rules include:

- All correspondence and all transactions must be reviewed and approved by the firm and maintained for three years.
- Disciplinary actions regarding employees must be reported to NASD.
- Registered representatives are prohibited from giving gifts to anyone (related to their broker activities) in excess of $100 per year.
- Disputes between registered representatives and firms must be resolved through an independent binding arbitration process. If agreed to by a customer, customer disputes can also be settled by binding arbitration.
- Firms must maintain fidelity bond coverage on all employees to protect against losses due to theft or misappropriation of securities.
- Registered representatives that leave the business for two years, lose their licenses, and must retake all required examinations.
- Continuing education requirements are imposed on all registered representatives to ensure that satisfactory knowledge is maintained. Firms are required to develop a training program for their employees.

Conduct of Customer Account Rules — were designed to provide a consistent and documented process to maintain customer records — in effect to protect customers from unsubstantiated or undocumented losses. The rules include:

- The financial goals and current financial situation must be assessed in order to make suitable investment recommendations. All new accounts must be approved by a principal in a firm.
- If a customer formally assigns power of attorney privileges to a representative, then all discretionary transactions must be approved by a principal in a firm.
- Registered representatives are prohibited from guaranteeing a customer's account against loss or from sharing in the losses or gains in an account.
- Registered representatives are prohibited from charging customers for investment advice.
- Private transactions conducted outside the firm are prohibited.
- If a firm's stock is publicly traded, employees of the firm may not recommend nor solicit purchases of the firm's stock. However, unsolicited purchases are acceptable.
- High risk ("penny stocks" selling for less than $5 that are not listed on an exchange or NASDAQ) stocks may not be sold to investors until the customer's financial position and market knowledge have been reviewed. In addition, the customer must sign a statement regarding the suitability of the investment prior to the actual transaction. Registered representatives are also prohibited from:
  - Excessively trading a customer's account.
  - Recommending purchases that are not suitable based on the customer's financial capacity.
  - Engaging in fraudulent activities such as trading without authorization or misappropriating funds.
  - Soliciting the purchase of stock before the dividend date to promote the receipt of dividends.
  - Trading in mutual fund shares (the registered representative may not make an inventory of mutual fund shares and act as a market maker for the company).

Trading and Market Rules — NASD also designed these rules to protect consumers and to provide a consistent and equitable method to sell and purchase securities. Some of the rules include:

- Trades cannot be executed by a broker-dealer unless they have reasonable assurance that the customer will pay (for a purchase) or deliver (for a sale) within three business days of the transaction.
- Trades must be executed under favorable pricing conditions for the customer. In other words, the member must obtain the most favorable pricing for the customer.
- All quotes and trade reports must be factual. Deceptive quotes are prohibited and members must honor all quotes (cannot back away).

- Commissions and markups must be fair and reasonable. Five percent has been set as a guideline; however, it should be noted that this is not a rule. However, the five percent guideline does not apply to mutual funds (8 ½ percent maximum sales charge rule), limited partnerships (10 percent maximum sales charge rule), new issues sold under a prospectus, exempt securities, and trades made on an exchange floor.
- Payments of any kind to influence the market price of a security are prohibited. This includes payments to influence newspaper articles or investment services.
- Payments designed to influence initial public offering price are also prohibited.
- Manipulative or deceptive practices are prohibited.
- Improper use of customer funds and securities is prohibited. This includes lending margin securities without a signed loan consent.

Communications with the Public — The NASD rules for communicating with the public are very similar to those used by the New York Stock Exchange. As with the NYSE, NASD wants to ensure that information disseminated to the public is fair and accurate, and does not mislead the public.

Some specific rules in this area include:

- Advertising and sales literature must be approved prior to its use by a principal and the documentation must be retained for three years. In a firm's first year of operation this literature must be submitted to the NASD 10 days prior to its use. The NASD also has the right to perform periodic checks of compliance. Advertising materials are defined as materials for the mass market, which includes mediums such as TV, newspapers, and periodicals. Sales literature includes form letters, seminars, research reports, and similar items.
- General standards for communication state that communications must be truthful and in good taste. They also must not mislead, make unwarranted claims, or promise specific results.
- Recommendations must be based in fact and the market price of the security must be included. In addition, if the firm has a relationship with the stock such as ownership or any other interest, such a relationship must be disclosed.
- Past performance statistics must be for at least a 12-month period. In addition, these materials must contain the statement that past performance does not indicate that future results must be made.
- Statements regarding investing advantages for a particular security must also include the corresponding risks.
- If compensated testimonials are used, it must be disclosed.
- All reports must be clearly dated and reasonably current (generally within the last six months).

If a customer files a complaint against a firm or employee, the NASD Code of procedures is used. The Code outlines the process for handling a grievance. There are multiple steps in the process and the length of the process depends upon the customer's and firm's satisfaction with the remedy.

The first step is the filing of the complaint (on a standard complaint form) to a NASD district office. The complaint is then forwarded to the District Business Conduct Committee (DBCC) which forwards the complaint to the firm. The firm must respond in writing to the DBCC and a copy of the response is sent to the customer. The DBCC then determines if a violation has occurred and what actions, if any, are appropriate. Depending upon the satisfaction of the remedy, the customer or firm may ask for a hearing and subsequently go through an appeal process if any of the remedies are not deemed acceptable.

Municipal Securities Rule-making Board (MSRB)

The MSRB was created in 1975 to develop rules and regulations to govern the municipal securities market. Prior to the board's creation, the municipal securities market was unregulated.

The MSRB is comprised of a 15-member board that creates regulations that apply to banks, brokers, and dealers engaged in municipal activities. It should be noted that the MSRB does not regulate municipal issuers, only the market participants. Although the MSRB promulgates regulations, it relies on other agencies to enforce its rules. These include the Federal Reserve Board, FDIC, SEC, and NASD, among others.

Registered Representative Rules — MSRB Rule G-2 requires that all parties effecting a municipal transaction must be qualified. Qualified is generally determined by the passing of an appropriate examination. Some example of individuals and examinations are:

- Municipal securities principal — any person engaged in management supervision or direction of municipal sales activities (underwriting, advising, communications, trading, processing, etc. of municipal securities). Such a person must have successfully passed the Series #53 (municipal securities principal) exam. Every firm must have at least one principal.
- Municipal securities financial and operations principal — any person engaged in (preparing or approving financial reports, supervision of accountants, supervision of individuals that process, clear, or store municipal securities, etc.). Such a person must have successfully passed the Series #27 (municipal securities financial and operations principal) exam.
- Municipal securities representative — any person who is not a principal, whose functions are not solely clerical, and who are engaged in (underwriting, advising, communications, trading, researching, etc. of municipal securities). Such a person must have successfully passed the Series #52 (municipal securities representative) exam or the Series #7 (general securities representative) exam.

- There is a 90-day apprentice period for new municipal securities representatives during which time they must pass the Series #52 or #7 exam. During this time, they are not authorized to transact municipal business or receive commissions on municipal transactions. However, they may be salaried employees during this period.
- Representatives may not solicit orders, new accounts, or new customers without passing the appropriate exam.
- If an exam is failed, it may not be taken again for 30 days. If an exam is failed three times, it may not be taken again for a period of six months. Also, if you leave the business for two years you must retake the exam(s).
- Firms or representatives may be disqualified if they willfully mislead the public, are convicted of "money" related crimes, or been expelled by other organizations such as the SEC, etc.
- New accounts must be promptly reviewed by a principal.
- Municipal broker-dealers are required to deal fairly with all persons and cannot engage in any deceptive or misleading practices.
- Municipal broker-dealers cannot give a gift greater than $100 to anyone (other than its employees) in the municipal securities business.
- A copy of the MSRB manual must be maintained in each office and available to customer's upon request.

Conduct of Customer Account Rules — The MSRB has established rules (similar to those discussed previously) to protect the customer. The MSRB requires that you assess the financial background, tax status, investment objectives, etc. in order to make effective recommendations. As mentioned previously, all new accounts must be approved in writing by a principal. Some specific provisions include:

- Account information must include the name, address, age, SSN, occupation, and type of account (Note: margin accounts must be authorized in writing). The form must be signed by the representative and a principal.
- All recommendations to customers must be based upon a knowledge of the customer and must be suitable for the customer. If a customer refuses to disclose financial information, a recommendation cannot be made.
- If a customer requests an unsuitable trade, it can be made if the representative informs the customer of the unsuitability and the customer still directs that the trade be executed.
- Discretionary accounts (those where the representative has the authority to make trades on behalf of the customer without specific transaction approval) must be authorized in writing. All discretionary transactions must be reviewed by a principal by the end of the day of the transaction.
- Municipal broker-dealers are prohibited from guaranteeing a customer's account against loss.
- Municipal broker-dealers are prohibited from sharing in the gain or loss of a customer's account.

- Municipal broker-dealers must disclose any relationships associated with a transaction in writing to a customer.
- Financial advisors to a municipality who assist in the structuring of a new offer, and who want to be the underwriter, must resign from the advisor relationship and notify the municipality in writing that a conflict of interest exists and disclose the expected financial remuneration from the issue.
- Customer complaints must be handled through a structured process and resolution must be approved by a principal. Also records of complaints must be retained for six years.

Trading and Market Rules — The MSRB has established rules to govern the municipal market. Some of the rules include:

- All quotes must be "bona fide" whether they are written or oral. Although, it should be noted that the quotes are subject to change and to prior purchase or sale by another party.
- All quotes must represent the broker-dealer's best judgment of the fair market value of the securities. The quotes do not have to be the exact fair market value, but a reasonable judgment based upon relevant factors such as possible market movements and the firm's inventory of the securities.
- Firms can quote securities that it does not own if it can deliver the security. Such quotcs are prohibited if the firm has knowledge that the security is not available.
- Quotes can be in the form of bids wanted (BW), offers wanted (OW), nominal quotes, and subject quotes. Nominal quotes are informational quotes that indicate that the firm is not willing to trade at those prices. Subject quotes are ones that are subject to some condition. This condition is often that the price is subject to change before the trade occurs.
- Broker-dealers are prohibited from reporting information on a trade unless it is known that a trade occurred at that price. False reports are considered to be a deceptive practice.
- Prices charged for municipal bond trades must be fair and reasonable. This applies to both principal and agency trades.

Advertising and Other Rules — The MSRB has established rules to control the dissemination of materials to the public. The basic definition of advertising is material designed for dissemination to the public through public media or promotional literature. This includes almost anything that is disseminated to the public such as notices, circulars, brochures, form letters, reprints, and market letters. It should be noted that internal memos or communications are excluded from this rule since they are not intended to be publicly distributed. Some of the rules include:

- Summaries or abstracts of official statement and offering circulars are included under these rules. Since these documents do not contain all of the information included in the official document, and may not be complete and accurate, they are considered advertisements. It should be noted that the complete official statement or offering circular is not considered an advertisement.
- Any advertisement may not contain false or misleading information.

- New issues may be advertised and the initial yield offering may be included in the advertisement as long as the date of the initial sale is included in the advertisement. However, the yields listed must have been in effect at the time of the publication. In addition, the new issue bonds must actually be available (not completely pre-sold) to be advertised.

Margin Lending

Margin accounts are accounts where the broker-dealer extends credit to the customer and only a percentage of the purchase price is actually paid. The advantage to a customer is the ability to leverage their money — in effect, buy additional securities with less cash. Some definitions associated with margin accounts are:

- Margin — the percentage of the sale price the customer must deposit. The margin percentage varies depending upon changes in federal regulations. It is usually between 40 percent and 60 percent. The margin amount is currently 50 percent, which means that a customer pays $.50 for every $1 of security purchased.
- Hypothecation — the practice of pledging securities as collateral.
- Rehypothecation — the practice of a broker pledging a customer's securities with a bank or other loan source.
- Loan Value — the percentage of the security's market value that the firm lends to the customer. If the margin requirement is 50 percent, then the loan value is 50 percent.

The Federal Reserve Board has set regulations for margin accounts:

- Regulation U — limits the amount that can be borrowed by brokers who use any customer securities as collateral.
- Regulation G — limits the amount a non-bank lender can lend to brokers who use customer securities (rehypothecate) as collateral.
- Regulation T — limits the amounts brokers can lend to customers on various types of securities.

There are special characteristics associated with margin accounts. Since they involve credit it was determined that special requirements were needed.

- New margin accounts must have a signed margin agreement in addition to the usual new account information. The margin agreement should state that all transactions are subject to pertinent laws and regulations. The customer must also agree to:
  - Allow the brokerage firm to pledge or repledge securities for broker loans.
  - The accrual of interest charges on debt balances in their account.
  - Permission to sell held securities with or without notifying the customer if equity is not adequate.

- Some individuals who work for exchanges (and their spouses) may require special approval from their employer before a margin account can be opened. Also, a registered representative may not open a margin account without branch manager approval.
- Only listed securities (those listed on national exchanges) and or securities listed on an OTC margin list (which is updated regularly) may be traded on margin per regulation T.
- Certain securities are exempted from regulation T margin requirements. These include federal government debt issues, state or municipal government issues, and other issues from taxing entities. Since these issues are exempt, firms can assign a higher loan value to them.

Other terms and definitions associated with margins are:

- Long market value — is the customer's gross cost and includes any charges and commission and is the amount used to calculate the margin requirement.
- Debit balance — is amount of the loan to the customer from the firm.
- Equity — the customer's net worth in their account. To calculate the equity, subtract the debit balance from the long market value.
- Restricted accounts — if the equity balance declines in an account due to a decline in the market price of security and the current equity position falls below margin requirements, the account is classified as restricted. Restricted accounts are subject to specific rules; however, no specific action on the account (i.e., increase the equity balance) is required per Regulation T. If additional securities are purchased, only the new purchases are subject to the original margin requirement.
- Industry requirements — NASD and NYSE have established some margin requirements (voluntarily) that are more strict than Regulation T. For example, new margin accounts have a $2,000 minimum value of an account that is added to the margin amount; thus, the actual margin amount is usually greater than 50 percent. In addition, NASD and NYSE have rules that require at least 25 percent equity in a long account.
- Maintenance calls — if the equity position in an account falls below the 25 percent threshold, the customer is required to place cash or securities in their account within 48 hours or be subject to the sale of shares from their account.
- Special memorandum account — if the market price of securities rises and the equity balance exceeds the margin requirement, the excess amount may be used to purchase additional securities on margin. Although no funds actually change hands, an additional line of credit is established for the customer.

B. Laws and Regulations

There are many laws and regulations that impact the business environment, and this section provides a broad overview of many of them. To provide accurate and detailed information, we provide excerpts from the specific laws and regulations. If more detailed information is required, please feel free to go to the source listed in the reference.

1. Equal Credit Opportunity/Antidiscrimination

Regulation B – Equal Credit Opportunity Act[6] promotes the availability of credit to all creditworthy applicants. Creditors are prohibited from discriminating on non-financial factors such as race, color, religion, national origin, sex, marital status, or age. Additionally, banks are required to provide applicants with a notice of action regarding the loan application and collect monitoring information regarding an applicant's race, color, religion, national origin, sex, marital status, and age. The following section is an excerpt of text of Regulation B.

TITLE 12 — BANKS AND BANKING
CHAPTER II — FEDERAL RESERVE SYSTEM
Sec. 202.1 Authority, scope, and purpose

(a) Authority and scope. This regulation is issued by the Board of Governors of the Federal Reserve System pursuant to title VII (Equal Credit Opportunity Act) of the Consumer Credit Protection Act, as amended (15 U.S.C. 1601 et seq.). Except as otherwise provided herein, the regulation applies to all persons who are creditors, as defined in Sec. 202.2(1). Information collection requirements contained in this regulation have been approved by the Office of Management and Budget under the provisions of 44 U.S.C. 3501 et seq. and have been assigned OMB number 7100-0201.

(b) Purpose. The purpose of this regulation is to promote the availability of credit to all creditworthy applicants without regard to race, color, religion, national origin, sex, marital status, or age (provided the applicant has the capacity to contract); to the fact that all or part of the applicant's income derives from a public assistance program; or to the fact that the applicant has in good faith exercised any right under the Consumer Credit Protection Act. The regulation prohibits creditor practices that discriminate on the basis of any of these factors. The regulation also requires creditors to notify applicants of action taken on their applications; to report credit history in the names of both spouses on an account; to retain records of credit applications; to collect information about the applicant's race and other personal characteristics in applications for certain dwelling-related loans; and to provide applicants with copies of appraisal reports used in connection with credit transactions.

2. Home Mortgage Disclosures

Regulation C – Home Mortgage Disclosure Act[7] provides the public with loan data that can be used to:

- Help determine whether financial institutions are serving the housing needs of their communities.
- Assist public officials in distributing public-sector investments so as to attract private investment to areas where it is needed.
- Assist in identifying possible discriminatory lending patterns and enforcing antidiscrimination statutes.

The following section is an excerpt of text of Regulation C.

TITLE 12 — BANKS AND BANKING
CHAPTER II — FEDERAL RESERVE SYSTEM
Sec. 203.1 Authority, purpose, and scope

(a) Authority. This regulation is issued by the Board of Governors of the Federal Reserve System ("Board") pursuant to the Home Mortgage Disclosure Act (12 U.S.C. 2801 et seq.), as amended. The information-collection requirements have been approved by the U.S. Office of Management and Budget under 44 U.S.C. 3501 et seq. and have been assigned OMB numbers for reporting data to the Office of the Comptroller of the Currency (1557-0159), the Federal Deposit Insurance Corporation (3064-0046), the Office of Thrift Supervision (1550-0021), the Federal Reserve System (7100-0247), and the Department of Housing and Urban Development ("HUD") (2502-0529). A number for the National Credit Union Administration is pending.

(b) Purpose. (1) This regulation implements the Home Mortgage Disclosure Act, which is intended to provide the public with loan data that can be used:

(i) To help determine whether financial institutions are serving the housing needs of their communities;

(ii) To assist public officials in distributing public-sector investments so as to attract private investment to areas where it is needed; and

(iii) To assist in identifying possible discriminatory lending patterns and enforcing antidiscrimination statutes.

(2) Neither the act nor this regulation is intended to encourage unsound lending practices or the allocation of credit.

(c) Scope. This regulation applies to certain financial institutions, including banks, saving associations, credit unions, and other mortgage lending institutions, as defined in Sec. 203.2(e). It requires an institution to report data to its supervisory agency about home purchase and home improvement loans it originates or purchases, or for which it receives applications; and to disclose certain data to the public.

3. Reserve Requirements

Regulation D – Reserve Requirements[8] relates to reserves that depository institutions are required to maintain for the purpose of facilitating the implementation of monetary policy by the Federal Reserve System. Depository institutions must maintain reserves in the form of vault cash or have an adequate balance at a Federal Reserve or corresponding bank. The following section is an excerpt of text of Regulation D.

TITLE 12 — BANKS AND BANKING
CHAPTER II — FEDERAL RESERVE SYSTEM
Sec. 204.1 Authority, purpose, and scope

(a) Authority. This part is issued under the authority of section 19 (12 U.S.C. 461 et seq.) and other provisions of the Federal Reserve Act and of section 7 of the International Banking Act of 1978 (12 U.S.C. 3105).

(b) Purpose. This part relates to reserves that depository institutions are required to maintain for the purpose of facilitating the implementation of monetary policy by the Federal Reserve System.

(c) Scope. (1) The following depository institutions are required to maintain reserves in accordance with this part:

- (i) Any insured bank as defined in section 3 of the Federal Deposit Insurance Act (12 U.S.C. 1813(h)) or any bank that is eligible to apply to become an insured bank under section 5 of such Act (12 U.S.C. 1815);
- (ii) Any savings bank or mutual savings bank as defined in section 3 of the Federal Deposit Insurance Act (12 U.S.C. 1813(f), (g));
- (iii) Any insured credit union as defined in section 101 of the Federal Credit Union Act (12 U.S.C. 1752(7)) or any credit union that is eligible to apply to become an insured credit union under section 201 of such Act (12 U.S.C. 1781);
- (iv) Any member as defined in section 2 of the Federal Home Loan Bank Act (12 U.S.C. 1422(4)); and
- (v) Any insured institution as defined in section 401 of the National Housing Act (12 U.S.C. 1724(a)) or any institution which is eligible to apply to become an insured institution under section 403 of such Act (12 U.S.C. 1726).

(2) Except as may be otherwise provided by the Board, a foreign bank's branch or agency located in the United States is required to comply with the provisions of this part in the same manner and to the same extent as if the branch or agency were a member bank, if its parent foreign bank

- (i) has total worldwide consolidated bank assets in excess of $1 billion; or
- (ii) is controlled by a foreign company or by a group of foreign companies that own or control foreign banks that in the aggregate have total worldwide consolidated bank assets in excess of $1 billion. In addition, any other foreign bank's branch located in the United States that is eligible to apply to become an insured bank

under section 5 of the Federal Deposit Insurance Act (12 U.S.C. 1815) is required to maintain reserves in accordance with this part as a nonmember depository institution.

(3) Except as may be otherwise provided by the Board, an Edge Corporation (12 U.S.C. 611 et seq.) or an Agreement Corporation (12 U.S.C. 601 et seq.) is required to comply with the provisions of this part in the same manner and to the same extent as a member bank.

(4) This part does not apply to any financial institution that (i) is organized solely to do business with other financial institutions; (ii) is owned primarily by the financial institutions with which it does business; and (iii) does not do business with the general public.

(5) The provisions of this part do not apply to any deposit that is payable only at an office located outside the United States.

4. Insider Transactions

Regulation O – Loans to Executive Officer[9] relates to prohibitions against providing preferential or treatment to insiders in the banking industry. The following section is an excerpt of text of Regulation O.

TITLE 12 — BANKS AND BANKING
CHAPTER II — FEDERAL RESERVE SYSTEM
Sec. 215.1 Authority, purpose, and scope

(a) Authority. This subpart is issued pursuant to sections 11(i), 22(g), and 22(h) of the Federal Reserve Act (12 U.S.C. 248(i), 375a, and 375b), 12 U.S.C. 1817(k), and section 306 of the Federal Deposit Insurance Corporation Improvement Act of 1991 (Pub. L. 102-242, 105 Stat. 2236 (1991)).

(b) Purpose and scope. This subpart A governs any extension of credit by a member bank to an executive officer, director, or principal shareholder of: The member bank; a bank holding company of which the member bank is a subsidiary; and any other subsidiary of that bank holding company. It also applies to any extension of credit by a member bank to: A company controlled by such a person; and a political or campaign committee that benefits or is controlled by such a person. This subpart A also implements the reporting requirements of 12 U.S.C. 375a concerning extensions of credit by a member bank to its executive officers and of 12 U.S.C. 1817(k) concerning extensions of credit by a member bank to its executive officers or principal shareholders, or the related interests of such persons

Sec. 215.4 General prohibitions.

(a) Terms and creditworthiness — (1) In general. No member bank may extend credit to any insider of the bank or insider of its affiliates unless the extension of credit:

(i) Is made on substantially the same terms (including interest rates and collateral) as, and following credit underwriting procedures that are not less stringent than, those prevailing at the time for comparable transactions by the bank with other persons that are not covered by this part and who are not employed by the bank; and
(ii) Does not involve more than the normal risk of repayment or present other unfavorable features.

5. Lending Disclosure

Regulation Z – Truth in Lending[10] purpose is to promote the informed use of consumer credit by requiring disclosures about its terms and cost. The regulation gives consumers the right to cancel certain credit transactions that involve a lien on a consumer's principal dwelling, regulates certain credit card practices, and provides a means for fair and timely resolution of credit billing disputes. The following section is an excerpt of text of Regulation Z.

TITLE 12 — BANKS AND BANKING
CHAPTER II — FEDERAL RESERVE SYSTEM
Sec. 226.1 Authority, purpose, coverage, organization, enforcement, and liability

(a) Authority. This regulation, known as Regulation Z, is issued by the Board of Governors of the Federal Reserve System to implement the Federal Truth in Lending Act, which is contained in title I of the Consumer Credit Protection Act, as amended (15 U.S.C. 1601 et seq.). This regulation also implements title XII, section 1204 of the Competitive Equality Banking Act of 1987 (Pub. L. 100-86, 101 Stat. 552). Information-collection requirements contained in this regulation have been approved by the Office of Management and Budget under the provisions of 44 U.S.C. 3501 et seq. and have been assigned OMB number 7100-0199.
(b) Purpose. The purpose of this regulation is to promote the informed use of consumer credit by requiring disclosures about its terms and cost. The regulation also gives consumers the right to cancel certain credit transactions that involve a lien on a consumer's principal dwelling, regulates certain credit card practices, and provides a means for fair and timely resolution of credit billing disputes. The regulation does not govern charges for consumer credit. The regulation requires a maximum interest rate to be stated in variable-rate contracts secured by the consumer's dwelling. It also imposes limitations on home equity plans that are subject to the requirements of Sec. 226.5b and mortgages that are subject to the requirements of Sec. 226.32. The regulation prohibits certain acts or practices in connection with credit secured by a consumer's principal dwelling.
(c) Coverage.
    (1) In general, this regulation applies to each individual or business that offers or extends credit when four conditions are met:

(i) The credit is offered or extended to consumers;
(ii) The offering or extension of credit is done regularly;
(iii) The credit is subject to a finance charge or is payable by a written agreement in more than four installments; and
(iv) The credit is primarily for personal, family, or household purposes.

(2) If a credit card is involved, however, certain provisions apply even if the credit is not subject to a finance charge, or is not payable by a written agreement in more than 4 installments, or if the credit card is to be used for business purposes.

(3) In addition, certain requirements of Sec. 226.5b apply to persons who are not creditors but who provide applications for home equity plans to consumers.

(d) Organization. The regulation is divided into subparts and appendices as follows:

(1) Subpart A contains general information. It sets forth:
(i) The authority, purpose, coverage, and organization of the regulation;
(ii) The definitions of basic terms;
(iii) The transactions that are exempt from coverage; and
(iv) The method of determining the finance charge.

(2) Subpart B contains the rules for open-end credit. It requires that initial disclosures and periodic statements be provided, as well as additional disclosures for credit and charge card applications and solicitations and for home equity plans subject to the requirements of Sec. Sec. 226.5a and 226.5b, respectively.

(3) Subpart C relates to closed-end credit. It contains rules on disclosures, treatment of credit balances, annual percentage rate calculations, rescission requirements, and advertising.

(4) Subpart D contains rules on oral disclosures, Spanish language disclosure in Puerto Rico, record retention, effect on state laws, state exemptions, and rate limitations.

(5) Subpart E contains special rules for mortgage transactions. Section 226.32 requires certain disclosures and provides limitations for loans that have rates and fees above specified amounts. Section 226.33 requires disclosures, including the total annual loan cost rate, for reverse mortgage transactions. Section 226.34 prohibits specific acts and practices in connection with mortgage transactions.

(6) Several appendices contain information such as the procedures for determinations about state laws, state exemptions and issuance of staff interpretations, special rules for certain kinds of credit plans, a list of enforcement agencies, and the rules for computing annual percentage rates in closed-end credit transactions and total annual loan cost rates for reverse mortgage transactions.

(e) Enforcement and liability. Section 108 of the act contains the administrative enforcement provisions. Sections 112, 113, 130, 131, and 134 contain provisions relating to liability for failure to comply with the requirements of the act and the regulation. Section 1204(c) of title XII of the Competitive Equality Banking Act of 1987, Pub. L. 100-86, 101 Stat. 552, incorporates by reference administrative enforcement and civil liability provisions of sections 108 and 130 of the act.

6. Deposits Disclosure

Regulation DD – Truth in Savings[11] purpose is to enable consumers to make informed decisions about accounts at depository institutions. This part requires depository institutions to provide disclosures so that consumers can make meaningful comparisons among depository institutions. The following section is an excerpt of text of Regulation DD.

TITLE 12 — BANKS AND BANKING
CHAPTER II — FEDERAL RESERVE SYSTEM
Sec. 230.1 Authority, purpose, coverage, and effect on state laws

(a) Authority. This part, known as Regulation DD, is issued by the Board of Governors of the Federal Reserve System to implement the Truth in Savings Act of 1991 (the act), contained in the Federal Deposit Insurance Corporation Improvement Act of 1991 (12 U.S.C. 4301 et seq., Pub. L. 102-242, 105 Stat. 2236). Information collection requirements contained in this part have been approved by the Office of Management and Budget under the provisions of 44 U.S.C. 3501 et seq. and have been assigned OMB No. 7100-0255.

(b) Purpose. The purpose of this part is to enable consumers to make informed decisions about accounts at depository institutions. This part requires depository institutions to provide disclosures so that consumers can make meaningful comparisons among depository institutions.

(c) Coverage. This part applies to depository institutions except for credit unions. In addition, the advertising rules in Sec. 230.8 of this part apply to any person who advertises an account offered by a depository institution, including deposit brokers.

(d) Effect on state laws. State law requirements that are inconsistent with the requirements of the act and this part are preempted to the extent of the inconsistency. Additional information on inconsistent state laws and the procedures for requesting a preemption determination from the Board are set forth in Appendix C of this part.

7. Real Estate Sales Disclosure

Regulation 34 – Real Estate Lending and Appraisals[12] purpose is to set forth standards for real estate-related lending and associated activities by national banks. The following section is an excerpt of text of Regulation 34.

TITLE 12 — BANKS AND BANKING
CHAPTER I — COMPTROLLER OF THE CURRENCY, DEPARTMENT OF THE TREASURY

Sec. 34.1 Purpose and scope.

(a) Purpose. The purpose of this part is to set forth standards for real estate-related lending and associated activities by national banks. (b) Scope. This part applies to national banks and their operating subsidiaries as provided in 12 CFR 5.34. For the purposes of 12 U.S.C. 371 and subparts A and B of this part, loans secured by liens on interests in real estate include loans made upon the security of condominiums, leaseholds, cooperatives, forest tracts, land sales contracts, and construction project loans. Construction project loans are not subject to subparts A and B of this part, however, if they have a maturity not exceeding 60 months and are made to finance the construction of either:

(1) A building where there is a valid and binding agreement entered into by a financially responsible lender or other party to advance the full amount of the bank's loan upon completion of the building; or

(2) A residential or farm building.

Sec. 34.2 Definitions.

(a) Due-on-sale clause means any clause that gives the lender or any assignee or transferee of the lender the power to declare the entire debt payable if all or part of the legal or equitable title or an equivalent contractual interest in the property securing the loan is transferred to another person, whether by deed, contract, or otherwise.

(b) State means any state of the United States of America, the District of Columbia, Puerto Rico, the Virgin Islands, the Northern Mariana Islands, American Samoa, and Guam.

(c) State law limitations means any state statute, regulation, or order of any state agency, or judicial decision interpreting state law.

Sec. 34.3 General rule.

A national bank may make, arrange, purchase, or sell loans or extensions of credit, or interests therein, that are secured by liens on, or interests in, real estate, subject to terms, conditions, and limitations prescribed by the Comptroller of the Currency by regulation or order.

8. Self-assessment of Internal Controls/Risk Management

The U.S. Sarbanes-Oxley Act of 2002, sponsored by U.S. Senator Paul Sarbanes and U.S. Representative Michael Oxley, represented a significant change to federal securities laws. The Act came as a result of the large corporate financial scandals involving Enron, WorldCom, Global Crossing, and Arthur Andersen. Effective in 2004, all publicly traded companies are required to submit an annual report of the effectiveness of their internal accounting controls to the SEC.

One of the primary requirements (probably the most well-known) is section 404 — "Management Assessment of Internal Controls" — which called on public companies to identify financial reporting risks, ascertain related controls, assess their effectiveness, fix any control deficiencies, and then retest and re-document anew. For companies of all sizes, but especially those with complex organizational structures, the provisions appeared to require an overwhelming task. In fact, so challenging was Section 404 implementation that the SEC thrice delayed compliance deadlines, once in 2003 and twice during 2004.

On May 27, 2003, the SEC adopted rules requiring an annual management report on an auditor attestation of a company's internal controls over financial reporting. Section 404 requires each annual report to contain an "internal control report," which shall:

- State the responsibility of management for establishing and maintaining an adequate internal control structure and procedures for financial reporting.
- Contain an assessment, as of the end of the issuer's fiscal year, of the effectiveness of the internal control structure and procedures of the issuer for financial reporting.

Auditor shall attest to, and report on, the assessment made by the management of the issuer. In addition, the SEC requires each reporting entity to disclose whether it has adopted a code of ethics for its senior financial officers and the contents of that code.

On May 16, 2005, the SEC released the following statement on issues that arose during the first year of experience with the implementation of Section 404 of the Sarbanes-Oxley Act of 2002.

> Commission Statement on Implementation of Internal Control Reporting Requirements
> Washington, D.C., May 16, 2005[13]
>
> From the Commission's April 13th Roundtable on Implementation of Internal Control Reporting Provisions — as well as from the extensive materials submitted in response to our request for feedback — we believe two messages came through clearly: First, compliance with Section 404 is producing benefits, including a heightened focus on internal controls at the top levels of public companies. We hope that this focus will produce better financial reporting. Second, implementation in the first year also resulted in significant costs. While a portion of the costs likely reflect startup expenses from this new requirement, it also appears that some nontrivial costs may have been unnecessary, due to excessive, duplicative, or misfocused efforts. As a result, we heard the implementation process needs to be improved going forward so that it is more effective and efficient.
>
> In response to those concerns, we asked the SEC staff, at the end of the roundtable, to consider whether additional guidance and clarification of certain issues was appropriate. Today the staff released a Staff Statement on Management's Report on Internal Control Over Financial Reporting to provide such guidance. An overarching principle of this guidance is the responsibility of management to determine the form and level of controls appropriate for each company and to scope their assessment and the testing accordingly. Registered public accounting firms should recognize that there is a zone of reasonable conduct by

companies that should be recognized as acceptable in the implementation of Section 404. The SEC staff guidance complements the guidance that the PCAOB will provide with respect to the application of its Auditing Standard No. 2, *An Audit of Internal Control over Financial Reporting Performed in Conjunction with an Audit of the Financial Statements*.

We wish to make clear that these actions are not the end of the process. The Commission staff will continue to monitor the implementation of the internal control reporting requirements, particularly for smaller public companies and foreign private issuers. In addition, because of the importance we place on effective and efficient implementation of Section 404, we believe the following broad concepts bear mention at this time.

Although it is not surprising that first-year implementation of Section 404 was challenging, almost all of the significant complaints we heard related not to the Sarbanes-Oxley Act or to the rules and auditing standards implementing Section 404, but rather to a mechanical, and even overly cautious, way in which those rules and standards apparently have been applied in many cases. Both management and external auditors must bring reasoned judgment and a top-down, risk-based approach to the 404 compliance process. A one-size fits all, bottom-up, check-the-box approach that treats all controls equally is less likely to improve internal controls and financial reporting than reasoned, good faith exercise of professional judgment focused on reasonable, as opposed to absolute, assurance.

In future years we expect the internal control audit to be better integrated with the audit of a company's financial statements. If management and auditors can achieve the goal of integrating the two audits, we expect that both internal and external costs of Section 404 compliance will fall for most companies.

Internal controls over financial reporting should reflect the nature and size of the company to which they relate. Particular attention should be paid to making sure that implementation of Section 404 is appropriately tailored to the operations of smaller companies. Again, this is an area where reasoned judgment and a risk-based approach must be brought to bear. We continue to be actively engaged in projects to evaluate and assess the effects of the internal control reporting rules on smaller companies. In addition to delaying the implementation of those rules for smaller companies, we have encouraged the Committee of Sponsoring Organizations (COSO) of the Treadway Commission to develop additional guidance in applying its internal control framework to smaller companies. We have established the Commission Advisory Committee on Smaller Public Companies to consider the impact of Commission rules — including the internal control reporting rules — on smaller companies.

We encourage frequent and frank dialogue among management, auditors, and audit committees with the goal of improving internal controls and the financial reports upon which investors rely. Management of all companies — large and small — should not fear that a discussion of internal controls with, or a request for assistance or clarification from, the auditor will, itself, be deemed a deficiency in internal control. Moreover, as long as management determines the accounting to be used and does not rely on the auditor to design or implement the controls, we do not believe that the auditor's providing advice or assistance, in itself, constitutes a violation of our independence rules. Both common sense and sound policy dictate that communications must be ongoing and open in order to create the best environment for producing high quality financial reporting and auditing; communications must not be so restricted or formalized that their value is lost.

The entire financial reporting community, including investors, auditors, management, and regulators, shares the common goal of improving the reliability of financial reporting and the information available to the market. With the experience of the first round of Section 404 implementation, we should continue to focus on the lessons learned and ways to improve the process going forward. Section 404 is too important not to get right, but getting it right requires both effective and efficient implementation.

9. Investor/Depositor Protection

Protecting the privacy of consumer information held by "financial institutions" is at the heart of the financial privacy provisions of the Gramm-Leach-Bliley Financial Modernization Act of 1999. The GLB Act requires companies to give consumers privacy notices that explain the institutions' information-sharing practices. In turn, consumers have the right to limit some — but not all — sharing of their information.

Below is a synopsis of the financial privacy requirements of the law.[14]

The GLB Act applies to "financial institutions" — companies that offer financial products or services to individuals, like loans, financial or investment advice, or insurance. The Federal Trade Commission has authority to enforce the law with respect to "financial institutions" that are not covered by the federal banking agencies, the Securities and Exchange Commission, the Commodity Futures Trading Commission, and state insurance authorities. Among the institutions that fall under FTC jurisdiction for purposes of the GLB Act are non-bank mortgage lenders, loan brokers, some financial or investment advisers, tax preparers, providers of real estate settlement services, and debt collectors. At the same time, the FTC's regulation applies only to companies that are "significantly engaged" in such financial activities.

The law requires that financial institutions protect information collected about individuals; it does not apply to information collected in business or commercial activities.

A company's obligations under the GLB Act depend on whether the company has consumers or customers who obtain its services. A *consumer* is an individual who obtains or has obtained a financial product or service from a financial institution for personal, family, or household reasons. A *customer* is a consumer with a continuing relationship with a financial institution. Generally, if the relationship between the financial institution and the individual is significant and/or long-term, the individual is a customer of the institution. For example, a person who gets a mortgage from a lender or hires a broker to get a personal loan is considered a customer of the lender or the broker, while a person who uses a check-cashing service is a consumer of that service.

Why is the difference between consumers and customers so important? Because only customers are entitled to receive a financial institution's privacy notice automatically. Consumers are entitled to receive a privacy notice from a financial institution only if the company shares the consumers' information with companies not affiliated with it, with some exceptions. Customers must receive a notice every year for as long as the customer relationship lasts.

The privacy notice must be given to individual customers or consumers by mail or in-person delivery; it may not, say, be posted on a wall. Reasonable ways to deliver a notice may depend on the type of business the institution is in. For example, an online lender may post its notice on its Web site and require online consumers to acknowledge receipt as a necessary part of a loan application.

The privacy notice must be a clear, conspicuous, and accurate statement of the company's privacy practices; it should include what information the company collects about its consumers and customers, with whom it shares the information, and how it protects or safeguards the information. The notice applies to the "nonpublic personal information" the company gathers and discloses about its consumers and customers; in practice, that may be most — or all — of the information a company has about them. For example, nonpublic personal information could be information that a consumer or customer puts on an application; information about the individual from another source, such as a credit bureau; or information about transactions between the individual and the company, such as an account balance. Indeed, even the fact that an individual is a consumer or customer of a particular financial institution is nonpublic person information. But information that the company has reason to believe is lawfully public — such as mortgage loan information in a jurisdiction where that information is publicly recorded — is not restricted by the GLB Act.

Consumers and customers have the right to opt out of — or say no to — having their information shared with certain third parties. The privacy notice must explain how — and offer a reasonable way — they can do that. For example, providing a toll-free telephone number or a detachable form with a preprinted address is a reasonable way for consumers or customers to opt out; requiring someone to write a letter as the only way to opt out is not.

The privacy notice also must explain that consumers have a right to say no to the sharing of certain information — credit report or application information — with the financial institution's affiliates. An affiliate is an entity that controls another company, is controlled by the company, or is under common control with the company. Consumers have this right under a different law, the Fair Credit

Reporting Act. The GLB Act does not give consumers the right to opt out when the financial institution shares other information with its affiliates.

The GLB Act provides no opt-out right in several other situations: For example, an individual cannot opt out if a financial institution shares information with outside companies that provide essential services like data processing or servicing accounts; the disclosure is legally required; a financial institution shares customer data with outside service providers that market the financial company's products or services.

The GLB Act puts some limits on how anyone that receives nonpublic personal information from a financial institution can use or re-disclose the information. Take the case of a lender that discloses customer information to a service provider responsible for mailing account statements, where the consumer has no right to opt out: The service provider may use the information for limited purposes — that is, for mailing account statements. It may not sell the information to other organizations or use it for marketing.

However, it is a different scenario when a company receives nonpublic personal information from a financial institution that provided an opt-out notice — and the consumer did not opt out. In this case, the recipient steps into the shoes of the disclosing financial institution, and may use the information for its own purposes or re-disclose it to a third party, consistent with the financial institution's privacy notice. That is, if the privacy notice of the financial institution allows for disclosure to other unaffiliated financial institutions — like insurance providers — the recipient may re-disclose the information to an unaffiliated insurance provider.

10. Financial and Personal Information Privacy

Regulation P – Privacy of Consumer Financial Information[15] purpose is to govern the treatment of nonpublic personal information. The following section is an excerpt of text of Regulation P.

TITLE 12 — BANKS AND BANKING
CHAPTER II — FEDERAL RESERVE SYSTEM

(a) Purpose. This part governs the treatment of nonpublic personal information about consumers by the financial institutions listed in paragraph (b) of this section. This part:
   (1) Requires a financial institution to provide notice to customers about its privacy policies and practices;
   (2) Describes the conditions under which a financial institution may disclose nonpublic personal information about consumers to nonaffiliated third parties; and
   (3) Provides a method for consumers to prevent a financial institution from disclosing that information to most nonaffiliated third parties by "opting out" of that disclosure, subject to the exceptions in Sec. Sec. 216.13, 216.14, and 216.15.

(b) Scope.

(1) This part applies only to nonpublic personal information about individuals who obtain financial products or services primarily for personal, family, or household purposes from the institutions listed below. This part does not apply to information about companies or about individuals who obtain financial products or services for business, commercial, or agricultural purposes. This part applies to the U.S. offices of entities for which the Board has primary supervisory authority. They are referred to in this part as "you." These are: State member banks, bank holding companies and certain of their nonbank subsidiaries or affiliates, state uninsured branches and agencies of foreign banks, commercial lending companies owned or controlled by foreign banks, and Edge and Agreement corporations.

(2) Nothing in this part modifies, limits, or supersedes the standards governing individually identifiable health information promulgated by the Secretary of Health and Human Services under the authority of sections 262 and 264 of the Health Insurance Portability and Accountability Act of 1996 (42 U.S.C. 1320d-1320d-8).

Another standard related to privacy is HIPAA (The Health Insurance Portability & Accountability Act of 1996) calls for a more efficient delivery of health care through the standardization of electronic data interchange, the protection of confidentiality, and the security of health data. The effect of this legislation requires major changes in most healthcare transactions and administrative information systems.

Health organizations must adopt standard code sets to be used in all health transactions. For example, coding systems that describe diseases, injuries, and other health problems, as well as their causes, symptoms, and actions taken, must become uniform. All parties to any transaction will have to use and accept the same coding. Privacy and Security Standards cover all individually identifiable health information in the hands of covered entities, regardless of whether the information is or has been in electronic form. The privacy standards limit the nonconsensual use and release of private health information; give patients new rights over access to their medical records; restrict most disclosure of health information; establish sanctions for improper use or disclosure; and establish new requirements for access to records by researchers and others. The security standards will provide a uniform level of protection of all health information that is stored or transmitted electronically and that pertains to an individual.

Additional information on HIPAA is available at http://aspe.hhs.gov/admnsimp/pl104191.htm

11. Anti-money Laundering

Bank Secrecy Act[16] was passed in 1970 to require banks to document and file certain transaction reports for possible use in criminal, tax, or regulatory proceedings. The purpose was to provide an audit trail of banking transactions to reduce the potential for money laundering activities by those involved in illegal activities. The regulations emphasize the development and implementation of "know your customer" policies and procedures by banks. Compliance with the Act is extremely important as civil and criminal penalties can be imposed, including the termination of banking licenses.

Each bank is required to develop and provide for the continued administration of a program reasonably designed to assure and monitor compliance with the recordkeeping and reporting requirements. The following section is an excerpt of text of the Bank Secrecy Act.

TITLE 12 — BANKS AND BANKING
CHAPTER I — COMPTROLLER OF THE CURRENCY, DEPARTMENT OF THE TREASURY

Sec. 21 (a)(1) The Congress finds that adequate records maintained by insured depository institutions have a high degree of usefulness in criminal, tax, and regulatory investigations and proceedings. The Congress further finds that microfilm or other reproductions and other records made by banks of checks, as well as records kept by banks of the identity of persons maintaining or authorized to act with respect to accounts therein, have been of particular value in this respect.
(2) It is the purpose of this section to require the maintenance of appropriate types of records by insured depository institutions in the United States where such records have a high degree of usefulness in criminal, tax, or regulatory investigations or proceedings.
Subpart C — Procedures for Monitoring Bank Secrecy Act Compliance
Sec. 21.21 Bank Secrecy Act compliance.

(a) Purpose. This subpart is issued to assure that all national banks establish and maintain procedures reasonably designed to assure and monitor their compliance with the requirements of subchapter II of chapter 53 of title 31, United States Code, and the implementing regulations promulgated thereunder by the Department of Treasury at 31 CFR part 103.

(b) Compliance procedures. On or before April 27, 1987, each bank shall develop and provide for the continued administration of a program reasonably designed to assure and monitor compliance with the recordkeeping and reporting requirements set forth in subchapter II of chapter 53 of title 31, United States Code, and the implementing regulations promulgated thereunder by the Department of Treasury at 31 CFR part 103. The compliance program shall be reduced to writing, approved by the board of directors and noted in the minutes.

(c) Contents of compliance program. The compliance program shall, at a minimum:
   (1) Provide for a system of internal controls to assure ongoing compliance;
   (2) Provide for independent testing for compliance to be conducted by bank personnel or by an outside party;
   (3) Designate an individual or individuals responsible for coordinating and monitoring day-to-day compliance; and
   (4) Provide training for appropriate personnel.

C. Stock Exchanges and Other Markets

The markets that manage the securities industry are complex. In order to understand the trading of negotiable securities, it is necessary to understand the financial markets. The following section will provide an overview of these financial markets.

Brokers and Dealers — Although they perform similar functions, brokers and dealers actually perform a separate and distinct function. The securities market must be liquid to function. That means that orders to buy and sell must be processed (filled) at all times; this is called "making a market." Dealers are expected to maintain an inventory of each security in which they make a market. Therefore, dealers are expected to have specific securities to sell if a customer wishes to buy them, and conversely, to buy these securities if a customer wishes to sell.

Dealers make their money through the "spread" — which is the difference between the "Ask" and "Bid" prices. The Ask price is the price at which the dealer will sell a security. The Bid price is the price at which the dealer will buy a security. The Bid price is always lower than the Ask price. For example, a dealer may market Stock A in the following fashion: Bid (10) and Ask (10.5). Thus, the spread or dealer profit is 0.5 point for each share bought and sold.

On stock exchanges, dealer firms are generally called specialist firms and have the sole (are the only ones who may sell) market for specific stocks on an exchange. The specialists deal with retail members or "brokers" of an exchange. Brokers are the middle person between dealers and the public. A public customer places an order with a broker and the broker executes the trade with a dealer. The broker receives a commission for the transaction from the public customer.

Dealers and brokers must be independent from each other. Additionally, dealers are prohibited from dealing directly with the public, except in the Over-the-Counter (OTC) market where a firm may perform either function, but cannot perform both on the same transaction. These firms are referred to as Broker-Dealer firms in the Over-the-Counter Market. The OTC market will be discussed later in this unit.

Types of Markets — Negotiable securities are traded in specific markets, primarily the primary and secondary markets.

The *primary market* is the market where new issues are sold. A new issue is a previously unissued security that is being sold to the public for the first time. Most new issues are traded in the OTC market, since the stock exchanges have more rigorous listing requirements. Transactions on the primary market are performed by an underwriter (the investment banking firm that is backing the transaction). After a security has been properly registered and priced in the primary market, it may be traded on the secondary market.

The *secondary market* is the market that promotes the trading (buying and selling) of issued securities. There are several component markets that comprise the secondary market. They are:

- First market — where listed securities are traded on the floor of a stock exchange. The largest first market is the New York Stock Exchange (NYSE).
- Second market — is the trading of securities that are *not* listed on an exchange, i.e., OTC. The secondary market actually has a greater trade volume than the exchanges and trades a greater number of companies. The OTC market is controlled by the National Association of Security Dealers (NASD). The market is generally called NASDAQ, which stands for NASD Automated Quotations.
- Third market — is the trading of listed securities (first market) which generally takes place outside of exchange trading hours. Third market companies stay open 24 hours a day and can perform trades of listed stocks even though the stock exchange is closed.
- Fourth market — is the direct trading of securities between institutions without a broker. This reduces the commissions paid to brokers by institutional investors (i.e., pension systems, mutual funds, or insurance companies).

Types of Orders — an order is the mechanism that is used by a registered representative of a broker to execute the trade for a public customer. An order ticket is used by a broker to convey the information to exchange floor traders (specialists) or OTC traders. Information that is included on an order ticket includes:

- Customer name and account number.
- Date submitted.
- Buy or sell indication.
- Order size (number of shares).
- Name and symbol of security being bought or sold.
- Price information (specific pricing information discussed below).
- Duration of the order (unless specified all orders not executed are canceled at the end of the day).

There are four basic types of orders:

Market orders are orders that are to be filled (executed) immediately at the current market price. There is no price specified on a market order. Market orders do not carry over to the next day.

Limit orders specify a price at which a security should be bought or sold. In most cases, limit orders will either be a buy or a sell limit order. A buy limit order would specify a target price for a security. To illustrate this, assuming that stock A's current market price is $20, a buy limit order for $18 is an order that will only be executed if the price drops to $18. A sell limit order is similar to a buy order except the public customer is hoping the market price rises. To illustrate this, assume stock A's current market price is $20, a sell limit order for $22 is an order that will only be executed if the price rises to $22. Note: in many instances limit orders are submitted as "good till canceled" (GTC) to stop the order from being canceled at the end of the day.

Stop orders are orders at specific prices that are used to limit losses on long and short positions. A sell stop order will not be executed until the market price reaches a specific target. To illustrate this, assume that a sell stop order was placed on stock A at a price of $20. Once a trade is made at $20 the sell order is triggered and executed as a market order (thus, the actual price could be higher or lower). Sell stop orders are used to limit losses on long positions (the public customer actually owns the stock) in falling markets; therefore, they are placed below current market levels. Similarly, a buy stop order will not be executed until the market price reaches a specific target and the trade is triggered the same as a sell stop order. Buy stop orders are used to limit losses on short positions (the public customer sold stock that they do not own and must deliver [buy the stock they sold] by a specified date) in rising markets; therefore, they are placed above current market levels.

Stop limit orders are similar to stop orders except that the order does not become a market order and must be filled at the limit price or better. To illustrate this, assume a sell stop limit order was placed on stock A with a stop of $20 and a limit of $18. Once a trade is made at $20 the sell order is triggered and turned into a limit order that will only be executed if the market price is $18 or higher.

New issues are used by corporations when they need to raise capital for long-term needs. In these cases, corporations often issue new securities. Although corporations can sell their own securities to investors, they usually work through an investment banking firm. Investment banking firms act as an intermediary between the corporation seeking capital and the individual or institutional investors.

Investment bankers often underwrite (buy the securities and resell them) the new issue. The dollar amounts of these transactions are very high and the investment banking business is extremely risky. Due to the high risk, commercial banks are prohibited from entering into the investment banking arena.

Before a new issue can be sold, the security must be registered with the SEC. This provides for full disclosure about the company and new issue to prospective investors. The SEC has a minimum of 20 days (called a cooling-off period) from registration to perform a review. While the SEC is performing its review, a preliminary prospectus (red herring) may be issued to provide information to potential investors. This prospectus contains information similar to the SEC registration document. Although a price may not be set in either the registration document or the red herring, an expected price range may be indicated.

The security also must be registered in each state in which it will be sold, in accordance with the laws of that state. At the end of the cooling off-period a meeting is held between the investment banking firm and the responsible officers of the corporation to establish the public offering price of the issue.

An amendment to the registration statement, setting the price must be messengered to the SEC. The following day the issue is effective and may be sold. The investment banking firm announces the new issue to the press. This is called a tombstone announcement. All buyers must receive a final prospectus prior to buying a new issue.

Depending on the market demand for an issue, the investment banking firm may need to stabilize the issue by buying back shares at a price below the initial public offering. On the other hand, there are some securities that sell for a premium on the secondary market immediately after initial issue. This is the result of the demand for the new issue exceeding the supply. In the late 1990s, a number of Internet-based companies fell into this category and the price on the secondary market rose substantially.

There are generally two types of offerings:

- Primary offering — called the initial public offering or IPO. The IPO is the first time that shares of a company are offered publicly. Proceeds from primary offerings generally go directly to the issuer.
- Secondary offering — when the investment banking firm distributes securities (often large blocks) held by individual owners.

Clearing and Settlement Process — is the process of delivering to the buyer and paying the seller for securities.

The securities must be delivered in "good" form to clear the deal. There are multiple requirements and conditions regarding good delivery. For example, a registered security must be "assigned" or properly endorsed on the back of the certificate exactly as indicated on the front of the certificate. If certificates are held by a brokerage firm (in which the holder has signed the power of transfer to a brokerage firm) the certificate can be transferred without a signature.

The settlement date for stock, municipal bond, and corporate bonds is three business days after the transaction date. This is called the *regular way* transaction. Other settlement dates are:

- Cash — a same-day settlement, usually before 2:30 p.m. Eastern Standard Time.
- U.S. government securities — a next business day settlement.
- Seller's and buyer's option — in both of these cases the settlement date is extended beyond three days at the request of seller or buyer.
- When, As, and If Issued (WAII) — the settlement is postponed until three days after certificates are issued. This is associated with a new issue and the certificates are not available on the transaction date. If the new issue is canceled, then the original trade is canceled.

The Stock Exchanges*

A stock exchange is the location where buyers and sellers trade securities. The largest and most widely known stock exchange is the New York Stock Exchange (NYSE).

Regional stock exchanges (see page 315) function in a similar manner and listed securities must be traded in the physical boundaries of the exchange floor. It should be noted that the NYSE handles over half of all securities transactions.

*To simplify discussions of exchanges most of the examples will be related to the NYSE; however, it should be noted that regional stock exchanges function in a similar manner.

How the Exchanges Function — Although exchanges are not involved in the market, they do have an enforcement role to ensure that trades conform to laws and regulations. An exchange board of directors sets policy, enforces rules, determines which stocks will be listed, and handles memberships. The board is comprised of an equal number of members (see below) and the general public. The board also includes an elected full-time chairman.

- Memberships on the NYSE are limited to 1,366 seats. These memberships are open only to individuals; corporations and partnerships may not hold seats. Seats are sold to any qualified person and prices range from thousands to millions of dollars. Although brokerage firms are not permitted to hold a seat, they may conduct business if a partner in the firm holds a seat. Categories of memberships are:
  - Commission house brokers — the members generally execute customer orders for a fee or commission. They may also execute trades for their own account.
  - Floor brokers — these members generally execute orders for other brokers when they are too busy.
  - Bond members — these members deal exclusively in bonds.
  - Market makers or specialists — these members stay in a particular floor location and are involved only in trades in which they specialize.
  - Registered traders — these members usually execute trades only for their own account.

Listing and delisting rules — To be listed on a stock exchange a company must meet specific requirements that are designated by the exchange. Only listed stocks can be bought and sold at the exchange. For example, the NYSE has some general and specific requirements (the requirements periodically change). The requirements for listing on the NYSE include:

- A minimum market value.
- A minimum number of outstanding shares.
- A minimum number of shareholders.
- A minimum threshold for corporate earnings.

- Financial condition of the corporation.
- Future prospects of the corporation.
- Corporation must permit full voting rights to common shareholders.
- Corporation must provide relevant information to investors on a timely basis.
- The NYSE Board also determines if there is sufficient national interest in the corporation.

Delisting can occur if the corporation falls below the minimum listing requirements described above. Additionally, a corporation can be delisted if they disallow common stock voting rights, file for bankruptcy, or fail to disclose financial statements.

A corporation may request an exchange to delist them. To delist a corporation on the NYSE, two-thirds of the common stockholders must vote to delist, holders of no more than 10 percent of the outstanding shares may object, and a majority of the corporation's board of directors must agree to the delisting.

The consolidated tape — stock transactions are shown on a tape within seconds of a transaction. The information on the tape is submitted by the selling broker and includes the number of shares and price. There are three tape networks:

- Network A — covers all stocks listed on the NYSE and includes all trades of the listed stocks (including regional exchange transactions and third and fourth market transactions).
- Network B — covers American Exchange (AMEX) transactions and trades from regional exchanges of stocks listed on the AMEX or NYSE.
- Consolidated quotation services — provides quotes on exchange listed securities traded in the OTC market.

The tape contains the following abbreviations and symbols:

- Ticker symbol or abbreviation for the stock is listed at the top of the line (for example, International Business machine is listed as IBM).
- Trades are listed in multiples of 100's and followed by an "s," with the exception of trade volume over 10,000, which is listed at the exact amount.
- Share price is listed in the dollar amount with the minimum value being one-sixteenth of a dollar.
- Preferred stocks are identified with a Pr.
- If a stock opening is delayed, the tape would have "OPD" or "OPENING DELAYED" next to that particular stock.
- If trading is halted, the tape would have "TRADING HALTED" next to that particular stock.
- Trades that are reported late are listed with "SLD."

Some basic examples of tape information follow:

IBM
11s90 (1,100 shares of IBM at $90)

SLD 9s91 (900 shares of IBM at $91 sometime earlier)

5sPr/110 (500 preferred shares of IBM at $110)

Specific Rules Relating to the NYSE — The NYSE has trading rules to ensure that the market functions effectively and that members and brokers do not have an unfair advantage over the public. A list of some of the NYSE trading rules follows:

- Prohibition of prearranged trades (rule 78) — prearranged trades to sell securities with an offer to buy back at a stated price is prohibited.
- Prohibition of crossing orders within a firm (rule 76) — a member firm holding a sell order and a buy order from two customers is prohibited from making the trade "within the firm." The firm must first send the trade to the exchange floor and if the order is not taken, then the firm may complete the trade within the firm.
- Trading limitations based on market volatility (rules 80A and 80B) — after the market crash in October, 1987, the NYSE instituted these rules to decrease market volatility. Rule 80A reduces computerized institutional orders by routing them to a specialist for approval. This rule is invoked if the Dow Jones Industrial Average (DJIA) moves by 50 points or more or if the Standard and Poor's 500 Index moves by 12 points or more. Rule 80B halts trading for all stocks for 1 hour if the DJIA declines by 250 points. If after trading reopens on that day and the DJIA decreases another 150 points, trading is halted for two hours.
- Customer orders must receive priority over firm orders (rule 92) — a customer's order must receive priority over an order for the firm's trading account for anyone associated with the firm.
- Trade records retained for three years (rule 410) — records of trade orders transmitted to the floor must be retained for three years with two years worth of these trades readily accessible.
- Firms are prohibited from the following activities (rule 435) —
  - Trading an account too frequently or trading an excessive amount in proportion to the account.
  - Participating in any customer manipulation.
  - Circulating rumors to influence market price.
  - Changing the price of a transaction before the settlement date.

For additional information on NYSE rules, go to http://rules.nyse.com/NYSE/NYSE_Rules/

Regional Stock Exchanges — A stock exchange is the location where buyers and sellers trade securities. Some of the regional stock exchanges and their Internet Web sites as of (November 2005) are listed below:

- The American Stock Exchange (http://www.amex.com/)
- Pacific Stock Exchange (http://www.pacificex.com/)
- Philadelphia Stock Exchange (http://www.phlx.com/index.stm)
- Boston Stock Exchange (http://www.bostonstock.com/)
- Montreal Stock Exchange (http://www.m-x.ca/accueil_en.php)
- Frankfurt Stock Exchange (http://deutsche-boerse.com/dbag/dispatch/en/kir/gdb_navigation/about_us/20_FWB_Frankfurt_Stock_Exchange)
- Tokyo Stock Exchange (http://www.tse.or.jp/english/index.shtml)

These exchanges perform the same function as the NYSE, but generally deal in smaller volumes.

Over-the-Counter (OTC) Market

The term Over-the-Counter, with the exception of trade volume over 10,000, which is listed at the exact amount is used to describe securities trading that does not take place on the floor of an exchange. There is no centralized location and individual firms "make a market" in a specific set of securities. All securities not listed on an exchange are traded on the OTC market; however, any stock may be traded OTC.

How the OTC functions — Unlike exchanges where prices are determined by bidding conducted on the floor, OTC prices are negotiated. For example, someone who wants to buy a security will make a bid (set a price at which they will buy a security) and someone wishing to sell will ask (set a price at which they will sell a security) for a price. The difference between the bid and ask is the spread. Some of the particulars of the OTC include:

- OTC transactions are governed by National Association of Securities Dealers (NASD).
- Smaller and newer companies tend to trade on the OTC (since they generally cannot meet the exchange listing requirements).
- All types of issues are traded OTC. For example, listed and unlisted securities, bank and insurance company shares, government securities, mutual fund shares, government bonds, and corporate bonds are all traded in the OTC market.
- A market maker (dealer) makes money through the spread (or markup) rather than through a commission.
- Brokers act as an agent for a buyer or seller and make money through commissions.
- Dealers may also be brokers; however, they cannot act a dealer and broker on the same transaction (i.e., earn a markup and charge a commission).
- Brokers must send written confirmations to the customer (for retail customers, confirmations must be sent on the settlement date).

NASDAQ includes 3 levels of quotes:

- Level 1 — for retail customers and includes the highest bid and lowest offer for a security.
- Level 2 — provides a listing of all market makers and their current bid and offers.
- Level 3 — for the use of market makers and permits the entry of their current quotes.

Listing and delisting and other OTC rules — Although not nearly as stringent as the listing requirement for an exchange, there are specific requirement for NASDAQ listing. The requirement for listing a security on NASDAQ include:

- Registration under the Securities Act of 1934 or the Investment Company Act of 1940.
- A minimum of 10,000 publicly held shares.
- A minimum of 300 stockholders.
- A minimum price of $5 per share.
- A minimum of $1 million to $2 million in capital and surplus.
- A minimum of two market makers for domestic companies and three for foreign companies.

Market makers on NASDAQ also have specific rules that they must follow. These requirements include:

- Maintain business hours of at least 8:30 a.m. to 4:30 p.m. (Eastern Standard Time).
- Require net capital position of at least $2,500 on each issue.
- Report trades within 90 seconds of execution.
- Require quotes for each issue.
- Require daily and monthly reporting regarding trading volume.

Options Market

The options market provides an opportunity to enter into a contract to buy or sell securities for a set price until a specified date. The individual who buys a contract is not required to finalize the trade, but has the option to do so. If the buyer exercises the option, the securities must be sold or bought at the specified price.

How the options market functions – To understand the options market, some basic terms must be defined:

- Long — A term used to describe the position of the holder (buyer) of the contract.
- Short — A term used to describe the position of the writer (seller) of the contract.
- Premium — the fee paid to the writer of an option by the holder. The premium is paid whether or not the option is exercised.
- Expiration date — the month (date) in which the option expires.
- Strike or exercise price — the specified price included in the contract.

- Call option — the holder of the option has the option (right) to buy securities from the writer for a specified price.
- Put option — the holder of the option has the option (right) to sell securities to the writer for a specified price.

To help explain options, two example are listed below:

- Example 1 – (Call Option) — Customer X buys an option for the month of January to buy 100 shares of stock Z at $40 per share for a premium of $300. If stock Z falls below $40, then customer X will let the option expire and lose the $300 premium. If stock Z rises to $50 then customer X may decide to exercise the option. In this case, customer X buys the stock for $4,000 ($40 x 100) and then sells it for $5,000 ($50 x 100). Customer X would realize a profit of $700 ($5,000 – $4,000 - $300 = $700).

- Example 2 – (Put Option) — Customer X buys an option for the month of January to sell 100 shares of stock Z at $40 per share for a premium of $300. If stock Z rises above $40, then customer X will let the option expire and lose the $300 premium. If stock Z falls to $32 then customer X may decide to exercise the option. In this case, customer X sells the stock for $4,000 ($40 x 100) and buys it for the sale $3,200 ($32 x 100). Customer X would realize a profit of $500 ($4,000 – $3,200 - $300 = $500).

One way to analyze options is through a breakeven analysis* for the holder and writer. The holder of a call has a breakeven point when the stock price equals the strike price plus the premium paid. Using example 1 outlined above, the breakeven price is $43 [($40X100 shares) + 300= $4300/100 shares = $43/share]. The holder of a put has a breakeven point when the stock price equals the strike price minus the premium received. The holder of the put in example 2 has a breakeven price of [($40X100 shares) - 300= $3700/100 shares = $37/share].

The writer of a call has the same breakeven point when writing an uncovered call (the writer will buy the stock at the time of the transaction). If the call is covered (the stock has already been purchased), then the breakeven analysis is a little more complex. Using example 1 outlined above and adding the writer's original purchase price of $38, the breakeven price is [($38x100 shares) – 300 = $3500/100 shares = $35/share]. The writer of a put has a breakeven point when the stock price = strike price – premium received. In example 2 the writer has a breakeven price of $37 [($40x100 shares) – 300 = $3700/100 shares = $37/share].

*Note: For simplicity, brokerage fees are omitted from the breakeven analysis.

D. Money and Banking

The financial sector and, in particular, the banking industry play an important role in the allocation of capital resources and monetary and growth in an economy. In the long term, a well-functioning banking system will facilitate increased growth and welfare, and even out business cycles.

Banks perform a variety of functions. They have provided money changing and payment processing services. Payment processing has gained relevance at the international level owing to the greater integration of financial services. Another critical role of banks is to manage and control risks. These functions also give banks a significant role in the process of saving and investment allocation. However, these functions also make banks vulnerable to market conditions and can have a negative effect on the economy because of banks' role in the economy. As a result, there is a case for strong regulations in a banking environment as banking and economic policy impact the performance of the overall financial market.

The following is a brief overview of money and banking concepts as these concepts are discussed in detail in other sections of this guide.

1. Role of Money and Banking

Broadly defined, money is anything of value that can function as a medium of exchange. The money supply in the world. typically refers to paper money, coins, and funds in checking accounts. "Near-monies" are highly liquid assets such as savings accounts and government bonds. A bank can lend money up to a specified amount based on the size of its excess reserves.

Money has value in relation to its purchasing power. Therefore, if prices rise, the value of money falls. If prices fall, the value of money increases.

Conceptually, money consists of instruments with certain characteristics. Money is generally defined as a medium of exchange, a standard of value, a standard of deferred payments, and a store of wealth. Thus, money represents generalized purchasing power, which should be reasonably well linked over time with the nominal value of the total spending and output of goods and services in the nation's economic system. Individuals and companies choose to hold money because its use simplifies a wide range of economic transactions. They may limit their money balances, however, because holding money may have costs in the form of lost opportunities from alternative investments. The amount of money that is consistent with a central bank's goals for prices and output depends upon the customs, practices, regulations, and political environment of its country's economy.

2. Bond and Stock Markets

- The financial markets help keep the economy function by giving individuals and businesses the opportunity to transfer and borrow money.
- Money can be transferred directly between individuals or companies, such as occurs when a company sells its stocks or directly to the public. Banks can increase the money supply and stimulate the economy through the funds its invests and loans.
- There are two types of financial asset markets: "Primary markets" deal in new issues of securities, and "secondary markets" trade in shares outstanding, mortgages, and loans.
- The two types of stock markets in the U.S. are the formal security exchanges (e.g., the New York Stock Exchange) and the "over-the-counter" market.

Note: other sections of this guide address the subject of financial markets in more detail.

3. Effect of Interest Rate Movements[17]

Interest is the price that someone pays for the temporary use of someone else's funds. To repay a loan, a borrower has to pay interest, as well as the principal, the amount originally borrowed. Interest is the compensation that someone receives for temporarily giving up the ability to spend money. Without interest, lenders would not be willing to lend, or to temporarily give up the ability to spend, and savers would be less willing to defer spending. Interest rates are expressed as percents per year. If the interest rate is 10 percent per year, and you borrow $100 for one year, you have to repay the $100 plus $10 in interest.

Lower interest rates make it easier for people to borrow in order to buy cars and homes. Purchases of homes, in turn, increase the demand for other items, such as furniture and appliances, thus providing an additional boost to the economy. Lower interest rates mean that consumers spend less on interest costs, leaving them with more of their income to spend on goods and services. Lower interest rates make it easier for farmers, manufacturers, and other businesses to borrow to invest in equipment, inventories, and buildings. Also, the returns that investments will produce in future years are worth more today when rates are low than when rates are high. That gives business more of an incentive to invest when rates are low. Increased business investment, in turn, makes the economy grow faster, as productivity, or output per worker, increases faster. Interest rates do not seem to affect the amount that people save. That is because higher interest rates have two conflicting effects on how much people save. First, the higher return that savings can earn gives people an incentive to save more. Second, however, the higher return makes savers feel richer, so they may spend more, rather than save more.

Because interest rates are expressed simply as percents per year, we can compare interest rates on different kinds of loans, and even interest rates in different countries that use different currencies (yen, dollar, etc.).

Interest rates can affect the value of the dollar versus that of other countries' currencies. All other things held constant, when real (inflation-adjusted) interest rates are higher in the United States than in other countries, foreigners want to invest their funds here in order to earn a high return. The resulting increase in the demand for the dollar pushes up the value of the dollar. The opposite can happen when U.S. interest rates are low.

The health of the economy affects interest rates by influencing the supply of, and the demand for, credit. For example:

- Incomes fall in a recession, so the amount people save also decreases.
- The demand for credit by business generally declines in a recession, as business spends less on new buildings, equipment, and inventories. Also, the Federal Reserve acts to reduce interest rates during recessions, in order to stimulate economic activity.
- The federal government's demand for credit generally rises in a recession, as the reduction in business and consumer incomes reduces tax revenues, and programs such as unemployment insurance require increased spending.
- The net effect of all of these changes is that interest rates often go down in a recession.

All other things held constant, the rising demand for credit in expansions pushes interest rates up. If the rates that consumers and businesses have to pay to borrow rise too rapidly, however, spending may decline, leading to an economic slowdown.

4. Monetary Management Theories

- Change the Discount Rate — The discount rate is the rate the Federal Reserve charges member banks to borrow funds. Decreasing the discount rate stimulates borrowing among member banks (which then lend more to customers). Therefore, if the Federal Reserve wished to decrease the money supply to try to reduce inflationary pressures, it would increase the discount rate to discourage borrowing.
- Buy or Sell Securities on the Open Market — The Federal Reserve buys government securities to increase the reserves of member banks and sells government securities to decrease in member banks' reserves.
- Moral Suasion — The Federal Reserve issues oral or written statements to encourage banks to increase or decrease their lending activities.
- Change Legal Reserve Requirements — Increasing legal reserve requirements decreases the amount of money that a bank has available to lend. Thus, increasing the legal reserve requirements decreases the money supply, and vice versa.

The Federal Reserve's monetary policies described above are designed to influence investment spending. Lower interest rates serve to stimulate investment activities.

References

[1]Federal Reserve System Web site, October 2005, http://www.federalreserve.gov/pubs/frseries/frseri.htm

[2]Bank for International Settlements Web site, October 2005, http://www.bis.org/

[3]European Central Bank Web site, October 2005, http://www.ecb.int/ecb/html/index.en.html

[4]European Central Bank Web site, October 2005, http://www.ecb.int/ecb/orga/tasks/html/index.en.html

[5]National Association of Insurance Commissioners Web site, October 2005, http://www.naic.org/index_about.htm

[6]Code of Federal Regulations Web site, October 2005, http://www.access.gpo.gov/nara/cfr/waisidx_05/12cfr202_05.html

[7]Code of Federal Regulations Web site, October 2005, http://www.access.gpo.gov/nara/cfr/waisidx_05/12cfr203_05.html

[8]Code of Federal Regulations Web site, November 2005, http://www.access.gpo.gov/nara/cfr/waisidx_05/12cfr204_05.html

[9]Code of Federal Regulations Web site, November 2005, http://www.access.gpo.gov/nara/cfr/waisidx_05/12cfr215_05.html

[10]Code of Federal Regulations Web site, November 2005, http://www.access.gpo.gov/nara/cfr/waisidx_05/12cfr226_05.html

[11]Code of Federal Regulations Web site, November 2005, http://www.access.gpo.gov/nara/cfr/waisidx_05/12cfr230_05.html

[12]Code of Federal Regulations Web site, November 2005, http://www.access.gpo.gov/nara/cfr/waisidx_05/12cfr34_05.html

[13] U.S. Securities and Exchange Commission Web site, November 2005, ttp://www.sec.gov/news/press/2005-74.htm

[14] Federal Trade Commission Web-site November 2005, http://www.ftc.gov/bcp/conline/pubs/buspubs/glbshort.htm

[15]Code of Federal Regulations Web site, November 2005, http://www.access.gpo.gov/nara/cfr/waisidx_05/12cfr216_05.html

[16]Code of Federal Regulations Web site, November 2005, http://frwebgate2.access.gpo.gov/cgi-bin/waisgate.cgi?WAISdocID=125958250987+1+0+0&WAISaction=retrieve

[17]Federal reserve bank of New York Web site, November 2005, http://www.newyorkfed.org/education/define.html